POPLAR FOREST

POPLAR FOREST

THOMAS JEFFERSON'S VILLA RETREAT

TRAVIS C. MCDONALD

UNIVERSITY OF VIRGINIA PRESS
Charlottesville and London

University of Virginia Press

Printed in the United States of America on acid-free paper

First published 2023

3 5 7 9 8 6 4 2
Library of Congress Cataloging-in-Publication Data

Names: McDonald, Travis C., author.
Title: Poplar Forest : Thomas Jefferson's villa retreat / Travis C. McDonald.
Description: Charlottesville : University of Virginia Press, 2023. | Includes bibliographical references and index.
Identifiers: LCCN 2022048767 (print) | LCCN 2022048768 (ebook) |
ISBN 9780813949635 (hardcover) | ISBN 9780813949642 (ebook)
Subjects: LCSH: Poplar Forest (Va.) | Jefferson, Thomas, 1743–1826—Homes and haunts—Virginia—Forest. | Octagonal houses—Virginia—Forest. | Historic house museums—Virginia—Forest. | Forest (Va.)—Buildings, structures, etc.
Classification: LCC E332.74 .M38 2023 (print) | LCC E332.74 (ebook) | DDC 975.5/671—dc23/eng/20221026
LC record available at https://lccn.loc.gov/2022048767
LC ebook record available at https://lccn.loc.gov/2022048768

Cover art: Poplar Forest's ornamental core, by L. Diane Johnson. (Courtesy of the artist)

For

Al Chambers
Architectural Historian

and

John Mesick
Historical Architect

CONTENTS

ILLUSTRATIONS

PREFACE

Poplar Forest tells the story of recovering one of Thomas Jefferson's most important and personal works of architecture. Late in the twentieth century Jefferson's private villa retreat was rescued, researched, investigated, analyzed, and slowly restored as a public history site. It represents one of the most interesting and unknown chapters of Thomas Jefferson's life in retirement, and as a missing link it completes our understanding of his personal style of architecture. This volume examines how and why the discoveries revealed during the investigation and restoration further our understanding of Thomas Jefferson's lifelong traditions as an architect and builder. Information from research and investigation imparted knowledge of what Jefferson designed and built, but it also generated questions: why did Thomas Jefferson build a second home, what made it architecturally distinctive, who labored on it and how was it constructed, and does the intimate nature of his retreat reveal something of Jefferson's character? Answering those questions is the principal objective of this book. Poplar Forest represents fresh perspectives, some just as complex and contradictory as any other aspects of his life. Thomas Jefferson was no ordinary man, and it should be no surprise that his special retreat would be extraordinary.

In 1809 Thomas Jefferson made a momentous transition from one chapter of his life to another. He finally retired from long public service to his country, thus ending what was commonly known about his life. The former president retired to his principal residence, Monticello, even then one of the best-known houses in the country and one just completed after a prolonged forty-year process. His family and close friends knew that in 1809 the retired president also began using a private retreat named Poplar Forest on his distant Bedford County plantation, a three-day's journey from Monticello. If the public knew anything about Jefferson's life from 1809 to his death in 1826, it might have been something about Monticello, or perhaps about his last big public legacy, the establishment of the University of Virginia. Few knew much about his private life, and those who did knew it from Monticello. When he died, the history of Jefferson's beloved retreat, used over a substantial fourteen-year period (1809–23), vanished from memory and from subsequent histories, absent even in some written in the twenty-first century. History is replete with people and events that disappear from the historical record, but for a sizable portion of Thomas Jefferson's life to disappear is more unusual for this extensively studied man. The only comprehensive history of Poplar Forest was written in 1993 in commemoration of the 250th anniversary of Jefferson's birth.[1] This architectural history fills in what we have learned since then and attempts to interpret what it means.

A significant dimension of this story is that Poplar Forest is the masterpiece of the enslaved craftsmen who executed all of its classical architectural elements. John Hemmings, who by this time had become the principal enslaved master craftsman at Monticello, had gained Jefferson's trust and was put in charge of the work. Hemmings's role at Poplar Forest is documented in the rare exchange of letters between this enslaved man and Jefferson. Working as apprentices in the joinery trade at Poplar Forest were John Hemmings's three nephews: William Beverly Hemings, James Madison Hemings, and Thomas Eston Hemings. (In his letters to Jefferson, John sometimes spelled his surname with one or two *m*'s; he seemed to prefer the latter, as evidenced by what he carved on his wife's tombstone.) Theirs was a family affair in more ways than one. These young enslaved men were Thomas Jefferson's illegitimate mixed-race children with his enslaved servant Sally Hemings. They would be engaged in close proximity with their father for many years (1815–26) constructing his dream house, but their critical role was unacknowledged. As Jefferson's "shadow family," these young men were invisible in the written record, referred to as "aids" to their uncle and only mentioned by name on the rolls of the enslaved. The poignant tableau of Jefferson's and his family's interaction with his sons has to be imagined. It is an overlooked intimate story of Poplar Forest and presents one of Thomas Jefferson's most conspicuous contradictions.

My restoration career as an architectural historian began at Colonial Williamsburg in the 1980s. It was a transitional time when new questions were being asked of buildings: what were the social and cultural intentions of a design, what does a close examination of details and finishes say about how various users interacted within a building, and what meanings might be determined through a wider view of the interconnected social and cultural landscapes?[2] Our architectural knowledge of Poplar Forest, what we know and how we know it, is based largely on what the walls of the house tell us. The subjective, close, even microscopic, analysis of Poplar Forest evidence has to first be recorded, studied, and merged with the written documents before it can yield fresh interpretations. This is the interesting forensic story of deciphering the architectural puzzle that was Poplar Forest in 1989. That detailed story of our investigation and restoration, encompassing both science and art, and upon which this architectural history rests, is a long one and more properly told in another volume. This work examines the larger meanings of what was discovered. When Jefferson's design for Poplar Forest was finally revealed through a long and intensive investigation, I explored some of the more obvious themes in articles and lectures, but writing this book stimulated still others and expanded the scope: what was Jefferson's history of using retreats, how unusual was Poplar Forest as an intellectual retreat for an individual, what was Jefferson's long tradition of using the octagon form, was it the first full octagon house in America, how did it compare with contemporary Virginian or American houses, what was the role of the Hemings family in building the house, were Jefferson's designs for the ornamental landscape unique in their relationship to the nature of the site and to his architectural design, and were there literary or intellectual influences connected to the creation and use of Poplar Forest?

It has been a rare professional privilege to have researched and contemplated Thomas Jefferson almost every day for the past thirty years. Long association with and study of any subject imparts an intuitive insight. I focus on details that are typically overlooked but illuminate Thomas Jefferson's development as an architect and builder. Yet it is also necessary to look beyond Poplar Forest in order to better understand the challenges he faced and the solutions he sought. I have tried to envision Poplar Forest by looking out of its windows and into them, situating the place in its ornamental and plantation landscapes, understanding who used the house and who made it work, and imagining how Jefferson fashioned his sense of self in the quiet environment he designed. Our accurate image of Poplar Forest now allows it to be seen in the pantheon of Jefferson's architecture. Some long-standing professional evaluations of Jefferson's architecture are true of Poplar Forest, but others need reevaluation. I conclude that Thomas Jefferson *was* exceptional both as an architect and builder when viewed in his time and place. His era encompassed many changes: new social domestic demands for houses, stimulating Enlightenment ideas of man's place in the world, and shifts in cultural expression, all of which bear on the design of Poplar Forest. Jefferson is due credit for his architectural accomplishments, although they are not completely free of their own contradictions. Architecture is called the most humanistic of the fine arts, one to be within and to feel as much as to visualize and contemplate, even if that experience might be intangible and subconscious. Authentically restoring Poplar Forest provides a spatial context for visitors—a type of portal—in which they might better sense and understand Jefferson's private place and vestiges of the past. Recovering this private chapter of Thomas Jefferson's story adds immeasurably to a seemingly unquenchable desire to know more about him as a talented person rather than an inapproachable myth.

ACKNOWLEDGMENTS

This book's genesis was in 1989, when I was hired to direct the architectural restoration of Poplar Forest. The subsequent years of architectural restoration, due to be substantially complete in 2022, involved so many people that a full accounting of debts owed, reaching back to the beginning of the project, is impossible. This architectural history encompasses the work of many staff, consultants, advisors, and colleagues who composed a "dream team" that investigated and restored Poplar Forest over a thirty-three-year period. More importantly, the restoration and current understanding of Poplar Forest would not have been possible without its rescue and formation as a nonprofit museum property in 1983. My first debt of gratitude must therefore go to the foundation's first director, Lynn A. Beebe, who quickly educated the board of directors and donors that this project would not be a fast one and that it had to be conducted with the highest-quality professional processes. After all, this was not just any house restoration; it was Thomas Jefferson's house! To the original and later members of the board—thank you for your unwavering trust in the professional team and your optimistic patience that it would be a long, exciting journey of discovery and restoration. Your conscientious stewardship and dedicated hard work of raising private funds made this one of the most idealistic projects in the country. Lynn Beebe's successor as president and CEO, Jeffrey Nichols, and his successor, Alyson Ramsey, are due special thanks for allowing me my own pursuit of privacy to write, and rewrite, this history, which, like Jefferson's own projects, took longer than expected.

The restoration team was composed of permanent staff, consulting architects, and advisory panel members, and while their contributions are more pertinent to a future restoration history volume, they need acknowledgment here. Key restoration staff members were Andrew Ladygo, architectural conservator (1990–95); Douglas Rideout, restoration supervisor (1995–98); Vincent Fastabend, restoration supervisor (1998–2019); Brian Foree, restoration supervisor (2019–21); and Canlin Frost, restoration supervisor (2021–). Working under these extraordinary lead craftsmen were many other restoration craftsmen who expertly restored the house in Jeffersonian ways. Other Poplar Forest colleagues in several disciplines contributed in many other ways; it has always been a team project. The Architectural Advisory Panel was formed in 1988 to guide the project and comprised one-third of the professional team (composed of staff, advisors, and consultants). This incomparable group of wise and experienced restoration experts was composed of William L. Beiswanger, Robert Burley, S. Allen Chambers, Edward A. Chappell, John Larson, Hugh C. Miller, Lee Nelson, Nicholas A. Pappas, Orlando Ridout V, and Robert Self. Their names are widely known and respected in the preservation world stretching back sixty years. The mutual respect among members of the restoration team ensured that we could debate opinions, question evidence, and suggest alternatives while always reaching a consensus that reflected the combined wisdom of the group. The critical third part of the team was the consulting architects. Mesick Cohen Wilson Baker, who were chosen in 1990 because they were the restoration architects working at Monticello and the University of Virginia, and they still are! John Mesick and Jeffrey Baker knew more details about Jefferson's architecture and construction than just about anyone else and were essential to the success of this project. Their continuity over more than thirty years in this "golden era" of Jeffersonian restoration facilitated a deep understanding of how Poplar Forest fit into Jefferson's work before and afterward. John's lifelong interest in Jefferson's architecture fortuitously led him to become an expert on the subject. It has been a great pleasure and privilege to work with him and Jeff Baker over several decades. Words fail to adequately thank all these dedicated team members who were entrusted by the Poplar Forest board to ensure that this was the best possible restoration project.

A deep debt is owed to Al Chambers for many reasons: he helped steer me toward a career in architectural history in 1975; as a native of Lynchburg, and its architectural history guru, he was an early advocate for saving Poplar Forest; he had Poplar Forest recorded by the Historic American Buildings Survey in 1985; he was an early and continuing advisor to Lynn Beebe and the Poplar Forest Board of Directors; he wrote the definitive history of Poplar Forest in 1993; and he has been a loyal supporter of the project in every conceivable way since its beginning. Most importantly, Al is an excellent writer and historian and offered wise recommendations for my manuscript. I owe him more than I can express for his editing, encouragement, and friendship.

Jefferson scholars have played important roles in the restoration of Poplar Forest, sharing in the exciting task of parsing out its meaning. William Beiswanger, Monticello's director of restoration, was the go-to oracle for anything related to Jefferson's role as an architect, builder, and landscape architect at Jefferson's most well-known house. As a member of the Architectural Advisory Panel, Bill also kept meticulous notes that document that group's assistance and was always quick to relay pertinent Jefferson documents and construction details; he was an indispensable Jefferson resource and fact-checker. Along with Bob Self, Monticello's architectural conservator, also an Advisory Panel member, they welcomed me to Monticello, on what I think is close to one hundred visits, documenting one critical and minuscule detail after another. Bill's successor as director of restoration, Gardiner Hallock, has continued the warm and extremely helpful assistance over the years. Colleagues in several other departments at Monticello were always a ready resource for any number of inquiries over several decades. Colleagues at the University of Virginia have also played a critical role in my research and comprehension of Jefferson the architect and builder. Over many years the ongoing restoration discoveries there were shared and followed up by hard-hat tours ranging from rooftops to basements. The University Architect's principal preservation staff of Brian Hogg, Jody Lahendro, James Zehmer, and Mark Kutney has always accommodated my constant trips to observe and learn from their excellent conservation and restoration work. And certainly the best unpublished Jefferson scholar of our time, and one who undoubtedly knows him as well as he can be known, is Bill Barker. Bill professionally portrayed Jefferson at Colonial Williamsburg for many years and is always available at Poplar Forest for special occasions. Whether it was describing new discoveries to Bill or thinking out loud with interpretive insights, it was like having a conversation with the man himself, someone who completely and intuitively understood what was conveyed like few others.

Colleagues and mentors undoubtedly contribute to one's professional development and expertise in ways large and small. I have been lucky to stand on the shoulders of teachers and mentors who kindled, furthered, and encouraged my career. I will be forever thankful to Professor Thomas S. Hines, who ignited my passion for architectural history and showed me a future course for my life's work. Mentors in the Office of Park Historic Preservation and in the office of the chief historical architect of the National Park Service in the mid-1970s took me in, guided my self-studies in Washington, DC, and encouraged me to attend graduate school. At the University of Virginia Freddy Nichols first turned me on to Jefferson's architecture in addition to early Virginia architecture. I first visited Poplar Forest on a Nichols class field trip in 1978, when the Watts family was still living there. Later for several years I had the opportunity to give Professor Nichols and his classes early glimpses of what was unfolding at Poplar Forest. Professor Richard Guy Wilson took over as the UVA Jefferson scholar, exposing me to the American Renaissance and modernism along the way, guiding my thesis work, and bringing his students to Poplar Forest. The nexus of architectural research and architectural restoration came at the beginning of my professional career with a project at Colonial Williamsburg in the 1980s. Colleagues in the Department of Architectural Research instilled in me good practices of fieldwork and how the close observation of details and materials must inform good restoration. Ed Chappell, Willie Graham, Carl Lounsbury, and Mark Wenger were incomparable colleagues recording and studying early Virginia and Chesapeake architecture like no others. Ed became a close friend and mentor and served on the Architectural Advisory Panel until his death in 2020. More than words can say I will always be indebted to my public history mentor and dear friend, William Seale, an outstanding historian and the country's premier interior furnishings restorer. William guided my career from the mid-1970s, bugged me to write articles, and always championed my restoration projects. His death in 2019 left a significant professional and personal void.

I would like to thank the Center for Palladian Studies in America for a grant that helped cover the expert editing services of Kenny Moratto, as did a grant from the Nicholas A. Pappas Fund. A fellowship at the International Center for Jefferson Studies in 2018 allowed me to conduct four weeks of blissful research in the Jefferson Library while living on its grounds; thanks go to Andrew O'Shaughnessy, Endrina Tay, Anna Berkes, and especially librarian Jack Robertson, who was always interested in Poplar Forest.

Various friends and colleagues were kind enough to read different sections of my manuscript, catching errors, and suggesting improvements: Al Chambers, John Mesick, Gail Pond, Barbara Heath, Bill Beiswanger, Mary Kesler, Ed Chappell, Peter Onuf, Cinder Stanton, Andrew O'Shaughnessy, and colleague Eric Proebsting, who provided essential information on the Poplar Forest landscape as revealed through archaeology and research. Thanks to Nat Case for his excellent maps, and to my friend Nancy Marion for her graphic design skills in depicting Jefferson's octagon designs in appendix C. I'm constantly reminded of a saying that there are no good writers, only good rewriters; this is borne out by the help from my readers, and rereaders. And, of course, no publication reaches the shelves without the essential expertise of the unsung editors and publication team. At the University of Virginia Press I'm beholden to Boyd Zenner, who first accepted my work, and Mark Mones, who kept it afloat. Andy Edwards became the production wizard who guided it through the final processes with other manuscript editors I have not had the pleasure of meeting. Alexander Trotter expertly created the index, and Susan Murray put in an extraordinary effort as copy editor, making this work all the better.

My family has shared me with Thomas Jefferson and Poplar Forest for several decades. My wife, Denise McDonald, never gets enough thanks for her love, support, and encouragement. My daughters, Margot and Madeleine, grew up with Poplar Forest, thinking it was Thomas Jefferson's primary home—my pride for them far outshines that which I feel for this project, which is considerable.

POPLAR FOREST

INTRODUCTION

Thomas Jefferson passionately embraced what awaited him in retirement at Monticello in 1809: a greatly expanded family of grandchildren, his completed "essay" in architecture, his maturing gardens, his beloved library, and the company of old friends. It was the new "friends" that created the dilemma. The public considered Jefferson public property and felt no remorse at showing up for a glimpse of him or expecting overnight accommodations as if Monticello were an inn. Jefferson's lingering belief in Virginia hospitality meant he was obligated to engage and dine with increasing numbers of guests. His longtime friends who came invited were eagerly anticipated, but he had lost control of others who showed up unexpected and uninvited. He juggled these intrusions on his private time by daily solitary horseback rides on his plantations and by restricting access to his chamber/library/cabinet suite. But to sit outside his suite now he had to build louvered enclosures for privacy. Time and space for his personal pursuits became more and more limited, but he had anticipated this. In the last few years of his presidency Jefferson's architectural ambitions had again been stimulated to design a retreat, an ultimate one in a lifetime of using them. This more anonymous retreat would be beyond the bounds of inquiring visitors, where his time and his companions would be of his own choosing. The retreat was named Poplar Forest, after his remote plantation, a three-day journey from Monticello and twice that distance from Washington. This distance, and wanting the retreat ready by his retirement in 1809, had challenged this experienced builder who typically supervised all aspects of his construction projects. After helping the bricklayer lay out the complex octagonal shape of its foundation in 1806, presidential duties kept Jefferson away from the project for two years. He was good at envisioning dreams of retired life and made extraordinary efforts that this one, contemplated for so long, would be a reality.

In 1812, after using his retirement retreat for three years, Jefferson described his second home to his son-in-law: "When finished it will be the best dwelling house in the state, except that of Monticello, perhaps preferable to that, as more proportioned to the faculties of a private citizen."[1] This short description captured the essence and personal significance of Poplar Forest. Jefferson acknowledged that it was still a work in progress. He acknowledged the comparative architectural quality of Monticello and hinted at the difference his second home signified and why he needed one. Most importantly, he indicated, it was proportioned for the faculties that could be exercised and pursued at a retreat. It would represent not only Jefferson's architectural masterpiece, classically proportioned in every way, but also that of the enslaved men who would expertly craft it. That one sentence from Jefferson outlines the questions in this book: what did he design, why did he design and build it, how did it function for a private citizen, and as "the best dwelling house," how was it different or similar in comparison to his designs and construction projects before and after Poplar Forest?

Why did Poplar Forest vanish from Jefferson history? The private nature of his retreat, the very reason for its establishment, made it virtually unknown to all but family members and local neighbors. Jefferson's distant friends with whom he corresponded from that place would have noticed the location name "Poplar Forest," but it would have signified little to them. To Thomas Jefferson it signified a great deal, representing his most private and intimate time in retirement, an astonishing fourteen-year period. To his closest friends Jefferson didn't hold back his exuberance when describing his precious time at Poplar Forest. But as important as it was to him, the memory of Jefferson's association with Poplar Forest pretty much vanished after his grandson Francis Eppes sold the property out of the family in 1828. Except for those who might have read Henry Randall's 1858 biography of Jefferson, with a significant reminiscence of Poplar Forest by his granddaughter Ellen Coolidge, little was known about this part of his life in retirement. The few architectural cognoscenti who happened to see Fiske Kimball's 1916 limited edition book on Jefferson's drawings would have gained some idea of Jefferson's creation. Virginians might have seen the house mentioned in some early twentieth-century books on homes and gardens. Jefferson fans reading Edwin Morris Betts's 1953 publication of Jefferson's Farm Book would have been curious to see that the end papers depicted a map of the route between Monticello and Poplar Forest and even a drawing of the house.[2] For the most part, however, Poplar Forest remained a sleeping historical beauty, privately lived in until 1979 and virtually unknown. The recovery of its story is one of the most substantial contributions to the corpus of Jefferson history in the past several decades, yet it remains relatively unknown to most Americans. An extensive online encyclopedia entry for Thomas Jefferson does not mention Poplar Forest. Recent scholarly and well-regarded general biographies of Jefferson of five to six hundred pages, and two that focus on his inner life and character of three hundred pages each, either fail to mention Poplar Forest at all or devote no more than a paragraph to it. While public recognition is understandable, continued professional oversight is a scholarly paradox.[3]

This is a specific history of one place and of one part of Jefferson's life, but it must also be seen in a larger context—aesthetically, culturally, socially, and economically. Once Poplar Forest was secured as a museum property, its basic and chronological history had to be constructed as the obvious starting point. Besides a few articles and two academic theses, published history of Poplar Forest was remarkably terra incognita until the 1990s. Architectural historian S. Allen Chambers Jr. solved that problem: sleuthing the vast Jefferson archival repositories around the country, he compiled research and then wrote a masterful general history of Poplar Forest.[4] President Jefferson's need to direct construction from the President's House resulted in a boon of explicit letters to and from the workers, making Poplar Forest one of the most documented of early American houses. Even in retirement there was two-way correspondence between Jefferson at Monticello and his enslaved craftsmen sent to work independently at Poplar Forest. Besides the trove of letters, information came from Jefferson's other habitual recordation: daily purchases in his Memorandum Book; plantation account books; his Garden and Farm Books; his construction notes and architectural drawings; land maps and surveys; and legal records.

Poplar Forest came late as a public history museum for one of America's most important founding fathers. The fundamental public history challenge is still to convey the history of Poplar Forest—why it existed, who created it, and why it is important. This is especially relevant given that its creator was Thomas Jefferson, who was said to have a "curious, inexplicable quality of elusiveness,"[5] and whose contemporaries "found him easy to know but impossible to know well."[6] As his most private residence, Poplar Forest offers the opportunity where we might come closer to glimpsing the private nature of Thomas Jefferson. If it is true that those who build their own houses reveal something of themselves, then Poplar Forest should have something to tell us. For Thomas Jefferson to have designed, built, and used two houses for himself over his

Fig. 1. Poplar Forest, northwest elevation, 2022.

Fig. 2. Poplar Forest, south elevation, 2022.

lifetime is an even rarer opportunity to decipher what that might reveal about his personal need to create his own dwellings. The second challenge, the focus of this book, is to convey both to the general public and to architectural historians what we've discovered of Jefferson's long-lost creation and how it completes and expands our knowledge of his architecture.

The reason for an extensive Poplar Forest restoration stemmed from two episodes one hundred years apart. In September 1846 Christian Hutter wrote to his son Edward: "I have no doubt that you have been able to make some valuable improvements in the rebuilding of your mansion, and that in some instances it is now more commodious than it was before the unfortunate fire occurred."[7] The letter to Edward Hutter, who owned Poplar Forest at that time, referred to the disastrous fire of November 21, 1845, that gutted the house, destroying the architectural forms and details John Hemmings and his nephews had crafted over many years. The valuable improvements making the house more commodious referred to what was rebuilt in 1846. Jefferson's innovative villa had been transformed into Hutter's more conventional farmhouse. The light and airy nature of the original design was severely darkened with eight bricked-up windows, walls inserted to divide rooms, doorways filled, triple windows made smaller, and staircases removed from the pavilions. Jefferson's central 20-foot cube decreased in volume by the insertion of an attic floor above and by a corner staircase that accessed it. The attic floor also meant the loss of light from the middle room's rare domestic skylight. Gone too were Jefferson's classical Roman features of interior moldings, exterior entablature, balustrade, Chinese railing, proper column capitals, and even the entire pediment to the south portico. Some of the new elements, like the fireplace mantels, door and window trim, and an entrance doorway featuring sidelights and transom were in the then-fashionable Greek Revival style. The four-room service wing was reduced by half, with the two rooms closest to the house demolished and the other two altered into

Fig. 3. Poplar Forest, west elevation, 1912.

Fig. 4. Poplar Forest, north elevation, ca. 1900.

two detached outbuildings. This critical episode in the house's history was the first of two that required extensive investigation and restoration in the late twentieth century.

The second era of alteration occurred one hundred years later, in the 1940s, when the Watts family transformed the Hutter farmhouse into an up-to-date country house. The conveniences required for domestic modernity at that time included three full bathrooms, two half baths, a large kitchen with butler's pantry, a family room, closets, and mechanical systems. Personal circumstance rather than professional appropriateness led the Watts family to engage a New York City architect for both the modern systems and amenities, and what they hoped would be a full restoration to Jefferson's design. The bricked-up windows were opened, and one room, the parlor, was restored to what was thought to be its original appearance but in a muddled way without a good understanding of what Jefferson had designed. The Watts family lived in their hybrid house until 1979. In 1983 the house and 49 acres were purchased as a nonprofit museum property, and the long restoration process began in 1989. The primary question was whether Jefferson's greatly altered personal masterpiece could be revealed through the best conceived documentary and investigative process.

A restoration team of staff, consultants, and advisors were assembled in 1989 to begin the exciting detective work of finding evidence that would reveal Jefferson's creation. This physical transformation of Jefferson's villa to a farmhouse and then to a country house left an architectural puzzle for the restoration team to decipher. One historian said of Jefferson's efforts at understanding Greek-language translations that he "attempted to unearth the original and exact truth beneath the accumulated strata of later transformations and reflections."[8] The same could be said of architectural investigation.

Fig. 5. Poplar Forest, outbuildings, 1943. The 1840s kitchen and smokehouse built in the location of rooms 3 and 4 of the original wing of offices.

Fig. 6. Poplar Forest, southwest elevation, 1989.

Fig. 7. Poplar Forest, section looking south, 1985.

Physical and documentary truths must be discovered, read, and interpreted, sometimes coaxed by the right question. As the architectural investigations examined accumulated vertical strata within the house, a parallel process of traditional archaeology examined horizontal ones in the adjacent landscape.[9] The architectural discoveries would continue past the initial five-year investigation well into the much longer restoration phase of more than twenty years. Our restoration project serendipitously coincided with an extraordinary era of Jeffersonian restorations conducted at the "architectural bookends" of Poplar Forest: Monticello and the University of Virginia. In addition to shared information among institutional colleagues, the fortuitous common factor between the three sites was shared restoration architects who provided unparalleled comparative knowledge of Jefferson's designs and construction at his most personal projects.[10] The restoration philosophy dictated for our project was both idealistic and unique.[11] The philosophical decision to restore Poplar Forest using Jefferson-era techniques, and to do so in the same historical sequence in which he originally finished the house, provided further insights into his use of idealistic forms and materials, and his patience for achieving those.[12] That exciting journey of unfolding revelations for one of Thomas Jefferson's most personal and near-perfect works of architecture forms the foundation on which this architectural history rests. We now know what Thomas Jefferson designed, how it was constructed, who built it, how it was used, and how and why it physically changed over time. Its restoration now allows others to know and understand it, adding to the ever-changing interpretations of Thomas Jefferson. This book offers an initial architectural interpretation of what the various aspects of Poplar Forest mean within the context of Jefferson's works and in American architecture.

The natural and plantation landscapes of Poplar Forest have been described in Barbara J. Heath and Jack Gary's *Jefferson's Poplar Forest: Unearthing a Virginia Plantation* and other scholarly publications that approach an understanding of the cultural landscape through archaeology. These ongoing archaeological investigations continue to be an active part of the Poplar Forest research and landscape restoration under the direction of Dr. Eric Proebsting.[13]

The themes explored in this history are all affected in one way or another by its raison d'être, the nature and use of the site as a private villa retreat. Understanding Jefferson's lifelong need for and use of retreats is paramount, leading to the conclusion that Poplar Forest was not only his ultimate one, but necessary for his retirement. The conceptual context for Poplar Forest is found in Jefferson's formal education, what he read, and in the intellectual currents of his time. Classical literature and history extolled the Roman culture of retirement and the benefits to be derived from rural villa retreats. The rural Italian villas famously depicted in Andrea Palladio's sixteenth-century book were another strong influence. Seventeenth- and eighteenth-century English literature and illustrated books that connected intellectual pursuits, new suburban retreats, and romantic picturesque landscapes were not lost on Jefferson. All of these influences, combined with Jefferson's habitual need for solitary quiet time and his use of various retreats, resulted in his final retreat. Whether Poplar Forest was unusual as an American second home and how it fits within the context of other summer and country houses requires some exploration and definition. Was it different as an intellectual retreat for one man? Monticello's redesign, intended for public display as well as for privacy, created an unfortunate bipolar tension for owner, family, and guests.[14] If Monticello has been characterized as both hermitage and villa, representing its private and public nature respectively, where does Poplar Forest fit in that scheme?[15] How Thomas Jefferson and family members used Poplar Forest is an important part of assessing its intentions in design and how that design facilitated aspects of their privacy.

Understanding Poplar Forest within Jefferson's many architectural designs requires a summary of his development as an architect. Architectural historians have been challenged to place Jefferson's domestic architecture within a larger American context, frequently viewing it as an isolated and idiosyncratic creation. Part of that reasoning is that Thomas Jefferson's long and consistent output of architectural designs, whether private or public, innovative or old-fashioned, is exceptional in America for its focused personal development within one style that evolved over a lengthy period. For this reason his architectural development must be examined to understand any one part, and especially Poplar Forest. The sheer volume of Jefferson's designs on paper, numbering in the hundreds, is a remarkable glimpse into the mind and development of a designer over a lifetime. Which architectural threads eventually weave together in Jefferson's final domestic design? How different was it from Monticello, or from other Virginia dwelling at the time? Jefferson's early, self-guided architectural education and his precocious design of the first Monticello helps us understand his subsequent works. Jefferson's study of ancient classical, Italian Renaissance, and eighteenth-century neoclassical designs from English sources are all reflected at Poplar Forest in his "melting pot" brand of neoclassicism. His experiential education in Europe, in particular Paris and France, is critical in understanding the rebuilt Monticello and modernistic features at Poplar Forest. For these reasons we must study these relevant developments of Jefferson as an amateur architect before discussing his designs for Poplar Forest. How his aesthetics were different at an occasional retreat, which by its nature could be more unconventional and ideal, and whether they were compromised by realities and circumstances, are pertinent questions to ask about the owner/designer/ builder/user. Because so many features of Jefferson's designs over his lifetime make them "Jeffersonian," appendix B explains his traditions of using certain elements and materials. His long and idiosyncratic personal style makes Poplar Forest both modern and old-fashioned.

Several aspects of Jefferson's design sensibilities and preferences for Poplar Forest are explored in the following chapters: his lifelong fascination with the octagon shape and the challenges for geometrical purity; his reliance on Palladian principles of classical design and how those relate to structure and components of ornamental landscape; and the devices of comfort, convenience, and privacy reflected in his final design and their subsequent alterations. Appendix C provides a glimpse of the many and various uses of the octagon shape that Jefferson primarily used in his domestic designs, almost all of which were unrealized.

By the time he began to construct Poplar Forest, Thomas Jefferson was also an experienced builder. That particular skill is perhaps his most unknown among many, and one covered extensively in this book for several reasons. This typically overlooked aspect of architecture—the structure and construction of a building—can be just as important as style in understanding the social and economic circumstances of its creation.[16] Jack McLaughlin's *Jefferson and Monticello: The Biography of a Builder* is the only in-depth work that interprets Jefferson's role as a builder.[17] McLaughlin observed that "those who construct their own shelter replicate themselves, at their deepest and most significant level, in their houses. They *are* what they build. By following the building process, therefore, one should be able to dig beneath externals and reveal unaccommodated man, the thing itself."[18] If Monticello can be called an autobiography in architecture, Poplar Forest might be considered the secret diary. Did this difference reflect any deviations from Jefferson's established traits for design, workers, materials, inspection, patience, and control?

Jefferson's characteristic need to control his building projects was frequently challenged by many factors, especially when he was absent: how well academically expressed designs were translated to workers, whether the obsessive mathematical precision of specifications were followed by hired or enslaved craftsmen, and how close the finished quality of any part matched the demanding expectations of this owner. Construction was a classic balance between design intention and the finished product, which was dependent upon inevitable circumstances. When first constructing Monticello Jefferson had taken on the role as undertaker, as building contractors were then known. This ambitious role was one he typically studied like any other of his interests, first in Virginia and then wherever he went. He observed the best buildings and construction practices in American cities (Annapolis, Philadelphia, and New York) and throughout Europe for five years. His notes reflect interviews with workers for comparative factors of time, materials, and labor. He practiced his knowledge and honed his supervisory skills when rebuilding Monticello, when directing the construction of major public buildings in Washington, DC, at Poplar Forest, and finally at what was then one of the largest construction projects in the country, the University of Virginia. For Thomas Jefferson the process of design and construction was personal and made all the more difficult by ambitious designs and his insistence on the best-quality construction, from a building's structure to the appearance of its finishes. The fact that Jefferson stretched this experience with the building process throughout his life, and documented it in many ways, provides a rare understanding of building practices in general and of his in particular. The construction story of Poplar Forest documents two related and common factors along this experiential journey: specified building materials and the workers who made and assembled them. It is both a common and an uncommon Jefferson story.

The long process of constructing and finishing Poplar Forest was a familiar one for its owner, but more challenging due to its remote location. The Bedford County site did not benefit from the shops found at Monticello. The workers, both free and enslaved, would travel back and forth between the two sites for many years. Jefferson's hired bricklayer and carpenters would have the house closed in for its owner's use by 1809, although it would remain an unfinished shell for years. The remaining finished joinery on the exterior and interior would be completed by the Hemings family over the next seventeen years, fourteen during Jefferson's residency (1809–23). Three members of that enslaved family, Jefferson's biracial sons, crafted his special place, yet their history represents the greatest unknown part in this larger missing chapter of Thomas Jefferson's life.

We must also ask why Jefferson would build such an architecturally impressive second home if it was not on display? His updated version of Monticello was undoubtedly meant to impress visitors as much as to satisfy its owner. His status as a social and cultural consumer was obviously on display there. Jefferson's neighbors who came to dine at Poplar Forest must have been impressed with his unusual house, but only a couple of foreign friends besides family ever saw his retreat. If few were intended to see it, Jefferson could have built a much simpler house, one easier and faster for an older man to construct and use. Instead, though, its design surpassed and transcended a quiet shelter as a place to read, write, and think. Jefferson seemed to be stimulated to create another domestic example of his synthetic brand of neoclassicism with familiar classical details. It was a creative urge for something special, with geometric purity, and as near perfect as he could make it for his own enjoyment. As he told the entablature ornament maker, his private second home was a chance to indulge his fancy. We have to imagine the personal fulfillment Jefferson's retreat afforded him in retirement—one of the more happy endings of his life.

The "construction factor" of building Poplar Forest reflected Jefferson's characteristic patience and optimism exhibited through many other things in his life. The process of creating and building seems to have been fundamentally important to him, and as great as the finished product. Our own parallel restoration journey took as much patience and offered insight into Jefferson's experience of seeing his conceptualized spaces, elements, and finishes slowly crafted and revealed over time. The recently handcrafted Doric order entablature for the dining room, with its more than 1,700 individual parts, gives more than an abstract understanding of what the Hemings family crafted. The process nevertheless comes to an end, and a restored Poplar Forest is ultimately the final word. It is a restored and physical historical truth, and like all historical truths from the past, it will be seen and interpreted in many different ways. In 1820 Thomas Jefferson was accused of appropriating from the College of William and Mary the Roman goddess Minerva for the new University of Virginia seal. Jefferson replied that William and Mary had chosen the shell (the image of Minerva's temple) and he had chosen the kernel (the figure of Minerva). At Poplar Forest we have restored the story's shell, an authentic context, as a means of understanding the kernel of its meaning. How it speaks to each visitor is part of their personal connection with the past and with Thomas Jefferson in his most intimate place.

1

THE RETREAT

Poplar Forest was the last of a number of retreats Thomas Jefferson used throughout his life. To understand Poplar Forest, we must understand Jefferson's history of using various retreats for uninterrupted time to focus on his studies or work during his public career. Once retired, why did he need Poplar Forest as a retreat? It is equally important to know how the long history and nature of rural retreats affected his conception and use of Poplar Forest. What did Jefferson know of villa retreats from Roman times or the famously published ones from the Italian Renaissance? What did he absorb from new types of suburban English retreats of the seventeenth and eighteenth centuries? What was his experience with contemporary European retreats from the 1780s? How different was Poplar Forest in comparison with other wealthy Americans' seasonal second homes? And what was the relationship between his retreat and the plantation on which it was located?

Why Poplar Forest?

The pleasure Jefferson took from his gardens and bespoke house at Monticello was compromised by his fame and consequently by the hospitality that fame entailed. After Mount Vernon, it was arguably the best-known private house in America. Jefferson rewarded friends and visitors who arrived with or without letters of introduction with lavish hospitality in a structure already bursting with family and servants. Anna Maria Thornton famously characterized Jefferson's private chamber/cabinet/library suite at Monticello as his "sanctum sanctorum."[1] "Sanctum" refers to a place where one is free from intrusion. The two-word Latin phrase derives from a Hebrew term that referred to the holiest place in a temple. Thornton's common usage of the term described the part of a building where few people were allowed to go. Visitors' description of Jefferson's suite as off-limits, even to some family members, portrays the master of Monticello locked away in his special intellectual space. For privacy outside his suite on the southern side of the house he built louvered "porticle" alcoves. A period painting shows a partial railing on the south terrace adjacent to Jefferson's suite that might also have been a barrier to keep others at a distance. Jefferson's small garden pavilion in the enormous vegetable garden beyond the south wing and Mulberry Row was yet another refuge of privacy outside the house.

Family members later gave their impressions of the frequent invasion of Jefferson's privacy to his biographer Henry Randall in 1858:

> With this constant influx of well-bred guests, came also swarms of impertinent gazers who, without introduction, permission or any ceremony whatever, thrust themselves into the most private of Mr. Jefferson's out-of-door resorts, and even into his house, and stared about as if they were at a public show. This nuisance increased as years advanced. There are a number of persons now living who have seen groups of utter strangers, of both sexes, planted in the passage between his study and dining room, consulting their watches, and waiting for him to pass from one to the other to his dinner, so that they could momentarily stare at him. A female once punched through a window-pane of the house, with her parasol, to get a better view of him. He was waylaid in his rides and walks. When sitting in the shade of his porticoes to enjoy the coolness of the approaching evening, parties of men and women would sometimes approach within a dozen yards, and gaze at him point-blank until they had looked their fill, as they would have gazed on a lion in a menagerie.[2]

Overseer Edmund Bacon's recollections of his time at Monticello painted the same picture of the burdens of Virginia hospitality:

> Mr. Jefferson always had a great deal of company. . . . One great reason why Mr. Jefferson built his house at Poplar Forest, in Bedford County, was that he might go there in the summer to get rid of entertaining so much company. He knew that it more than used up all his income from the plantation and everything else, but he was so kind and polite that he received all his visitors with a smile and made them welcome. They pretended to come out of respect and regard to him, but I think that the fact that they saved a tavern bill had a good deal to do with it with a good many of them. I can assure you I got tired of seeing them come and waiting on them.[3]

When he was absent, Jefferson's daughter Martha Jefferson Randolph complained of still having to entertain guests who treated Monticello as an exquisite tavern, consuming food and wine. Jefferson reminded her that they were obligated to offer traditional hospitality.

When this portrait of unattainable privacy at Monticello is understood, the need for Poplar Forest as a quiet retreat becomes clear. As Henry Randall put it, Jefferson's convenience, spirits, and health "demanded that he have a roof to which he could occasionally fly for relief and rest from the traveller-thronged caravansera of Monticello."[4] Poplar Forest provided an effective sanctum, a three-day remove from Monticello where few outside of family were invited and very few others intruded uninvited. Poplar Forest might also be called a sanctuary, a place of refuge and protection, and even a sanatorium, providing mental rest and recuperation. Monticello does not fit the classic definition of a villa. In classical times the villa was a rural and pleasurable retreat to which one escaped from an urban environment. Monticello, while not an urban environment, was the busy place from which Jefferson escaped to his satellite rural retreat. In this way Poplar Forest does fit the definition of a true villa retreat. In his lifelong use and need of using retreats, Poplar Forest seems inevitable, a psychological necessity for Jefferson's introverted personality, which, as one historian put it, was "scholarly and reclusive by taste and training."[5]

"At the Poplar Forest"

Poplar Forest's other inescapable function was of course economic, as a plantation worked by enslaved laborers. Building a second home on this plantation did provide its owner a place to stay when he came to oversee its agricultural cash crops, but that was not its purpose. This inherited property was remote from Monticello and thus served as a retreat to distance Jefferson from his obligations of hospitality.

The Poplar Forest tract of land traded hands several times in the eighteenth century just as the county in which it sat would continue to change names as colonial counties in Virginia were divided for new ones. When granted 4,000 acres in 1745, William Stith's land was then in Albemarle County and included the location "at the Poplar Forest." This was the first known reference to this place-name referring to its distinctive natural feature. This area of rolling piedmont hills up against the east side of the Blue Ridge Mountains had streams, some of whose names recalled earlier eras: Bear Creek, Tomahawk Creek, Buffalo Creek, Elk Creek, Otter Creek, and Wolf Branch. Like his own father, Peter Jefferson, Thomas Jefferson's father-in-law, John Wayles, speculated in and accumulated various parcels of land, including Stith's Poplar Forest tract. By the time Wayles bought the Poplar Forest tract in 1764, now comprising 5,800 acres, the name of its county had changed twice: to Lunenburg in 1746 and to Bedford in 1753. Interestingly, Thomas Jefferson's father had once owned land adjacent to Wayles's two parcels in Bedford County. At Wayles's death in May 1773 these two properties, Poplar Forest and Judith's Creek, totaling 6,861 acres, passed to his daughter, Martha Wayles Jefferson, along with 135 enslaved people in four different counties and considerable debt. In September of that year Thomas Jefferson traveled to Bedford County to inspect the properties there. He chose to keep the Poplar Forest tract, perhaps because of its old-growth forest, selling the Judith's Creek land. A county record in 1766 indicates that Wayles had been working his Bedford County land with enslaved workers, but at his death the enslaved population was not great by plantation standards, being eleven people at Poplar Forest and Wingo's (an adjacent tract), and nine at Judith's Creek. Jefferson soon increased the numbers to seventeen and eighteen respectively. After gifting the Wingo's land to his daughter Martha on her wedding in 1790, Jefferson was left with 4,627 acres at Poplar Forest, out of a total of 10,647 acres on his nine separate Virginia plantations. By 1783 the enslaved population at Poplar Forest numbered thirty-five and would continue to grow as Jefferson moved people from one plantation to another and came to rely on the income produced by its tobacco crops. Eventually the enslaved population at Poplar Forest would number more than ninety people in seven families, with as many as four generations present at one time.[6]

When Jefferson first visited Poplar Forest in 1773, the closest town was New London, established in 1757 as the Bedford County seat. That same year a Quaker teenager named John Lynch would establish a ferry crossing on the Fluvanna River, as the upper portion of the James River was then called, about ten miles north of Poplar Forest. On that trip Jefferson noted that he paid Lynch to ferry him across to the north side of the river. In 1786 that crossing would become the thriving town of Lynchburg, where warehouses stored hogsheads of tobacco before they were sent downstream on locally designed bateaux to the inland seaport of Richmond. Lynchburg would also become the hub for manufactured goods Jefferson ordered from Europe via Richmond that made the more difficult journey poled upstream on the same riverboats.

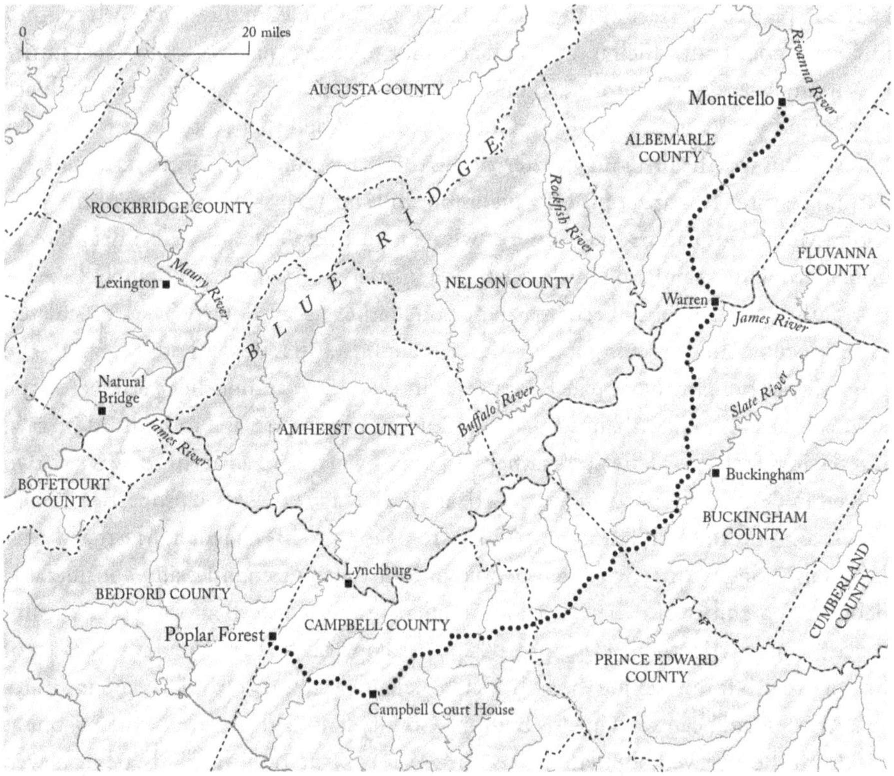

Fig. 8. Map showing route between Monticello and Poplar Forest.

Retreats of a Lifetime

Jefferson's predisposition for isolated quiet time had a long history that started early. His daughter Martha recounted that as a boy her father enjoyed retreating to the wooded mountaintop adjacent to his boyhood home at Shadwell: "I have heard my father say that when quite a boy the top of this mountain was his favorite retreat, here he would bring his books to study, here would pass his holiday and leisure hours; that he never wearied of gazing on the sublime and beautiful scenery that spread around, bounded only by the horizon, or the far off mountains."[7] This small mountaintop in Albemarle County that Jefferson first called "the hermitage" became "Monticello" (meaning small mountain in Italian) when Jefferson started building there in 1769.[8] The first completed structure, in keeping with traditions of large plantation houses that could take years to complete, was the South Pavilion, which served the unmarried Jefferson as an interim dwelling. Jefferson famously told a friend: "I have here but one room which, like the cobbler, serves me for parlour, for kitchen and hall. I may add, for bed chamber and study too."[9]

While Virginia's governor (1779–81), Jefferson would retreat to his Elk Hill plantation in Goochland Country, about halfway between Richmond and Monticello. Enslaved blacksmith Isaac Jefferson recalled: "Old Master had a small brick house there where he used to stay, about a mile from Elk Island. . . . When Mr. Jefferson was Governor, he used to stay thar a month or sich a matter; and when he was at the mountain, he would come and stay a month or so and then go back again."[10] After destroying Elk Hill in 1781, Lord Cornwallis sought to capture Governor Jefferson, who narrowly escaped from Monticello with his family and literally retreated to the Poplar Forest plantation, where they lived for two months in a simple overseer's house. He used the time there to write part of his book *Notes on the State of Virginia.* A house plan he sketched on a Poplar Forest plat on that visit indicates Jefferson's desire for a future house on the property. When confined to the overseer's house by heavy rains, Jefferson supposedly calculated how to retire the nation's debt.[11] This story must have been retold by family members to Jefferson biographer Henry Randall, who called it the genesis of "an uninterrupted retreat for the solitary study of high problems."[12] Whether this is true or not, Jefferson was already prone by his introverted nature to seek retreats.

While living in Paris, Jefferson wrote to a friend in 1787, "The sky is clearing and I shall away to my hermitage."[13] This real hermitage on a hill overlooking Paris took in paying guests who enjoyed the good air, a magnificent view of the city, and found comfort for body as well as for soul. Jefferson's daughter Martha recalled, "Whenever he had a press of business, he was in the habit of taking his papers and going to the hermitage, where he spent sometimes a week or more til he had finished his work."[14] This experience undoubtedly spurred him to write from Paris to another friend, "I sometimes think of building a little hermitage at the Natural Bridge and of passing there a part of the year at least."[15] He referred to one of early America's natural wonders that was just over the mountain from Poplar Forest and a "sublime" work of nature he had purchased in 1774. He had written still another friend from Paris, "I had rather be shut up in a very modest cottage, with my books, my family and a few old friends, dining on simple bacon, and letting the world roll on as it liked, than to occupy the most splendid post which any human power can give."[16] Retreats not so modest occupied landscaped gardens all around Paris. Jefferson was taken with one in particular, the Désert de Retz folly he visited outside of Paris. This summer residence that resembled an enormous broken column was the prototype for a circular retreat Jefferson would later design.

When he returned for a visit to Virginia in 1789 after spending five years in Europe, Jefferson reluctantly accepted George Washington's call to be secretary of state and moved to the government seat in Philadelphia. In 1792, in the backyard of his rented townhouse, Jefferson tried to build a very small building to use as a retreat. This, he said, was needed as "a place to retire & write in when I wished to be unseen & undisturbed even by my servants, and for this purpose it was to have a sky-light and no lateral windows."[17] In his absence the workers could not conceive of the anomaly of no windows and built it with two window-doors. Jefferson pronounced it "absolutely useless for my purpose."[18]

The following year Jefferson found a much more useful retreat on the Schuylkill River outside of Philadelphia when he rented a house there for the summer. At the beginning of April 1793 he wrote a friend that he was "determined to remove from this city into a small house in the country."[19] Jefferson's use of the summer house near Gray's Ferry provided uninterrupted time he had needed to focus his mind on work or to communicate with friends and family. This brief but valuable time undoubtedly revived and enforced Jefferson's ideas for a permanent personal retreat that he had wistfully dreamed of in Paris. The following year, about the time Jefferson resigned as Washington's secretary of state, he designed an intriguing 54-foot-diameter circular retreat.[20] As Fiske Kimball noted, it was "a sort of Trianon . . . to which he could retire, attended only by a single servant."[21] The most obvious reference for a circular retreat with oval rooms was the Désert de Retz outside of Paris he had admired.[22]

A series of unidentified drawings Jefferson possibly produced between 1789 and 1794 Kimball labeled "studies for retreats."[23] These designs show various room plans with unequal octagons, projecting octagons, and semi-octagons.[24] Some of these might be early studies for a general retreat or preliminary studies for Poplar Forest.[25] Regardless of their attribution, we can safely conclude that after Paris Thomas Jefferson had future retreats on his mind that he characteristically explored on paper in a variety of forms.

With the prospect of retirement within sight in 1808, Jefferson directed alterations at Monticello that would provide additional private spaces in which to retreat. The South Pavilion, which had famously served as Jefferson's first "hermit's room," now became a "scholar's" room that he filled with books that overflowed from his principal library space.[26] For outdoor privacy he built "porticles" or "Venetian porches" on the south piazza adjacent to his greenhouse and chamber suite. These were louvered "rooms" that allowed outdoor privacy and were important enough to Jefferson that he allowed

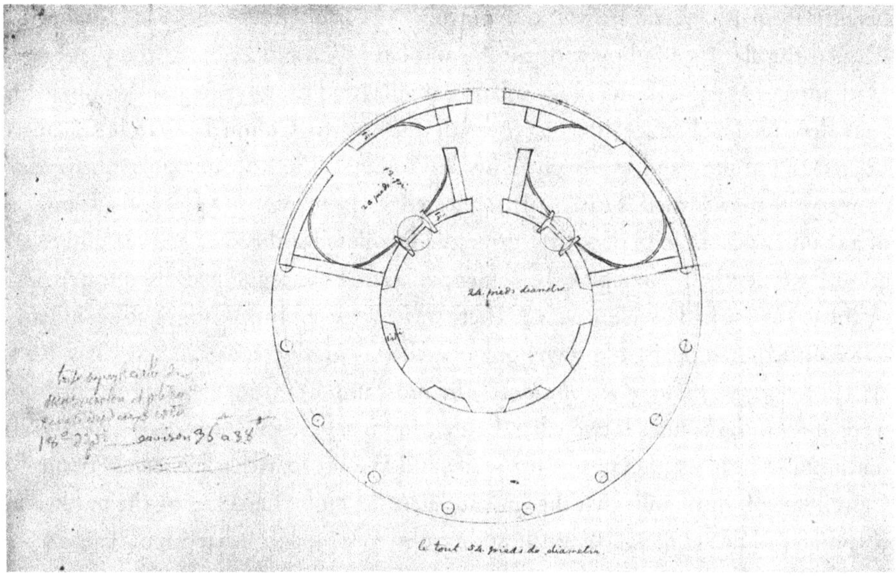

Fig. 9. Jefferson drawing (ca. 1793) of a circular retreat based on the Désert de Retz folly near Paris.

them to trump the symmetrical appearance of the house.[27] To retreat farther outdoors at Monticello and to more fully enjoy nature, Jefferson created a pavilion on the retaining wall of his large vegetable garden. Originally conceived as one of four octagonal garden pavilions or lodges representing different styles of architecture, or miniature imitations of famous buildings, the pavilion "box" was open on all four sides with oversize double-sash windows extending to the floor.[28] This small and very transparent retreat was similar to garden houses and summer houses in American gardens where one could retreat for short periods. A visitor to Monticello said the garden pavilion was Jefferson's favorite place to "read and sit."[29]

Jefferson's various retreats, large or small, imagined or constructed, show that a "retreat" was not a particular type of structure but rather a building or place that offered shelter from worldly pressures. Poplar Forest fits perfectly into this long tradition of Jefferson's conception of retreats. In the spectrum of Jefferson's retreats, Poplar Forest was the ultimate solution and was characteristically unique both in style and in function.

Traditions of the Villa Retreat

When Jefferson spoke of Monticello as an idealized pastoral setting using classical villa references, it reflected a long lineage of classical, Renaissance, and eighteenth-century European villas. James Ackerman's history of the villa argues that it is unique as a building type whose program has remained unchanged for over two thousand years.[30] Ancient villa retreats of wealthy Romans and the concomitant healthful and intellectual benefits from using them are well known from classical literature and history. Jefferson studied the classics as a boy with tutors, and later with professors at the College of William and Mary.[31] The ideology of ancient villas and the advantages of country life were described by Horace, Martial, Juvenal, Cato, Varro, Columella, Virgil, Epicurus, Lucretius, Catullus, and, especially, Pliny the Younger. The Romans spoke of the ideal country life they termed "Otium." This referred to the mental and physical advantages of a country villa that, in opposition to city life, offered seclusion, serenity, and relaxation.[32] Readers had to imagine the ancient villa since almost all had disappeared, and by the 1780s few had been excavated. There was one exception. While residing in Paris, Jefferson acquired the best-known book of archaeologically reconstructed villas: Robert Castell's 1728 *Villas of the Ancients.* The most important images and descriptions were of Pliny the Younger's two villas, Laurentinum and Tusci.[33] Castell described Laurentinum as "a Place rather proper for Study, and to retire to with a few select Friends."[34] Castell said of Pliny's villa that the "private spaces[,] more than eluding the public, incorporated understandings of retreat, study, solitude, and décor that might offer release from social and political dimensions of consciousness."[35]

Renaissance architects continued the traditions of the villa. The most famous were those designed by Andrea Palladio in the sixteenth century. Following territorial wars in the early fifteenth century, wealthy Venetians turned to agricultural development of the "terraferma" mainland and the Veneto hills beyond. This economic revolution created the opportunity for a new type of farmhouse where owners could supervise their agricultural production and laborers. Seasonal life in the country then became more desirable culturally and socially. Palladio responded to this contemporary need by designing new fashionable houses at the center of these agricultural complexes. The villa house itself might be used for agricultural storage, but the attached "barchesse" (barn wings) for agricultural use became a signature part of Palladio's designs. In his famous book of 1570, *The Four Books of Architecture,* Palladio described the villa and its site, "where the mind, fatigued by the agitations of the city, will be greatly restor'd and comforted, and be able quietly to attend the studies of letters, and contemplation" and where one "could easily attain to as much happiness as can be attained here below."[36] Leon Battista Alberti, a Renaissance architect whose influential fifteenth-century work Jefferson had purchased in Paris, described the nature of villas as conducive "to the repose, tranquility or delicacy of life"; "the owner would be 'at liberty to do just what he pleases.'"[37]

In important ways Palladio's architectural legacy in eighteenth-century England had just as great an impact on Jefferson. Published works by the "British Palladians" were critical in forming Jefferson's early study of architecture. By the mid-eighteenth century, literature extolled the rural and suburban villas with their associated picturesque gardens. Associated with this architectural movement were much deeper philosophical, economic, political, and social currents that were to significantly bear on Thomas Jefferson's life and architecture.

Modern Prototypes

The ideological underpinnings of modern eighteenth-century English villa retreats are found in the profuse literary references Jefferson and his contemporaries knew so well. It is an influence that bears on Poplar Forest as a retreat as well as one more intangibly explaining Jefferson's development as an individual needing a retreat. Its genesis was in Elizabethan England during the sixteenth century.[38] This movement would come to strongly associate an individual's personal development and identity with his rural villa retreat. It started with hunting lodges that were located some distance from the main house that eventually took on more entertainment functions and where dessert courses were served. As Mark Girouard explained, "Apart from their purely sporting functions they served a distinct purpose as a retreat from the formality and pomp of the great house, a place to which the owner could retire with a few friends and a reduced staff, when he kept what was known as a 'secret house.'"[39] These "garden houses," "summer houses," "belvederes," "prospect rooms," or "secret houses" were related to a new appreciation of nature. Some lodges could house a family for a short time, but others became more refined as a retreat for study and reflection. William Cecil's Theobald Lodge of the 1590s was where he "retyred from Buysnes of so much Companie, [and was] his greatest Greatnes & onlie Happiness."[40] William Lawson remarked in 1618 that some property owners could "withdraw themselves from the troublesome affayres of their estate."[41] One of Jefferson's famous triumvirates of history's greatest men (Bacon, Locke, and Newton), Sir Francis Bacon, created a writing retreat in 1595 at his Twickenham house. It had an associated garden, referencing ancient villas with elevated loggias and mounts, where Bacon was very productive "in studious retirement."[42] Lord Halifax said of his own retreat on his estate at Horton: "It is a room for reflection: a belvedere with its wide views over trees and grass and water; a banqueting room, for convivial gatherings of old friends; and, at the same time, a hermitage for study and for solitude. No one could ask for more."[43] Roger North's 1698 essay *Of Building* described a "villa" as "quasy a lodge, for the sake of a garden, to retire to injoy and sleep, without pretense of entertainement of many persons."[44] By the early eighteenth century the casinos, follies, and pleasure pavilions on older country house estates were now associated features of the landscape garden movement and were joined by entire villa estates associated with retirement, pleasure, and relaxation.[45] By the mid-eighteenth century the English had a well-established culture of retirement with an association of retreats and gardens.

Revolutionary political writers like John Locke, who was most admired by Jefferson, also influenced these cultural shifts that associated dwellings with their owner's character and identity. Locke's "Essay Concerning Human Understanding" (1690) argued for the politically free self, for private property, and for home ownership as a way to articulate and develop one's individuality and selfhood.[46] Personalized spaces, thought Locke, shaped personal identities and formed an intimate relationship between architecture, self, and knowledge.[47] The ancient villa had been revived for country and suburban retreats: "What was known in early eighteenth-century Britain about ancient Roman and Renaissance villas, villa life, and villa ideology made the villa a potentially attractive paradigm for the emerging British bourgeoisie. Associated with retreat, leisure, and pastoralism, the villa could suit any social stratum with sufficient surplus time and wealth."[48] This ideology associating architecture and landscapes with an owner's need for contemplation, study, and privacy found fertile ground in Thomas Jefferson's intellectual development. Toward that development his use of retreats would continue to enforce their benefits.

Providing architectural examples for the growing culture of retirement was British Palladian Robert Morris, whose book *Select Architecture* (1755) had a major impact on Thomas Jefferson's early architectural development, in particular as a main source for octagonal houses.[49] Robert Morris's *Lectures in Architecture,* published in 1734, advocated for private dwellings of a secluded and solitary character where individuals could pursue their personal intellectual enlightenment within his harmonious designs. Morris linked seclusion at a small retreat to an individual's intellect and pleasure, where

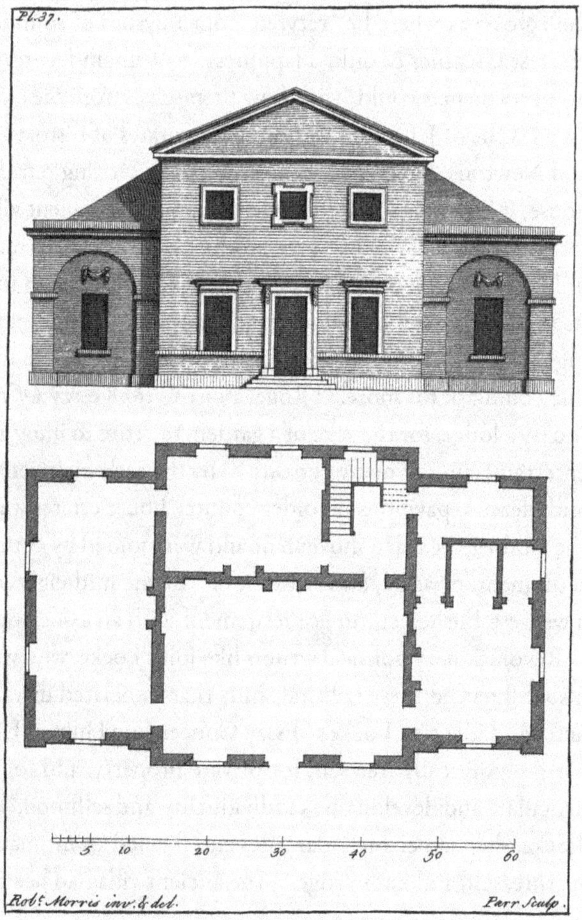

Fig. 10. "Design for a Retired Person," plate 37, Robert Morris, *Select Architecture* (1757).

the dwelling was a "perfect geometric balance that afforded the mind a state of harmonic awareness conducive to such elevated thoughts" and where the owner could "secrete himself" and "contemplate the important Themes of Human Life."[50] Morris's designs for "a contemplative Genius" in retirement in a "necessarily secluded and remote locale" must have resonated with Jefferson and lodged in his fertile mind. By the eighteenth century the connection of retirement, retreats, and an individual's pursuit of happiness in solitude was well established in literature and architecture.

English country houses and villa retreats now expressed a new relationship with the natural environment: the picturesque landscaped garden.[51] William Kent, one of Jefferson's early British Palladian mentors whose books also introduced him to octagon designs, was greatly influential in the landscape garden movement. Kent's garden design for Alexander Pope's villa at Twickenham had been one of the sites Jefferson visited on his famous English landscape garden trip with John Adams in 1786. Jefferson later wrote to John Page that "gardening in that country is the article in which it surpasses all the earth. I mean their pleasure gardening. This indeed went far beyond my ideas."[52] This interconnected movement of suburban houses and landscapes was promoted in the British poetry found in Jefferson's library that linked retirement, intimate spaces indoors or out, and the intellectual benefits of solitude. Some even associated the virtues of retreat with "opposition retirement," an antidote from corrupt political trends and a theme discussed by Jefferson and John Adams in their retirement years.[53]

It is hard to overestimate the impact these interrelated intellectual concepts of life, liberty, and pursuits of happiness had on colonial American elites. They seem like abstract concepts, but these ideas wove themselves into eighteenth-century American culture, society, and politics.[54] Notions of political selfhood from the seventeenth century affected aspects of privacy and personal spaces in house designs on both sides of the Atlantic in the eighteenth century. Subsequent shifts in domesticity and intimacy changed the way individuals and families interacted with each other, with visitors, and with servants. Notions of the self, privacy, retirement retreats, and connections to nature were powerful ideas absorbed by Thomas Jefferson for many years.

Monticello certainly reflects some of the ideology of a classical villa with its landscaped gardens, but Poplar Forest does far more. Ackerman defines the villa as: "A building in the country designed for its owner's enjoyment and relaxation. Though it may also be the center of an agricultural enterprise, the pleasure factor is what essentially distinguishes the villa residence from the farmhouse and the villa estate from the farm. The farmhouse tends to be simple in structure and to conserve ancient forms that do not require the intervention of a designer. The villa is typically the product of an architect's imagination and asserts its modernity."[55] The economic system of eighteenth-century Virginia was one of isolated plantations where the owner's principal residence might be architecturally distinctive and surrounded by pleasure gardens, and even spoken of in classical terms, but they were not satellite properties in counterpoint to principal houses in the city. Just the opposite was often true in Virginia, where planters maintained a secondary house in town.[56] The impulse behind the villa, in the words of

Ackerman, is "generated by psychological rather than utilitarian needs; it is quintessentially ideological."[57] In this way Poplar Forest more than Monticello exemplified the ideological prototype of the villa retreat.

American Traditions

Seventeenth-century America was composed of rural houses as a matter of circumstance. Once it became safe to leave the security of an early settlement, the individualistic impulse to disperse and own a separate piece of property became an American characteristic. Subsequently there were many houses in the country as opposed to country houses in the English manner. The settlement pattern of the Chesapeake region and the colonial South produced country plantation houses due to geography and economy. As settlements moved into the Piedmont, the model still held, as long as transportation to a port was viable. Monticello is a classic example, located inland but linked by river to its essential seaport. Although Poplar Forest can also be called both a Piedmont plantation house, or a country house, its role as a secondary residence distinguishes it. The English tradition of villa retreats transferred to the American colonies early on. From the banqueting houses and lodges of the seventeenth-century gentry to the suburban villas of the eighteenth-century wealthy, the secondary American country house has a rich but largely undocumented history. What distinguishes Poplar Forest within this tradition requires some sorting out between the distinctions of "lodge," "country house," "summer house," "country seat," and "retirement villa." Unlike the southern "country seat" of Monticello, and almost any other secondary seasonal houses, Poplar Forest was a rare intellectual retreat for an individual.

Not surprisingly, the earliest references to country retreats in America are those of aristocratic English governors who had come with that tradition. In the early summer of 1775 John Murray, the Fourth Earl of Dunmore, and the last colonial governor of Virginia, literally retreated from the Governor's Palace in Williamsburg and its rebellious citizens to his farm outside of town named Porto Bello. An earlier 1717 reference indicates Virginia governor Alexander Spotswood originally built it as a "country place."[58] In the English tradition Dunmore described this house as a hunting lodge. The term "lodge" refers to that tradition in England of banqueting houses where guests retired from the main house for food, drink, and entertainment. A surprising discovery documents an early tradition of banqueting houses by leading aristocrats in Virginia.[59] Virginia governor William Berkeley's impressive house Green Spring, begun in 1643, was expanded by 1674 with a large new wing functioning as a country banqueting and party house. His wealthy Virginia peers Lewis Burwell and Robert Carter likewise constructed remote secondary banqueting houses at Fairfield (1694) and Corotoman (1726). Maryland's royal governor Charles Calvert was said to retire around 1672 to his "summer house," Zekiah Manor, outside of Annapolis.[60] Similarly, Maryland governor Horatio Sharpe built White Hall near Annapolis in 1765 as a lavish entertainment and fishing lodge in the same tradition.[61] Hunting and fishing lodges became common among those who could afford second homes. Dr. Thomas Walker built his hunting lodge named "Turkey Hill" near Keswick, Virginia, in 1764.[62] Benjamin Chew built his summer retreat and his "lake house" outside Philadelphia. The Coles family house, Enniscorthy, in Albemarle County, where Jefferson frequently stayed on his trips to Poplar Forest, started as a summer residence and hunting lodge before 1769.[63] The tradition continued in the nineteenth century with examples like Huntley in Fairfax County, Virginia, constructed by Thomson Mason in 1825 as a summer house and hunting lodge.[64]

A clarification of terms and definitions for the American "summer house" is necessary. The term "summer house" could mean two different things. One is synonymous with "garden house" and refers to a small decorative structure in a landscaped garden that was very much part of that traditional English ethos. Examples are many and often in octagonal forms, like those George Washington constructed at Mount Vernon as decorative gardening sheds that resembled his octagonal privies. Other examples include Thomas Mifflin's 1778 octagonal summer house at his country house outside of Philadelphia; Isaac Royal's highly articulated hexagonal garden house with cupola situated on a mound in his eighteenth-century garden in Medford, Massachusetts; Samuel McIntire's 1799 architecturally significant summer house in Salem, Massachusetts; Abraham Redwood's elegant summer house at his Redwood Farm in Portsmouth, New Hampshire (New England's first botanical garden); and John Burgwin's 1760s "English style" gardens at his Hermitage plantation on the Cape Fear River in North Carolina, which boasted an octagonal summer house and a brick garden house on a mound that served as library and chapel.[65] Nicholas Biddle's two-story temple-form building on the grounds of his house Andalusia (1750–95) outside of Philadelphia served as a billiard and card house.[66] Some of these buildings served utilitarian purposes for gardeners or as the covering for icehouses, but most were small buildings in landscaped gardens built exclusively for their owners' retreat and repose. No better example is Jefferson's own ca. 1796 design for an unexecuted temple-form greenhouse/lodge at Monticello. His 1804–7 "General ideas for the improvement of Monticello" included plans for garden temples based on the Lantern of Demosthenes, the domed temple at Chiswick, and a Chinese pavilion based on the Menagerie at Kew Gardens.[67] These were unexecuted, but again in 1807 he proposed a wonderful variety of garden temples for Monticello that would have imitated the Maison Carrée, the Pantheon, the Monument of Lysicrates, a Gothic temple, and a Chinese temple.[68] Jefferson gave instructions to Hugh Chisolm to make the bricks for these garden buildings, but they were never built. Finally, as we have seen, in 1812 he built his small garden house on the edge of the Monticello vegetable garden that served as his miniature retreat. Lady Jean Skipwith's early nineteenth-century octagonal garden house at Preswould plantation in Southside Virginia served the same purpose. Public examples and the continued usage of the ambiguous term "summer house" existed well into the twentieth century. A 1940s description of Alum Springs, a resort hotel in New London near Poplar Forest, mentioned that "summer houses were sprinkled all over the wide lawn."[69]

A more common usage of the term "summer house" referred to a seasonal second house. The earlier English traditions of banqueting houses, casinos, and lodges of the royal and upper classes, and later the bourgeois, became more democratic in America by the middle of the eighteenth century. The tradition of wealthy eighteenth-century Americans retreating from their urban homes to a summer place became widespread by the end of the eighteenth century. Jefferson's rented house outside Philadelphia is a good example, where a country setting connoted a healthier repose for the summer. A traveler to Philadelphia in 1795 remarked, "During the summer, the people that can make it convenient retire to country houses in the neighborhood of the town."[70] When arriving in New York in 1807, Augustus John Foster found himself "at a season when many of the best families of the place were at their country houses."[71] The greatest concentrations of summer houses were logically located near the eighteenth-century cities where wealth had accumulated: Boston, New York, Philadelphia, and Baltimore. Even when Washington, DC, was being laid out in the 1790s, the older settlers in the eighteenth-century town of Georgetown looked to the nearby country for sites. Rosedale was built in 1793 "as a summer retreat when well-to-do Georgetowners were beginning to establish country seats."[72] Charlestonian families from the low country of South Carolina retreated to summer houses in the cooler North Carolina mountains.[73] Older buildings could be converted into seasonal houses. An 1831 Virginia newspaper ad suggested that the older brick house Reveille, just outside Richmond, "at moderate expense might be repaired and made a desirable place for a family residing in town to retire during the summer months."[74]

Terminology can still be misleading as a "country house" could be a seasonal "summer house," or it could be a full-time "country seat." A "retirement villa" in the country could be where one retired to the suburbs during the summer or it could be where one retired from working life and business to a full-time country house. Monticello was both, the country seat as the principal dwelling at the center of a southern plantation to which Jefferson joyfully retired from public life. Alexander Hamilton built "The Grange" in 1802 as his principal dwelling in the upper Manhattan countryside on the Hudson River. The fashionable house in its landscaped gardens was described by the owner as "a retreat" and a "sweet asylum from care and pain."[75] Hamilton was not alone. In 1787 the upper part of Manhattan was filled with "elegant country-seats" that were also quickly springing up on Staten Island, Long Island, in Brooklyn, and along the Hudson and East Rivers to the point where "Every commanding eminence is occupied by Gentlemen's Houses, some of them most delightfully situated."[76] James Fenimore Cooper could write about the Hudson River Valley, "There is scarcely an eligible site for a dwelling that is not occupied by a villa, or one of the convenient and respectable looking farm-houses of the country."[77] By the 1850s travelers now making use of steamboats could report that "elegant summer residences" lined the Hudson River halfway to Albany. By 1850 seasonal country houses for the cultured elites of America were de rigueur, and the growth of country houses or "villas" exploded in numbers around large cities, both as second homes and for the new suburban middle classes.[78]

Tamara Plakins Thornton's study of country houses of the Boston elite describes virtues other than those extolled by the ancient Romans. Bostonian elites escaped political realms to become prominent scientific farmers pursuing agricultural reforms. Thornton argues that this is tied to the 1790s political debates of Republican ideology, echoing the earlier British political principles and virtues of "opposition retirement," like Christopher Gore, who retreated from Boston to his fashionable house in Waltham to escape politics for his books and his farm.[79] Similarly George Cabot was "abstracted from the political world" on his Brookline farm.[80] John Archer also argues that Americans added a layer of republican individualism and domesticity that uniquely defined the connection between virtue, character, and retirement architecture.[81] Fisher Ames wrote that his tranquility centered on his farm, where his books, his friends, and his family provided "a refuge from the terrors & vexations of politics."[82] Retirement to family, friends, farm, and books resonated with Jefferson's own pregnant hopes and desires in his last years of public life as he also retreated from politics. Jefferson had also been very interested in progressive techniques of scientific farming, but his exceptional skills as a "revolutionary gardener" focused on flowers and vegetables.[83]

The most comprehensive history of early American country houses is one that documents that building type around Philadelphia. In their masterful study of colonial-era buildings and landscapes around Philadelphia, Mark Reinberger and Elizabeth McLean trace the British architectural heritage of the bourgeois country house to its eighteenth-century transformation in this American region.[84] They define three types of country houses: a full-time country seat, a weekend or summer retreat, and a house in the city that was rural in character. The first two types are similar to those mentioned around Boston and New York. A map drawn of the Philadelphia area in 1754 shows 150 such country houses. Traveler Andrew Barnaby recorded in 1759 that "the whole country [around Philadelphia] is covered with villas, gardens, and luxuriant orchards." Philadelphia estates were known for their landscaped gardens in the English style with equally distinctive lodges, garden houses, pavilions, temples and "summer house" buildings.[85] This area on the Schuylkill River was described by Emily Cooperman as "the most developed villa district in the young nation, perhaps rivaling only the Thames upriver from London for its concentration of suburban country houses."[86] By the mid-eighteenth century the terms "retirement," "country seat," and "villa" were commonly used in reference to these pastoral retreats that were close enough to be used on weekends. Socializing between villas encouraged competitive architectural, artistic, intellectual, and epicurean experiences, especially when President George Washington and his cabinet, residing in Philadelphia, were the invited guests! Andrew Hamilton's Bush Hill was described as a "kind of art museum" with numerous paintings and statues.[87] John Adams was impressed with Lansdowne and its landscaped gardens and described it to his wife as "very retired, but very beautiful—a splendid house, gravel walks, shrubberies, and clumps of trees in the English style"[88] Robert Gilmer described it as "the best country house in America," noting that it "commands a noble view of the Schuylkill."[89] One Schuylkill River house advertised for sale in 1767 was "particularly calculated to form a pleasant Country Retirement in Summer, for a Gentleman and his Family."[90]

For five months in the spring and summer of 1793 Jefferson joined wealthy Philadelphians in pastoral retirement on the east bank of the Schuylkill River. That September Jefferson made reference to "the malady prevailing in this city, and which has nearly suspended all business" and noting that the "season for the country will be nearly over."[91] The "season" referred to the common practice of wealthy elites living in cities or low-lying regions who would escape to the hills, mountains, or country site, to avoid real or imagined summer-time "diseases." Some fled to medicinal spring resorts for curative and social vacations. This tradition in Virginia remained for Jefferson's overseer Edmund Bacon a distinctive memory: he recalled that in the middle of June throngs of visitors heading to the springs would descend upon Monticello, eating Jefferson "out of house and home."[92] Bacon even associated this seasonal onslaught with Poplar Forest: "One great reason why Mr. Jefferson built his house at Poplar Forest, in Bedford County, was that he might go there in the summer to get rid of entertaining so much company."[93]

The "noble" setting of Jefferson's small rental house just below Gray's Ferry elicited a joy that could hardly be contained in a letter to his daughter Martha: "I never go into the house but at the hour of bed. I never before knew the full value of trees. My house is intirely embosomed in high plane trees, and good grass below, and under them I breakfast, dine, write, read and receive my company. What would I not give that the trees planted nearest round the house at Monticello were full grown."[94] A mid- to late nineteenth-century watercolor by David Johnson Kennedy shows the Gray's Ferry house with an open lawn sloping to the nearby river and tall groves of trees on the opposite side.[95] The geographical advantage of Gray's Ferry put Jefferson in proximity to two significant gardens. One was owned by John Bartram, scientist, horticulturalist, and America's most notable naturalist. Bartram's famous garden, still in existence, supplied Jefferson with plants and seeds for the Monticello grounds. More important was the nearby Woodlands, owned by Jefferson's good friend William Hamilton. After spending time in England and on the Continent, Hamilton remodeled an earlier house on the Schuylkill River in 1789 in a fashionable Adamesque style.[96] The Woodlands featured oval bows, alcove beds, and sash doors along with Venetian windows and porticos that opened to the landscape and views of the nearby river. Hamilton created one of the most important English-style picturesque gardens in America, which elicited a long letter from Jefferson inviting him to Monticello with hope he would "have an opportunity of indulging on a new field some of the taste which has made the Woodlands the only rival which I have known in America to what may be seen in England. thither we are to go without doubt for the first models in this art."[97] Perhaps inspired by the Woodlands, Jefferson drew a plan of how he would alter his small rental house, with an oval saloon that projected as a semi-octagonal bow out onto the landscape and toward the river beyond. Hamilton's creation, both architecture and gardens, stimulated Jefferson's fertile collection of ideas that fed into the 1796 rebuilding of Monticello.

Jefferson's enjoyable summer sojourn at Gray's Ferry would have provided yet another impetus for a future retreat, especially one with large mature trees. That summer Jefferson might have visited two other nearby houses on the Schuylkill: Doctor William Smith's octagon house and John Penn's The Solitude, the former a possible source for a full octagon house sketched by Jefferson and the latter an example of a rare intellectual retreat used by an individual.

In this long and rich history of American country house retreats, Poplar Forest is uncommon for three reasons: its location, its year-round use, and its use by an individual. As a second home, its distance from the principal home was unusual. It was land Jefferson inherited, but its isolated three-day distance by horse or carriage from Monticello made it perfectly suited for retreating from too many visitors. Country houses were typically located within a day's travel from the principal home and close enough to be used on weekends. Although Jefferson did engage with plantation neighbors at Poplar Forest, this was not the social interaction and entertainment common among the country-house elites around Philadelphia. The fact that Jefferson used Poplar Forest at all seasons of the year also made it unusual. Other second homes are routinely referred to as "summer" houses and only used in the mild or summer season. Use of a country retreat for purely intellectual reasons, by an individual, might not be unique, but examples are rare and hard to document. Most seasonal country houses were used by families with the expectation of visitors. Rural retirement did not mean rural seclusion. This is not to say that family retreats were not used by individuals from time to time and used for intellectual pursuits of reading and writing. In 1798 George Cabot remarked about his country house that "when I have no living company, I call upon the Dead who are always ready to come from my Library & entertain me."[98] Other individuals used convenient retreats when necessary. From 1811 Secretary of State, and then President, James Monroe retreated from official duties to an early eighteenth-century stone cottage on property he owned in Loudoun County, Virginia, before eventually building his retirement home there in the 1820s.[99]

If summer retreats were used by individuals, men were the norm, but two exceptions are known. About 1766, following the death of her husband, Rebecca Warner Rawle Shoemaker built a small country house on the Schuylkill River. She and her daughter used the small but architecturally fashionable house that was "finely situated for prospect, beauty, and pleasure, on that delightful river."[100] Charles Carroll, barrister, of Baltimore, died in 1783 and left his estate to his widow, Margaret Tilghman Carroll. On part of the estate called The Caves was a small frame octagon building, 24′ × 24′, that Margaret used as a summer retreat, calling it "Little Lodge at the Caves."[101]

As an intellectual retreat, the closest analogue to Poplar Forest might be John Penn's house, The Solitude, constructed on the Schuylkill River in 1785.[102] John, the bachelor grandson of William Penn, the Founder, returned to Philadelphia from England in 1783 to reclaim family lands. The twenty-four-year-old Penn had a master of arts degree from Cambridge University, had traveled extensively in Europe, and was characterized as "a liberal patron of art, something of a poet, and an idealist."[103] Penn built his "elegant box" for a "bachelor of quite [*sic*] tastes" on the west bank of the Schuylkill River. He named it after Castle Solitude, a neoclassical hunting lodge, or "refugium," a place of quiet reflection and solitude, built for the Duke of Württemberg in 1764.[104] The 26′ × 26′ house had a parlor on the ground floor that opened with floor-to-ceiling windows onto a small Ionic order portico with eastern views of the river. Along with two small bed chambers on the second floor was Penn's fifteen-foot-square library that "held a goodly collection of the classics, English poets and standard works appealing to a scholarly taste."[105] Though small, the house was articulated with "exquisite plaster decorations of the ceilings and cornice," "carved woodwork," and an "intricately hand-wrought" iron stair balustrade.[106] It also featured a rare European-style bed alcove. Penn was known as an "enthusiastic" and "intelligent arboriculturist" and set his refined house in a notable English-style landscaped garden with "clumps" of trees and bushes, bowling green, flower garden, ha-ha ditch, and "wilderness" garden. A 1784 plan of the estate shows this expertly composed and compact 15-acre site. George Washington visited Solitude, but Penn left for England in 1788 before Jefferson took up residence in Philadelphia. It is tempting to speculate that Jefferson would have known about and visited the site. Penn's reclusive and intellectual nature, and his refined year-round house and landscaped gardens, come close as an American example to what Thomas Jefferson would create at Poplar Forest. Like the seventeenth-century literary retreat of Francis Bacon, the nature of a retreat was determined by the character of the owner and how the retreat was used.

In 1806 when Elizabeth Trist heard Jefferson was building a second home, she reasonably assumed that "you mean to pass your summers there."[107] Only his family and close friends would come to realize that Poplar Forest was Jefferson's retreat in all seasons. Still, the ingrained and persistent tradition of escaping to summer houses remained strong well into the twentieth century and perpetuated the assumptions made for Poplar Forest. George Hutter, writing in 1838 to his brother Edward, who would marry into the Cobbs family that owned Poplar Forest after 1828, referred to Poplar Forest as "the old summer residence of the great and good Thomas Jefferson."[108] The earliest mention of Poplar Forest by a historian was Henry Howe's in 1845. He also assumed that it "was his [Jefferson's] residence in the summer months."[109] By the end of the nineteenth century those accustomed to retreating to summer houses would find it inconceivable that one would do so at other times of the year, especially in winter. Many summer houses were not even designed for wintertime use. Some old family homes in the country became the designated summer place when the family moved to a nearby town or city. Rebecca Yancey Williams fondly remembered her summers outside of Lynchburg, Virginia: "In the summer we always went to Bedford County to stay with my father's mother. She was Grandma. She lived about twelve miles out of Lynchburg in a sweet old place which had been the summer home of my father's family."[110] During the summer her father, Robert Yancey, commuted daily via railroad into the city. Rebecca described the excitement of an elaborate picnic with their Hutter family friends who had encamped to nearby Poplar Forest for the summer. Claudine

Hutter's 1930 description of Poplar Forest still called it Jefferson's "summer home." She could be excused because her ancestors who purchased the property from Jefferson's grandson in 1828 had used it only as a summer house after 1889. Hutter children would come to love their summer experience at Poplar Forest as they escaped the city of Lynchburg. One cousin wrote to another, "We summer there & it is the place we all gather during the hot months of June July & August."[111] This strong Virginia tradition of summer houses accounts for the persistence to this day that Poplar Forest was Jefferson's summer house retreat. It was the year-round madding crowd of visitors from which Jefferson escaped, not the Virginia summer heat. Jefferson's conceptual ideas for his ultimate retirement retreat, contemplated for many years, certainly reflected many well-known references, both ancient and modern. But in comparison with American traditions of second homes, it would be very different.

2

THOMAS JEFFERSON'S EDUCATION AS ARCHITECT AND BUILDER

In September 1802 Dr. William Thornton and his wife, Anna Maria, visited Jefferson at Monticello. Anna Maria left one of the most observant and descriptive accounts of the still unfinished and remodeled Monticello. Her most poignant and pregnant statement, no doubt shared by all of Jefferson's close friends, was that he took "a very long time maturing his projects."[1] This factor is key to understanding what makes Thomas Jefferson an exceptional architect and builder. The lifetime evolution of Jefferson's process in design and construction reflects his fundamental characteristics—a penchant for precision, an obsessive need to control the process, and an amazing patience for achieving idealistic goals.

Thomas Jefferson began construction of Monticello as a twenty-six-year-old bachelor. The unfinished work lasted forty years, from 1769 to 1809, interrupted by time in Europe and in public office. In 1796, at age fifty-three, he began the selective demolition and rebuilding of his ambitiously enlarged and more sophisticated house. This protracted process spanned from 1796 to 1809. In 1806, at age sixty-two, he began construction of Poplar Forest and directed its long, slow completion until just before he died in 1826, a twenty-year project. Even before finishing Poplar Forest, at age seventy-six, he began the "hobby" of his old age, the University of Virginia. Construction of these university buildings designed and supervised by Jefferson began in 1817 and was effectively finished in 1826, the year of his death, a nine-year project. Any one of these accomplishments would be notable for a Virginian gentleman architect. Together they are the very remarkable product of one man, but even as phenomenal as they are, they are not the principal achievements for which he is remembered. Without the intellectual, political, educational, and scientific achievements of Thomas Jefferson, his architectural works would still stand as extraordinary for their time and place. How did Jefferson come to be so accomplished an architect and builder?

It would be almost 150 years before the full extent of Thomas Jefferson's precocious role as an architect and builder was known to the general public, and even then it was a very limited exposure.[2] Although a number of editions of Jefferson's letters had been published by the early twentieth century, his architectural drawings and building notes had remained hidden in Boston, where they had been thankfully saved by the Coolidge family.[3] Fiske Kimball's monumental work, *Thomas Jefferson, Architect,* published in 1916 in a private limited edition, finally gave to Jefferson another feather in his already crowded hat. The importance of Kimball's book—in addition to the author's excellent initial analysis of Jefferson's whole life's architectural works—was found in the generous quantity of its illustrations, which were competently sorted by project and date. The quantity, detail, and breadth of this treasure trove would have been apparent to anyone who saw it. As an architectural historian Kimball had recognized in these papers something just as important as the drawings and had insisted on illustrating them as well. These were samples of Jefferson's many pages of notes that showed not only his mathematical precision of design, based on his architectural books, but the detailed and comparative notes and specifications for materials and construction. What Kimball understood about Jefferson's conceptual and executed building process for the first Monticello was that his grasp of historical precedent combined with a mathematical precision was exceptional compared with contemporary American gentry architects and master builders.

Kimball characterized Jefferson's approach to architecture as a "relish for precision in all departments of life, coupled with historical passion." Jefferson's "determined effort at formulation," Kimball said, led him to create an "art of retrospection and science."[4] These insightful characteristics still seem valid, especially with our current understanding of Poplar Forest. Stated in a different way, other historians point out that Jefferson was trained for a profession in the law and that this training emphasized a precision and logic based on rules derived from historical precedent.[5] As an attorney might apply and interpret that logic and history to current circumstances, Jefferson typically had to rectify his idealistic intent in architecture with circumstances and their consequences. Mitigating circumstances, in addition to materials, workers, and workmanship, were the necessary considerations of comfort, convenience, beauty, and privacy, both for himself, his family and guests, and in relationship to the enslaved people who interacted within these spaces. These social and cultural aspects were also part of Jefferson's Virginia heritage that had an influence on his architecture, even if filtered through his idiosyncratic and innovative designs.[6] By 1780 Thomas Jefferson's formal liberal arts education and his informal but studious architectural education had given him the confidence to express critical assessments of Virginia's architecture. He infamously did this in his only published book, *Notes on the State of Virginia,* first published in 1785 while Jefferson was in Paris. While intended as a natural history of the state, it also included Jefferson's critique of Virginia buildings in general and public ones in Williamsburg specifically. The "reformation in this elegant and useful art [of architecture]" was one he had personally undertaken with the design and construction of Monticello.[7]

The "eye" of Jefferson, a theme used so brilliantly by William Howard Adams for his aesthetic biography of the man, focuses on the visual influences that affected his architectural development.[8] Jefferson's eye first observed his native Virginia architecture, the best of which was Georgian-Palladian but something he sought to criticize in *Notes on Virginia.* He then absorbed bookish visions from the remains of classical architecture and images of newer British Palladian houses. He saw the best of current architecture in Annapolis, Philadelphia, and New York on his travels to those places in 1766. His eye took in some of the best colonial buildings in Philadelphia when there with the Continental Congress in 1775–76. After his eye-opening experience in Europe from 1784 to 1789, he again saw the latest styles, still traditional, in Philadelphia in 1791 to 1800. From New York, Jefferson made a quick trip to Boston and as far as Portsmouth, New Hampshire, in 1784, but he doesn't leave us any impressions of seeing the early work of Charles Bulfinch or William McIntire, who were working in the new Federal style. Bulfinch would become better known for the work he did after his European tour in the 1780s, staying with Jefferson for a time in Paris. From 1800 to 1809 President Jefferson saw the few new distinguished buildings in Washington, DC, from James Hoban, William Thornton, and George Hadfield. He didn't get to Savannah to see the innovative Regency-style designs of William Jay. He most likely did not see the stylish work of various French émigré architects working in the mid-Atlantic states and stylish suburban houses around Baltimore.[9] The most up-to-date architecture Jefferson saw was the neoclassical work of Benjamin Henry Latrobe, but that seems to have had little influence on his own architecture other than ideas Latrobe later submitted for the University of Virginia. Jefferson's and Latrobe's student Robert Mills became part of the new Greek Revival movement of American neoclassicism, but that was a new generation of American architects, not a new fashion for someone still diligently working on his own older neoclassical style. Some architectural historians position Jefferson's architecture in a conflicting realm that was provincial and cosmopolitan, innovative and old-fashioned, backward looking and contemporary, idealistic and practical.[10] Latrobe complimented Jefferson on being the father of the arts in the United States—and at the same time told others that Jefferson was old-fashioned and fished things out of old French books. Jefferson's architectural works—considered provincial or hailed as revolutionary in his time and ours—often have been greatly misunderstood. His was a personal style that is not unreasonably labeled as the development of a personal style. That uniqueness is reflected at Poplar Forest but requires some background history for full comprehension.

Amateur Architect

Jefferson's education and development as an architect had begun with the initial construction of Monticello in 1769 and kept pace thereafter through his hundreds of designs and a lifetime of constructing his own works. The initial preparation for an architect, the first-century architect Marcus Vitruvius Polio had advised, before studying ancient and contemporary buildings, and before understanding how to construct them, was obtaining a good liberal arts education. In that regard Thomas Jefferson acquired the best academic and intellectual foundation he could have hoped for in colonial Virginia. He entered the College of William and Mary in 1760 at the age of sixteen, having arrived with a good grounding in classical studies from two private tutors.[11] The academic opportunity at William and Mary was not lost on this serious and precocious "hard student" with a "canine appetite" for reading, who typically studied for fifteen hours a day. There is no better account of Jefferson's singular and fortunate education than his own autobiography, in which he credits William Small, a Scottish Enlightenment professor; George Wythe, one of the best classical scholars in America; and the worldly Governor Francis Fauquier as his academic and professional mentors.[12] They comprise one of two important circumstances in Williamsburg that would direct and form Jefferson's interest and extracurricular study of architecture.[13] Jefferson's exposure to books on all subjects comprises the other most important influential and formative factor. Along with his formal education, books cannot be overestimated as an essential part of his persona, life, and everything he accomplished in that full life. In 1769, Jefferson wrote of the importance of books: "The only help a youth wants is to be directed what books to read, and in what order to read them . . . one difficulty only occurs, that is, the want of books."[14] As Daniel Boorstin remarked, "the building of libraries concentrated Jefferson's intellectual energies again and again," and "books inform and guide Jefferson's life in a way with no precedent and few equals among American statesmen."[15] The subject of Jefferson's education and preparation as an architect was critically related to his books. William B. O'Neal observed that books made possible Jefferson's architectural achievements that were second only to his political contributions.[16]

Jefferson's serious self-study of the subject led him to become an architectural scholar. His wide range of books taught him the theory behind the architectural forms he would design. His architectural process stands out for its time and place because of his tendency to synthesize various forms from different sources and to fashion something new rather than merely copying a design. Still, it would become a very long learning curve, with new experiential observations and many additional books. Jefferson obstinately relied on some of these earliest architectural books that represented a preferred and repeated personal style he would practice all his life, one we can call "Jeffersonian."

The formation of Jefferson's library was very important. In colonial Virginia, libraries reflected the education, tastes, and status of their owners. Jefferson had inherited a modest library from his father but went about book acquisition in a significant way in Williamsburg. He purchased books sold by the publishers of the *Virginia Gazette* newspaper and acquired others through estate sales. Jefferson bought books from Philip Ludwell's estate sale at Greenspring in 1768, and in 1770 he acquired some of the "valuable collection of English, Latin, French and Italian" books from the estate of Nicholas Walthoes.[17] He ordered books directly from London, undoubtedly those recommended by his mentors.[18] The most extensive private library in Virginia was William Byrd II's 3,500 books of enormous breadth in subjects, with twenty-three titles on architecture. After Byrd's death Jefferson calculated whether he could afford to buy the entire library and sadly concluded he could not.[19] Jefferson might have picked up architectural books from the auction of Governor John Murray's library of 1,300 books in 1775 or from Williamsburg cabinetmaker Maurice Eventon's sale in 1779 that contained from twelve to fifteen books on architecture.[20] Other architectural books might have come from Jefferson's purchase of estate libraries from Peyton Randolph, Richard Bland, James Horrocks, Samuel Henley, or Thomas Gwatkin.[21] His initial library at Shadwell, his boyhood home, was lost in a fire in 1770. He eagerly acquired more books and replaced important ones that had been lost. By that time he had already started using his architectural books in the preliminary designs for Monticello. Among his earliest architectural books acquired before 1770 were Leoni's edition of Andrea Palladio's *Four Books of Architecture* (1742), James Gibbs's *Rules for Drawing Buildings* (1753) and *Book of Architecture* (1728), and Robert Morris's *Select Architecture* (1755). Jefferson used all four in his design for Monticello I. Another important early book he bought was William Kent's *The Designs of Inigo Jones* (1727). From these books Jefferson learned the formulas and proportions of Roman classical design, Roman-derived details, the system of design described by Palladio, and modern British interpretations of Palladio's architecture. We can imagine that Jefferson's love of and inclination toward the precision of mathematics, instilled in him by William Small, coincided with the mathematical formulas and proportions of classical architecture. Architecture offered the harmony, order, and logical arrangement of parts to whole, just as the harmony of numbers made mathematics his favorite study.[22] From Gibbs, Morris, and Kent, who were part of the British Palladian movement, Jefferson drew his love of the geometrical octagon shape that he would explore in many works throughout his lifetime. By 1780 Jefferson's book collection, referred to as his second library after his losing the first in the Shadwell fire, was considerable. His design books represented a precocious list of what one would want to consult as an architect and builder.[23] Five years in Paris allowed Jefferson to add another 2,000 books to his library, including some important architectural volumes and some that were already hundreds of years old and not easily acquired in America.

Whether serious or not, Jefferson first mentioned the idea of building a house for himself and his occasional friends in 1763.[24] Whether he had learned enough skills of architecture and construction by that time is doubtful, but he may have started to think about what kind of house he might want. This was still earlier than his 1766 three-month trip to Philadelphia to get inoculated against smallpox. On that trip, which included Annapolis and New York, he had the opportunity to observe and compare colonial buildings and regional construction outside of Virginia.[25] Philadelphia, the "Athens of America," had the best British colonial architecture at this time, styles Jefferson came to reject. His journals on this and subsequent travels, either local or abroad, are frustratingly mute on important buildings he saw. One exception was the fashionable Hammond-Harwood House (1774) in Annapolis with its semi-octagonal wings that he sketched. Given Jefferson's very busy time training and practicing as an attorney in Williamsburg, he still managed to squeeze in a serious study of architecture by the late 1760s that came from a synthesis of books, mentors, and observation. His early designs were already leaning toward a true architect's skill of combining ideas from several printed sources, with unique results, rather than the more common colonial practice of wholesale copying.

Thomas Jefferson's legacy of extensive writings gives him an exceptional place in American history. The same legacy documents his development as an architect and builder. In 1767 Thomas Jefferson began a "scrupulous fidelity" of recording daily his legal transactions, his financial expenses, and "miscellaneous memorandums." The editors of these published "Memorandum Books" called them the "first flowering of what can only be described as a passion for making daily records."[26] The year before he had started his "Garden Book," and in 1774 he began his "Farm Book." To these are added his voluminous building notebooks, memoranda and general notes, drawings, public papers, scientific notes, and personal letters. From these various sources we see the mind of Jefferson the builder developing concomitant with his skill as architect. Jefferson had approached architectural design in what we would consider a modern process by first considering every aspect of a building on paper.[27] His characteristic practice of design and construction started with a mathematically precise design, preliminary studies, drawings of structural details, and even full-size working drawings. He calculated and specified every type of building materials, knew the process of producing these materials, and recruited the best workmen for construction. His control of the process and close supervision of the work stemmed from Jefferson's obsessive personality. His character further instilled an incredible patience to obtain the desired quality of the end product, no matter how long it took.

Jefferson's novice skill as a gentleman architect and builder is understood by looking at three different but interrelated sets of documents for the first Monticello. The most visual of these are architectural drawings.[28] Fiske Kimball, who had the first professional look at Jefferson's drawings, numbering more than seven hundred, stated that "they are of a number and elaborateness unexampled in America until long afterwards."[29] Eighteenth-century American architectural drawings were relatively few in number and simple in scope and detail.[30] As a self-trained draftsman, Jefferson's drawings for Monticello have been described as "remarkably sophisticated drawings—sophisticated in technique and sophisticated as an index of his intent in design."[31] Employing the typical eighteenth-century drafting style, of pricking, scoring, and using ink, Jefferson's early drawings were "brought to a peak of purity and elegance."[32] They are very accomplished for their precision, especially in full-size detailed drawings. They were the intellectual tools Jefferson used to work out the proportions and details of the classical orders and to help visualize and calculate the various materials and construction tasks. They were unambiguous visual instructions for untried workers from the owner/contractor, who even at this early age displayed a compulsion for attempting ideal forms. Jefferson's studied formulations of proportions and the mathematical purity in his intent cannot be appreciated solely by examining the built results but only by seeing his drawings that reflect his mind at work. His concentration on creating what

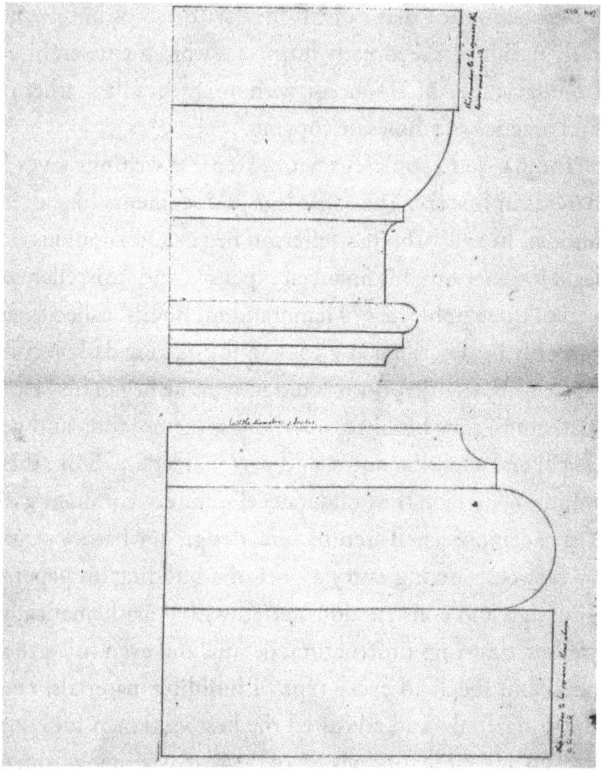

Fig. 11. Jefferson detail drawing for Tuscan column.

has been called "a museum" of the use of classical orders was unusual for the time and part of his reformation of architecture in Virginia.[33]

Jefferson's early drawings alone would be sufficient to demonstrate his significance as a self-trained architect, but they must be seen together with his second set of interrelated written documents. The "miscellaneous memorandums" recorded in his Memorandum Books include a section on design and construction dated 1767–69. These earliest notes by Jefferson for specifications and quantities of materials for the first Monticello show his developing grasp and understanding of building processes and techniques. His other early building notes in the Farm Book display a similar knowledge. Written specifications show an unusual attention to all of Monticello's elements: doors, roofs, windows, chimneys, fireplaces, entablatures, wallpaper, lead flashings, leader pipes, and similar features not only for the mansion but also for all the outbuildings. These notes provide a glimpse of his three-dimensional mental imagery of what was to be built and how it would be constructed. They further detail the different finished materials according to location, the hierarchy of classical orders through the house, the named parts of complex classical moldings, the book sources for decorative ornaments, and even colors for the walls. It was Jefferson's virtual reality clearly envisioned.

The third set of design documents consists of Jefferson's "Building Notebook" that started in 1770. This is yet another set of written specifications that accompanied the drawings and the memo notes. They document design and dimensional information of all the different building elements and their different materials. Most importantly, they show Jefferson's obsessive mathematical number-crunching for proportions of every interior and exterior aspect of classical design. Jefferson's reliance on Andrea Palladio's architectural canon of Roman orders had to be mathematically interpreted. Palladio gave the Roman system of dividing each type of architectural order and of each part of an order, down to the various moldings, in "minutes" that were the subdivided portions of each order's column diameter. Jefferson's love for precision and the authority of precedent is easily seen on the many pages where he converted Palladio's regional Italian inches into English inches. For instance, he calculated that Palladio's dimension of 1 Doric minute equaled 0.38319 inches. The cap molding of the Doric pedestal equaled 7.66386 inches. These minuscule dimensions can only be seen as Jefferson's delight in formulating mathematical equations. They were more than mere numbers; they represented ancient Greek and Roman ideals of classical architectural beauty that Jefferson, like other architects in the neoclassical era, felt had never been equaled. Later in life Jefferson told a friend that Palladio was the Bible and he should stick to it closely.[34] Jefferson did rely almost exclusively on Palladio for his system of proportional design and antique precedent and would come to own six different editions of his work. James Gibbs, Robert Morris, and William Kent offered eighteenth-century British interpretations of Palladio, especially in the form of octagonal shapes, but Palladio offered the basic foundation for Jefferson's process of design and the one he considered closer to the classical truth. He was not slavish, however, and combined details from different sources, creating new forms as Palladio had done in the sixteenth century.[35] This

Fig. 12. Perspective sketch, Monticello I.

flexibility would be true of his design and details for Poplar Forest, which relied on both Palladio and Gibbs and followed the rules and bent them.

Jefferson's early architecture came from a studious knowledge and practice "out of the books of a bookish movement."[36] Jefferson's work as a neoclassicist has been characterized as the culmination of the English neo-Palladian movement but not innovative in the broader movement and even conservative, being fifty years out of date.[37] Benjamin Latrobe's impression of Virginia architecture in 1796 saw it as "plain and decent but of a fashion of 30 years ago."[38] By the time Jefferson was rebuilding Monticello and designing Poplar Forest, the more neoclassical Federal style based on Robert Adam's English works had taken root in America. Jefferson retained his Roman Revival style. New England architect Asher Benjamin remarked in 1806: "Old fashioned workmen, who have for many years followed the footsteps of Palladio and Langley, will no doubt leave their old path with great reluctance."[39] Jefferson's architectural pupil Robert Mills, who later studied under Latrobe and who would practice his own American style, paid homage to his first mentor, saying: "Mr. Jefferson was peculiarly partial to Architecture, and possessed a good taste in this branch of the fine Arts."[40] Jefferson seems to

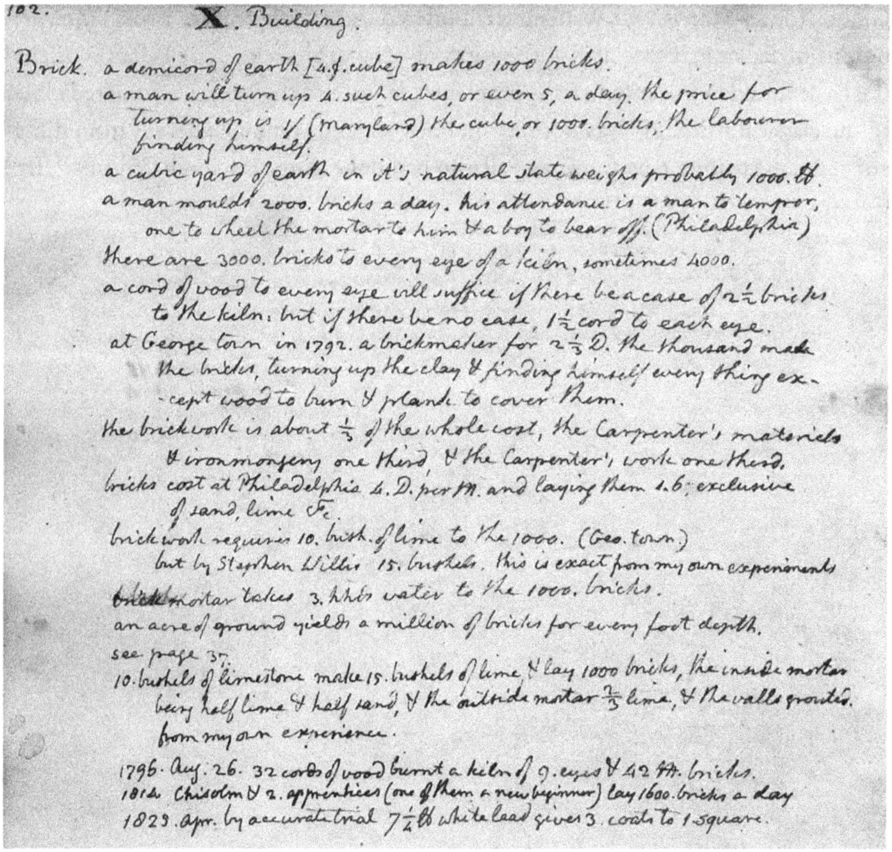

102.

X. Building.

Brick. a demicord of earth [4.f. cube] makes 1000 bricks.
a man will turn up 4. such cubes, or even 5, a day. the price for turning up is 1/ (Maryland) the cube, or 1000. bricks, the labourer finding himself.
a cubic yard of earth in it's natural state weighs probably 1000. ℔.
a man moulds 2000. bricks a day. his attendance is a man to temper, one to wheel the mortar to him & a boy to bear off. (Philadelphia)
there are 3000. bricks to every eye of a kiln, sometimes 4000.
a cord of wood to every eye will suffice if there be a case of 2½ bricks to the kiln: but if there be no case, 1½ cord to each eye.
at George town in 1792. a brickmaker for 2⅔ D. the thousand made the bricks, turning up the clay & finding himself every thing except wood to burn & plank to cover them.
the brickwork is about ⅓ of the whole cost, the Carpenter's materials & ironmongery one third, & the Carpenter's work one third.
bricks cost at Philadelphia 4. D. per M. and laying them 1.6; exclusive of sand, lime &c.
brickwork requires 10. bush. of lime to the 1000. (Geo. town)
but by Stephen Willis 15. bushels. this is exact from my own experiments
~~brick~~ mortar takes 3. hhds water to the 1000. bricks.
an acre of ground yields a million of bricks for every foot depth.
see page 37.
10. bushels of limestone make 15. bushels of lime, & lay 1000 bricks, the inside mortar being half lime & half sand, & the outside mortar ⅔ lime, & the walls grouted. from my own experience.
1796. Aug. 26. 32 cords of wood burnt a kiln of 9. eyes & 42 M. bricks.
1814. Chisolm & 2. apprentices (one of them a new beginner) lay 1600. bricks a day
1823. apr. by accurate trial 7¼ ℔ white lead gives 3. coats to 1. square.

Fig. 13. Jefferson's notes on brick, Farm Book, 1774–1824, p. 102.

have imparted his theory of flexible precedent to Mills, who wrote: "I have always deprecated the servile copying of the buildings of antiquity; we have the same principles and materials to work upon that the ancients had, and we should adapt these materials to the habits and customs of our people as they did to theirs."[41] Jefferson had passed the torch and recognized a new generation's progress but was content to maintain his own consistent style, which was innovative for America in the 1770s, but out-of-date by the 1820s.[42]

Ambitious Builder: Monticello I

Jefferson's initial study of architecture included a beginner's uncommon interest in learning how to construct the designs he put to paper. Jefferson was unusual in taking on the role of a builder that in colonial Virginia had traditionally been enacted by a master builder, called an undertaker, or by better individual craftsmen. Providentially he had followed the advice handed down by Vitruvius that a proper architect had to know construction techniques as well as aesthetic design. Whether from books, observation, or both, by 1768 he had learned enough to attempt his own ambitious building project, taking on the role of a master builder. Where did Jefferson acquire this construction knowledge? We can trace his academic education with more certainty, but his experiential learning has to be imagined. We can imagine he absorbed experiences as a boy in Virginia's traditional built environment, living in the social and cultural middle ground of the Piedmont between older Tidewater settlements and the expanding westward frontier settlements. We can assume that his father, Peter Jefferson, land surveyor and coauthor of a famous early map of Virginia, imparted certain skills and lessons of various kinds to his son. Did Thomas learn drafting skills from his father? What lessons were learned from typical plantation practices of construction? At the impressionable and curious age of ten Thomas undoubtedly observed scenes around him as he lived in and adjacent to construction projects at his childhood home, Shadwell. Peter Jefferson hired builder John Biswell to expand the family home and, with other carpenters free and enslaved, to construct a nearby mill. At an earlier age young Thomas would have also seen the work of house joiner Francis West, who executed work at Tuckahoe Plantation during the Jefferson family's residence there from 1746 to 1753.[43] Thomas would have observed the common practice among building tradesmen and plantation owners of relying on enslaved craftsmen for both unskilled and skilled tasks. Peter Jefferson's enslaved men Jupiter and Sampson probably worked on Shadwell's expansion since they were also hired out to Biswell to construct the mill.[44] Thomas Jefferson would later lease Jupiter from his mother as his enslaved manservant. The practice of using enslaved laborers—whether "owned" or hired—was common, and the relatively higher "property" value of skilled tradesmen is seen in deed and will records.[45] Skilled enslaved workers were important for one's own plantation needs, but more importantly, they could be hired out to others by the day, week, month, or year. Whatever lessons he learned as a boy, Thomas Jefferson would become obsessed with owning, training, and supervising his own enslaved workers, even his own sons, for his own long-duration projects.

In July 1768 Jefferson engaged John Moore to start leveling the mountaintop where Monticello would be built. The same month he ordered from England "the best crown glass" and 150 yards of "window line." The following year he asked a friend going to England to procure, among other things, rising dovetail door hinges, Venetian hinges, Chinese brass bells with wire and cranks, pulleys and cord for Venetian blinds, and mortise locks for doors.[46] This order indicates several things: Jefferson was confident enough in his design to be ordering certain items directly from England rather than settling for what he could get in Virginia. He ordered specific fashionable and expensive items like the door hinges and Venetian blinds. His order of the bells with wires and cranks indicated his anticipated use of enslaved house servants. Referencing specifications from Palladio's book, Jefferson ordered paneled doors around 1768 from house joiner John Saunders in Williamsburg.[47] While Saunders could also have made his window sash, Jefferson opted for something better and ordered his from London in 1774.[48] Acquiring the best materials and the most-skilled workers for all of these trades would prove a challenge to Jefferson as a novice undertaker. He even tried unsuccessfully in 1777 to secure skilled house joiners and stonecutters from among British prisoners-of-war being held in Maryland, confiding to his friend John Harvie that there was a "scarcity of skilled hands now following this Branch of Business."[49]

Typically, as with any of his interests, Jefferson's education as a builder came from intense study and observation. It would be his lifelong habit to question and converse with mechanics of every sort and to record their useful information. Thomas Jefferson Randolph observed of his grandfather that his "powers of conversation were great, yet he always turned to subjects most familiar to those with whom he conversed, whether laborer, mechanic, or other; and if they displayed sound judgment and a knowledge of the subject, entered the information they gave, under appropriate heads, for reference."[50] His copious notes on construction techniques, material specifications, and workers began with the design and planning of Monticello ca. 1768, when he was still living in Williamsburg. Jefferson first recorded in his building notes the amount of water needed to make a quantity of bricks, which was important since water was a scarce resource on the Monticello mountaintop. His first datable record of construction techniques occurred in his Garden Book on July 27, 1769, when he noted that "a bed of mortar which makes 2000 bricks takes 6 hhds of water."[51] This information most likely came from Jefferson's brickmaker, George Dudley, who started making bricks for Monticello on July 14, 1769.[52] The following year Jefferson hired brickmaker William Bishop to help with the process, the same year that bricklayer Stephen Willis would begin to lay them.[53] He continued noting information in the Garden Book on September 7, 1771: "Stephen Willis sais [*sic*] it takes 15. Bushels of lime to lay 1000 bricks."[54] On the same day he recorded: "Old Sharpe sais a bushel of Lime-stone will weigh 114 lb. and if well burnt will make 2. Bushels of slacked lime."[55] The following year he continued this comparison: "William Gillum sais it will take a bushel of Limestone (which he sais is equal to 2 bushels of slacked lime) to a perch of stonework 18. I thick.—but Anderson sais 3. Bushels of Lime."[56] Jefferson's education in material production and labor efficiency would be recorded for all manner of activities, whether given by hired hands or enslaved workers. He would frequently note that the information came from Philadelphia, or Georgetown, or a European location, but he would identify notes from his own experience by the occasional phrase "this is exact from my own experiments."[57] Other plantation activities of every kind were similarly recorded in his Farm Book, which he began in 1774. On the subject of brick construction alone this would be the most complete layman's understanding and documentation of its kind: describing the quantities of earth, wood, and water that were required to make and fire brick; the quantities of limestone, lime, water, and sand to make mortar; the time and labor for making the same; and the time, labor, and quantity for laying brick or stone, and whether it was by master or apprentice.

When Jefferson took on the role as "undertaker," as a master builder was called, he had to recruit the most skilled workers to execute the stone, brick, and wooden parts of the building. Usually an owner engaged the undertaker, who used his own workers, free or enslaved, and hired others in the various trades needed for the job. Coordination and supervision were critical. In addition to his own enslaved workers, Jefferson would hire more than one hundred men to construct Monticello from 1768 to 1809. His relationship with some of them would become extraordinary for its scope and duration. The longer-term benefit was Jefferson's practice of apprenticing his enslaved workers to these hired tradesmen. When he came to rebuild the more complex Monticello II, the slave apprentice system would be more important for its scope and duration, and for the eventual skills needed at Poplar Forest.

Jefferson noted in his Memorandum Book on January 24, 1774, "Agreed with Humphry Gaines that he shall work with my carpenters and I am to give him £30 a year and find him provisions."[58] Jefferson's reference that Gaines "shall work with my carpenters" acknowledges the beginning of his apprenticeship system for enslaved labor. Who were Jefferson's enslaved carpenters at this time? When Jefferson turned twenty-one in 1764, he inherited about sixty enslaved people along with land from his father's estate. It is uncertain whether there were skilled tradesmen among them. In his first recorded roll of the enslaved in 1774 there are four enslaved men who are not identified as field laborers who might have been tradesmen. One of these was Jupiter, who had helped build Peter Jefferson's buildings. That same year Jefferson recorded the significant roll of enslaved people inherited from his father-in-law, John Wayles. The list starts off with "Tradesmen" and lists two carpenters, two blacksmiths, a shoemaker, and three watermen among 187 enslaved people on ten separate plantation sites. The carpenters were Sanco from the Elkhill plantation, and Abram from the Guinea plantation. Phill from the Guinea plantation was identified as a shoemaker. It is most likely that Sanco and Abram were the carpenters Jefferson apprenticed to Humphry Gaines. By the time Jefferson recorded another roll of the enslaved for Monticello in 1794 that included occupations, he listed as carpenters John, Davy, Lewis, Abram, Phill Shoemaker, Johnny,

Phill Waggoner, Tom Shackelford, Goliah, and Mingo. Five of these men had been listed in 1774 as field hands but had been brought to the Monticello plantation and by 1783 were listed as carpenters. As work progressed on the first Monticello from 1774 to 1784, these enslaved men were trained by the first hired carpenters and then by two skilled British army deserters Jefferson hired in 1781, David Watson and Billy Orr.

Monticello enslaved boys at the age of fourteen would start working with the "out carpenters," who felled trees for firewood, fences, lumber, or charcoal. They might also be put to work in the blacksmith shop and after 1796 in the nailery shop. At the age of sixteen enslaved boys were chosen to "go into the ground" as field hands or to learn a trade.[59] If chosen for a trade, they might be apprenticed to another skilled slave or to a hired worker. On his 1792 roll of the enslaved Jefferson listed the name "Johnny 75," which refers to John Hemmings and the year in which he was born, although Jefferson later changes the date to 1776. Birth years helped Jefferson keep track of enslaved people who might have the same given name but seldom a last name. John was the eleventh child of house slave Betty Hemings and house joiner Joseph Neilson, whom Jefferson had hired to work on the first Monticello. After three years as an out carpenter John started his skilled training at age seventeen under Englishman David Watson.[60] He might also have learned his trade from helping enslaved carpenters Lewis and Abram. Still later in the 1790s John learned more refined skills from the Irish joiners James Dinsmore and John Neilson. The joinery workshop on Monticello's Mulberry Row would be the scene where carpentry and joinery skills were practiced, but for the initial construction of Monticello the house itself had been the workshop. The same would be true for Poplar Forest, where John Hemmings would become the master craftsman directing his nephew apprentices who were learning the joinery trade.

Thomas Jefferson's trials and tribulations in constructing his first house were highly instructive imparting knowledgeable and practical skills that would continue to improve. He never stopped studying innovative building materials or observing the best practices of construction. The "long time in maturing his projects" would also become characteristic, as would his trait of closely supervising and inspecting his expanding workforce and their products, and having the patience to wait decades to see a finished result. Jefferson's design for Monticello, even if unfinished, was distinctive for its time and place due to the diligent effort expended on its conception and creation as an "authentic" Roman classicism.[61] A German officer imprisoned near Charlottesville in 1780, invited by Jefferson to Monticello and given "free Access to a Copius and well chosen Library," described him as having "a Noble Spirit of Building, he is now finishing an elegant building projected according to his own fancy."[62] The best description of the first Monticello, and of its owner, comes from the Marquis de Chastellux, who visited Jefferson in 1782. In part the Marquis said that the house, "of which Mr. Jefferson was the architect, and often the builder," was "constructed in an Italian style, and is quite tasteful" and "is to be decorated entirely in the antique style. . . . [I]t resembles none of the others seen in this country. . . . Mr. Jefferson is the first American who has consulted the Fine Arts to know how he should shelter himself from the weather."[63]

Chastellux's full description captured several other important aspects of what he observed: Palladian prototypes; Jefferson's preference for antique orders and antique Roman decoration; the second-largest space in the house devoted to a library; and Jefferson's idea for terrace walks above the service rooms. Surely there were grander and more expensive displays of domestic architecture, but the marquis understood Jefferson's approach as different, drawn from the "Fine Arts." Chastellux's description regarding the fine arts might refer to Jefferson's desiderata for "Statues, Paintings &c," which was noted in his early Building Notebooks of ca. 1771; Jefferson would have proudly shared his wish list with Chastellux.[64] The vision Jefferson shared with Chastellux was impressive as an imaginative sum greater than its unfinished parts. It was to be trimmed out in antique details and filled with copies of European paintings and classical sculpture. Jefferson's unique "shelter" on his mountaintop would then be set in a landscaped garden that reflected romantic literature and advanced theories of the English picturesque landscape movement. Like his early architectural preferences for Palladian and Roman sources, which would withstand later European influences, "his ideas on landscape gardening were well established and were surprisingly little altered in succeeding years."[65] Had Jefferson just completed his initial plans for Monticello, his house would have been noteworthy, or, as Irishman Isaac Weld Jr. projected, "it will be one of the most elegant private habitations in the United States."[66] But before Jefferson could complete his inaugural accomplishment, circumstances pushed him onto the "vaunted scene of Europe" and profoundly expanded his architectural horizons, rendering his first essay in architecture inadequate.

Having just completed his *Notes on Virginia* manuscript with its scathing comments on colonial public architecture, Jefferson carried it with him in 1784 for publishing in Paris the scene of his next immersive and significant architectural education. Five years in Europe gave him the opportunity to acquire two thousand of the best and rarest books related to America and the fine arts, and to see the best contemporary designs in architecture and landscape as well as those from the Renaissance and the ancient world.

A European Education

After a year in Paris Thomas Jefferson gleefully wrote a friend: "Were I to proceed to tell you how much I enjoy their architecture, sculpture, painting, music, I should want words. It is in these arts they shine."[67] Jefferson's appointment as minister plenipotentiary to France in 1784 would change his life in many ways. Based in Paris for five years, Jefferson found himself in a city undergoing an extraordinary modernization architecturally, socially, culturally, and politically. New urban spaces, modern houses, and public venues abounded through wholesale urban transformations. One-third of the city's buildings were less than twenty years old. Enlightenment thought and philosophy echoed in all manner of arts, society, and science. "For the first time in his life, Jefferson was living in a rarefied cosmopolitan environment where every day he could meet and talk on equal terms with men and women who shared his own wide-ranging interests."[68] Some historians have pointed out that despite his anticipation of becoming more enlightened, cultivated, and polite, Jefferson, at age forty-one, "would not be so vulnerable to the attractions—and seductions—of the 'vaunted scene' . . . and could benefit from the glories of European civilization without succumbing to its vices."[69] If anything, he came to see the American republic more clearly from afar, with a moralistic view of European royalty, societal manners, and horror at the stratification of classes. Still, he could say, "I do love this people with all my heart."[70] For all the impressive urban squares, landscaped parks, and new suburbs that he approvingly observed, his anti-urban opinions were also strengthened by what remained of medieval Paris.

Jefferson's documentation of his remarkable five years in Europe has been thoroughly described by historians.[71] The significance of his experience, as detailed as it is, lies more in what his observant eye took in than in what he chanced to write down. Daniel Boorstin observed about Jefferson histories in general, which could stand for his architectural influences as well, that "Those who have been mainly interested in distinguishing the 'new' from the 'old,' the 'original' from the 'borrowed,' the 'native' from the 'foreign,' have often become so preoccupied with separating the threads which make up the Jeffersonian mind that they have failed to see its texture."[72] Even the broad texture of Jefferson's overwhelming artistic experience is not easily described. Eleanor Berman characterized Jefferson's philosophy of art as a "formal inconsistency," saying, "his aesthetic ideas express in effect a constellation of attitudes which are communicated via hundreds of observations occurring in all sorts of other connections."[73] His insatiable curiosity engaged all manner of European traditions and customs, both ancient and modern, in conversations with field workers or ministers of state, from the smallest vernacular details to revolutionary philosophical ideas. Enlightened discussions in philosophic Parisian salons and in the scientific frontiers of the French écoles and academies were intoxicating, but it was the fine arts that particularly vied for Jefferson's attention. In a letter from Paris to James Madison, Jefferson had written that he was "an enthusiast on the subject of the arts," and Paris in the 1780s rivaled any city of Europe in art, architecture, and urban planning.[74] Of the European fine arts, architecture played the most significant role in Jefferson's education and would be reflected at Monticello and Poplar Forest. Landscape gardening in the picturesque English style that was also practiced in France was a close second.

In Paris Jefferson found himself surrounded by a remarkable range of royal, private, and ecclesiastical buildings. Baroque- and rococo-style buildings of the seventeenth and early eighteenth centuries had given way in the Age of Reason to a wave in the 1750s of neoclassical buildings. Medieval streetscapes were still evident, but the city was "every day enlarging and beautifying."[75] The transformative urban changes taking place across Europe came with new attitudes in art and architecture that were fueled by published works detailing archaeological discoveries and interests in Greek and Roman remains.[76] France, more than any other country, had been steeped in a vigorous architectural academic debate for more than a century regarding appropriate forms of classicism. Jefferson quickly developed a discerning and critical eye for the many

Fig. 14. East elevation of Louvre, Paris, from A. W. Pugin, *Paris and Its Environs* (London, 1830).

visual delights that assailed him as he made his long habitual walking tours around Paris. It was said that Jefferson "sailed with remarkable skill through the confusing and often contradictory currents of artistic expressions in Europe."[77] He focused on particular aspects of private dwellings that he could personally adapt. For future American public buildings, in the yet to be built District of Columbia, Jefferson chose as models buildings from the seventeenth century (Perrault's East Louvre facade) and the mid-eighteenth century (Gabriel's Place Louis XV buildings). Jefferson pronounced the Halle aux Bleds (the grain market) "the most superb thing on earth" and used its structural system for the Monticello dome and its skylight design as a suggestion for the later U.S. Capitol Building.[78] The new Palais Royal development of underground shops and restaurants, lighted by an enormous skylight, Jefferson proposed as the model for a similar scheme in the still-developing capital at Richmond, Virginia. He focused more on construction technology and plans for convenience and privacy than on architectural or decorative style. French architectural qualities of light and air stuck with him. Despite Jefferson's insatiable curiosity and observation of the world around him in Europe, he failed to comment on so much, especially architecture both old and new. He failed to mention interior decoration or new furniture styles. He did not record his opinion of French picturesque gardens or new neoclassical buildings like Sainte-Genevieve or the École de Chirurgie. He observed but did not comment on new fashionable city residences, the exception being the Hotel de Salm. He knew and corresponded with architects like J. D. le Roy but said nothing about their new books or the much-debated theories of French architecture.[79]

French domestic architecture had the greatest impact on Jefferson. Private city houses for the ancien régime families and the growing middle class reflected French ideas of interior planning with purer neoclassical exterior forms. Jefferson was most taken with these townhouse "hotels" of the 1770s and 1780s that were spreading out in the new suburban areas in which he lived, first in the Chaussée d'Antin neighborhood and then in the Faubourg-du-Roule. Jefferson's favorite new hotel was Pierre Rousseau's Hotel de Salm, a version of French Palladianism, under construction on the banks of the Seine across from the Tuileries Garden. In his own words, Jefferson was "violently smitten" with this city mansion. His own rental residence on the Champs-Élysées, J. F-T. Chalgrin's 1768 Hotel de Langeac, featured the typical interior arrangement for which the French hotel became known. The distribution, or "dégagement," of asymmetrical interior spaces, based on a rational and practical arrangement of plan, was disguised by regular exterior forms.[80] The light and airy nature of hotels, indoor toilets, emphasis of the central dining room with skylight followed en suite by the salon, and the deemphasis of staircases were features Jefferson would use at Monticello and Poplar Forest. George Flower's description of Poplar Forest as being like a French chateau aptly referenced the prototypes.

Just as influential were the garden pavilions. "Maisons de plaisance" were created as retreats, large and small, by the royal families in the eighteenth century, and then by nobles retreating from courtly responsibilities.[81] King Louis XIV's retreat at Marly and Louis XV's Petit Trianon at Versailles were two royal examples that impressed Jefferson. Comte and Comtesse Du Barry's Pavillon de Louveciennes by Ledoux and

Fig. 15. Hotel de Salm, Paris, from A. W. Pugin, *Paris and Its Environs* (London, 1830).

Comte D'Artois's Pavilion Bagatelle by Belanger in the Bois de Boulogne park were two notable private examples, both, like the Petit Trianon, set within English Romantic landscape gardens. The fashionable jardin anglais, England's contribution to France, could also be found at a number of new private houses in the city and in the Parc Monceau, all near Jefferson's last two residences. Jefferson's favorite English-style garden with accompanying follies was Francois Racine de Monville's Désert de Retz on the outskirts of Paris. Serving as a retreat house was a gigantic broken column of fifty-foot diameter with interior oval rooms that Jefferson would copy for a retreat in the 1790s.[82]

From the seventeenth century onward, many royal and private garden and retreat pavilions took the shape of octagons. A great number of the new city townhouses also featured central octagonal dining rooms and salons, many lighted by skylights, stoking Jefferson's increasing love of that shape.[83] Claude Perrault's seventeenth-century Paris observatory, a cubistic building with three octagonal corner towers, inspired Jefferson to design an observatory for the University of Virginia, unexecuted, with four octagonal corner towers. Jacques Gondoin's celebrated École de Chirurgie (1769–79) in the Latin Quarter, with its anatomical theater lighted by a large skylight, was no doubt an inspiration for Jefferson's design for the Anatomical Theater at the University of Virginia. Jefferson's design, with its octagonal seating and large skylight, was the last of his buildings to be constructed there (1826) and the only one to have been demolished (1940s).[84]

Two tourist trips outside of Paris have become famously important in Jefferson's European history. In March 1786 Jefferson went to London, visiting John and Abigail Adams in addition to performing a few duties as trade minister. Jefferson and Adams took the opportunity to spend most of the month of April visiting gardens associated with great estates, comparing them with descriptions contained in Thomas Whateley's famous *Observations on Modern Gardening* (1770). Jefferson concluded that Whateley's "fine imagination had never been able to seduce him from the truth."[85] The books on English picturesque gardening Jefferson had studied in Virginia paled in comparison with the real prototypes. His letter to John Page gushed in his excitement: "The gardening in that country is the article in which it excels all the earth. I mean their pleasure-gardening. This, indeed, went far beyond my ideas."[86] Similar to his practical discernment of overwhelming currents of architecture in Europe, Jefferson focused on garden details that might be useful back at home, "such practical things as might enable me to estimate the expense of making and maintaining a garden in that style."[87] While he critically noted "ill effects" of some English landscapes, his few notes on the grand country houses and garden pavilions made harsher critiques. As with so many architectural monuments he observed and visited in Europe, he failed to mention those he saw in London, even those by his British Palladian mentors.

The following spring Jefferson journeyed to southern France and northern Italy, where he was "nourished with the remains of Roman grandeur."[88] Roman buildings and ruins in Nîmes, Arles, Avignon, St-Rémy, and Orange instilled a particular excitement, being "precious remains of antiquity" he had theretofore known only from

Fig. 16. Maison Carrée, Nîmes, France.

books.[89] The Pont du Gard aqueduct he considered "a sublime antiquity," reflecting "Roman taste, genius, and magnificence."[90] The outstanding example of a Roman building he had anticipated seeing was a small first-century temple in Nîmes, already chosen as his model for the Virginia State Capitol. Jefferson had engaged the architect, archaeologist, and artist Charles-Louis Clérisseau to design the Capitol and knew the prototype, the Maison Carrée, through Clérisseau's book on the antiquities of Nîmes. On the basis of drawings and prints alone, Jefferson already called the temple "the most beautiful and precious morsel left us by antiquity."[91] His inspection of the actual building did not disappoint. In a letter to Madame de Tessé, he uncharacteristically revealed the emotional power ancient buildings had on him: "Here I am, Madam, gazing whole hours at the Maison Carrée, like a lover at his mistress."[92] In the same letter he confessed that his strong love of buildings was not without precedent, because in Paris he had been "violently smitten" with the modern Hotel de Salm. When he did comment on medieval alterations to classical buildings, or, rarely, on monumental Gothic buildings, they generally drew the epithet of "barbarism." Ironically, Jefferson "scarcely got into classical ground" in Italy before duty called him back to Paris, coming within one day's journey of the Veneto region and Palladio's villas.[93] Still, the Roman remains Jefferson did see, and his relationship with Clérisseau, reinforced his long-standing predilection for classical architecture, just as English-style gardens, in France as well as England, became even stronger references for Monticello and Poplar Forest landscapes.[94] The modernity of private Parisian houses would have the greatest impact on his two residences. The "fabric" of Jefferson's European experience, even if not fully documented, cannot be overestimated.

Monticello II

The story of Monticello II is that of a "reboot" of Monticello I, or of a "Monticello 2.0," with enhanced architectural ideas. Would Jefferson have been content with completing his first house if he had not gone to Europe for five years? Given his deep dive into architectural theory and practice in the 1770s, he most likely would have continued his architectural education as he acquired additional books and came into contact with more sophisticated architecture. Jefferson's process of rebuilding—of design, materials, and construction—followed the traits he had developed as an architect and builder in his first project but in more intense and refined ways. Jefferson's aesthetic approach to design was still based on three-dimensional conceptual planning, detailed drawings of structure and details, precise mathematical dimensions, proportions from antique classical sources, and correct classical ornaments. He now used two additional architectural handbooks, Roland Freart de Chambray's *Parallèle de l'architecture antique avec la moderne* (Jombert edition, Paris, 1766) and Antoine Desgodetz's *Edifices antiques de Rome* (Jombert edition, Paris, 1779). His preference in materials was still for quality, efficiency, and permanence. Stone, brick, and lumber were processed from his own land, but other finished or superior materials came from outside Virginia and outside the country with great difficulty and expense. Putting these materials together required constant recruitment of the best workers in and out of Virginia. Developing a skilled cadre of enslaved workers trained by the various hired craftsmen was now a constant and important practice. When living in Philadelphia in 1792, he had even asked a Scottish stonemason working there whether he could recruit a stonemason and house joiner from Scotland to work on Monticello. This failed, which was probably for the best, since Jefferson could not fully turn his attention to the remodeling until years later.

Jefferson's deep-rooted need for controlling the process and for the best-quality work, as well as his patience in getting it accomplished, were ever more evident as his new architectural vision became more sophisticated and required greater effort. All of these characteristic traditions would be true for Poplar Forest and would be severely tested at the University of Virginia.[95] The extremely detailed information on materials, labor, and construction that Jefferson started recording in his Building Notebooks for the first house greatly expanded for the second, including information gathered in Europe. His Memorandum Book offers an indispensable chronological record of purchases, hiring of white workers, use of enslaved workers, and the construction process. Added to this unique documentation for an American building is the voluminous correspondence between Jefferson and family members, friends, merchants and suppliers, overseers, and workers.[96] The correspondence for this period of the second house, from 1789 to 1809, is much greater in quantity than pertaining to either the first house or Poplar Forest, due to Jefferson's long absences from Monticello. Altogether these remarkably detailed accounts paint an early, accurate portrait of Jefferson the architect and builder.

When Thomas Jefferson departed France for a visit home on September 26, 1789, he could not have foreseen that he would still be engaged in public life for the next nineteen years, with only a two-year hiatus. Immediately upon his return to America he reluctantly agreed to serve as President Washington's secretary of state, which he did from 1790 until the end of 1794, moving with the government to New York City and then to Philadelphia, going back and forth to Monticello when he could. After five busy political years he gladly retired back to Virginia in 1795 to his still unfinished house with the expectation of staying put and supervising his ongoing ambitious project. Jefferson had returned from Europe filled with new ideas for remodeling and enlarging Monticello. Although still a widower, Jefferson's plans for a larger house was also due to his daughter's growing family that he wanted to permanently host in the "bosom" of Monticello. During a brief time as a private citizen in 1795 Jefferson had written to a friend, "I have returned, with infinite appetite, to the enjoyment of my farm, my family & my books, and had determined to meddle in nothing beyond their limits."[97] Jefferson's greatly expanded library alone, with an additional two thousand books acquired in Paris, necessitated a larger house. He also envisioned an appropriate tasteful place to entertain and converse with old and new friends as he had in Paris salons. His earlier desideratum of paintings and sculptures had been actualized by his many purchases in Paris and would, along with his fashionable French furniture, impress and educate his guests. His observation of European "cabinets of curiosity" gave him the idea to create a unique American domestic space in his lofty and spacious entry hall that visitors would later call his "museum," with its "strange furniture on the walls" exhibiting Native American artifacts and natural curiosities. But those ambitious ideas, like all of his projects, would take a longer, interrupted route to completion. While still living in the unfinished first house, Jefferson invited George Wythe to come visit but warned him: "We are now living in a brick-kiln, for my house, in it's present state, is nothing better. I shall recommence my operations on it the next summer, and no small part of the pleasure I promise myself in it's future accomodations [*sic*], is founded in the hope of possessing you here sometimes, and of gratifying your taste for books, by introducing you to a collection now certainly the best in America."[98] Jefferson couldn't wait to share his new books with his beloved mentor, who had encouraged his youthful ambition to collect as many books as he could. Jefferson's library would greatly expand all at once in 1806, when Wythe bequeathed his to his former pupil. Wythe knew better than anyone where Jefferson's treasure lay, explaining in his will that his books were "the most valuable to him [Jefferson] of any thing which I have power to bestow."[99]

For two years, 1795–96, Jefferson joyfully resumed full-time civilian life at Monticello with his family, his farm, and his books. But the house he returned to had suffered greatly since his absence for five years in Paris and another four in America. The unfinished brick shell Jefferson invited Wythe to share was devoid of plaster and its intended "antique style" architectural embellishments. Indeed, it resembled a large brick kiln that would become even more ruinous in appearance and more challenging as a habitation when selected demolition started. In March 1796 Jefferson reported that his workers had begun demolishing the upper brick walls he had so proudly erected in 1770. He wrote to a friend that month: "I am now engaged in taking down the upper story of my house and building it on the ground, so as to spread all my rooms on one floor. We shall this summer therefore live under the tent of heaven."[100] Jefferson had made a point of constructing his first house for permanence and would come to regret it. As his workmen took down the solid brick walls, he lamented: "We are in dreadful confusion with the demolition of our walls, which is more tedious than I expected. The walls are so soled [solid] that 7. Men get down but between 3. And 4000 bricks a day. They would make new ones as fast. The tumbling brickbats keeps us in constant danger, we have as yet had but one accident of a man knocked down."[101] Still, he invited friends to come, saying that the "noise, confusion, and discomfort of the scene will require all your philosophy and patience" and that they would "find comfort in a comparison of our covering with that of an Arabian tent."[102]

Jefferson's optimism would flag as he impatiently complained of the lack of progress that summer and fall before being drawn away into public office again by an election in December 1796, this time as vice president. He once again moved to Philadelphia for the following three years, interrupting construction work at a critical time. Work mostly ground to a halt for the winter of 1796–97, leaving the partially demolished house still open to the weather. Absence from the site was the key factor since Jefferson did not trust his workforce to proceed without personal supervision. As he wrote from Philadelphia in June 1791, "as there are generally things to be done by the carpenters which can only be done when I am present to direct them."[103] When work resumed in earnest in 1796, Jefferson wrote again from Philadelphia that workers "must suspend their work during my absence."[104]

Ironically it was during the period of demolition in 1796 that we have one of the best descriptions of Jefferson's vision for his new house, again from a European visitor. For seven days in late June that year the Duc de La Rochefoucauld-Liancourt visited Monticello. He had been a friend in Paris and a former leader of the French Revolution. Despite the unfinished and ever more ruinous state of the house, Jefferson spread out his drawings and gave his visitor an optimistic vision of what would come. La Rochefoucauld-Liancourt described Monticello as "infinitely superior to all other houses in America, in point of taste and convenience . . . the house will certainly deserve to be ranked with the most pleasant mansions in France and England."[105]

La Rochefoucauld-Liancourt's takeaway impression was that Jefferson's bookish taste, superior in the first house, had expanded through his experiential education in Europe. He described the mezzanine floors disguised on the exterior and the convenient "apartments" modeled on French interior planning that emphasized convenience and privacy. That convenience had come as a design challenge that Jefferson felt compelled to explain to architect Benjamin Henry Latrobe: "My essay in architecture has been so much subordinated to the law of convenience, & affected also by the circumstance of change in the original design, that it is liable to some unfavorable & just criticism."[106] Jefferson's revised essay was very French in its innovative use of maximum light and airiness, and in its relationship to the designed landscape. The use of a dome set the house apart from anything in the country. It was extremely complex in form, structure, and detail. William Beiswanger characterized the challenge: "Indeed the puzzle for Jefferson, as for all architects, was how to bring into balance both program and architectural form and, in Jefferson's case, how to do this while still observing classical rules of proportion. But the ultimate test or justification for Jefferson—at least at Monticello—came from subjecting his design to the 'law of convenience.'"[107] Jefferson had retained his strong belief in classical rules and precedents for design. The greater challenge had been to open a house to the exterior and to conveniently separate private, public, and service spaces.

In the rebuilding of Monticello, Jefferson had not abandoned his fundamental use of classical rules and proportions of the first Monticello's essay in architectural orders, but he used them now with a confident flexibility and freedom. He continued to rely on Andrea Palladio's and James Gibbs's books as in the first house but used Chambray's, and Desgodetz's, acquired in Paris, for entablature details.[108] The various Roman orders constituted a consistent design element throughout all of his work from Monticello I to the University of Virginia.[109] Jefferson's use of the various hierarchical orders would be very complex, unorthodox, and probably not understood or appreciated by those who saw it except for the few equipped with a classical architectural literacy. One visitor who did appreciate Jefferson's efforts was Baron de Montlezun, who visited Monticello in 1816: "The interior of the house is decorated in the different styles of architecture, with the exception of the composite. The vestibule is Ionic, the dining room Doric, the drawing room Corinthian and the dome Attic. The rooms are decorated with various forms of these styles, in their true proportions, after Palladio."[110] In his Building Notebook Jefferson noted the use of Tuscan, Doric, Ionic, and Corinthian orders for each room.[111] He indicated the source—for example "Tuscan. Palladio's from the Arena of Verona"—and whether he was adding or subtracting certain details, e.g., "Doric. With dentils the Thermae of Diocletian (Errand)." He typically translated Roman and Renaissance modules of dimension into minute inches. For example, the plinth of the exterior Doric order pedestal was 0–26 modules that was figured as 0–9.96301 feet and inches. In the many pages of calculations of this sort, for both the first and the second house designs, Jefferson never had fewer than five decimal places, a clear illustration of continued obsession with mathematical precision, even if on paper.[112]

Jefferson continued to conceive of every element and material in a three-dimensional way. Pages of calculations estimate the sizes and quantities of raw materials and the same for the finished parts, whether they were stone, brick, or wood. These written specifications were accompanied by detailed working drawings like those for the first house. Quantitative lists include structural and finished elements for joists, sills, plates, rafters, studs, girders, shingles, sheeting, purlins, floor plank, and the innovative system for constructing the dome. He specified Palladian proportions in vertical and horizontal dimensions, and even the dimensions for individual parts, for every door, window, and fireplace, including those of the outbuildings. The complexity of the reimagined

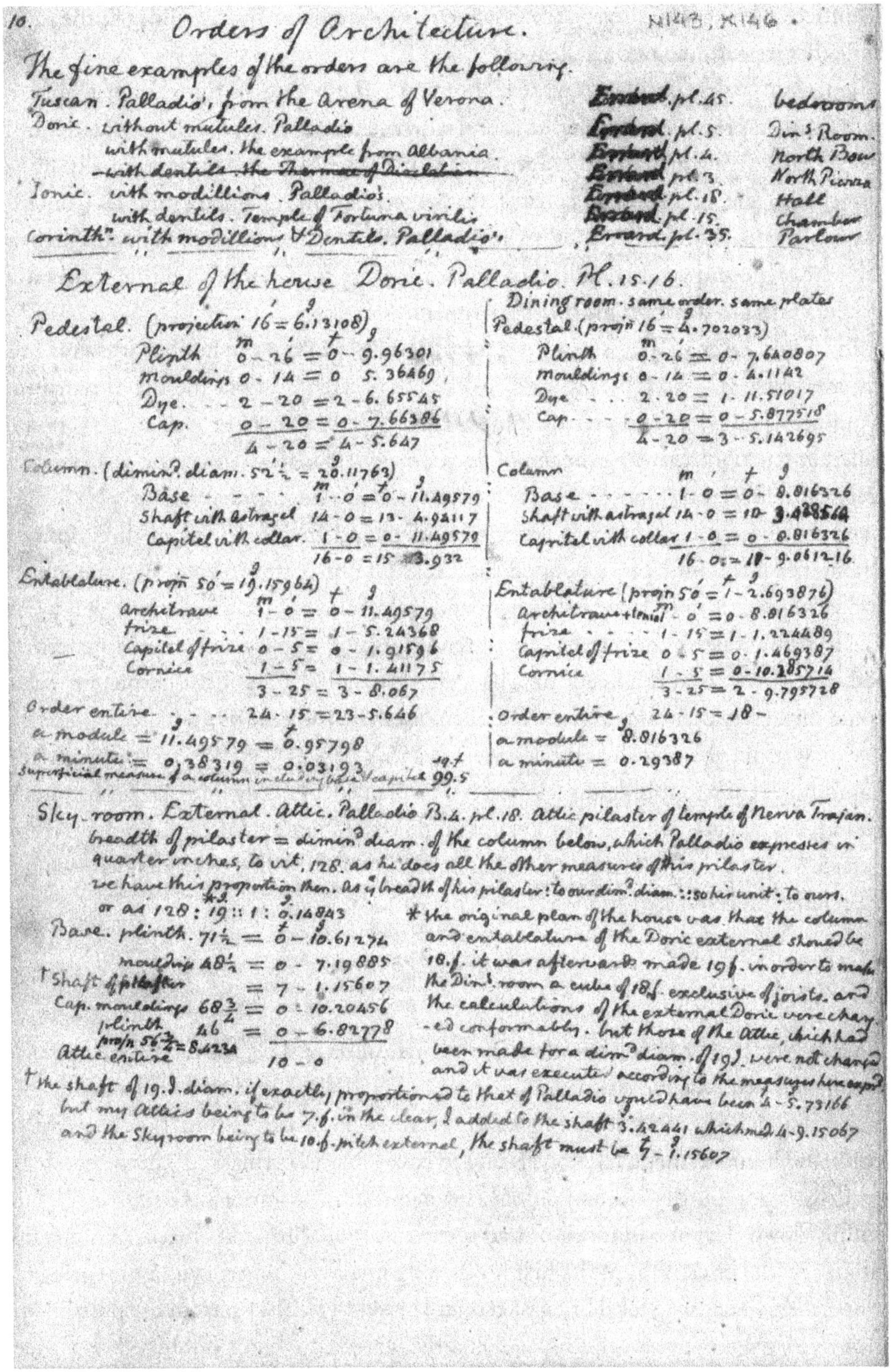

10. Orders of Architecture.

The fine examples of the orders are the following.

Tuscan.	Palladio's, from the arena of Verona.	pl. 45.	bedrooms
Doric.	without mutules. Palladio	pl. 5.	Din^g Room.
	with mutules. the example from Albania.	pl. 4.	North Bow
	~~with dentils. the Thermae of Diocletian~~	pl. 3.	North Piazza
Ionic.	with modillions. Palladio's.	pl. 18.	Hall
	with dentils. Temple of Fortuna virilis	pl. 15.	Chamber
Corinth^n.	with modillions & Dentils. Palladio's.	pl. 35.	Parlour

External of the house Doric. Palladio. Pl. 15.16.

Pedestal. (projection 16 = 6.13108)
- Plinth 0 - 26 = 0 - 9.96301
- mouldings 0 - 14 = 0 5.36469
- Dye 2 - 20 = 2 - 6.65545
- Cap. 0 - 20 = 0 - 7.66386
- 4 - 20 = 4 - 5.647

Column. (dimin^d diam. 52½ = 20.11763)
- Base 1 - 0 = 0 - 11.49579
- Shaft with astragal 14 - 0 = 13 - 4.98117
- Capitel with collar. 1 - 0 = 0 - 11.49579
- 16 - 0 = 15 - 3.932

Entablature. (proj^n 50′ = 19.15964)
- architrave 1 - 0 = 0 - 11.49579
- frize 1 - 15 = 1 - 5.24368
- Capitel of frize 0 - 5 = 0 - 1.91596
- Cornice 1 - 5 = 1 - 1.41175
- 3 - 25 = 3 - 8.067

Order entire 24 - 15 = 23 - 5.646
a module = 11.49579 = 0.95798
a minute = 0.38319 = 0.03193
superficial measure of a column including base & capitel 99.5

Dining room. same order. same plates

Pedestal. (proj^n 16 = 4.702033)
- Plinth 0 - 26 = 0 - 7.640807
- mouldings 0 - 14 = 0 - 4.1142
- Dye 2 - 20 = 1 - 11.51017
- Cap. 0 - 20 = 0 - 5.877518
- 4 - 20 = 3 - 5.142695

Column
- Base 1 - 0 = 0 - 8.816326
- Shaft with astragal 14 - 0 = 10 - 3.428564
- Capitel with collar 1 - 0 = 0 - 8.816326
- 16 - 0 = 12 - 9.061216

Entablature (proj^n 50′ = 1 - 2.693876)
- Architrave + [illegible] - 0 = 0 - 8.816326
- frize 1 - 15 = 1 - 1.224489
- Capitel of frize 0 - 5 = 0 - 1.469387
- Cornice 1 - 5 = 0 - 10.285714
- 3 - 25 = 2 - 9.795728

Order entire 24 - 15 = 18 -
a module = 8.816326
a minute = 0.29387

Sky-room. External. Attic. Palladio B. 4. pl. 18. Attic pilaster of temple of Nerva Trajan. breadth of pilaster = dimin^d diam. of the column below, which Palladio expresses in quarter inches, to wit, 128. as he does all the other measures of this pilaster. we have this proportion then. As y^e breadth of his pilaster : to our dim^d diam. :: so his unit : to ours. or as 128 : 19 :: 1 : 0.14843

- Base. plinth. 71½ = 0 - 10.61274
- mouldings 48½ = 0 - 7.19885
- † Shaft of pilaster = 7 - 1.15607
- Cap. mouldings 68¾ = 0 - 10.20456
- plinth 46 = 0 - 6.82778
- proj^n 56¾ = 8.4234
- Attic entire 10 - 0

* the original plan of the house was that the column and entablature of the Doric external should be 18. f. it was afterwards made 19 f. in order to make the Din^g room a cube of 18 f. exclusive of joists. and the calculations of the external Doric were changed conformably. but those of the Attic, which had been made for a dim^d diam. of 19 I. were not changed and it was executed according to the measures here copied.

† the shaft of 19. I. diam. if exactly proportioned to that of Palladio would have been 4 - 5.73166 but my Attic being to be 7. f. in the clear, I added to the shaft 3.42441 which made 4 - 9.15067 and the Skyroom being to be 10. f. pitch external, the shaft must be 7 - 1.15607

Fig. 17. Jefferson's notes for Monticello II, Building Notebook, 1774–1824.

Monticello expanded Jefferson's learning curve as architect and a builder at the same time that it presented new challenges.

Jefferson's notes continued on the techniques and processes of turning raw materials into finished products wherever he found workmen to interview. This provided him a better basis with which to judge a workman's proposed cost and to occasionally argue for a better one. His notes on construction practices now included examples from his stays in Europe, Philadelphia, and Washington. He continued to record details such as "an acre of ground yields a million of bricks for every foot depth," and sometimes still noted, "This is exact from my own experiments."[113]

In certain cases Jefferson was even particular about how the lumber was cut. His enslaved sawyers, who typically used enslaved boys starting about the age of fourteen, would cut, haul, hew, and prepare lumber from Jefferson's own property. His very detailed instruction regarding the use of geometry to efficiently cut up the sections of a tree was followed by a note to his son-in-law acknowledging that his sawyers would need to be instructed once or twice to understand the complicated directions.[114] Thomas Mann Randolph responded that "it would be better to employ some industrious white person to labor with them and lay off their work for them. It will be of greatest advantage to them to be superintended by one who is a tolerable carpenter."[115] Randolph reiterated the need for what Jefferson called a "resident carpenter" who could direct all other carpenters, hired or enslaved. At the time of this correspondence David Watson, the British army deserter, was that person. Jefferson's 1793 list of enslaved people at Monticello mentioned ten carpenters, but only one on that list, John Hemmings, would rise to become a skilled and master joiner.[116] Of all the imports from outside Virginia during this era, the most important were skilled workmen who would train Jefferson's enslaved workers.

Workers

Jefferson's search for the best workers was even more crucial for the rebuilt Monticello than it had been for the less complex original design. This time the challenge for the owner/builder was carefully taking apart certain walls of the existing house and substantially adding to them. Jefferson is said to have famously remarked, "Architecture is my delight, and putting up, and pulling down, one of my favorite amusements."[117] The pulling-down part of Monticello I had started in 1796 during his hiatus as a private citizen. As the brick walls of the first house were finally coming down in the spring of 1796, Jefferson engaged local brickmakers and bricklayers. They started the putting-up process in 1797, the year Jefferson reluctantly agreed to reenter public office as vice president. In his absence the work would continue, but it would suffer as he once again took up residence in Philadelphia in March 1797. By that summer new bricks were being made by Stephen Willis and Willis's enslaved assistant Ned. Reclaimed bricks from the old walls and new bricks were being laid by bricklayers Richard Richardson and Hugh Chisolm, both of whom would later work at Poplar Forest. If they met his exacting standards, Jefferson endeavored to retain competent workers. Richardson would work at Monticello from 1796 to 1801 and Chisolm from 1796 to 1797, 1801 to 1814, and 1820 to 1826 at Monticello and Poplar Forest, and briefly at the University of Virginia. Jefferson's Memorandum Book records payments for "Chisolm's Lewis," one of his enslaved assistants.

The enslaved men, women, and boys who carried out the brickmaking tasks were usually not mentioned when the work was invoiced and paid. Brickmakers, who might also be the bricklayers, typically used their own enslaved laborers for the laborious process: tempering and mixing the clay, molding it, laying out the green bricks for sun-drying, hauling and stacking the green bricks in a clamp, burning the bricks for several days, dismantling and hauling the bricks to the building site, carrying bricks up the scaffold, and finally laying the bricks in a wall. For making mortar the labor force would have hauled limestone to the site, found firewood, burned the rick for several days, hauled good river sand and water to the site, and then beat the sand and burned/slaked lime together with water. Jefferson had calculated a price per thousand bricks based on his comparative notes for time, materials, and labor. Whether a hired worker had his own "hands" or not, Jefferson continued the practice of assigning his own slaves to help them in order to acquire his own skilled workforce. Yet Jefferson never relied solely on his enslaved bricklayers as he would on some of his enslaved carpenters and joiners. Troublesome hired workers would be indulged if their transferable skills warranted it. Overseer Edmund Bacon described how Jefferson put up with blacksmith William Stewart's drunken sprees for six years, "a good many years long [*sic*] than he would have done because he wanted him to teach some of his own hands."[118]

Enslaved workers not "owned" by Jefferson were either "owned" by the individual craftsmen or hired for the job. Bricklayer Richard Richardson was paid in 1801 for the hire of seven men. Richardson's own enslaved assistant Joe was presumably skilled with mortar, plaster, or bricklaying.[119] Two enslaved workers, Simon and Stepney, were hired from bricklayer Henry Duke, most likely for their skill in making mortar or laying brick. Jefferson's account for building expenses for 1802–3 simply listed "negro hire."[120] The practice of hiring out skilled enslaved workers was common, yet Jefferson did not seem to hire out his own enslaved workers from the building trades. His 1801 list of "negroes leased" versus "negroes retained" showed all of the carpenters on the retained list.[121] Payable accounts for the hired workers might fail to mention enslaved assistants who might occasionally be mentioned as "Perry's people" or "Perry's hands." Jefferson's own skilled enslaved workers performed many unrecorded construction tasks but are seldom mentioned except in correspondence with whoever was in charge when Jefferson was away.

When the masonry shell of the enlarged house had been completed, the work turned to the carpenters. Carpenters were responsible for framing the structural parts of a building: windows, doors, floors, roof systems, and interior partition walls. David Watson, the British army deserter, worked once again as the resident carpenter from 1792 until 1797. Working under him at various times on various plantation duties were enslaved carpenters George, Davy, John, Abram, Phill, Lewis, Johnny, Jupiter, King, Goliah, Mingo, Fanny, Tom Shackelford, and Moses.[122] Some of these men had acquired their initial skills working on the first house or on various plantation outbuildings. By 1797 Lewis was thirty-seven, John forty-four, Davy forty-two, Abram fifty-four, Phill S. fifty-seven, Phill forty-three, Johnny Hemmings twenty-two, Goliah sixty-six, Moses eighteen, and Jupiter fifty-four. "Johnny" Hemmings had obviously showed early promise and continued to do so. If the Scottish workers had showed up in 1793, Jefferson had instructed that John should work with the house joiner and Moses as the "disciple" of the stonemason.[123] John continued to learn valuable skills working under David Watson from 1793 to 1797. Early in 1798 Jefferson had written his son-in-law, "If you could sometimes take the trouble to make John and Davy come to you and bring their written instructions, and question them as to their progress, it would probably keep them to their metal."[124] Like John and Davy, two of the older and more reliable carpenters who were evidently literate, John Hemmings would also become literate, taught by Jefferson's granddaughters. His literacy would pay great dividends for Jefferson in the completion of Poplar Forest in the years to come.

Despite Jefferson's ill luck with getting his house covered in 1798, there was a bright note that year. On April 5 Jefferson could scarcely contain his delight when he wrote from Philadelphia to his daughter, "I have engaged a fine housejoiner here to go on with me."[125] This signaled Jefferson's great luck in finding James Dinsmore, an experienced Irish house joiner newly arrived in Philadelphia. Jefferson might have swayed his catch with descriptions of Monticello and by allowing him to pick out a new set of tools.[126] Jefferson had a good feeling for Dinsmore's capability and would come to appreciate him even more in the years to come, eventually recruiting him for the University of Virginia in 1817. Dinsmore was more than capable of executing all of the minutely detailed and specified building components voluminously listed in Jefferson's Building Notebooks for Monticello II. When Dinsmore arrived at Monticello, the house still resembled a brick kiln, having been partially demolished, and now stood ready for the finished joinery trim. His skill was exactly what Jefferson hoped for, confirmed by the fact that Dinsmore would later send Jefferson suggested details for Monticello based on architectural books in Jefferson's library.[127] Perhaps more importantly, Dinsmore could supervise work in Jefferson's absence.[128] Jefferson later recommended Dinsmore, saying, "A more faithful, sober, discrete, honest, and respectable man I have never known," and characterized his work as having "nothing superior in the U.S."[129] Jefferson would also have good luck with Lynchburg joiner Reuben Perry. Perry worked on Monticello from 1799 to 1803, and his carpenter brother John would work there from 1800 to 1811. Both Perrys would work at Poplar Forest, and John would later be responsible for a lion's share of contract work at the University. Both Perry brothers used their own enslaved assistants, as evidenced by references to their "people" or their "hands."

In the spring of 1800 Jefferson once again said goodbye to public life and returned to Monticello, where he hoped he could speed its rebuilding. His return home as a private citizen was agonizingly short, since he would be elected president the following February. In the fall of 1801 he again left his mountaintop and took up residence in the President's House in the visionary, but barely begun, federal city of Washington, DC. This symbolic building must have seemed familiar as an unfinished shell of a house where he tried to make himself comfortable in a few rooms. Characteristically, Jefferson drew up unrealized plans to enhance the interior with French apartment schemes suitable to his expanded architectural tastes. His plans for a picturesque landscape garden there also failed to reach fruition. His principal architectural contribution consisted of two 100-foot service wings having his signature flat "terras" roofs.[130] President Jefferson satisfied his urge as an architect and builder by supervising the construction of public buildings, especially the completion of the President's House and the Capitol. His own house was only just under roof and still an unfinished shell. If long-distance control and supervision had been difficult before, presidential duties would greatly increase that challenge of finishing Monticello, and starting Poplar Forest.

Jefferson's Memorandum Book offers an expenditure history of his life, including construction projects and payments to workers. In March 1802 his "Analysis of expenditures" recorded the expenses for the previous year, including those for running the President's House, which had to be taken out of his presidential salary. The private expenses in the list included books, debts, acquisitions, furniture, building, and household expenses for Monticello. For "building," he spent $2,076, about half the amount spent for the household and plantation. In the building list were materials such as lime, window sash, glass, and composition ornaments. Payments to workers included James Dinsmore, with the large payment of $430, John Holmes, James Oldham, Martin Wanscher, Hugh Chisolm, Joseph Moran (stonemason), John Perry, and Reuben Perry.[131] The following year the building expenses totaled $3,587. Dinsmore was not on the list, probably due to the large payment the year before and the fact that Jefferson frequently owed his workers back pay. He gave his workers ten to thirty dollars per month throughout the year, but the greater debt might not be paid off for years. James Dinsmore would come to perform a very important role at Monticello (1798–1809) as the instructor who would train Jefferson's enslaved carpenters. In particular he trained John Hemmings, who would rise above the carpenter trade to that of joiner.[132]

John Hemmings's life and fate were tied to two notations in Jefferson's Memorandum Book, one related to the construction of Monticello I and the other to Monticello II. On January 28, 1775, Jefferson noted in his Memorandum Book, "Joseph Neilson & his apprentice began to work for me the 23d inst. @ 50/per month."[133] Neilson (no relation to John Neilson) was a carpenter/joiner who worked at Monticello with his apprentice William Fosset for four years (1775–79). In that time he impregnated an enslaved house maid, Betty Hemings, the illegitimate daughter of Martha Jefferson's father, John Wayles, resulting in John Hemmings's birth in 1776.[134] The second Memorandum Book reference came in 1781. On April 3 Governor Jefferson noted from Richmond: "Sent David Watson a British deserter, house joiner by trade, to work at Monticello @ 3000 lb. tobo. a year or its worth in paper." Watson would work on Monticello I from 1781 to 1784, and on Monticello II in 1792, and then again from 1793 to 1797. Watson's reputation was as a heavy drinker but a skilled joiner who as a wheelwright, carriage maker, and cabinetmaker made Jefferson's phaeton carriage and writing desk, and supervised the out carpenters. Jefferson's October 1793 "Memorandum with respect to Watson" mentioned that he and his wife would temporarily live "in the shop near the sawpit" and would make wheels for a mule cart, two oxcarts, the phaeton, wheelbarrows, and a wagon. In the same memorandum: "Johnny is to work with him for the purpose of learning to make wheels and all sorts of work."[135] John Hemmings would indeed learn all sorts of work under Watson and Fosset until they left in 1797.

In February 1793 Jefferson listed his enslaved carpenters as: "George, Davy, John, Abram, Phill, Lewis, Johnny, Jupiter, King, Goliah, Mingo, Fanny, and Moses."[136] In May 1793 Jefferson's son-in-law wrote him to complain about the "dullness" of operations performed by the carpenters and recommended that "it would be better to employ some industrious white person to labor with them and lay off their work for them."[137] Jefferson responded that he agreed supervision was needed and that he was awaiting a Scottish stonemason and house joiner; "as to the house joiner, I mean Johnny (Betty Heming's [*sic*] son) to work with him. The first plain and simple job for him will be to make 10. Window frames, exactly of the size of those now in the house and of the same moldings, but without entablatures. . . . He will have to vamp up my old set of tools and make the most of them."[138] John Hemmings was evidently good enough by that time to be chosen to work with the prized Scottish house joiner, who never arrived. Watson would assume the supervisory resident carpenter role, and Jefferson was relieved to have him, despite his drinking sprees. Carpenter job lists for 1793 included making wheels, felling trees, hewing logs, pit-sawing stocks, mending fences, hauling wood, preparing wood for the joinery for "remodeling the house," working on the mill canal, building a stable, and making shingles. Hemmings would also have learned basic carpentry skills from working with enslaved carpenters Lewis, John, and Davy. He could also have learned his trade by working with or observing Monticello carpenter/joiners William Davenport (1797–98), James McGee (1798–99), Reuben Perry (1799–1803), and John Perry (1800–1811), but after 1798 James Dinsmore would be his principal instructor in the art of joinery.

Hemmings's more skilled training came from working with the joiners who fashioned windows, doors, and all of the detailed classical moldings. Jefferson's memorandum from autumn of 1799 noted: "Dinsmore and Johnny prepared and put up the oval arch in do. [the 'cabinet' room of Jefferson's suite]."[139] Dinsmore had taken over as Hemmings's principal instructor, although he could have benefited from working alongside joiners John Holmes (1800–1801), James Oldham (1801–4) and John Neilson (1805–9). "To-do" lists for Dinsmore, with Hemmings as his aide, included the dome room, the exterior dome base and cap, paneled doors, venetian blinds, window sashes, bases, sur bases (chair rails), architraves, floors, sash doors, window shutters, gallery balustrade, staircases, exterior balustrade, roof gutters, interior entablatures, the NW Pavilion, Chinese railing, the south piazza entablature, and the SW portico.[140] In Jefferson's "Distribution of blankets" list for the years 1793–1802, the word "joiner" appears after "Johnny," the only instance of that designation for all of the enslaved carpenters.[141] By September 1804 there is no doubt John Hemmings was considered an accomplished joiner and capable of working independently. That month Jefferson wrote out a number of lists of who would be responsible for certain tasks. One was "reserved for J. Hemings" and listed "All the Chinese railing. Venetian blinds for the Porticos. the 3 remaing. Angular portals. the Aviary. Facings [&c] of windows of covered ways. Folds of window shutters. closet of my bed chamber. store rooms in the loft."[142] On another list Jefferson placed "Dinsmore" at the head of one column and "John Hem" at the head of an adjacent column of tasks, indicating that they were working together but on different parts of the building. All of these tasks would prepare Hemmings to execute some of the same features at Poplar Forest.

Dinsmore also instructed Hemmings in the content and use of important architectural pattern books. The first December of Dinsmore's tenure, Jefferson had written his son-in-law, "Mr. Dinsmore asked me to lend him Gibbs's Rules for drawing, and I forgot to lay it out for him."[143] Jefferson would also have made available his Palladio, Chambray, and Desgodetz volumes that were sources for the finished moldings. Hemmings would come to use the same Gibbs and Palladio books for his work at Poplar Forest. Monticello overseer Edmund Bacon's autobiography primarily associated John Hemmings with Dinsmore: "John Hemings was a carpenter. He was a first rate workman—a very extra workman. He could make anything that was wanted in woodwork. He learned his trade of Dinsmore. He made most of the woodwork of Mr. Jefferson's fine carriage."[144] Hemmings would continue to put finishing touches on Monticello like the Venetian blinds in 1812, and, most significantly, he would turn his skills to making fine furniture for Monticello and Poplar Forest in addition to Jefferson's Landau carriage in 1814.[145]

By 1808 Hemmings had earned a privileged status at Monticello. Whether skilled or not, all enslaved workers of certain age were expected to pitch in at the critical plantation harvest time. This is indicated in Jefferson's 1797 note to his son-in-law regarding his enslaved workers who assisted the hired bricklayers: "There will be a difficulty as to the bricklayers. They should reserve for the harvest season that sort of work which will require least attendance, and do with the least possible."[146] Some, however, like the privileged house servants and skilled tradesmen, like John Hemmings, were exempt from field work. Jefferson wrote his overseer in 1808: "At harvest, give your whole force to Mr. Randolph, to assist in his harvest, the nailers, as well as all the rest, except Johnny Hemings and Lewis."[147] Hemmings had proven himself by this time and enjoyed a better status.

Learning their trade under John Hemmings were his three nephews, sons of Sally Hemings and Thomas Jefferson: William Beverly Hemings (1798–1822+), James Madison Hemings (1805–1877), and Thomas Eston Hemings (1808–1856). They would have typically started working in the Mulberry Row nailery at age ten, and by age fourteen they would either "go to ground" and become field hands or become apprentices learning a trade. If they were destined for a woodworking trade, they would typically start as an "out carpenter" at age fourteen, as their uncle had done. Jefferson's sons were an exception. Beverly started working for his uncle at age ten (1808), Madison at age eleven (1815), and Eston at age eleven (1819). Annette Gordon-Reed remarked that these Hemings boys were comparatively privileged. They were favored by Jefferson over other enslaved workers and were "measurably happy," as Madison recalled, and possibly grew up knowing they would someday be freed according to Jefferson's purported verbal promise to their mother.[148] Still, Madison later stated that their father was not in the habit of showing "fatherly affection" to them as compared with his other children and grandchildren. Gordon-Reed also believes that their association with their uncle was a favored decision by Jefferson: "So Jefferson's decision to put his sons in the daily care and under the tutelage of their uncle was not only a sound practical move; it served an important affective goal as well. Standing in Jefferson's place, the much respected carpenter and joiner [John Hemmings] could be the father they could not have, and they could be like sons to Hemings."[149] Madison and Eston would be among the lucky few who gained their freedom when Jefferson died, put in the custody of their uncle John until age twenty-one; they were freed in 1827. The other freed enslaved men were John Hemmings, painter/glazier Burwell Colbert, and blacksmith Joe Fossett; the other enslaved men, women, and children were sold off, like Monticello and its furniture, to satisfy Jefferson's debts.[150]

It would take Jefferson his entire eight-year tenure (1801–9) as president to complete Monticello. Halfway through that period he would start designing and supervising the construction of his retirement retreat house, using the same craftsmen, hired and enslaved, who had not yet finished the other, and who would go back and forth between the two. Monticello's floors were still being installed by John Perry in 1804 as the plastering reached its long completion. The joiners were busy with interior and exterior trim. The doors, made in Richmond by James Oldham, finally arrived on site in 1805 and were faux-painted and varnished by Richard Barry, who had arrived that year from Washington, DC. Barry would also glaze the Monticello and Poplar Forest window sash made by Dinsmore in 1807–8.

On March 11, 1809, retired president Thomas Jefferson paid a one-dollar ferry fee to cross the Potomac River at Georgetown and headed south toward home, this time to remain a private citizen. The four-day trip, in a "tremendous snowstorm," was difficult with Jefferson in a carriage followed by three wagons filled with boxes of personal items and shrubbery from a nursery. The house he finally reached was at last something that resembled a finished project, the result of many frustrating years of using and keeping competent workmen. The year 1809 was also when Jefferson started using his long-awaited villa retreat that, like his first and second projects at Monticello, and even the President's House, would still resemble a brick kiln for many years. By the time Thomas Jefferson finally retired from public life in 1809, his ideas about architecture, especially domestic works, were solidified. His personal style of Roman classicism remained consistent, if not old-fashioned. His aesthetic designs, even if ideal, were blended with native colonial traditions of plans and elements from which he could never really

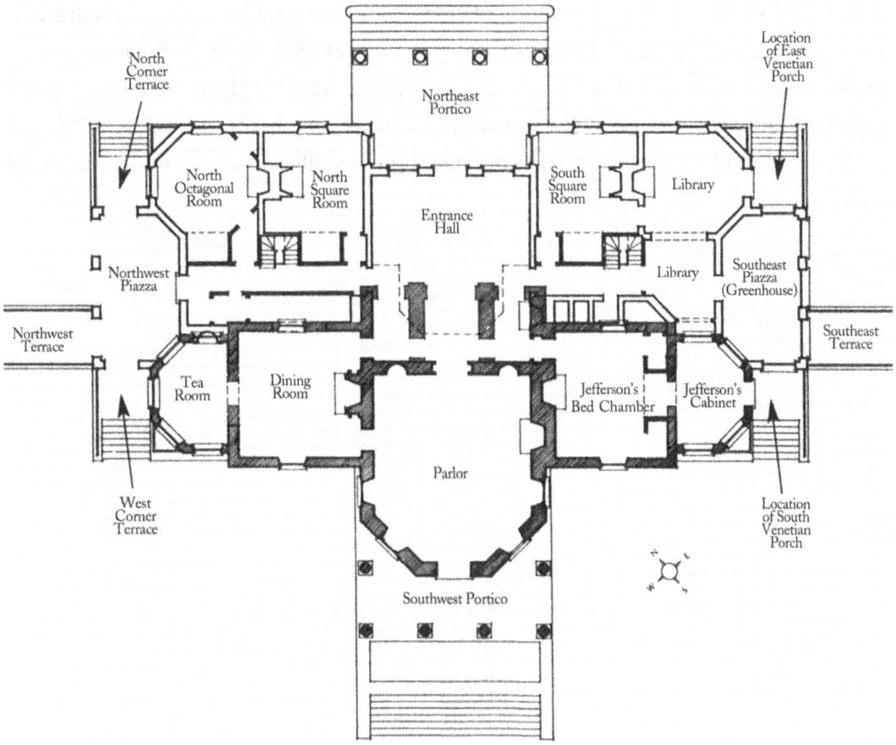

Fig. 18. Plan of Monticello II. Darker lines represent original construction.

escape.[151] His personality trait of needing to control every aspect of construction, with great patience and a faithful optimism to steer toward a vision or an ideal achievement, was not unlike his long role in forming a new nation. Jefferson's personal visions for all aspects of the new country were constantly under siege by circumstances beyond his control, but ones he felt could be ameliorated in some future way or perhaps by another generation. Jefferson's need for change and his restlessness for improvement were parts of his life and character, extending from architectural details to any number of political, educational, agricultural, and scientific endeavors. The energy spent to improve his nation now focused on two retirement projects, one very personal. Could he accomplish his quest for complete privacy at Poplar Forest? Could his idealistic design be achieved without compromise for convenience?

Building and rebuilding Monticello had given Jefferson an experience that would serve him well at Poplar Forest, even if his new project had unique challenges. He had contemplated and designed precise architectural details for his retreat and could specify familiar materials down to the quantity of bricks and the ratio of lime and sand for the mortar that would hold them together. Jefferson knew all too well from Monticello that the wild card in construction was the workforce. His strategy, especially for a long-distant project that he couldn't routinely inspect, was to rely on workmen who had proven their worth at Monticello. Jefferson gambled that the known quality of a workman, even flawed, outweighed that of a more local but untested workman. The consequence of this tried-but-true approach was the logistical challenge of getting workmen and materials from Monticello to Poplar Forest. As the finished woodwork stretched on year after year, Jefferson would come to rely without qualms on the expertise of John Hemmings, who had practiced those skills at Monticello and was now without peer.

3

DESIGNING A RETREAT

Thomas Jefferson's architectural output for designs both public and private surpasses that of any other amateur architect of his time and place. From the 1760s to the 1820s the number of his designs was extraordinary for the variety of building types and for his evolving ideas of appropriate public and private forms. However, although Jefferson designed a great many domestic works, there is only a small number that were built and an even smaller number built to his design and specifications. For himself he designed and used two houses, the initial Monticello and its rebuilt version, and Poplar Forest. For his daughter Martha Randolph, he designed Edge Hill (1797) near Monticello.[1] Jefferson's friends recognized his talent and asked for advice on new houses or remodeling old ones. New house designs included a design (1796) for Wilson Cary Nicholas that featured two octagon rooms; a town house (unexecuted) for an unidentified friend (ca. 1800); a house (unexecuted) for Mrs. Mary E. Higginbotham in Albemarle Country (ca. 1809); Farmington (1810) in Lexington, Kentucky, for John Speed; and Barboursville (1817) in Orange County, Virginia, for James Barbour.[2] Attributed house designs with some bit of verification include Brandon (1789) for Benjamin Harrison; Edgemont (1806) in Albemarle County, Virginia, for James Powell Cocke; and Ampthill (1815) in Cumberland, County, Virginia, for Randolph Harrison.[3] Less solid are attributions for Belle Grove (1794) in the Shenandoah Valley and The Residence (1793) in Orange County, Virginia. For others he designed additions: Montpelier (1797) in Orange County, Virginia, for James Madison; Farmington (1802) in Albemarle County, Virginia, for George Divers; and Eppington (1798) in Chesterfield County, Virginia, for Francis Wayles Eppes.[4]

Jefferson drew designs on a variety of papers: large and small sheets of writing paper, scraps of paper, printed graph paper, and even reused envelopes. By remarkable good fortune most of these drawings were saved and still exist due to the value Jefferson's family placed on them. The largest collection passed through the Coolidge Family in Boston, which Fiske Kimball examined at the Massachusetts Historical Society, resulting in his important work *Thomas Jefferson, Architect.* Frederick Nichols updated Kimball's catalogue with his own numbering system, added additional drawings, and revised some of Kimball's attributions.[5] Many of these drawings reveal Jefferson's design process. Preliminary ideas for room function and use were turned into plans that fit into a building's preferred size and shape, governed by the client's economic and social status. The outward style of the building came from an accepted or traditional regional prototype, in this case Jefferson's Roman classicism. Jefferson's architectural designs reflect his ever-changing ideas about comfort, convenience, privacy, and architectural correctness, but in a consistent exterior style. What makes Jefferson's surviving collection of drawings important is the continuity of designs that span his lifetime and show his evolution as an architect and builder. Jefferson saved many preliminary studies of designs that give insight into his thought process for addressing any particular building's needs, function, and appearance.

Jefferson's designs for domestic works can be grouped into general types regarding size and plan, many using octagons or semi-octagons. The first Monticello evolved from a three-room (numbers of rooms are for first floors), two-story rectangular house to one with a two-story center block with one-story wings and attached service rooms. Other types include square houses of three to six rooms that featured semi-octagonal rooms with or without centered canted bows. The design for Monticello II is exceptional in American architecture as a complex four-story house with a dome, having eleven rooms on the first floor including octagon rooms, semi-octagon rooms, and canted bows. An unusual variant of Jefferson's domestic designs is the centralized rotunda house with dome, with and without wings. Other rectangular or square designs of four to six rooms used a centered regular octagon room projecting as a canted bow. Variations on this type include plans with two full octagonal rooms with canted bows having one or two porticos. One unique design was for a circular retreat house based on one Jefferson saw outside of Paris. One large "urban dwelling" design had nine rooms with oval rooms and two porticos. An unusual full octagon house plan features four projecting corner rooms with canted bows. And finally there is the full idealized octagon house used for Poplar Forest with its preliminary designs. These many forms and their variations clearly show an architect grappling with room shapes and sizes, various means of communication between rooms, efficient use of spaces and staircases for public and private interaction, and various exterior expressions. This was Jefferson's flexible design typology, discussed later in this chapter, of mixing spatial, structural, and ornamental elements within codified mathematical rules and classical proportions. Jefferson eventually used his design typology in a much more idealized way at Poplar Forest than the compromised design for Monticello II that he admitted was "subordinated by law of convenience and affected by circumstance of change."[6]

Octagons

Just why Thomas Jefferson loved the octagon shape remains a mystery.[7] Perhaps it was the love of mathematical formulation for someone steeped in classical theories of harmonic numbers and mathematical reason. Jefferson never says. The only clue is tied to the qualities of light and air, but his affection reflected more than recognition of certain practicalities. In 1816 Jefferson allowed John Neilson to share the Poplar Forest design with a friend, eliciting this response: "He is a great advocate for light and air—as you predicted he was for giving you Octagons. They were charming. They gave you a semi-circle of light and air."[8] Jefferson associated octagons and airiness in a more dramatic manner at Monticello when he invited his friend William Giles to visit in 1796. As the house was being demolished and rebuilt, Jefferson stated that its "re-edification" should not deter a visit: "We shall have the eye of a brick-kiln to poke you into, or an Octagon to air you in."[9] What is certain is that Thomas Jefferson tenaciously used the octagon shape from his earliest designs to his latest. Poplar Forest was his ultimate and most innovative use of that geometric shape.

Throughout history the octagon shape has been commonly used for many designs and types of buildings. It can be found in ancient times onward on different continents for Roman temples, medieval cathedrals, Muslim mosques, and on countless European and American churches for cupolas and steeples. It became religiously symbolic in the Middle Ages throughout Europe as a ubiquitous form for baptisteries and baptismal fonts. It appeared frequently in Renaissance designs. It is tied to Masonic symbolism. The shape appears in designs for tile and parquet floors, for coffered ceilings, and for furniture. Octagonal buildings large and small were built in the British Isles and on the European Continent in the sixteenth, seventeenth, and eighteenth centuries as lodges, pavilions and casinos. Actor David Garrick's villa featured an octagonal temple dedicated to Shakespeare. King Louis XIV's seventeenth-century chateau at Marly featured an octagonal salon, as did any number of Parisian mansions and French chateaus of the eighteenth century. The Dutch Reformed Church in the Hudson River Valley and in New Jersey chose the octagon as their favored form and constructed more than twenty octagonal churches between 1660 and 1750. When Jefferson arrived in Williamsburg in 1760, he laid eyes on the earliest free-standing octagonal building in Virginia: the 1715 brick Powder Magazine.

Small octagonal buildings were scattered across the landscape of colonial America. They appeared as various outbuildings used as dairies, privies, dovecotes, garden sheds, offices, and icehouses.[10] George Washington designed octagonal sheds for seeds and tools at Mount Vernon. In Virginia the octagonal privies at Poplar Forest were preceded by those that graced the garden yards at Brandon and Mount Vernon. The most public octagonal privy sat next to the impressive domed Maryland Capitol in Annapolis. Landscaped gardens featured octagonal "garden houses" or "summer houses" where one could retreat like Charles Carroll and William Paca in Annapolis. Octagonal

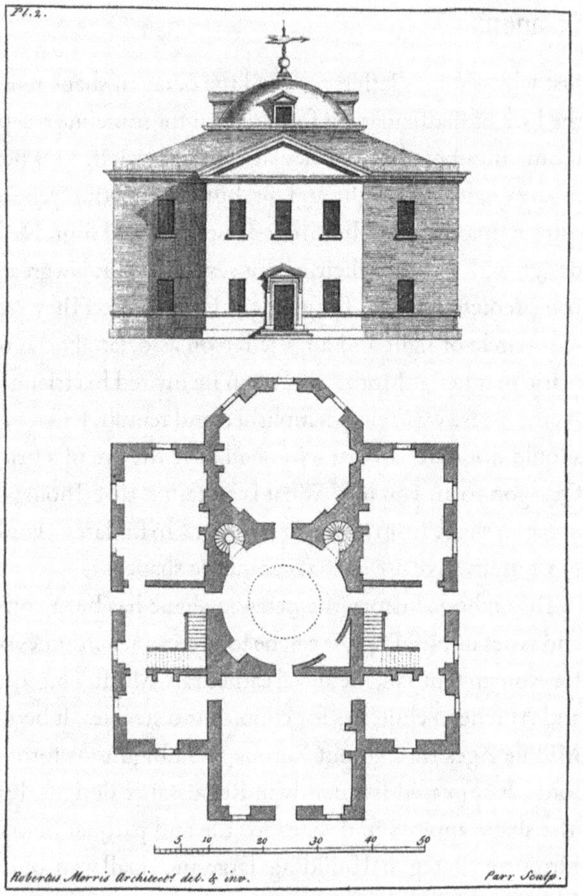

Fig. 19. Two houses and a chapel with octagon forms from Robert Morris *Select Architecture* (1755), plates 2, 30, 32.

garden summer houses could be found up and down the East Coast: at John Burgwin's plantation in North Carolina; at Thomas Mifflin's country house outside Philadelphia; at Jean Garesche's house in Delaware; and at Isaac Royal's house in Massachusetts.

Jefferson saw octagonal buildings and designs in any number of his books depicting classical remains. Palladio did not use octagons in his own designs but depicted ancient Roman examples in his book. Where Jefferson saw a proliferation of octagonal building designs was in architectural books by the British Palladians. It is almost certain Jefferson developed his love of octagons from three of his earliest architectural acquisitions: James Gibbs's *Book of Architecture* (1728), Robert Morris's *Select Architecture* (1755), and William Kent's *Designs of Inigo Jones* (1727). A fourth source that included octagon designs was William Chambers's *Treatise on the Decorative Parts of Civil Architecture* (1759). While it is reasonable to consider only the architectural books owned by Jefferson, the chance is great that he perused those in other private libraries in America and in Europe.

The earliest American octagonal room Jefferson might have seen was in Colonel Roger Morris's 1765 summer house called Mount Morris on Manhattan Island. Morris

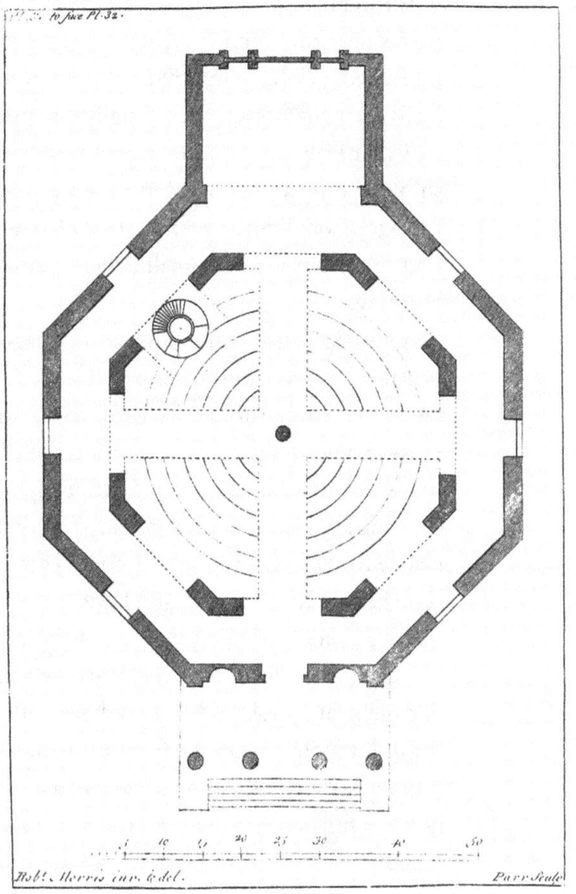

was the son of the London architect Roger Morris, a British Palladian who developed a popular version of the neo-Palladian villa in the 1730s.[11] He was also the nephew of the more famous British Palladian architect Robert Morris, whose book Jefferson owned. We can imagine Colonel Morris returning from England with new ideas suggested by his father or uncle. Mount Morris was a typical Georgian-Palladian design with the exception of its unusual octagonal drawing room wing.[12] By 1785 the house had become a tavern that hosted a dinner party in July 1790 that included Jefferson along with President Washington's cabinet.[13] While the dinner party was reported to have taken place on the lawn, Jefferson must have sneaked a peek inside at the octagonal room.

One well-known "octagon" that Jefferson couldn't fail to see was John Tayloe's winter town home just to the west of the President's House.[14] The house was started in 1799 from designs by William Thornton, who had won the Capitol design competition. It must have irked President Jefferson, an expert in the use of that shape, that the Tayloes christened their new six-sided home "the Octagon."

The earliest-known full-size octagonal house might be a country seat on the banks of the Schuylkill River near Philadelphia. Jefferson most likely knew this house since it was near the summer residence he rented in 1793. Dr. William Smith constructed his suburban villa in the 1760s in the fashion of Philadelphians who wished to "retire" from their city houses in the English manner.[15] Little is known of this house other than a distant view in a 1794 illustration of the Schuylkill Falls and in a 1925 photograph showing only a portion of the then-altered house.[16] The illustration shows "Smith's Octagon," or "Smith's Folly," on a hill as a two-story building with a cupola. The photograph shows a rather small octagon bow attached to a much larger and later school building.

An intriguing and mysterious full octagonal house is one Jefferson undoubtedly saw because he sketched it on the back of a dinner invitation (fig. 20). The undated invitation was from Thomas McKean to George Washington and is most likely from the 1790s, when the government resided in Philadelphia. Was Jefferson in the company of Washington at this dinner and using his invitation for an impromptu sketch? At that time McKean, a distinguished soldier and signer of the Declaration, was chief justice for Pennsylvania and lived at Third and Pine Streets in Philadelphia, but there is no known McKean octagon house, or any other of that type in Philadelphia for that matter. Could Washington and Jefferson have been at Dr. William Smith's octagonal house on the Schuylkill River? This invitation was discovered in 1896 in a secret compartment of a desk said to have been Jefferson's and later owned by Jefferson's niece Sarah Randolph.[17] On the front of the invitation are pencil sketches of an eighteenth-century-style pediment window and a period chair. On the back are two sketches of a house, a full octagon plan and its partial elevation showing it as a two-story house. The plan shows two 20′ × 20′ center rooms and a portico with four columns. The sketches would indicate Jefferson was drawing in-situ. It is a mysterious link of Jefferson and octagons, possibly the first full-size American octagon house he had seen, and perhaps the earliest one.[18]

The octagon shape remained supreme throughout all of Jefferson's domestic designs. Along with classical design, the octagon shape defines Jefferson's most consistent architectural signature, used mostly in domestic designs (see appendix C). He used the shape in any number of ways, beginning with the first Monticello in 1769 to his ultimate octagon at Poplar Forest, and finally in two unusual ways at the University of Virginia.[19] His most popular expression of the shape was a semi-octagonal canted bow that projected from an exterior wall. His use of this form for Monticello I was not novel compared with the use of that device in England, but it was innovative for the colonies. The use of a semi-octagonal "canted bay" had its genesis in seventeenth-century England, but its real popularity came in designs by the British Palladians, who were at their peak in the 1750s, when their influence was beginning to be felt in America.[20] That influence ran to about 1800, with the exception of Jefferson, who continued his personal style into the 1820s. Jefferson's early use of the semi-octagonal projecting bow for Monticello I would soon find company in America as the interest in octagonal shapes gained in popularity beginning in the 1770s.[21] By the time Jefferson came to remodel

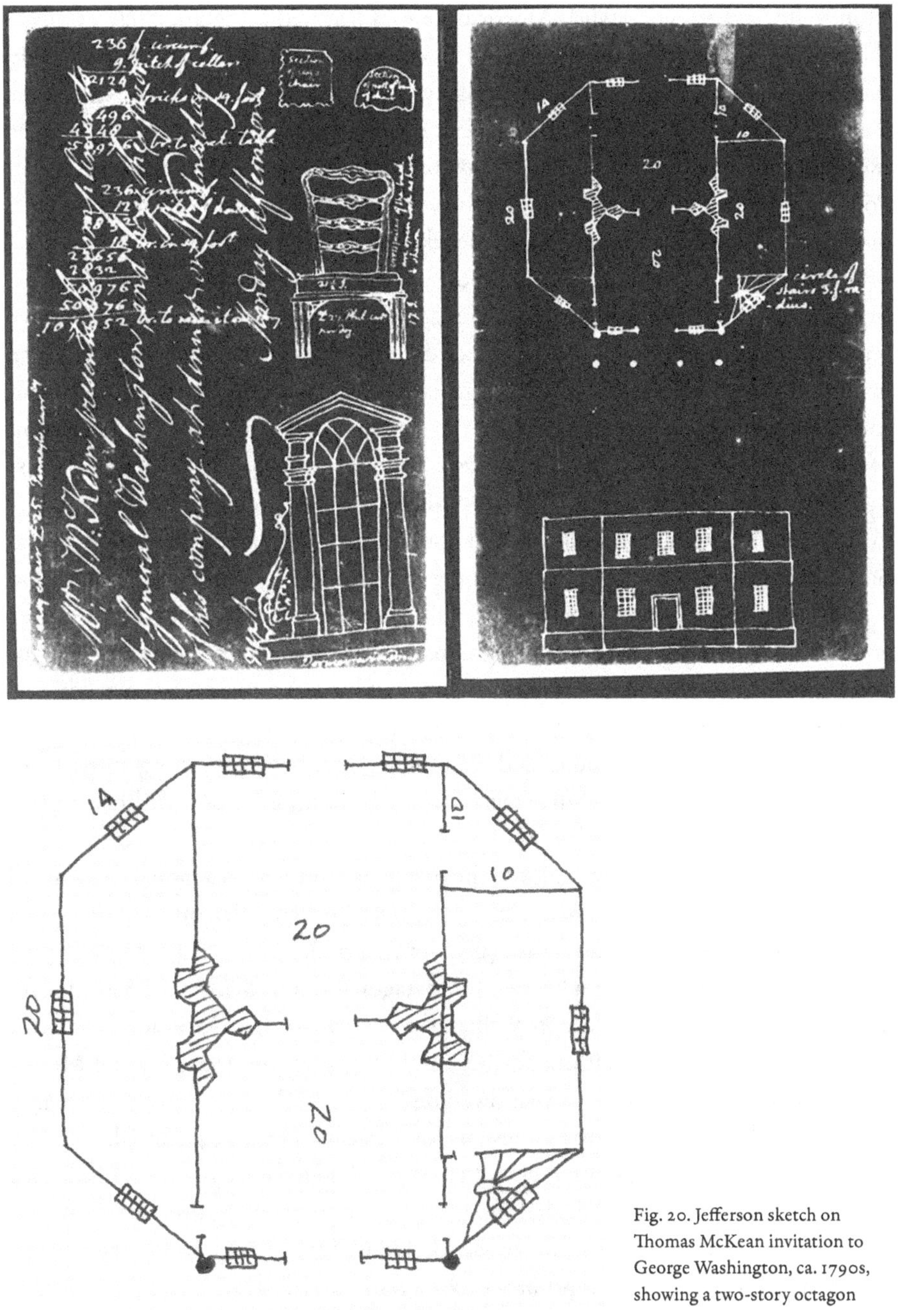

Fig. 20. Jefferson sketch on Thomas McKean invitation to George Washington, ca. 1790s, showing a two-story octagon house and tracing of plan by the author.

Monticello in the 1790s, stylish American houses featured octagons, circles, or ovals that protruded from exterior walls in the new neoclassical "Adam," or "Federal," style. A regional collection of houses featuring octagonal shapes was built in Richmond, Virginia, from 1795 to 1815. Whether Jefferson saw any of these on his last trip there in 1809 he doesn't say.[22] He most certainly saw, but failed to comment on, George Cabell's Point of Honor house in Lynchburg (1815), with two canted bays in front, that was most likely modeled on the Michael Hancock House in Richmond.

Jefferson used the projecting canted bow or bay in a variety of ways. The final design for Monticello I featured one for the projecting parlor and for each of the two semi-octagonal wings. In another instance of Jefferson sketching on the back of an invitation, this time one of his own and an early one from the 1770s, he shows a four-room house with two full 20-foot octagonal rooms projecting to either side at the front of the house (fig. 22). This scheme of two octagonal rooms in the center of a house was more elegantly accomplished in his design for John Speed's house, Farmington, in Kentucky. In other designs the canted bow could encompass the entire rear elevation of a building; it could extend from the center square or rectangular room; and it could form the ends of wings. The variation Jefferson came to favor was the canted bow extending from a rear central octagon room, a good example being his design for Barboursville (fig. 23). With very few exceptions, if he designed a central octagonal or a semi-octagonal room, it projected outward as a canted bow. Canted bows could also be used with nonoctagonal rooms and even some center bows projecting onto a front portico.[23] Three examples of a full octagonal room projecting as a bow within a portico featured rare domestic domes.[24]

To say Jefferson obsessively explored the octagonal and semi-octagonal shape in all its variations is an understatement. In chronological order, Jefferson used octagonal shapes for the first Monticello house (1770–72); a design for a chapel in Williamsburg (ca. 1772); a house plan with two full octagonal rooms (ca. 1776); plans for remodeling the Governor's Palace in Williamsburg (1779–81); a Governor's House in Richmond (1779–81); alterations for his Elk Hill plantation house (1784); Monticello II (1785–89); designs of "urban dwellings" (1789–94); alterations of his rented Philadelphia house (1793); various designs for "retreats" (1789–94); an addition for Eppington (1798); a design for Edgehill (1796); a design for Edgemont (? indicates an unconfirmed design) (1796); alterations for Farmington in Virginia (1802); Poplar Forest (1789, 1804–6); the Alexander McRae House (?) in Richmond (1809); Farmington in Kentucky (1810); Ampthill (?) (1815); Barboursville (1817); and Buckingham County Court House (1821). Jefferson used two other unusual octagonal designs at the University of Virginia. The Anatomical Theater was a brick cube having only exterior lunette windows and a long skylight lighting the central operating table that was surrounded by tiered seats forming an octagon.[25] His other design, unexecuted, was for an observatory composed of four regular octagons joined in their center, inspired by the Paris observatory.[26] Rarely did an architect work so long and hard using a special

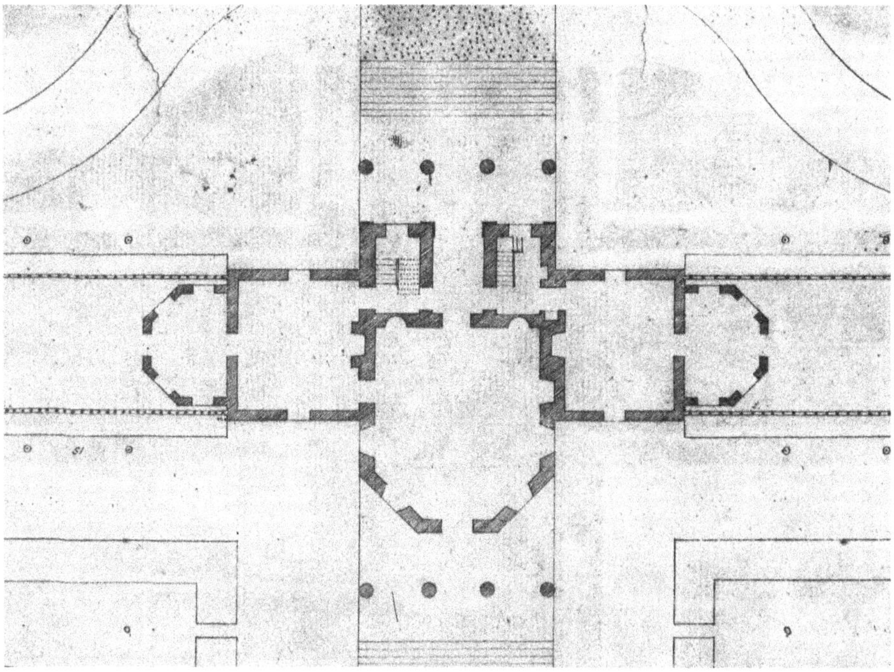

Fig. 21. Jefferson drawing of Monticello I plan.

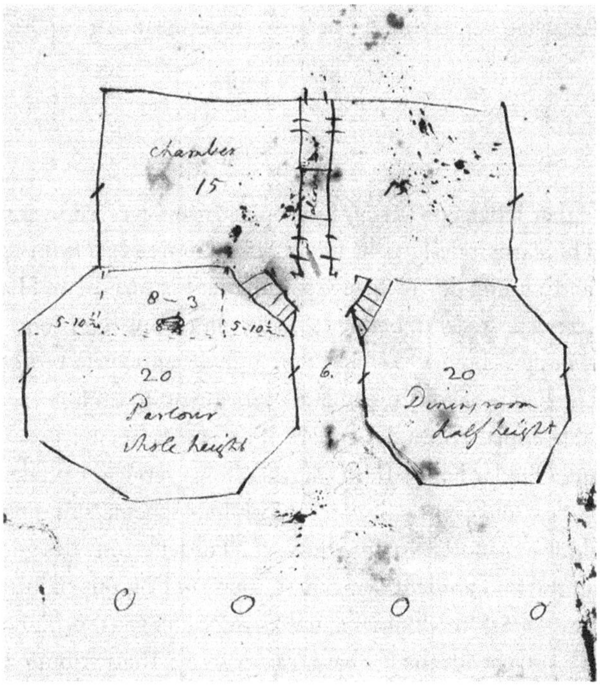

Fig. 22. Jefferson drawing of a house with two octagon rooms, ca. 1770s.

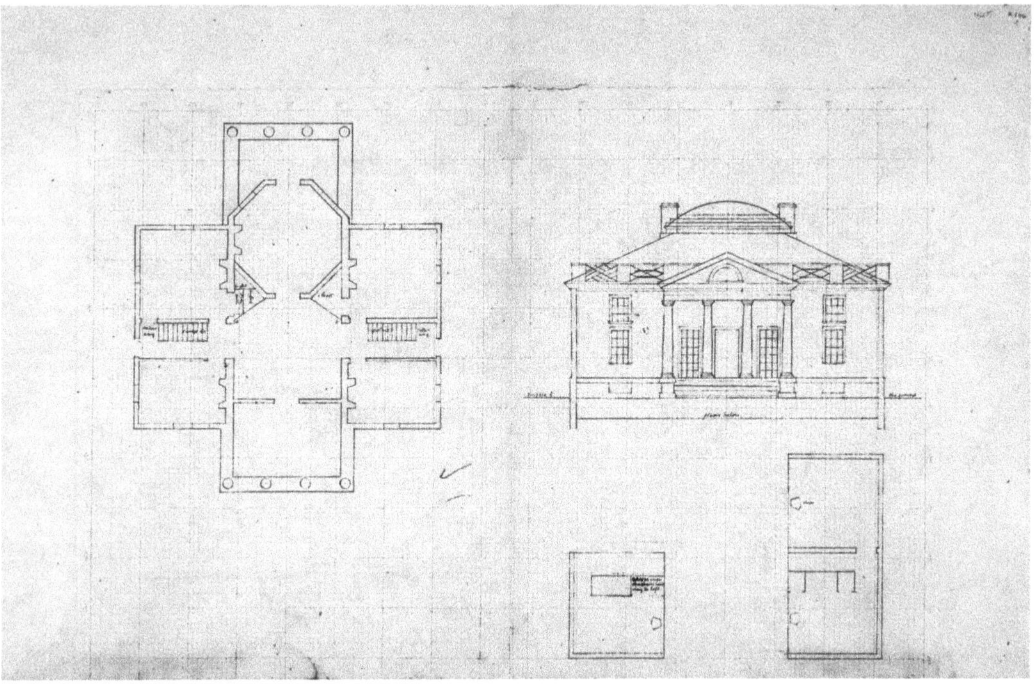

Fig. 23. Jefferson drawing of Barboursville, 1817.

shape in so many variations. For whatever reason, the octagon shape meant a great deal to Thomas Jefferson.

Retreat Designs

It should come as no surprise that Jefferson's design for Poplar Forest evolved over a long period. Had he executed his earliest designs, he might have repeated his "favorite amusement" of "putting up and pulling down" before settling on his final plan. His earliest design for Poplar Forest dates to 1781, before he had even completed Monticello I. He settled on his final design about 1804–5, when he could anticipate retirement in 1809. In that interim he had time to contemplate a retreat and to explore various schemes on paper. Verifiable Poplar Forest designs are of two types; so, in a sense, there was a Poplar Forest I and a Poplar Forest II. In this case, however, Jefferson delayed construction of his early ideas and eventually executed his final scheme, skipping the messy rebuilding he had done at Monticello. If we look at all of Jefferson's designs for retreats, those for Poplar Forest and unidentified others, they can be grouped into four phases: the Premature Phase (1781), the Experimental Phase (ca. 1789–1800), the Mature Phase (ca. 1800–1804), and the Idealistic Phase (ca. 1805–6). The attribution of some designs and their sequence remains frustratingly unknown for the two middle phases. Regardless, it is obvious that Jefferson continuously thought about and experimented with many design solutions for retreats.

Jefferson's first known but pre-mature design for a dwelling at Poplar Forest was more suited to the needs of his family than it was a retirement retreat. Jefferson drew a house plan, oddly enough labeled in Anglo-Saxon, having a central octagon room with a canted bow and flanking wing pavilions also with canted bows (fig. 24). This drawing is the same plan depicted in miniature on the back of a 1781 Poplar Forest land plat (fig. 34).[27] At the time Jefferson had designed changes to the Williamsburg Governor's Palace where he was living and a design for a future governor's house for Richmond, both of which were similar to the early Poplar Forest plan. Jefferson and his family had literally retreated to Poplar Forest to avoid capture by the British in 1781, giving Jefferson time to think about a future house on that property. The scale of that house plan was not suited to a retired man's retreat but resembled a full-scale domestic design, incorporating ideas he had considered for Williamsburg and Richmond. The significance of this early drawing is that it defined a plan using a center octagon room with a canted bow. Jefferson would continue to use this scheme for decades, including in later preliminary designs for Poplar Forest.

Jefferson's five years in Europe (1784–89) gave him the chance to see many types of retreats, some for daily use in gardens and parks, some royal and some private, and many of architectural distinction. Jefferson's use of a real hermitage near Paris led him to write a friend that he contemplated his own "little hermitage" at Natural Bridge.[28] Jefferson returned from Paris full of ideas for retreats as evidenced by a series of the designs for small buildings that can only be attributed to such a function. Despite his busy duties with the new government from 1789 to 1800, and with his fits and starts for remodeling Monticello, Jefferson experimented on paper with various ideas for a retreat. This represents his Experimental Phase. Whether he intended these for Poplar Forest is unclear, but they show he was thinking about how he would retreat from the world. One scheme from about 1794 resembled a familiar prototype: a design for a circular retreat, labeled in French, and featuring oval rooms like the Désert de Retz retreat he had seen outside of Paris.[29]

Other drawings by Jefferson, by their scale of having only three principal rooms,

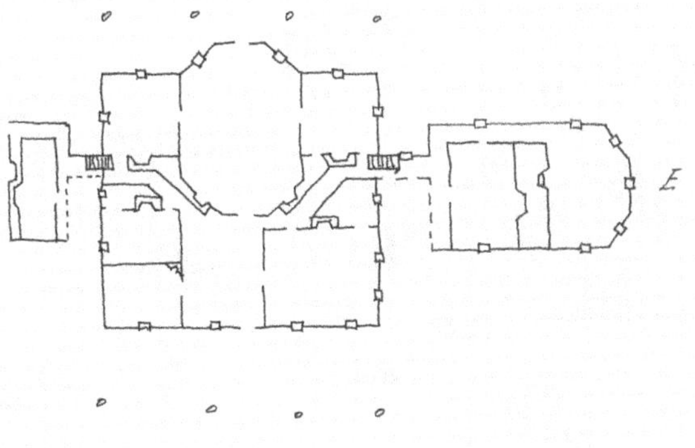

Fig. 24. Jefferson drawing of first Poplar Forest plan, ca. 1781, on verso of a Poplar Forest land plat; rooms labeled in Anglo-Saxon; tracing of plan by the author.

appear to be experiments for a retreat.[30] These can be seen as the traditional Virginia combination of chamber, dining room, and parlor. Four other designs on a single sheet show a progression from more successful three-room plans using semi-octagons to a larger one of six rooms (fig. 25). Whether using full or semi-octagons that project in various fashions, these schemes show Jefferson using a flexible typology of shapes that expanded or contracted depending on the scale of a house.

For this next-to-last design for Poplar Forest, in his Mature Phase, Jefferson recycled one of his earliest and most consistent schemes. This familiar six-room plan with projecting octagonal bow probably dates to the period 1800–1804. He had used this design before, and he would continue to use it after Poplar Forest (fig. 26).[31] Confirmation that this is a design for Poplar Forest is revealed by the label "Plan for Bedford" written on the drawing.[32] Four other designs using this basic scheme are related to the Poplar Forest design. Two of these were noted by Kimball as being Poplar Forest studies (fig. 27).[33] Two were unknown to Kimball, one from the Huntington Library and one from the University of North Carolina Library (the "Trist" plan, fig. 29).[34] With the exception of the Huntington drawing, on a paper dated to ca. 1803–5, all the other designs are on graph paper, which Jefferson started using after his time in Paris, post-1789.

The sequence of these plans is hard to determine. They all have a general rectangular shape but with different room arrangements. In most cases the internal walls defining the entry hall and parlor contain the fireplaces, with one example showing the use of stoves. The plans range from having one bed chamber to four, most with alcove beds,

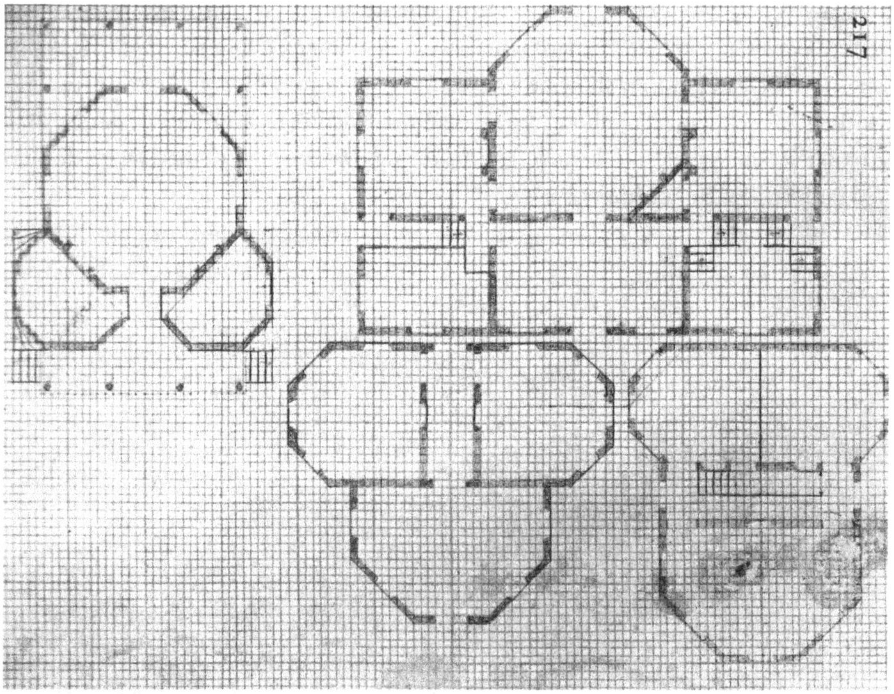

Fig. 25. Jefferson studies for retreats.

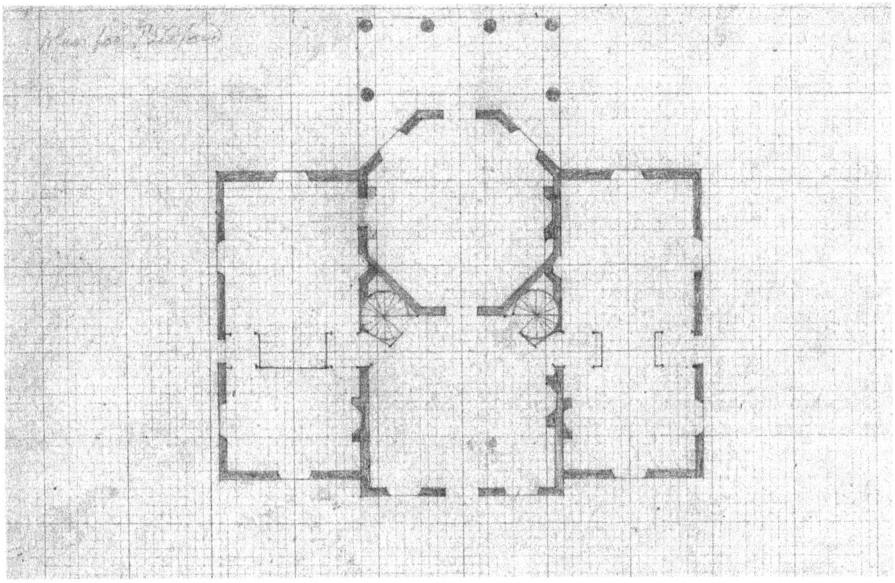

Fig. 26. Jefferson study for Poplar Forest.

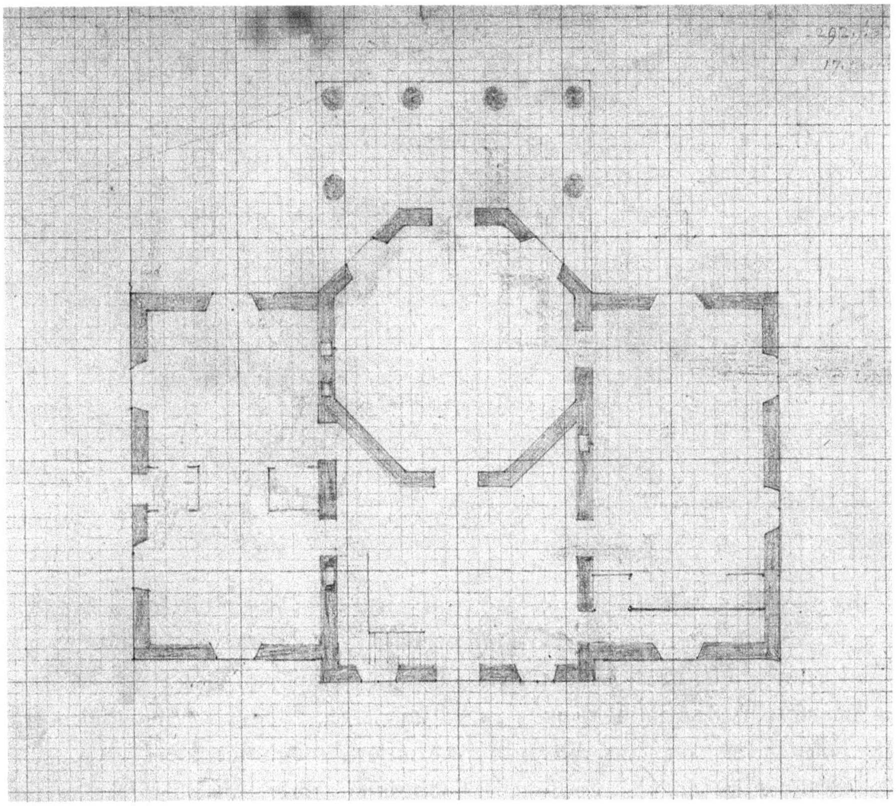

Fig. 27. Jefferson drawing, possible study for Poplar Forest.

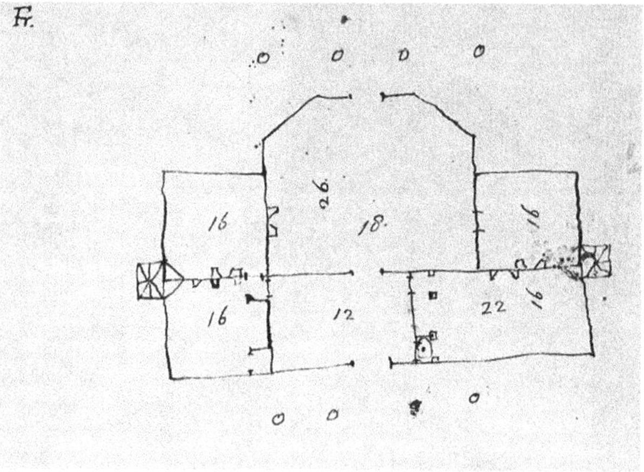

Fig. 28. Jefferson drawing, possible study for Poplar Forest.

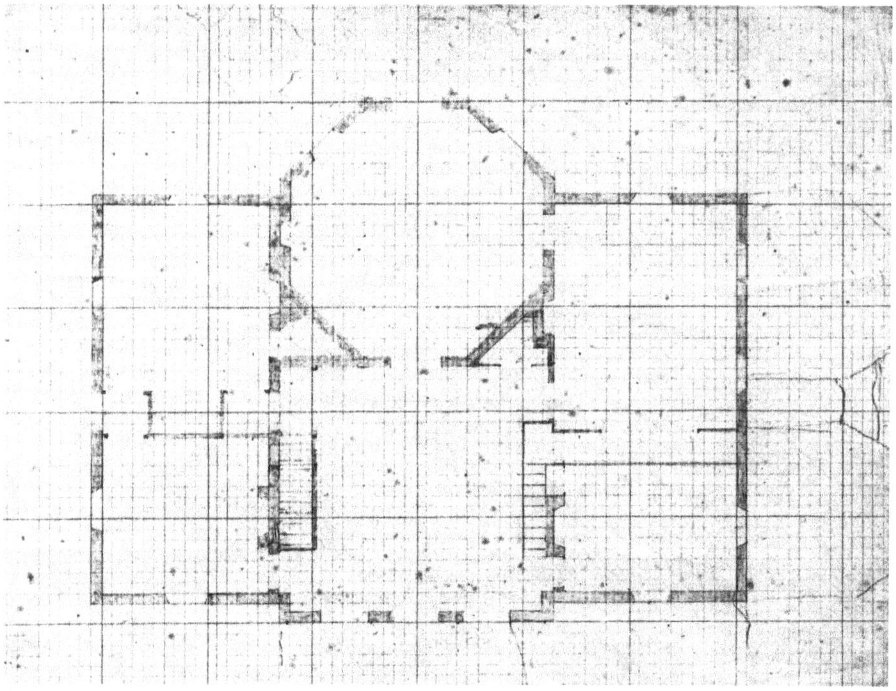

Fig. 29. Jefferson drawing, possible study for Poplar Forest.

both one- and two-sided. All have a large entry hall and a rear projecting parlor that is semi-octagonal in two cases and a full octagon in three cases. Stairs, indicating a two-level structure, are shown in the entry hall, in exterior pavilions, and in one case as circular stairs. The dining rooms are small and large, variously served by sideboard vestibules and servant stairs. Access to the exterior through side doors is through a transverse passage (one plan) or through a bed chamber (three plans). In three plans the dining room communicates with the parlor, and in one it also communicates with the exterior. Facades and entry halls vary in size, but the perimeter rooms of chambers or dining room are a consistent 16-foot width.[35] Three show porticos on the rear, one on both sides, and two having none, but front porticos by necessity can be imagined. Access for family and servants between floors and to the exterior seemed to be the biggest challenge for Jefferson. Together these various schemes give some insight into Jefferson's effort to solve the programmatic public/private needs of chamber suites, smaller chambers, serviceable dining rooms, upper- and lower-floor access, and exterior access.

Jefferson's final design for Poplar Forest, like the earlier schemes, was a sequential process of unknown dates and just as mysterious as earlier retreat studies. If some of the "retreat" designs using various combinations of octagonal rooms were a precursor, the final phase shows a move toward an ultimate and innovative full octagon design that represents Jefferson's Idealistic Phase. When Jefferson settled upon this final scheme we cannot say. If we take him at his word that the full octagon house was "exactly on the plan once thought of for Pantops [near Monticello] and intended from the beginning for Francis," then it could date from 1801, when his grandson Francis Eppes was born to Mary Jefferson and John W. Eppes. After Mary's death in 1804 Jefferson still promised to build a house and wrote to John Eppes that he expected "some day [it will] become the residence of Francis. I may only take more time of it."[36] Jefferson now intended that Francis's future house would be in Bedford County. That final statement meant that in the meantime Jefferson intended to build and use the house for himself; its design would now be intended for two purposes but more suited as an occasional retreat.

It has been suggested that Jefferson's design for Poplar Forest was inspired by a German landscape gardening book he purchased in June 1805.[37] Wilhelm Gottlieb Becker's *Neue Garten- und Landschafts-Gebäude* (1798–99) illustrated a garden temple in the shape of an octagon with a square center room surrounded by three long rectangular rooms. Did Jefferson use the Becker design months before sending Hugh Chisolm to start the foundations? Jefferson had seen octagonal buildings from his earliest architectural books by the British Palladians. He had seen numerous octagonal buildings and garden pavilions in Europe. He had sketched the mysterious octagonal house near Philadelphia in the 1790s. He had consistently used the octagon shape throughout his life. Jefferson seldom, if ever, used any single source or prototype without adapting it with other sources and ideas. It is not easy to establish a single genesis for any of his ideas. The Becker plan might be one source, but Jefferson had already been working with three full octagonal house designs, one of which is undoubtedly a preliminary Poplar Forest plan.

Jefferson was clearly challenged by a full octagonal plan. One unidentified plan of his shows a full octagonal house measuring 33.8 feet from side to side and having four rooms with canted ends projecting from the four shorter facets of the octagon (fig. 32).[38] This odd plan of radiating rooms could have been inspired by plate 47 in Robert Morris's *Select Architecture,* which depicts a building with a similar plan. Another possible source was the 1670 octagonal chapel at Salpêtrière Hospital in Paris with four octagonal projecting wings.[39] The challenge was the spatial relationship of

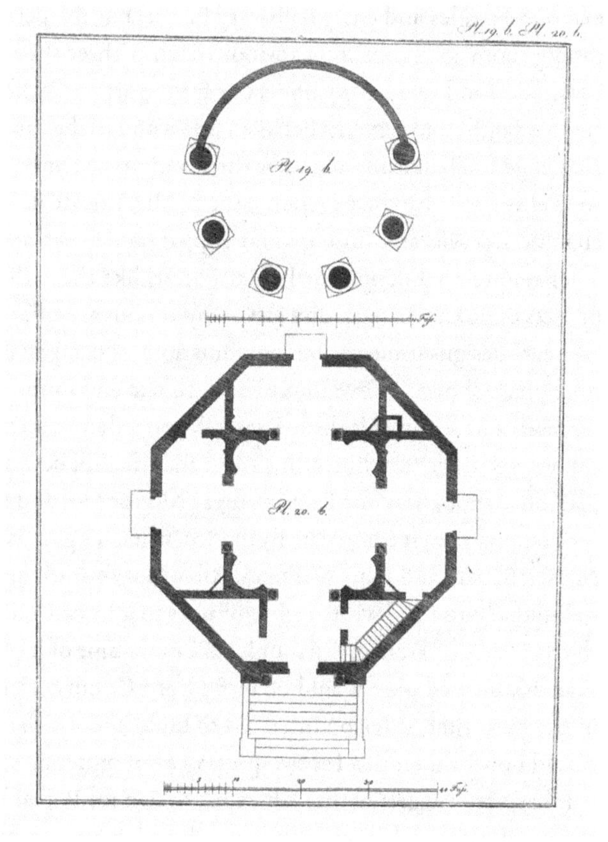

Fig. 30. Octagon garden pavilion, from Wilhelm Gottlieb Becker, *Neue Garten- und Landschafts-Gebäude* (1805).

rooms to walls, passages, and fireplaces. We get clues to his solutions by looking at another of his full octagonal designs. This one shows an irregular large octagonal house of 64 feet diameter, with a 32-foot-square room in the center (fig. 31). In this plan Jefferson had worked out the placement of four symmetrical chimney masses that served the eight small rooms off each passage. Four symmetrical chimneys would be part of his ingenious solution in the final design of Poplar Forest.

It is more reasonable to see this big octagonal house plan scaled down and altered for Poplar Forest than it is to see the Becker plan as a prototype. Characteristic of Jefferson's work, this plan constituted a merging of ideas. The big octagonal house plan (fig. 31) shows the basic scheme of a square center room within the outer octagonal walls. This same idea is transformed into the preliminary designs for Poplar Forest (fig. 33).[40] One plan shows the arrangement of the 20-foot-square center room connected by corner walls to the outer walls of the now-regular octagonal shape. Jefferson then developed the internal arrangement of chimney masses, entry passage, windows, and doors. Jefferson reduced the entrance passage to one-quarter the size of the middle room and pulled the four symmetrical corner chimney masses outward in order to create the end octagon angles of each room.[41] This also allowed for two doorways in the diagonal walls that Jefferson added during construction. The preliminary plan shows

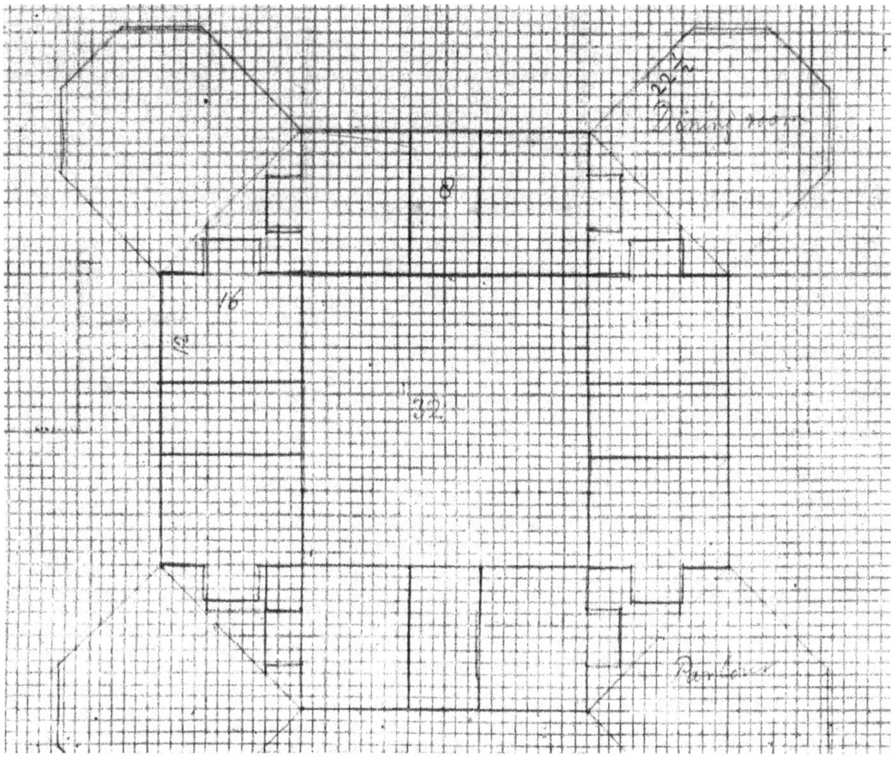

Fig. 31. Jefferson drawing, octagon house.

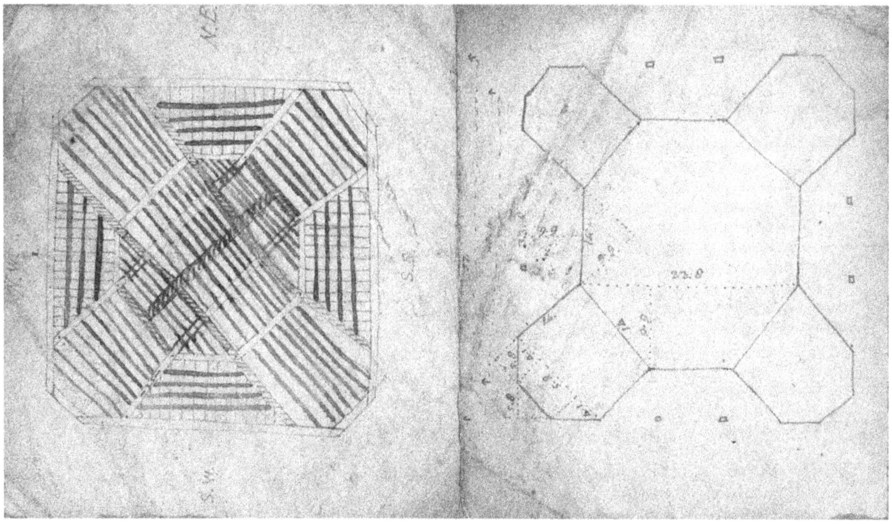

Fig. 32. Jefferson drawing, octagon house.

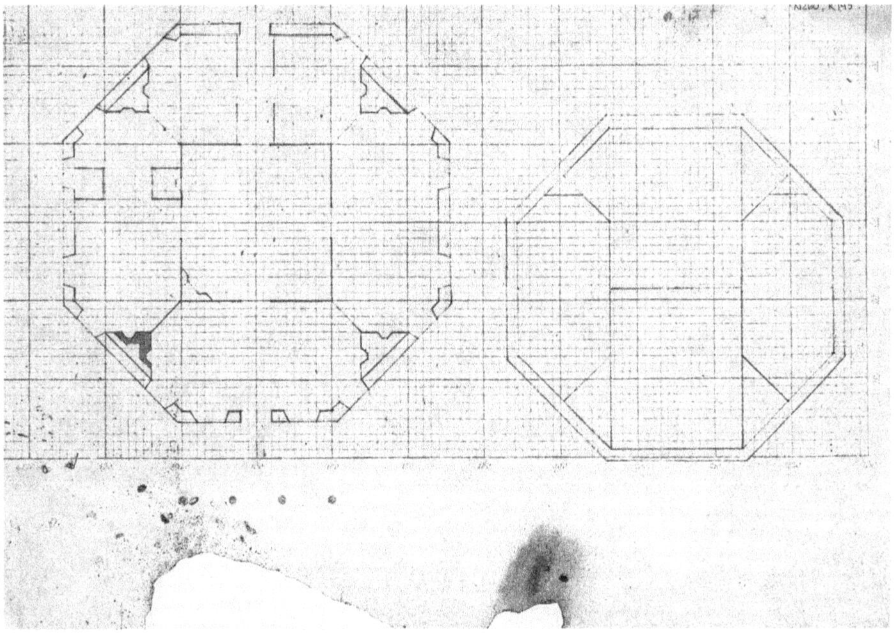

Fig. 33. Jefferson drawing, study for Poplar Forest.

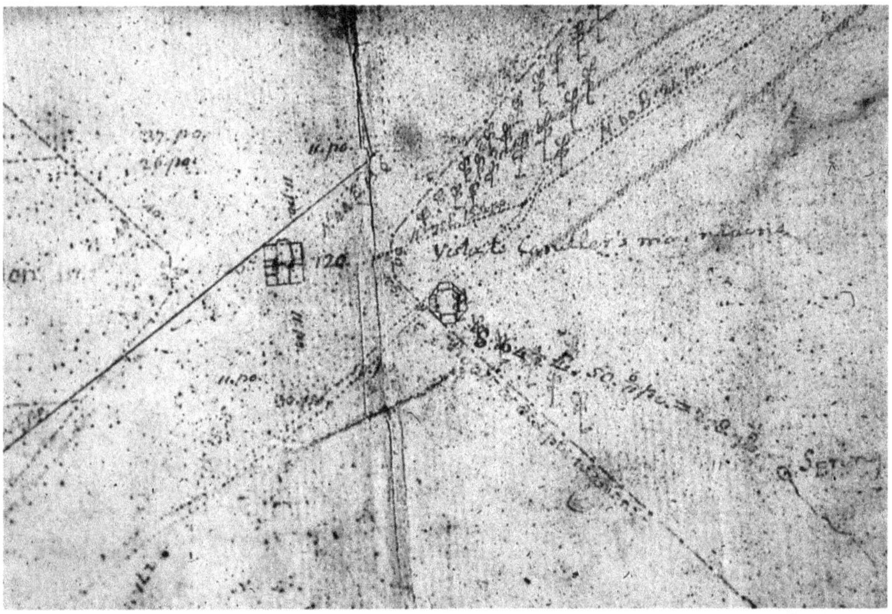

Fig. 34. Detail, Jefferson 1781 Poplar Forest plat showing first proposed house plan (*left*) and final full octagon plan (*right*).

an off-center bed alcove with vestibules on each side, one possibly for a closet and one straddling a window, presumably for borrowed light. On the opposite side Jefferson showed a large undivided room. This was still an evolving design that showed no windows on the front wall, the center fireplace in a different corner, no stairs, no communicating doors, a rear but not a front portico, and no side doors. Jefferson worked with this plan and arrived at an almost final design sometime by the fall of 1805.

A Compromised Solution

In September 1805 Jefferson sent Monticello bricklayer Hugh Chisolm to Poplar Forest to start making the many bricks that would be required for the house. The following July Jefferson was forced to leave presidential duties in Washington to help Chisolm with the geometric challenge of "laying out the foundations."[42] Jefferson's ideas were still germinating after seeing the actual foundation of the house, and he contemplated some final changes for more convenience. Writing Chisolm from Monticello on September 7, 1806, Jefferson sent revised instructions:

> It occurred to me after leaving Poplar Forest that there ought to be some more doors of communication in the rooms of the house below, than what I had marked in the plan given you. I therefore sketched them with a pencil and sent the sketch to you by Mr. Griffin. I now send you a sketch in ink, wherein you will find the following alterations:
>
> 1. 4 doors of communication between the rooms below.
> 2. 2" between the rooms above.
> 3. The two porches which I told you I should add.
> 4. Two stairways necessary for communicating between the upper and lower floors without going from under cover.
>
> The porticos & stairways will require more digging. You must make the space between window & window on the East & West sides, exactly 10 ft. so that the stairways may be placed between without blocking up the windows. Everything is drawn so plainly that no further explanation is necessary. Take care of the drawings as they will be necessary for Mr. Perry, & I do not reserve another copy for him. Accept my best wishes.[43]

The plans and sketches mentioned are not known to survive, but they indicate that Jefferson continued to work through the solutions. When helping Chisolm lay out the foundations, Jefferson had evidently already decided to alter the pure octagon form with porticos, "which I told you I should add." He tweaked his preliminary design to center a bed alcove in one large bed chamber and had added a symmetrical one in the other. Windows were added to the front wall flanking the doorway, and he shifted the center room's fireplace to another corner.

The only finished drawings of the Poplar Forest plan and elevation known to exist

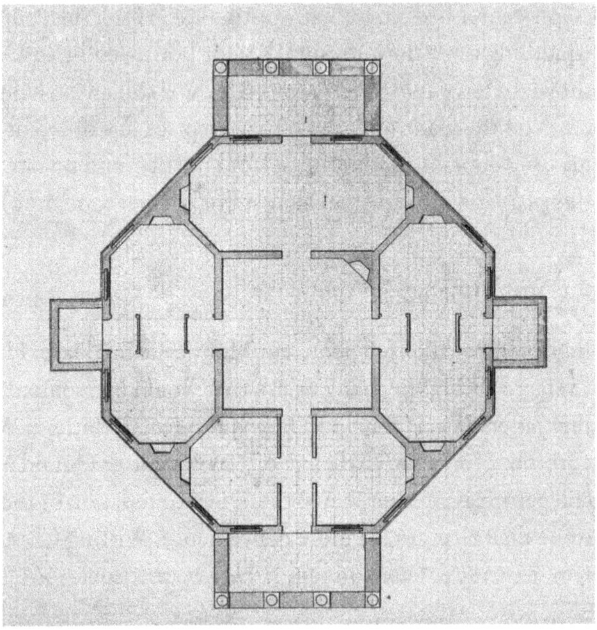

Fig. 35. John Neilson octagon plan after Poplar Forest, 1817.

Fig. 36. John Neilson elevation after Poplar Forest, 1817.

are actually not for Poplar Forest. These two "Poplar Forest" drawings are by Jefferson's worker John Neilson, who is believed to have copied Jefferson's Poplar Forest drawings for another project. Jefferson was apparently willing to share his personal retreat design with his friend John Hartwell Cocke, who was about to build his house in 1817. Neilson became the architect / builder for Bremo, designing Cocke's house in a different form.

Neilson's "Poplar Forest" drawings show the changes Jefferson had made in 1806: the front and rear Tuscan order porticos and the two external stair pavilions. The plan drawing does not show the two "communicating" doors in the northeast and northwest diagonal walls, and it shows the center fireplace in a different corner. The elevation drawing does not have a full Tuscan entablature, the Chinese railing on the upper roof, or a lunette window in the pediment. Inexplicably the drawing shows the flat terras roof above the dining room that Jefferson added in 1819, perhaps indicating that this had been an idea years before it actually happened. Thus what we see in Neilson's drawings is a hybrid, reflecting some changes to the original design, not showing others, and showing one change that had not yet happened. It is assumed that Neilson was copying drawings Jefferson had at Monticello, and the two drawings remain the closest we have to Jefferson's long-lost ones. Poplar Forest was born of long gestation from a mind that continuously turned over new solutions to problems of structure, convenience, privacy, and beauty and represented mature ideas and personal choices that had accumulated over a lifetime.

On one other drawing Jefferson had noted the word "Bedford." On a sheet of graph paper Jefferson drew four outbuildings, two rectangular ones 25′ × 35′ and two 22′ square.[44] The square buildings of one room each were unidentified. The other can be partially identified. One with two rooms separated by a chimney was identified as a kitchen and washhouse. The other rectangular building of two rooms had closets and alcove beds that seem to indicate this as quarters for enslaved household workers. Between the two rectangular buildings Jefferson wrote "100 f. between." A separate drawing on paper dating to 1800–1806 had a more detailed drawing of the kitchen/washhouse that included detailed written specifications characteristic of Jefferson regarding proportions, materials, structure, function, and appearance. This document specifies that the buildings were to be built in stone rather than brick, which seems unusual for outbuildings that would closely flank the main house. The larger two buildings were meant to flank the house according to the direction: "having driven a pin in the center of the spot destined for a dwelling house hereafter, measure 50 f. due East from that pin, and there make the center of the door as at a."[45] A specific location must have been chosen since the drawing had directional notes and the specifications say, "the ends of the house are to look to the North & South, the sides to the East and West." Which house scheme was this to accompany? The phrase "destined for a dwelling house hereafter" indicates that the outbuildings were to be built first, and as Chambers suggested, perhaps they would serve as temporary quarters while the house was built, not unlike the South Pavilion at Monticello. The flanking buildings would create a symmetrical five-part Palladian scheme.[46] The note specifying that the Poplar Forest pavilions be oriented with their long sides toward the house would make this identical to Jefferson's ca. 1781 design for the Governor's House.[47] The two square outbuildings remain a mystery as to purpose or location.[48] It seems likely that these outbuildings were meant for the earlier "mature" Poplar Forest designs rather than for the final retreat house. Nevertheless, the outbuildings were not constructed.

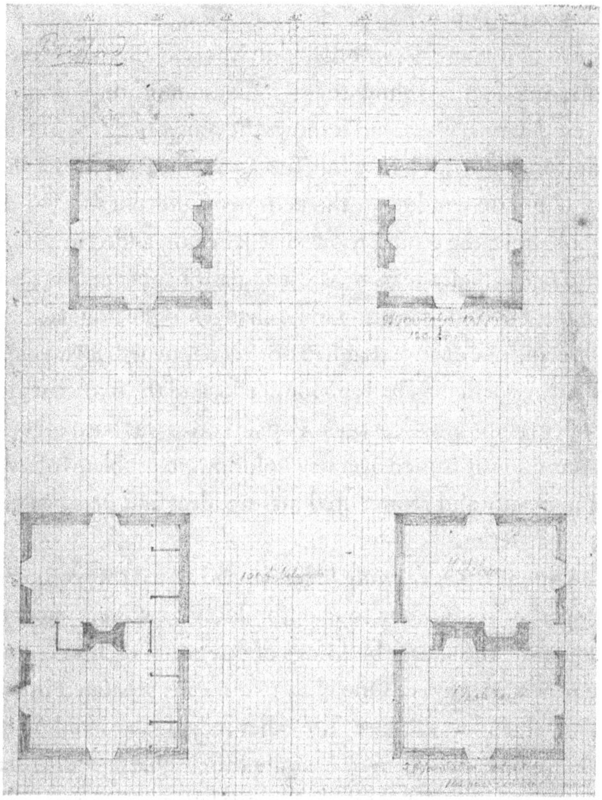

Fig. 37. Jefferson drawing, Poplar Forest outbuildings.

When he had settled on the final octagon house design, did Jefferson intend to build the outbuildings "destined for a dwelling house hereafter?" In 1808 Chisolm reported he was ready to build the kitchen. This would have been a single building that perhaps also had a laundry room as indicated on the earlier drawing. If it was built, its location is unknown. Did Jefferson construct the initial kitchen building and then include one five years later as part of the east wing? If so, the one kitchen building, even with a washhouse, would not have been sufficient unless additional outbuildings were intended. The completed wing had four rooms: an unheated room (spinning room?), kitchen, washhouse (laundry), and smokehouse. There is no further written evidence that a kitchen was built by Chisolm, there is no mention of a kitchen building being demolished, and archaeological excavation of the wing revealed no former building on that site. The 100-foot service wing at Poplar Forest, built in 1814–15, was the same size as the two wings Jefferson had just added to the President's House. His drawings for those wings were done in 1804, and construction began in 1805, about the time he finalized his designs for Poplar Forest.[49] It seems odd he wouldn't have initially considered service wings for Poplar Forest, making the 1808 reference to a kitchen puzzling. The answer might lie in Anna Maria Thornton's observation that Jefferson took "a very long time maturing his projects," even with one as mature as Poplar Forest.

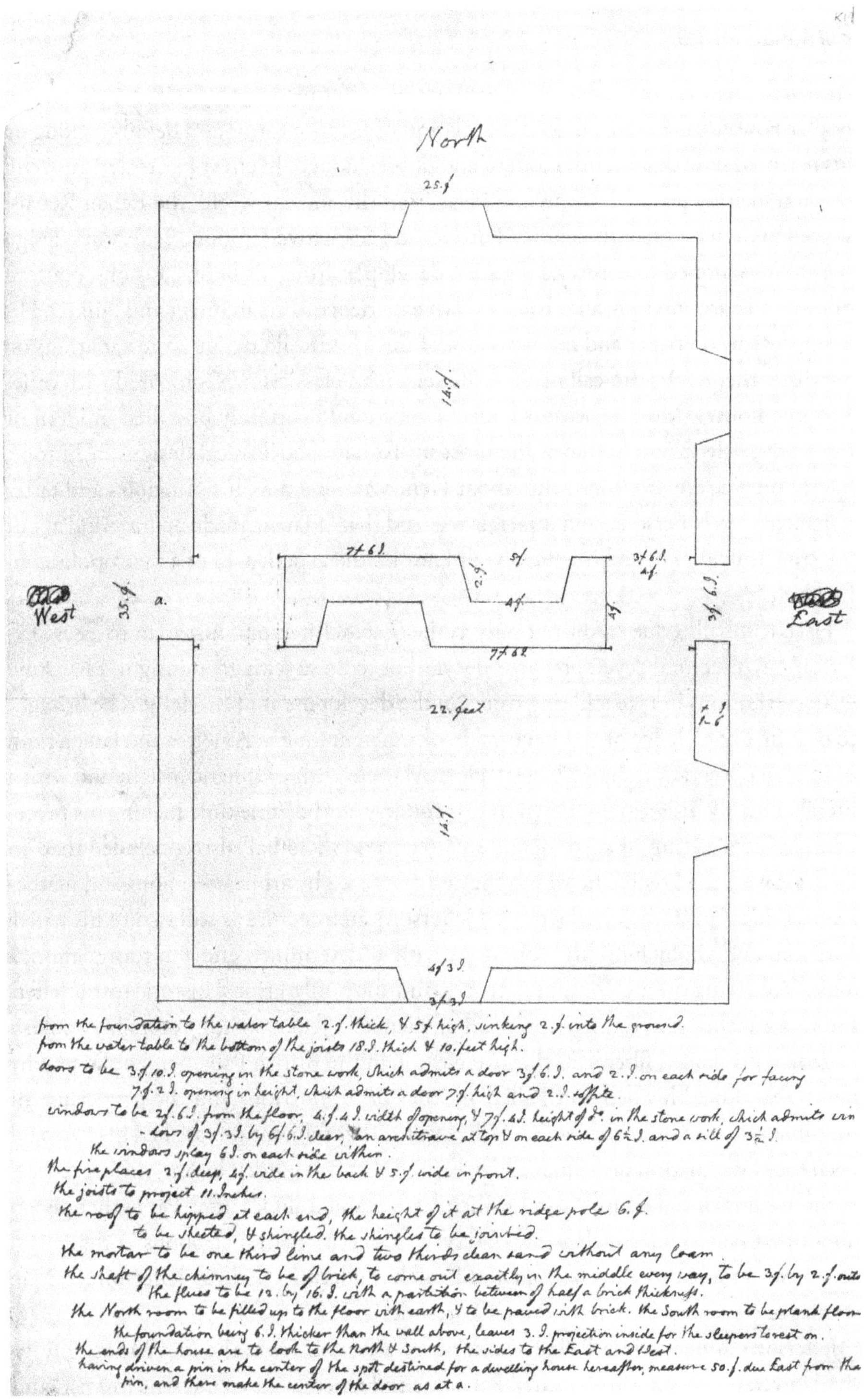

Fig. 38. Jefferson drawing, Poplar Forest kitchen building.

Personal Forms

As a great synthesizer, Jefferson incorporated a lifetime of ideas into his design for Poplar Forest.[50] He drew on an accumulation of favorite forms and details making up his personal style that is both modern and old-fashioned. In effect he created an architectural melting pot with forms and ideas from the ancient world, the Italian Renaissance, modern eighteenth-century Europe, and his native Virginia. Jefferson's design sensibilities, honed over several decades, developed from his books, his observations of the world around him, and from his own experience as an architect and builder. His many designs on paper and his evolution of the Monticello design were variations on a stylistic theme. We can call his style "Jeffersonian classicism." Compared with other Virginia houses, Monticello and Poplar Forest could certainly be called modern or innovative.[51] Jefferson had seen the most up-to-date neoclassical designs in Europe, but despite his effusive comments about French architecture, his principles and tastes remained largely personal and intact. It was said that "Having made up his mind about the true principles of architecture, he did not let the experiences of a metropolis confuse him."[52]

Fiske Kimball is due credit not only as the first architectural historian to assess Jefferson's architectural development and style, but to do so with great insight. His astute characterizations in 1916 still ring true: "In the development of his designs he brought to bear first knowledge of architectural books then unique in America and later a fund of foreign observation shared by few. He used them with prophetic insight and with a literal accuracy hitherto unknown in this country, at the same time making his precedents his own as truly as an academic architect can."[53] Kimball also concluded that "in contrast with the French, he was to the end restricted by arbitrary canons and mathematical rules."[54] Kimball characterized Jefferson's architecture as still tied to his native Virginia, not wholly innovative but done with a "determined effort at formulation, a logical following through of consequences, and above all a critical historic spirit. Jefferson's art was the art of retrospection and of science."[55] Jefferson hung on to his bookish Palladian principles, filtered as they were through the British Palladian books, and he never abandoned his belief in Palladian rules of proportions and the proper use of simplified Roman orders, as varied as they were. That foundation satisfied his personal need for mathematical principles and precision that was guided by antique precedent. Although his initial architectural principles remained intact after Paris, there is no doubt that he assimilated elements observed in that modern metropolis in the 1780s. These two influences, Palladianism and French modernity, meld in Jefferson's unique species of classicism seen in his Poplar Forest design.[56]

Jefferson's adherence to Palladianism never wavered. From the first Monticello to the University of Virginia, Andrea Palladio's influence was ever present in form and detail, never more so than at Poplar Forest. From his initial collection of architectural treatises Palladio showed Jefferson the way to the antique; As Jefferson famously told a friend, Palladio was "the bible. You should get it and stick close to it."[57] Whereas

Fig. 39. Poplar Forest, north elevation.

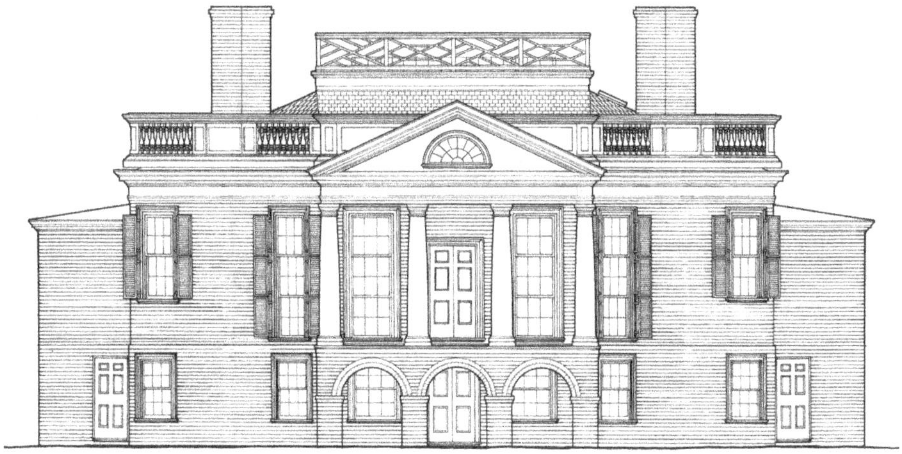

Fig. 40. Poplar Forest, south elevation.

many "Palladian" buildings mirrored an exterior style only, Jefferson absorbed Palladio's fundamental lessons of design. As Kimball recognized, "the preponderance of spiritual agreement between them [was] overwhelming."[58] Palladio's had been a holistic approach to design that integrated structure, function, and site planning.[59] His compositional designs synthesized ancient forms and contemporary models into his own modern and idealized style. In his system of design, beauty resulted from a building's organization and the relationship of its form and details. Palladio described this as the "correspondence of the parts to the parts, of the parts among themselves, and of the parts to the whole."[60] Palladio's vocabulary of selected favorite ancient details allowed for flexibility and modification, using them in various combinations for his different

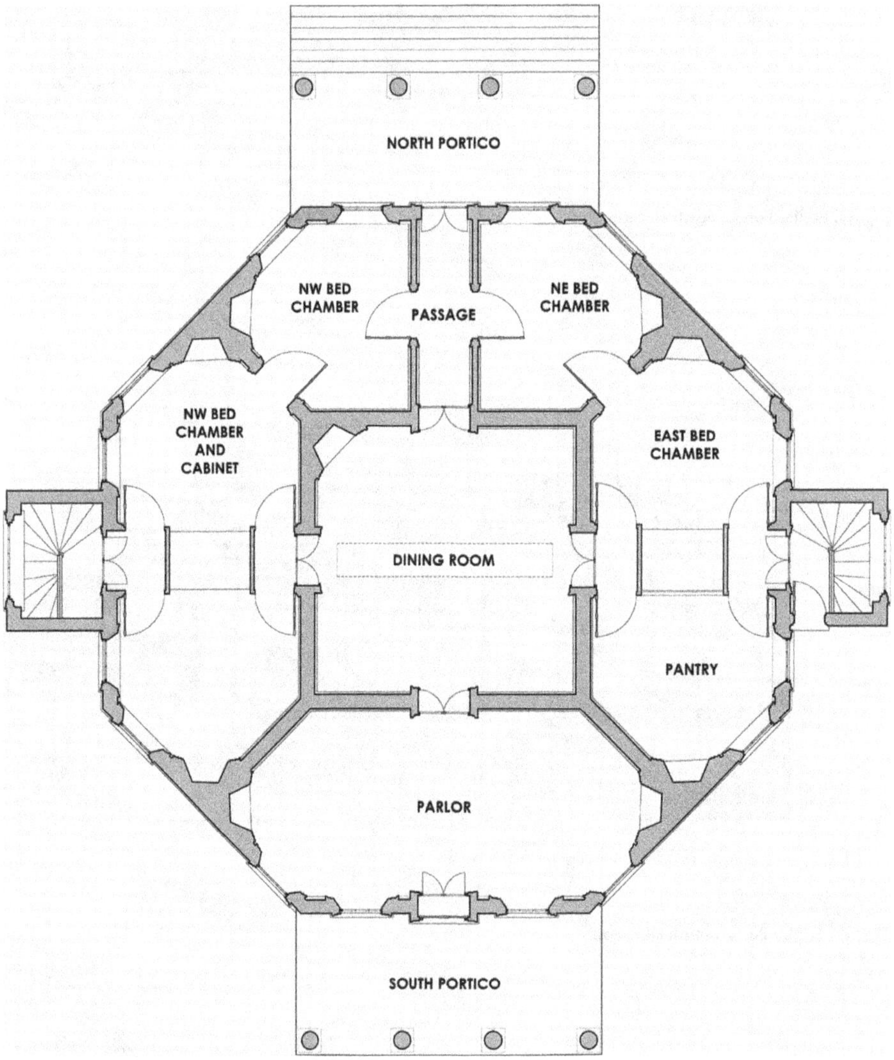

Fig. 41. Poplar Forest, upper-level plan.

Fig. 42. Poplar Forest, section looking east.

typologies of buildings. The hundreds of designs Jefferson developed over his lifetime show that he also absorbed from Palladio's system a three-dimensional approach combining function and structure, a typology of room shapes and sizes, and his own vocabulary of classical details with which to finish and ornament his designs.

Jefferson's "determined effort at formulation" in the final octagon design allowed him to achieve an ideal centralized plan with bilateral symmetry. Palladio's most centralized design, the Villa Capra (or Villa Rotonda), Jefferson admired and twice tried to copy it for the Virginia Governor's House and the President's House. Most of Palladio's villas featured a tall central public "sala" space around which were rooms with lower ceilings. Jefferson's tall central dining room gave him a centralized rotunda space—the closest he would get to achieving a rotunda house.[61] If Poplar Forest represented Jefferson's ideal dream house, it was only fitting that he could create a design that referenced Palladio.

Jefferson's love of precision and the idealized nature of the Poplar Forest design echoed Renaissance ideals of mathematical harmonies. Whether Palladio used whole number golden ratios exclusively, dynamic root symmetry equations, or a more straightforward geometric process, a mathematical system of design using numbers had always been important from the Greeks, to the Romans, and through the Renaissance. Rachel Fletcher believes that some of Palladio's designs are more than whole number golden ratios and that he used a more complex dynamic symmetry and root ratios.[62] She notes that Jefferson was proficient in arithmetic, algebra, geometry, trigonometry, Newtonian calculus, and other natural and mechanical mathematical applications, but that geometry was his special interest. Jefferson's notebooks show two different calculations of how to draw the sides of an octagon. Jefferson's design for Poplar Forest

Fig. 43. Poplar Forest plan showing Jefferson's use of root-2 mathematical analysis (Rachel Fletcher).

was very much determined from the authority of geometry, which generated the pure ideal octagon plan before the addition of the porticos and pavilions.[63] The preliminary octagon house designs show Jefferson struggling with the geometries and with the functional aspects.[64] From the pure octagon shape Fletcher demonstrated how the Poplar Forest internal plan can be determined by a root-two ratio process. Starting with the outer size of an octagon, a circle, this process can determine sides of the outer octagon walls, the size and placement of the cube room, the entrance passage, the width of the perimeter rooms, the octagonal ends of the perimeter rooms, the fireplace masses that define the octagonal perimeter rooms, the stair pavilions, and the north and south portico sizes.[65] Numbers, measure, arrangements, and proportions were critical components of Jefferson's architecture, especially at Poplar Forest, and suited his mathematical mind perfectly. The redesigned complex plan and structure of Monticello certainly resulted from great formulated thoughts and calculations, but the plan of Poplar Forest was excessively clear and ideal, the opposite of complex, yet requiring just as much formulation.

Jefferson found Palladio's system of design most useful for its codified dimensional rules for imitating Roman architecture. Jefferson characteristically adhered to these classical all'antica (antique) principles of design and proportions put down by Palladio. This classical system of design suited Jefferson's personality, combining—as Kimball said—a relish for precision and a passion for antiquity. As he had done at Monticello, Jefferson translated Palladian modules into English inches. At Poplar Forest all the vertical dimensions and proportions of the house are precisely based on these modules, starting with the exterior brick Tuscan order columns, covered with plaster to resemble stone, a practice Palladio credited to the ancient Romans.[66] The height of the interior perimeter rooms was determined by the 2/9 roof pitch favored by Palladio, with rafters spanning from the top of the cube room walls to the outer perimeter walls. This gave a 12′ ceiling height that worked perfectly with the 3′3″ chair rail height, the 6′6″ window height, the 6 ½″ window architrave, and the 1′9″ Tuscan entablature. The interior hierarchical Tuscan, Doric, and Ionic entablatures are appropriately proportioned based on imaginary columns below. Door and window architraves are the typical Palladian one-sixth of the opening. Like Palladio, Jefferson chose his favorite classical molding

Fig. 44. Poplar Forest, south portico, 2019.

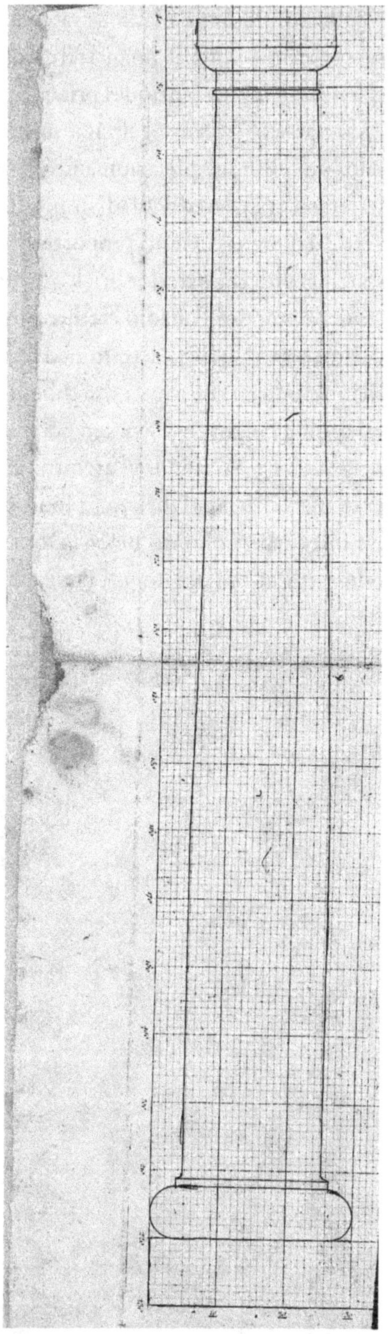

Fig. 45. Jefferson drawing of Tuscan order column.

details, his "vocabulary," and then used them repeatedly as his "grammar" in his different designs. For the Roman moldings favored for interior trim, Jefferson used those in James Gibbs's *Book of Architecture.* At the University of Virginia Jefferson instructed a worker to make some moldings simpler, "finding the simplicity of those in Palladio preferable."[67]

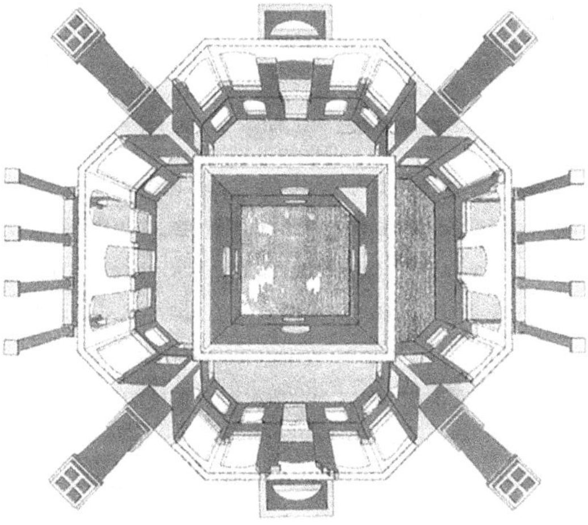

Fig. 46. Axonometric drawing of Poplar Forest brick walls, chimneys, and columns.

Palladio used certain room sizes and shapes in a hierarchical and symmetrical arrangement of squares, circles, and rectangles. Jefferson had his own typology of shapes used at Poplar Forest, including his own favorite shapes—the octagon and half octagon. The placement of the four chimneys on the corner angles of the central cube space created perimeter rooms that are a full octagon (south parlor) or half octagons (bed chambers). The two smallest shapes in the hierarchy are the rectangular stair pavilions. Palladio explained that his symmetrical plans were better for an even roof load on the walls. Jefferson's genius regarding the spatial arrangement and structural forces is that the tall 12-inch-thick central brick walls of the cube are not only buttressed at the top by the perimeter roof rafters, but more importantly on their corners by the large solid chimney masses that act like buttresses. The placement of the four chimneys also provided fireplaces for each adjacent room and created an octagonal end shape for the perimeter rooms.

Palladio and architects of his time believed that ancient Roman architecture was based on laws of nature. This doctrine had been reiterated by the British Palladians, who believed nature, along with antiquity and reason, were the principal authorities on which all true architecture was derived.[68] Nature was a major component of Jefferson's Enlightenment education and beliefs, and his view of the world. The authority of nature is easily seen at Poplar Forest beginning with Jefferson's choice of a building site. Palladio made it clear that the choice of a villa's site, and its orientation, was critical. Jefferson's decision to build on a particular small rise of land within his 5,000 acres seems related to a distinctive place of nature.[69] The name "Poplar Forest" went back to long before Jefferson's 1773 ownership and referred to this old-growth stand of tulip poplar trees, a species Jefferson referred to as the "Junos of our groves."[70] Jefferson sited the house on the north side of the hill that had already been cleared of trees for tobacco fields. To create a naturalistic setting just north of the house within the circular road, he planted additional poplars as early as 1806. House and wing not only engaged the landscape but were actually nestled in the ground, seeming to rise out of it. The large windows of the house and the south portico furthered the connection.[71] In the most unusual way of referencing Palladio, Jefferson created a five-part Palladian composition using the house in the center flanked by earthen mounds standing in as pavilions and connected to the house on each side by a double row of trees acting as architectural hyphens.[72] Each mound, cleverly used as a place to put the dirt from the sunken south lawn, was made more vertical with three rows of trees featuring a "dome" of four willows on top, a middle row of Golden Willows, and a columnar row of slender aspen trees around the base. The two octagonal brick privies, with their Palladian domes and perfectly proportioned cornices, stood on the outer side of each mound, creating a seven-part composition. This unique landscape design featured the naturalistic design of a forested grove on one side, a combination of architecture and landscape in the center, and man-made gardens on the other side.

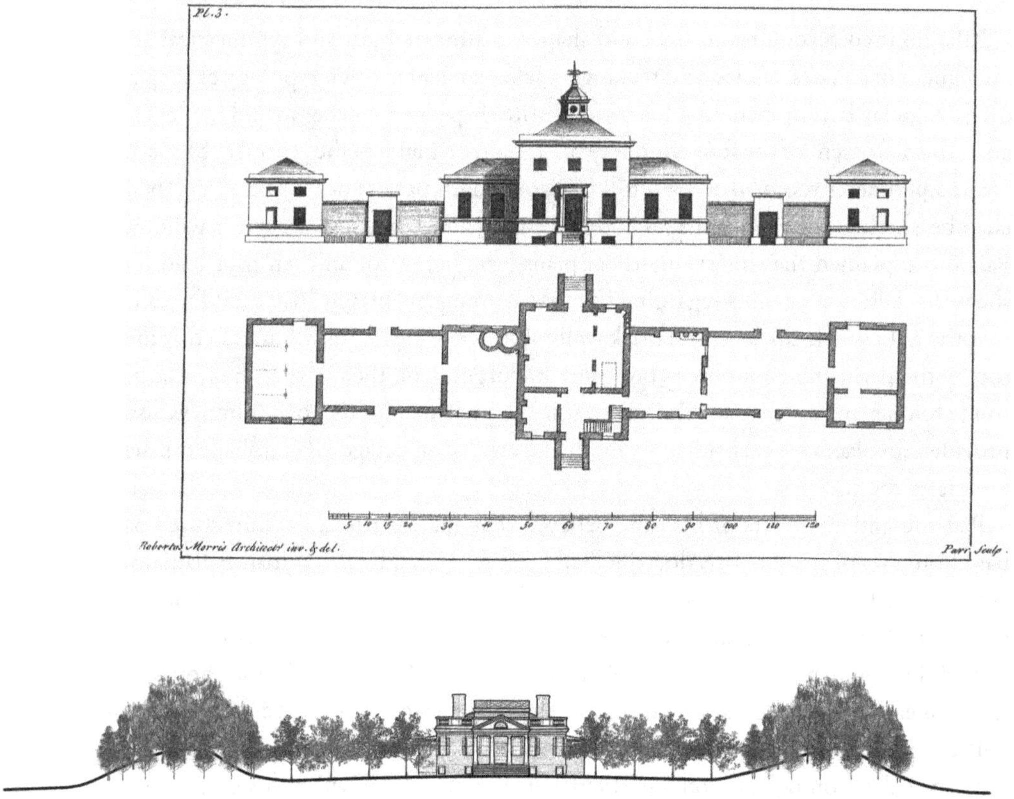

Fig. 47. Comparison of Jefferson's design of Poplar Forest with typical British or Virginia five-part Palladian composition designs from Robert Morris, *Select Architecture* (1755), plate 3; and drawing by Rieley & Associates Landscape Architects.

Fig. 48. Poplar Forest, west octagonal privy, 2022.

The most obvious Palladian reference was the 100-foot-long service wing Jefferson added to the east side of the house in 1814, replacing the double row of trees as a connection to the east mound. Jefferson had adopted Palladian service wings, seen in Palladio's book, in his first designs for Monticello. This was not a "barchesse" in the sense of the attached agricultural buildings of Palladio's Veneto villas but related to the typical outbuilding functions that served Virginia plantation houses. By placing his outbuilding functions in wings rather than scattered near the house, Jefferson reserved the space for his ornamental gardens. Strictly imitating Palladio, Jefferson should have built a balanced west service wing connecting the house to the west mound. Jefferson's symmetrical service wings at Monticello, and the two 100-foot service wings he had just added to the President's House in Washington, suggest that he preferred a balanced scheme.[73] The logical conclusion is that one wing satisfied the simpler service needs at the retreat. Jefferson improved upon Palladio's wing design by designing his terras roof that allowed for a flat deck above.[74] This allowed Jefferson to use the top deck and to engage Nature on one side and the ornamental landscape on the other. Although there

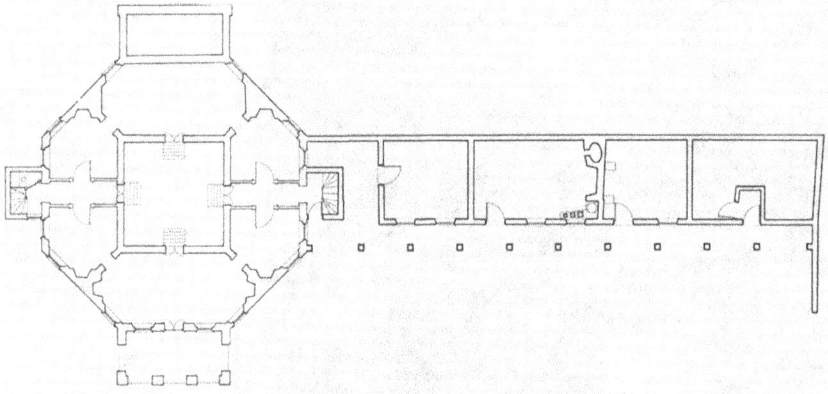

Fig. 49. Poplar Forest, lower-level and service wing plan.

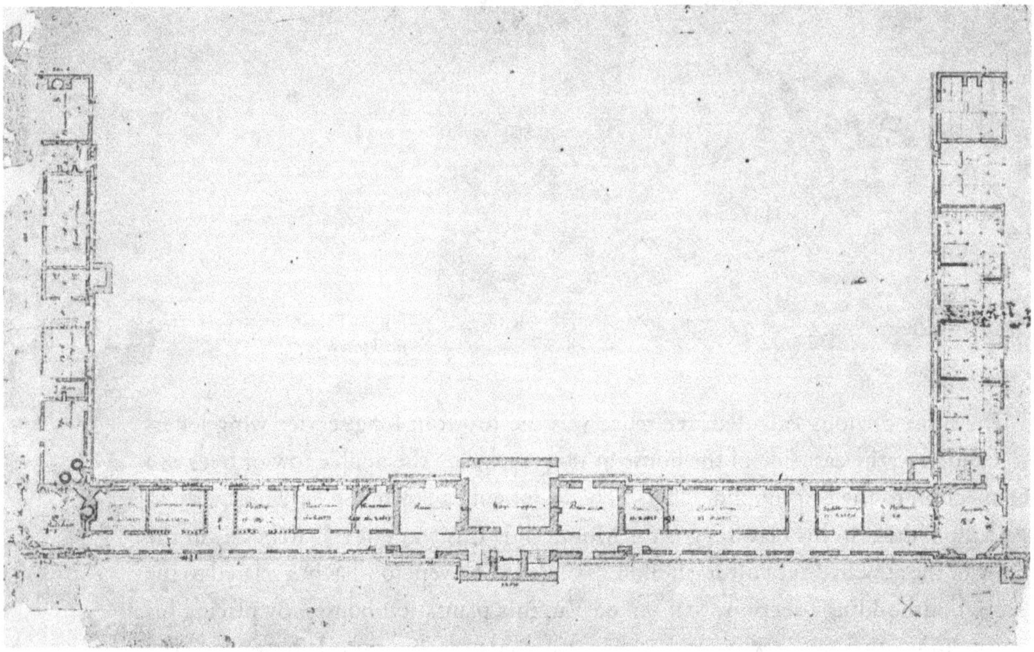

Fig. 50. Jefferson drawing, Monticello I with house and service wings.

are other examples of service wings at Virginia houses, Jefferson's use of his was unique. Palladio's ensemble of villa and wings fit within a surrounding vernacular landscape. Jefferson's surrounding ornamental gardens was more in the tradition of ancient Roman villas or the European country houses he had seen.[75]

Jefferson had absorbed the holistic design approach used centuries earlier by Palladio, creating good contemporary architecture. Palladio had learned from Marcus Vitruvius Polio, a first-century Roman architect, that architects should innovatively use

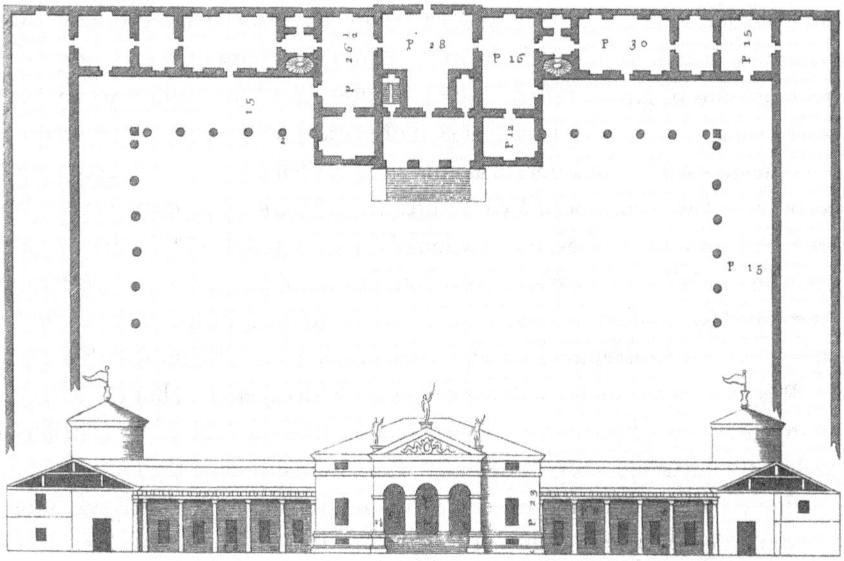

Fig. 51. Andrea Palladio, Villa Saraceno, from *The Architecture of A. Palladio in Four Books,* Giacomo Leoni (1721 ed.).

models from the past so that architecture would be "an open system of design capable of accommodating steady progress and innovation."[76] In other words an architect must have the confidence to synthesize both tradition and contemporary influences. This philosophy helps explain the legacy of Palladio's very modern works and, consequently, those of Jefferson. In his design for Poplar Forest Jefferson returned to a purer Palladian essay than he had tried with his first bookish design for Monticello. Facilitating this approach was the nature of Poplar Forest as a more authentic example of a classical and Renaissance villa that served as an occasional retreat. Architectural historians have recognized Jefferson as the inheritor of Palladio's heritage in England and also as "intellectually the most significant spokesman" for American Palladianism.[77] In both respects Jefferson gave Poplar Forest an unmistakable essence of Palladianism that can also be called Jeffersonian.

Private Dictates

Jefferson's final design for Poplar Forest was also dictated by privacy. Jefferson required more privacy than most his entire life, and though greater privacy was possible at Monticello II, he desired and required even more. If privacy became the struggle at Monticello, it reigned at Poplar Forest, being its raison d'être, and this was reflected in its design. The public and private conflict of social interaction and room use had been playing out in other Virginia houses throughout the eighteenth century.[78] By the end of the eighteenth-century old customs of hospitality diminished, and families retreated more to their private spaces with less public interaction with visitors and servants.[79]

An interesting study of the Cabell family's Palladian-style houses in Virginia between Monticello and Poplar Forest showed a relationship of social and economic status shown through architecture with the dimensioning tradition of hospitality and the increasing forms of privacy reflected in new house plans.[80] In a different way Poplar Forest's plan also fulfilled its principal goal of privacy, being much more intentional than contemporary Virginia houses as conceived for Jefferson alone or accompanied by a couple of family members. Two features of the interior plan made Poplar Forest unique, both affecting privacy: the location of the stairs and that of the dining room.

Jefferson's initial ideal design for Poplar Forest as a pure octagon, as we have seen, was compromised by comfort and convenience. Access to the principal floor would have been by the single front entry door, and there was no communication with the lower floor. This seems incomprehensible for a designer with experience, but the letter confirms this great oversight, apparently clouded by an idealistic vision of purity. Jefferson's letter to Chisolm acknowledged the practical circumstances and the remedy, "subordinated to the law of convenience" as he had said of Monticello.[81] This was another struggle in which Jefferson's ideals were compromised through union with practical circumstances.[82] Jefferson's addition of the two stair pavilions fulfilled a necessity for both enslaver and enslaved workers, but their location reveals the most telling quality of the house. They are not publicly accessed, and their use is only gained through the east and west bed chambers. There was no expectation of public need. The west stairs allowed Jefferson the freedom to go to the lower level "without going from under cover" or to the exterior. The stairs were also necessary for enslaved workers using the lower-level storage and service spaces.

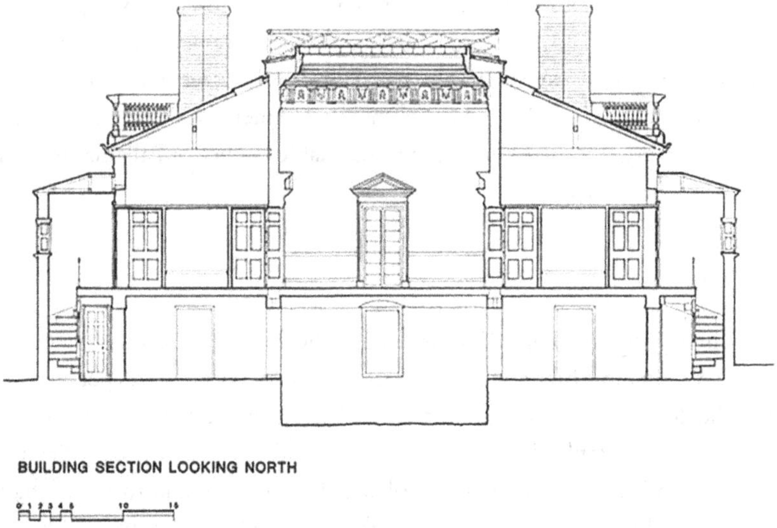

Fig. 52. Poplar Forest, section looking north.

Two retrofits also involved the stair pavilions and privacy. Jefferson squeezed a personal privy under the stairs off his chamber, cleaned from the exterior, further limiting the interaction with enslaved servants in the house. Jefferson had installed water closets at the President's House and indoor privies at Monticello, a convenience he had grown accustomed to in Paris.[83] The other retrofit was on the opposite side of the house. When the east service wing was completed in 1815, Jefferson opened a doorway in the upper south wall of the east stair pavilion in order to access the wing's deck from the upper level of the house, being adamant that his decks be "absolutely in the level of the floor of the house."[84] Jefferson's route to the deck necessitated passing through the east chamber. Servants bringing food from the wing kitchen to the dining room traversed the opposite route. This posed no problem when the east chamber was unoccupied, but once Ellen and Cornelia Randolph started using the east chamber their privacy was at issue. The solution was to close the south side of the bed alcove, making it a one-sided opening like most of those at Monticello.[85] With this alteration the south end of the east room was now a separate room, later identified as a pantry.[86] Jefferson's innovation of the dual open-sided alcove for cross-ventilation had its disadvantage at Monticello as well. There he had been forced to shield one side of his own bed alcove with a movable screen for more privacy.

The location of the dining room connoted another difference from Monticello. Located in the center of the house, it was the first room entered from the dark, narrow entrance passage. There was no need for a waiting space for visitors like the entry hall at Monticello. Still, it was unusual for the dining room to be the first room entered. We could read Jefferson's placement of the dining room in the center of the house as the only logical space for one of two public rooms, especially when he preferred to site his parlor and library in the large, sunny southern room. The central dining room undoubtedly served multiple functions like the old traditional Virginia hall.[87] In fact, Jefferson, his granddaughter, his grandson, and John Hemmings referred to the center room as the "hall."[88] Although without windows in the center of the house, the dining room might also have reminded some of the "summer hall" function of center-passage houses where the coolest breezes were found in the hottest weather. The extra perimeter windows made possible by the octagon shape, and the fact that the upper window sash could also open, meant greater cross-ventilation through the center room. Jefferson's granddaughter Ellen Randolph remarked that louvered blinds were closed over the dining room's skylight in the summer, which made the middle room "deliciously cool."[89]

The location of the dining room might have been the logical one in the centralized octagon plan, but it also reflected another strong tradition that was not common in America. A compelling prototype for this placement came from the smaller fashionable houses of Paris, where guests went directly to the table.[90] A good number of late eighteenth-century French houses in Paris show the sequence of entrance vestibule, dining room, and salon.[91] The likelihood of this prototype for Poplar Forest is only strengthened by the fact that many of these central dining rooms were also lighted from above by a skylight. Jefferson knew this practice, but his memory would have been refreshed when he purchased Kraft and Ransonnette's *Les plus belles maisons de Paris* (1802) at the end of 1804, when final plans for Poplar Forest were coming together. This remarkable work illustrated the best works by forty-three architects with plans, elevations, sections, details, picturesque landscapes, and garden buildings. Round, oval, and octagon rooms were frequent shapes in the sequence of vestibule, dining room, and salon. Jefferson's reliance on this work is documented in an interesting faux pas that happened while he was president. Benjamin Latrobe complained about Jefferson in an 1805 letter to John Lenthall, saying, "I am cramped in this design by his [Jefferson's] prejudices in favor of the old French books, out of which he fishes everything."[92] Latrobe accidentally addressed the letter to Jefferson, who returned it, stating he had not read it. When Jefferson asked Latrobe to return his Kraft and Ransonnette book, he slyly indicated he had read the letter, saying, "Being about to build some little temples in my grounds at Monticello, I must pray the return of the *Plans de Maisons des Paris* . . . as I expect to find some good designs in that."[93] In other words, Jefferson chided Latrobe by saying he planned a fishing expedition in his French books.

Revised Architectural Aesthetics

Jefferson brought to bear in the rebuilt Monticello and at Poplar Forest new sensibilities in a French manner. This resulted in opening up buildings to light and air, with a consequence of connecting the interiors to the exterior's landscape gardens. Light and air made up an important aspect of Jefferson's post-Paris aesthetic with large panes of glass, glass doors, triple-sash windows, and skylights. This quality gave them a modern feeling compared to typical houses in Virginia. Some of the best descriptions of Monticello came from European visitors who compared it with other American houses and found it different. The only contemporary description of Poplar Forest, by Englishman George Flower in 1816, was telling: "His house was built after the fashion of a French chateau, Octagon rooms, floors of polished oak, lofty ceilings, large mirrors betokened his French taste, acquired by his long residence in France."[94] Only a European could make this appraisal. These few features were but mere shadows of the opulent French houses of late eighteenth-Paris that Jefferson knew. One of the most common and ubiquitous elements in French and other European houses was "floors of polished oak." When instructing his workmen to install the herringbone pattern oak floor in the dining room. Jefferson remarked, "all the floors of Europe are of oak."[95] What made the floors European was not simply the material (oak) but, as Flower noted, that they were "polished." American floors, oak or other species, did not have the oil and wax finish. One of the servants Jefferson hired for his Parisian house was Saget, Le Frotteur (floor polisher). "The sole duty of this indispensable functionary of a French household was to wax the floors on footbrushes."[96]

Jefferson's "French taste" at Poplar Forest was distinctly related to light and air. The outer octagonal shape of Poplar Forest allowed more windows than a conventional

Fig. 53. Poplar Forest, stair pavilion lunette window, 2022.

Fig. 54. Poplar Forest, sash doors, view from entrance passage into dining room, 2020.

Fig. 55. Poplar Forest, dining room skylight with louvered blinds, 2019.

Fig. 56. Poplar Forest, parlor with southern triple-sash windows, 2022.

Fig. 57. Poplar Forest, south portico, 2022.

square design. Jefferson's choice for central bed alcoves allowed for an extra window rather than wall space for bed furniture. In his Building Notebook, Jefferson noted the size of windows: "Light. Rule for the quantity requisite for a room. Multiply the length, breadth & height together in feet & extract the square root of their product. This must be the sum of the areas of all the windows."[97] The varnished walnut window sashes had thin muntins that held large 12″ × 18″ glass, a size not readily available in Virginia. When ordering more glass after the 1819 hailstorm, Jefferson's overseer remarked that he had "never seen any there as large panes, as those in your windows and doors."[98] Later when Mary Elizabeth Eppes was living at Poplar Forest, she wrote an unfavorable note regarding Poplar Forest and winter winds: "I often wish that I could exchange those large windows (altho in the summer, nothing can be more agreeable) for the little closely chincked windows at Ashton."[99] Even the smallest bed chambers on the north had two windows each. These sashes were not only modern by being hung with weights but were double-hung, with the top sash giving many more options of convection ventilation. The oversize lunette windows of each stair pavilion opened for ventilation and served to light the tight dogleg stairs. In the west pavilion, a transom window opposite the lunette threw borrowed light into the storage space above the bed alcove. When entering the front door into the narrow passage, one's eye was drawn ahead through the entire house by three sets of sash doors, two of the dining room and the third being the parlor's southern door to the portico. The greatest surprise of illumination lay ahead in the tall central dining room, lighted like a Parisian house with its sixteen-foot-long skylight. The 18″ × 18″ glass in the four sash doors of the central room threw borrowed light into the dark spaces of the north passage and into the east and west bed alcove vestibules. Passing through the center room to the southern octagonal parlor revealed the brightest room. Its octagonal facets allowed for a total of four floor-to-ceiling triple-sash windows, all hung and operable, flanking the transparent southern sash door. The amount of glass in this southern brick wall tested structural limits.[100] When the lower and middle sashes were raised, the wall opened with both feeling and sight to connect with the landscape. In the winter the mostly glazed southern wall took advantage of the lower angle of the sun for great solar gain. The parlor's two middle windows and sash door opened to the south portico, which acted as an extended outdoor room set farther within the landscape on the private side of the house.

At Poplar Forest there was no need to sit in the louvered "porticle" rooms Jefferson had added to Monticello for outdoor privacy.[101] Jefferson happily sat on his rear portico, or on the wing deck, openly engaging nature and landscaped gardens. Jefferson's description in *Notes on the State of Virginia* that the Capitol Building in Williamsburg was "light and airy" was a relative term in colonial Virginia that took on a completely different connotation after he experienced Paris. The octagon shape of Poplar Forest facilitated a more open and airy nature that set it apart from most American houses of the time and that struck George Flower as something more European.

4

THE CONSTRUCTION SAGA

On July 15, 1805, President Jefferson left the hot, humid Federal City and headed south for a short summer reprieve at his beloved Monticello. He noted in his Memorandum Book $487.20 cash on hand, welcome funds from his presidential salary with which to pay anticipated debts when he arrived home.[1] He arrived on July 18 and immediately began disbursing funds to various people, including workers James Dinsmore, John Perry, and Hugh Chisolm, who among others were still in the process of rebuilding Monticello. Eight days later Jefferson headed southwest for a quick trip to Poplar Forest, a typical three-day journey each way. The principal purpose of this four-day visit was to rearrange boundaries of land promised his two sons-in-law. Jefferson's visit served another more immediate purpose of choosing the final site for his retreat house. In the unfinished President's House, his retreat had been on his mind as he settled on its final plan. Now the important first step was to choose its site in his almost 5,000 acres that comprised the Poplar Forest property in Bedford County. On that land were three areas of plantation activity, quarter farms: Tomahawk Creek, Bear Creek, and Wingos. The initial house site indicated on the 1781 plat placed it between Tomahawk Creek and Bear Creek. He now chose a small rise between two branches of Tomahawk Creek near the distinctive grove of poplar trees. Back at Monticello during the next two months Jefferson would prepare detailed drawings and specifications for his new house before departing for Washington on September 29. On that day he noted cash on hand had diminished to $67.55. He handed $10.00 of that amount to bricklayer Hugh Chisolm, followed by the note: "Chisolm goes to Bedford to work at 20 D. per month. Hhd. Exp. 10.50."[2] Jefferson's last notation on September 29 was, "set out from Monticello," meaning he headed north back to Washington in the opposite direction of Chisolm.[3]

This long-distance circumstance, between Washington and Monticello and Poplar Forest, made this project one of the most challenging for a man obsessed with control and supervision. The many circumstances imposed by a remote location would define some major aspects of the Poplar Forest project, affecting Jefferson's control of workers, their materials, and the quality of their work. Jefferson had of course supervised building projects at Monticello from a distance; the difference now would be that two simultaneous projects shared workers and workshops. A rational option would have been to delay construction of his retreat until retirement so he could personally supervise the building process. Another rational choice would have been to delay Poplar Forest until Monticello was finished. We can only conclude that the impatient desire and need for solitude at a retreat could not wait. The burden of presidential duties and the crush of visitors at Monticello pushed a faster timeline. The purpose of the classic villa, as Ackerman characterized it, was as much psychological as recreational. Getting Poplar Forest built and finished would try Jefferson's patience, but the immediate benefit of putting it in motion would give him great satisfaction and optimistic daydreams for the future use of his retreat and the privacy he continually craved.

Jefferson's skills and traits as a builder were codified and keenly developed by the time he began construction of Poplar Forest. His earliest experience with Monticello revealed several characteristic traits of his personality that had only become more prominent with its rebuilding: belief and reliance on historical precedent and classical canons of architecture; architectural forms and details based on mathematical precision; detailed specifications for materials and construction; use of high-quality and innovative materials; finding and using the most talented craftsmen and retaining those who had proved their worth; apprenticing his own enslaved tradesmen to those master craftsmen; the need to inspect the work and to control all parts of the process; an unusual patience to achieve idealistic goals at the expense of earlier completion; and the inclusion of integrated landscaped gardens. He approached the Poplar Forest project with this experience. The remote location of Poplar Forest would continue to be a challenge during the characteristically long period it took Jefferson to complete it. Once he started living in the unfinished shell in 1809, it would take another seventeen years to complete every last part of it. Still, he patiently and optimistically met the challenges and turned them into acceptable and even better solutions when circumstances demanded.

The two most fundamental components of any building process, materials and workmen, describe and define Jefferson's role and traditions as a builder.[4] Accumulated ideas, turned over and over in his mind for years, eventually emerged on paper as a final design. Turning those three-dimensional ideas into a building was something altogether different, governed by realities and circumstances hard to control. Construction was a complex and coordinated effort involving many people with their own myriad quirks and faults. Despite differences in design, scale, and use, building traditions and processes at Poplar Forest are more similar than not when compared with Monticello. Monticello I and II represented Jefferson's learning curve as evidenced by notes on labor, materials, and building techniques that filled his various and voluminous notebooks, in particular his Farm Book and Building Notebook. The former has only two dated entries after 1796, and only one of those might refer to Poplar Forest.[5] The latter book's extraordinary quantity of specified details and construction data was clearly preparatory for the construction of the first and second Monticello. Jefferson could have used these detailed notes as a ready reference for Poplar Forest, not that he even needed them. He had no further need to quiz craftsmen or to study time and labor processes. Oddly, the initial calculations for quantities of materials seen for the Monticello projects would have also been necessary for Poplar Forest as well but are absent in surviving documents. Sitting in the unfinished shell of the President's House, Jefferson no doubt worked out preliminary details, material estimates, and specifications, as was his practice. Later he produced drawings necessary for bricklayers, carpenters, and joiners. These construction drawings, of the very detailed type drawn for Monticello, are missing for Poplar Forest, although mentioned in letters.

When away from Monticello building projects, Jefferson relied on supervision by family members or trusted "resident carpenters." The remote location of Poplar Forest necessitated a similar correspondence, but without family members on-site he relied on plantation overseers more as intermediaries to relay instructions to workers and to report on their progress. His impatience to get the retreat underway meant a reliance on his bricklayer and carpenter to work unsupervised. His optimistic hopes for the best were not always realized. Other traditions of using classical details, favored materials, and particular features of comfort and convenience would be continued at Poplar Forest. The one significant difference from the construction at Monticello was the reliance on John Hemmings and his three nephew apprentices to execute all of the finished wood joinery, inside and out. Hemmings had been the enslaved craftsman apprentice working with the hired craftsmen to complete Monticello. Now, after 1809, he was the master craftsman and entrusted to complete Jefferson's retreat house. Perhaps more importantly, Beverly, Eston, and Madison Hemings learned their trade working alongside their uncle to create their father's special place. The distinction of their craftsmanship would not be acknowledged in any way.

The remote location of Poplar Forest on the east Piedmont slope of the Blue Ridge Mountains in central Virginia only increased the difficulty of transportation for both materials and workers. Jefferson's hired and enslaved workers and workshops at Monticello were a three-day journey to the northeast. When fragile goods could not travel by wagon from Monticello to Poplar Forest, they were sent on bateaux down the Rivanna River to the James River and then laboriously poled upriver to Lynchburg, still ten miles away from the site. The port of Richmond, where domestic or imported international goods arrived by ship, lay farther east on the James at the fall line in the upper Tidewater. Fragile goods would travel on the more difficult journey upriver on the same flat-bottomed bateaux that had carried hogsheads of tobacco downriver. Regardless, these distances failed to hamper Jefferson's desire and patience for specific materials that could not be found in Virginia, or even in the United States. We can consider it fortunate that President Jefferson was occupied with affairs of state and needed to supervise the first two years of construction by letter. Explicit letters from the President's House to the workers in Charlottesville or in Bedford County, and their return letters to Washington, comprise the greatest documentation for the construction history. During the period 1806–9, work to complete Monticello II was in high gear at the same time that work proceeded at Poplar Forest. The number of letters for each, written from or to the President's House, shows the proportion of work at each site. In 1806, for example, Jefferson corresponded about construction-related projects at Monticello in at least forty-five letters but in only two for Poplar Forest. In 1807 he wrote or received sixty-seven letters for Monticello and nine for Poplar Forest. In 1808 the ratio started to change, with thirty-six for Monticello and twenty-four for Poplar Forest. This correspondence provides not only valuable information about work at each site but insight into Jefferson's relationship with his workers. It is rare documentation for any early American domestic building project.

Of equal importance in understanding the construction story were the physical facts. Physical details discovered during the investigation comprise evidence that either corroborated Jefferson's initial instructions to the workmen or confirmed changes mentioned in the workmen's letters. With Jefferson we can rely on a third type of information termed prototypical. When documentary or physical evidence is lacking, knowledge of Jefferson's consistent traditions of design and construction fill the gap. His use of the same workers before and after Poplar Forest, comparing similar elements designed by the same man, offers this additional research methodology.[6] Together, the differing sources provide a very complete knowledge of how and by whom Poplar Forest was constructed.

The Poplar Forest construction history from 1805 to 1826 can be divided into four phases: 1805–9; 1810–14; 1815–23; and 1823–26. The initial phase is defined by Jefferson's last term as president and his absence from the building site in Bedford County. Once construction started in 1806, he made only one brief trip to the site in 1807, relying on Monticello workers and workshops and supervising the work by correspondence. Once retired, Jefferson first stayed in the incomplete shell of his retreat house in November 1809, beginning the second phase of construction when he could oversee the work directly. It was still a challenge to use the same workers at two sites. Phase three constitutes the longest period when the finished joinery was executed on the exterior and interior by John Hemmings and his nephew apprentices. In the final phase Francis Eppes was in residence, and although Jefferson had stopped using Poplar Forest, he was still directing its completion.

The Process Begins: 1805–9

The nature of the retreat did not affect the basic manner in which it was constructed, which was similar to that of Monticello. Common building materials such as brick, stone, mortar, plaster, and lumber were traditionally produced at the remote site. What Poplar Forest lacked was shops, and even accommodations, for the workers, who would travel back and forth to Monticello. Monticello's Joinery Shop, still under the control of James Dinsmore until 1809, produced some items like doors and windows that then required several days' journey on a wagon to reach Poplar Forest.

Fig. 58. Poplar Forest, squint brick with angles used for the octagon corners.

The principal actor in scene one of this construction drama was bricklayer Hugh Chisolm, with supporting roles by his brother John and two unnamed enslaved boys. Chisolm's initial task in the fall of 1805 and in the winter that followed was to start the brickmaking process in Bedford County.[7] Jefferson would have given him precise estimates for the number of bricks needed, the shapes and sizes of special bricks to be molded, and mathematically correct drawings. Chisolm had been working at Monticello for some time, but nothing was left to chance, especially on this long-distance project. Jefferson knew exactly what Chisolm and his "hands" would be doing. In 1771 he had noted that it took two men and three boys to mold and burn bricks.[8] During the process of building and rebuilding Monticello Jefferson had used twenty-two different brickmakers and bricklayers. Jefferson could estimate the exact number of bricks needed and judge their proposed costs. Using bricks "of our usual size of the neatest make," Jefferson gave precise dimensions for the height and thickness of foundations, walls, fireplaces, and chimneys.[9] This practical knowledge was another means of controlling the process, at least psychologically. However, detailed knowledge of the builders' process did not always ensure quality control, just as Jefferson's daily record of every penny spent provided an optimistic sense, even if false, of fiscal reality.

Jefferson's confidence in his bricklayer was soon jarred in the summer of 1806. Hugh Chisolm knew enough about the expectations of his client to write the president that June asking for help. On June 16, 1806, Jefferson wrote to his daughter Martha Randolph: "I find by a letter from Chisolm that I shall have to proceed to Bedford almost without stopping in Albemarle. I shall probably be kept there a week or 10 days laying the foundation of the house, which he is not equal to himself."[10] Chisolm most likely needed help with the geometry of laying out a full octagon house. Jefferson ended up spending six days at the site, "being so much engaged." Being on-site and setting Chisolm straight on his angles for the initial pure octagon design pushed Jefferson to the realization that his ideal design had practical faults. This resulted in the "change order" letter of September 7, 1806, where Jefferson added the stair pavilions and portico appendages and six internal doorways. Jefferson had given Chisolm a pencil sketch for these changes but wanted to take no chances, writing, "I now send you a sketch in ink" where "Everything is drawn so plainly that no further explanation is necessary. Take care of the drawings as they will be necessary for Mr. Perry & I do not reserve another copy for him."[11] After this visit Jefferson might have guessed presidential duties would unfortunately keep him from the site for some time. Indeed, he would not return to the site until the fall of 1807, and then not again for two more years.

Hugh Chisolm, of course, did not work alone. Most craftsmen of means "owned" enslaved workers or rented them by the day, week, month, or year, according to the established practice in Virginia.[12] Chisolm's brother John worked with him at Poplar Forest, as he had at Monticello, but the labor for making bricks and mortar was performed by Chisolm's "two boys." These two might be Lewis and Stepney, who were mentioned in an 1822 ad by Chisolm warning the public not to hire them independently. In November 1807 Chisolm mentioned to Jefferson, "I have made a purches [*sic*] of a negro Boy for which I gave three hundred and sixty dollars."[13] Slave boys performed the labor for making bricks and mortar. The same boy purchased in 1807 might have been the one Jefferson mentioned regarding plastering the cisterns at Monticello: "Chisolm, Hugh. Began to work with his negro boy 1811."[14] Jefferson supplied the critical assistance of enslaved laborer Jerry, who hauled bricks, limestone, wood, and sand for the brickmakers in his wagon. Jerry would go back and forth between Monticello and Poplar Forest for many years, ferrying supplies and workers in addition to performing various duties at the site.

Chisolm wrote Jefferson in June 1807 that Jerry was again hauling sand for mortar in preparation for more bricks that he was now ready to burn.[15] Jefferson's Building Notebook gives an indication of how much hauling Jerry would have done: a bushel of limestone weighed 114 pounds and when burned would produce mortar for one perch of stone or 1,000 bricks. A bushel of sand weighed 100 pounds, and four of those, added to the lime putty, would produce mortar for one perch of stone; 15 bushels of sand were required for mortar to lay 1,000 bricks.[16] Jerry's job was indeed a "very tegerous Job," as Chisolm described it. Chisolm reported that the main walls were all level and that he was waiting on a stonemason to lay the stone walls of the central 20-foot-square deep cellar on the lower level of the house. The walls of the south "piazer" were up to the water table (where the exterior wall decreased in thickness at the first-floor level), but he was holding off on the stair pavilions. Chisolm said he didn't want to proceed above the water table because "it will be the best plan to Lay on the sleepers before I put the next story as they have so little bearing."[17]

In June 1807 Jefferson wrote Chisolm that he wanted him back at Monticello, "where I wish some work done under my own eye."[18] On his only visit to Poplar Forest that year Jefferson noticed Chisolm's poor-quality brickwork that had been done without his supervision. Jefferson instructed Chisolm that he was not to wait for the doors and windows coming from the Monticello shops but "work up the proper opening for them which you will find in your instructions, & if the window frames are ready it is better to put them up & work the wall to them, but if not ready, they are not to be waited for. They can be put in afterwards, tho' with more trouble."[19] The doors and windows would

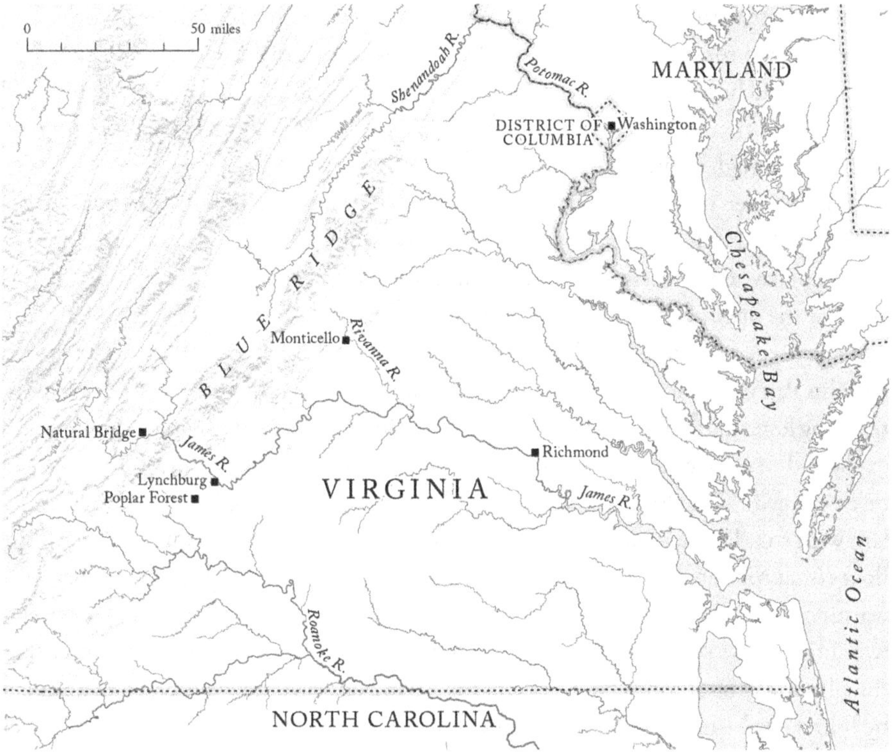

Fig. 59. Map of Virginia showing location of Washington, DC, Richmond, Monticello, and Poplar Forest.

not come for another year, and Chisolm would indeed construct the brick openings but without following Jefferson's precise dimensions. When James Dinsmore's windows finally arrived, the brick openings were too large, and Chisolm resorted to the sloppy practice of filling the gaps with mortar.

As Chisolm and his crew laid bricks in the summer of 1807 Jerry was "hauling for Mr. Perry." This was carpenter John Perry, performing the critical role of framing the floors, ceilings, and roof as Chisolm's brickwork rose to receive them. Perry had worked at Monticello from 1800 to 1811 and in the summer of 1807 was still engaged there and late in getting to Poplar Forest, one of the challenges of having the same workmen working at two sites simultaneously. Jefferson preferred trusted workers from Monticello rather than local workers with whom he had no relationship. What Jerry hauled for John Perry were the large framing members for floor joists, ceiling joists, roof rafters, and roof sheathing.[20] Perry used 700 pounds of wrought nails that Jerry had also hauled from the Monticello nailery that year. There are no references that Jefferson paid separately for water-mill sawing at this time, so the lumber, cut from the poplar forest, was pit-sawn by hand. The labor was done by Perry's enslaved men, and the cost absorbed without itemization in invoices or payments. Jefferson would later refer to the "belted poplars" as stock for his lumber. "Belting" refers to the practice of girdling a tree to kill it but leaving it standing until time to harvest it for "stocks," and then sending those with a "bill of scantling" to a sawmill.[21] Trees were best cut in the winter before the sap rose. Jefferson of course knew this, as one of his letters indicates: "the stocks should be got as soon as possible lest the sap should begin to rise, which would occasion the timbers to rot very soon."[22] This was common knowledge, but Jefferson was good enough to provide the rationale.

In December 1807 Perry wrote Jefferson with important news: "The ruff [roof] of the Bedford house is framed and will be sheeted by Christmas."[23] A better present could not have been received. Unlike Monticello, where a temporary tent structure had covered the open roof to protect the floors and plaster underneath, extra protection was not needed for the brick shell of Poplar Forest, as it still had no floors. This would be John Perry's last work at Poplar Forest, although Jefferson would write him an interesting letter anticipating other work to be performed there. In March 1808 Jefferson explained in a letter to Perry his rationale for a certain material and how it would be assembled: "The floor at Poplar Forest being intended for an under floor must be laid with oak. Poplar would not hold the nails, and pine is too distant & dear. All the floors of Europe are of oak, so are the decks of ships. Good nailing will secure it against warping. Perhaps it may be easier done in herring bone, as the hall floor at Monticello was. In that case your sleepers should be but 14 I. from center to center, in order that the plank may be cut into two feet lengths."[24] The floor would eventually be installed by John Perry's brother, but the extraordinary letter is an example that Jefferson sometimes took the time to explain his rationale in a mentoring way.

The year 1808 was a busy one. Hugh Chisolm had been detained at Monticello in the winter and spring of 1808 and sent his brother John and "boys" to Poplar Forest to prepare for another season of brickmaking. Hugh could report to Jefferson in early July: "It is my wish to inform you, how we are coming on with our work at this place. We have burnt the bricks, and a finer kiln I never burnt in my life, it contains seventy five thousand. We made the bricks for the bases and capts. Of the columns as I thought it would make a better job than to have them of wood. We are now running the stairways."[25] It is inconceivable that Jefferson would have left to Chisolm an important

Fig. 60. Poplar Forest, nailing block inserted into brickwork for attachment of wood trim, showing cut finish nail.

Fig. 61. Poplar Forest, portico pediment framing, 1997.

decision regarding the bases and capitals of the Tuscan order columns. Chisolm confirmed in a letter of September 4 that "we have run the columns for the South portico and I think they will, when finished be elegant."[26] Proper classical columns mattered greatly to Jefferson. This was the first time he had used the Roman and Renaissance method of making brick columns that would be rendered (covered with lime stucco) to resemble a solid carved piece of stone. When corresponding with Benjamin Latrobe in 1804 regarding the United States Capitol, Jefferson noted that most of Palladio's buildings had brick columns covered with stucco.[27] If brick columns were good enough for Palladio, they would suit Jefferson. His only use of solid stone columns at Monticello had resulted in a bad experience he was reluctant to repeat, especially when he was not on-site to supervise the construction.[28] He had used brick columns on the President's House wings and would do so again at the University of Virginia. When he finally replaced the temporary poplar tree columns on the west portico of Monticello, he used brick for the shafts and stone for the bases and capitals. The molded brick bases and capitals at Poplar Forest were a rare occurrence used only there.[29]

Jefferson's visit to the site in September 1808 had been canceled due to a fall from his horse. His anxiety must have matched Chisolm's since he had not been to the site for a year to inspect the brickwork. Anticipating his visit that July, Chisolm had written, "Mr. Perry has laid the flow [floor] in west rooms and is now studing the alcove, as soon as he is done that I shall bricknog and plaster it for your reception."[30] If Jefferson had come that summer or fall, his room alone on the west side of the house would have been usable in the shell that still contained no floors, plaster, or any other interior feature. Walking on boards laid across floor joists would have been familiar to Jefferson, who had experienced that condition twice at Monticello. "Mr. Perry" referred to another member of that family who had taken up work at Poplar Forest after John resumed work at Monticello. Reuben Perry was a house joiner from Lynchburg who had worked at Monticello since 1799 and would work at Poplar Forest until 1814, executing some of the more exacting carpentry work. Perry started in the summer of 1808 where his brother left off: preparing chestnut shingles for the roof, installing the floor joists, and framing the interior bed alcoves and entrance passage walls.[31] As Chisolm completed brickwork for the stair pavilions, the octagonal privies, and the two porticos, Perry installed the two staircases, the portico floors and pediments, and all the wooden elements of the privies. He would also install the exterior doors and windows coming from the Monticello shop. The third Perry brother, Jesse, was not as skilled and is generally listed as a laborer, as were Reuben's enslaved carpenters, Hal and Matt.[32]

Letters document the close relationship and trust between Jefferson and his hired workers, as well as the difficulties typically encountered. A few days after Christmas in 1806 Jefferson instructed James Dinsmore, who was working in the Monticello joinery shop: "The window frames at Poplar Forest may be of poplar dug out of the solid, with locust sills, tho I do not know why the sides and top might not also be of locust dug out of the solid."[33] This is the first letter mentioning any Poplar Forest parts being made at Monticello. This letter reveals that Jefferson could at times think out loud in correspondence with his most trusted workers, whose opinions he valued and with whose decisions he could usually live. Circumstances occasionally determined the matter, as when Dinsmore wrote ten months later that he questioned the quality of the walnut

Fig. 62. Poplar Forest, north portico with rendered Tuscan order columns, 2022.

Fig. 63. Poplar Forest, bed alcove framing in east bed chamber, 2019.

Fig. 64. Reuben Perry's signature.

he could get. Jefferson then allowed Dinsmore the choice based on his best judgment: "I should certainly prefer walnut for the Bedford sashes, because well rubbed on the inside and unpainted it has a richer look than a painted sash, and I believe no wood is more durable but if you cannot get it good, then certainly good pine will be preferable to bad walnut. It must therefore depend on your being able to get good walnut and without delaying the work. The sashes for the lower rooms may be pine."[34] Jefferson again took the time to explain his aesthetic rationale with a practical caveat that respected Dinsmore's discretion for the outcome.

Jefferson was particular about the window sash he entrusted Dinsmore to make. The quality of light in a room became an important issue for Jefferson after his Paris years. This quality depended upon a large, 12″ × 18″ glass size for the panes of six-over-six double-hung sash. Jefferson ordered this glass from Philadelphia and was explicit that it had "to be very exactly cut to their measures, because in the country those who could trim them are few & awkward & occasion great loss. To be of the same quality you formerly furnished me, that is to say Hamburg or Bohemian glass of the middle thickness."[35] Precision and quality always mattered. Subsequent letters in October and December 1807, and then January 1808, lament the delay of the glass. The glass was eventually shipped from Europe to Philadelphia and then in March to Washington, where it was transferred to another ship in the port of Alexandria. That ship then sailed down the Potomac River to the Chesapeake Bay, down to the mouth of the James River at Norfolk, and then up the James River to the inland port of Richmond. By late April it had at last arrived at Monticello. Two months later Jefferson instructed that when the windows were completed, they should be sent by boat, the safest means, to Lynchburg, meaning they would travel down the Rivanna River to the James and then upriver to Lynchburg, which was still a ten-mile distance from the building site. Dinsmore responded to Jefferson in June that the windows had not yet been glazed and that he lacked sufficient sash cord and pulleys. The windows were finally sent by wagon in July, but the fifty-seven metal sash weights would come later. Thus ended the lengthy ordeal of getting the finished windows to the site. There was also the real possibility that a certain quantity of glass would arrive broken. This long process was exacerbated by the use of the shops and craftsmen at Monticello, by Jefferson's insistence on hard-to-obtain materials, and by the challenges of long-distance transportation by ship, boat, and wagon. Jefferson's patience was tested as he constantly learned from these experiences and optimistically took measures to rectify similar future problems.

Jefferson sometimes delayed the Poplar Forest work to take advantage of the best craftsmen at one site instead of two. Such was the case with master painter Richard Barry, who arrived from Washington to glaze and varnish the Monticello window sash and to faux-paint all the interior doors. Jefferson instructed Barry to glaze the Poplar Forest sashes, still at Monticello, and finish them in a manner similar to the Monticello sashes with a varnished interior treatment. Having delayed the sashes so Barry could finish and glaze them, Jefferson had responded to Chisolm's request for the door and window frames by saying he could install them later, after the openings had been built. Barry also had the opportunity to faux-paint some of the Poplar Forest doors being made in the Monticello joinery at that time.[36] Jefferson apprenticed his enslaved manservant Burwell Colbert to Barry to continue to learn the art of painting and glazing. Colbert would later be able to repair the Poplar Forest windows as well as to paint the house inside and out. Freed in Jefferson's will, he would be employed for years as a painter and glazier at the University of Virginia.

Simultaneous projects at Monticello and Poplar Forest were at various stages during this overlap period. They shared the same protracted and frustrating sequence of difficult procurement, transportation, and construction. Poplar Forest's remote building site created numerous needs for Jerry and his wagon. In the summer of 1808, he and

Fig. 65. Poplar Forest, double-hung walnut window sash, 2022.

his wagon carried four tables, bedding, two stoves, metal sash weights, sheet iron, and sheet lead. Letters to and from the workers provide a dense and dizzying paper trail of construction details squeezed into the busy life of a president. On December 28, 1806, a day of great distraction, President Jefferson even found time to write James Dinsmore a detailed letter discussing choice of wood for the Poplar Forest window sash; that day Meriwether Lewis had miraculously arrived back at the President's House from his long, incredible trip with William Clark![37]

In March 1809 Thomas Jefferson resumed life as a private citizen at Monticello, where his work crew, both hired and enslaved, fittingly labored to complete his greatly expanded house. He was busy enough that spring and summer that he could not make his long-awaited trip to Bedford County until November. If 1808 constituted a busy year at Poplar Forest, 1809 was relatively slow, without much documented work except "digging about the house," which had been the primary job of enslaved laborer Phil Hubbard.[38] Reuben Perry would have been completing some carpentry jobs, and Jefferson ordered 1,000 feet of heart plank for the next season, suggesting how it should be cut for more efficiency.[39] On his trip to the site that November, his first in two years, he would have laid anxious eyes on the completed exterior shell of his retreat. What his eyes took in was the unusual but personally familiar shape of a large octagon. The house still lacked its exterior Tuscan entablature, its balustrade, and the large lunette windows for the pavilions and portico pediments. Jefferson would have engaged John Richardson, who was plastering the ceilings with the help of Phil Hubbard.[40] It was a precarious time of year to plaster, but the overseer reported that "by keeping good fiers thare will not be any danger of the plastering."[41] Richardson would have disputes with the overseer and quit without finishing the work. Four and a half years would pass before the owner would experience a fully plastered house. The year 1809 was important, though, because Jefferson could now make more frequent trips to supervise the work and, most importantly, could begin using his retreat. His gleeful anticipation of that moment shines unmistakably through his letters. Before leaving office, he wrote to his good friend Madame de Corny in Paris: "I at length detach myself from public life, which I never loved, to retire to the bosom of my family my friends, my farm and books, which I have always loved. I retire in hearty affection with the world, because indeed the world has been kinder to me than I claimed."[42] The very same day he wrote

Fig. 66. Poplar Forest, sash doors originally made by John Hemmings, view from dining room into north passage, 2022.

another friend in Paris: "Within a few days I retire to my family, my books, and farms & having gained the harbor myself, shall look on my friends still buffeting the storm, with anxiety indeed, but not with envy. Never did a prisoner, released from his chains, feel such relief as I shall on shaking off the shackles of power."[43]

Second Era of Construction: 1810–14

The second era of construction, 1810–14, resembles the previous era's processes regarding workers and materials. Hugh Chisolm and Reuben Perry continued working at the site; some materials were produced on-site, and others came from the Monticello joinery; and enslaved workers owned by the hired workers or by Jefferson continued to play an important part in the construction. The biggest difference came from Jefferson's more frequent interaction with the workers and work he observed under his own eye. For the very first time Jefferson was able to pay a springtime visit, spending fourteen days at the site in March and April 1810. The following year he paid a fourteen-day visit in August and a twenty-seven-day visit in November and December, satisfying his great need for controlling the building process, but, most importantly, enjoying his retreat.

Monticello was largely complete by 1809. Any construction work remaining was left in the hands of others as the skilled Irish house joiners James Dinsmore (at Monticello from 1798 to 1809) and John Neilson (at Monticello from 1805 to 1809) left to remodel Montpelier for James Madison. They left Jefferson with their well-trained enslaved apprentice John Hemmings. Even though Jefferson still hired "resident carpenters" who directed the plantation work of enslaved carpenters, Hemmings took over as the most skilled woodworker at Monticello. He had risen to the skill of a house joiner and cabinetmaker who made furniture as well as finished architectural trim. Elements made for Poplar Forest in the Monticello joinery shop would now be made by Hemmings or under his direction.

The principal work for this second era consisted of preparing for the wall plaster, plastering the walls, and constructing a service wing dependency. Jefferson spent considerable time at the site, visiting three times in 1810 and three times in 1811. His enjoyment is contained in a most revealing letter to his good friend Dr. Benjamin Rush:

> I write to you from a place, 90 miles from Monticello, near the New London of this state, which I visit three or four times a year, & stay from a fortnight to a month at a time. I have fixed myself comfortably, keep some books here, bring others occasionally, am in the solitude of a hermit, and quite at leisure to attend to my absent friends. . . . Mathematics, I have resumed that study with great avidity, it was ever my favorite one. We have no theories there, no uncertainties remain on the mind; all is demonstration & satisfaction. . . . I take moderate rides without much fatigue: but my journey to this place, in a hard-going gig, gave me great sufferings, which I expect will be renewed on my return, as soon as I am able. . . . I find friendship to be like wine, raw when new, ripened with age, the true old man's milk, & restorative cordial.[44]

In this second era a significant new craftsman entered the saga of Poplar Forest construction. On September 26, 1810, Jefferson wrote James Dinsmore, "Johnny Hemings is just entering on a job of sash doors for the house at Poplar forest [*sic*], and tells me he cannot proceed without his sash planes and the templet belonging to them in your possession."[45] John Hemmings needed a specific molding plane Dinsmore had borrowed from Jefferson. Jefferson had stocked the joinery shop with a substantial collection of woodworking tools, which Dinsmore inventoried on April 15, 1809. Jefferson desired a particular window sash muntin (the thin elements that hold and divide the glass panes), and Dinsmore had borrowed the plane that could produce it.[46] At the bottom of the joinery shop inventory Dinsmore had noted: "planes borrowed by Jas. Dinsmore. 1 Tuscan Cornice plane, 1 Sash astragal, 1 ogee & quarter round." The "Sash astragal" would have been what Hemmings needed. He would also come to need the Tuscan cornice plane for Poplar Forest. The term "sash doors" referred to a door with glass rather than wood panels for greater visibility and light. In Paris these were ubiquitous, and Jefferson wanted them for the four doorways on each side of the dining room and for the south parlor door. Hemmings did not come to Poplar Forest to install his doors because the following spring Jefferson wrote Reuben Perry: "My boat will start to Lynchburg as soon as it has got all my flour down from hence; which will be in about one trip more. She will carry the 4. Pair of glass doors with their jambs & soffites, & the semicircular windows, all ready glazed for hanging. I must pray you to be in readiness to come the moment of my arrival at Poplar Forest to put them all up, that it may be done while I am there."[47] During Jefferson's twenty-three-day visit that August he observed Perry installing the sash doors and the four lunette windows of the porticos and stair pavilions.[48] After that visit Jefferson had written a friend: "I am just returned from a place I possess in Bedford County near Lynchburg, and where I pass certain portions of the year. It is the most valuable of my possessions and will become the residence of the greater part of my family."[49] This hope for his family had been encouraged when Jefferson's daughter Martha had given her portion of the Poplar Forest land to her daughter Anne, who married in 1808. In between his last two visits in 1812, Jefferson wrote his famous letter to his son-in-law John Wayles Eppes regarding grandson Francis's eventual ownership of Poplar Forest: "It is an Octagon of 50.f. diameter, of brick, well built, will be plaistered this fall, when nothing will be wanting to finish it completely but the cornices and some of the doors. When finished it will be the best dwelling house in the state, except that of Monticello, perhaps preferable to that as more proportioned to the faculties of a private citizen. I shall probably go on with the cornices and doors at my leisure at Monticello."[50]

Jefferson's description was mostly correct, especially the statement that missing items would be finished at his leisure. His description characterized the full size of the octagon, without appendages, and stated that, like all of his building projects, it was well built. The statement about its being more proportioned to the faculties of a private citizen was certainly much more relevant to himself than to his grandson. As to its completion, he was less than honest. There was much more than cornices and doors to complete, and most of that would be made on-site for years to come by John Hemmings and his nephews.

Jefferson was desperate to have his retreat plastered in the fall of 1812. When he headed to Poplar Forest in August on the second of three trips that year, he pleaded with Reuben Perry, "be ready to come there on notice of my arrival and lay all the grounds for the plaistering while I am there."[51] "Grounds" referred to the more time-consuming and precise method of putting boards on the brick walls and ceiling joists to ensure the plaster would be plumb and level. In Jefferson's perfect house this precision mattered, and having measured the grounds, he wrote Perry, "I find that for wanting of plumbing the grounds in the parlour, several of them will be to take down when we go putting up the architraves & cornices. I pray you to have strict attention paid to this in the rooms still to be done."[52] Chisolm would finish the plaster job that Richardson had abandoned years before. For the best result Jefferson specified a "very clear gritty sand" and suggested which creek might supply it, having once observed the geologic quality of its sand. Jefferson asked that his two overseers each furnish Chisolm "one hand to make his mortar [plaster] & attend on him," and "that had better be Phil Hubbard because he understands the making mortar so well."[53] Jefferson was nervous about the late December season, "when plaistering becomes very precarious," and resorted to borrowing some plaster of Paris from a neighbor to avoid a "permanent eyesore."[54] Jefferson was a little disingenuous, since Monticello I had never been plastered, and Monticello II looked like a brick kiln for so long. Jefferson could not return home that Christmas with the satisfaction of a plastered retreat, but progress had been made. Reuben Perry itemized plaster grounds for doors, windows, chimneys, bases, surbases (chair rails), and cornices (entablatures). In addition he had made and installed three chimney screens, window panels, window sills, curtain boards (for window curtains), and two trap doors for the closets above each bed alcove. Perry still owed Jefferson a wooden model for casting seven iron firebacks.

The house would remain unplastered for another year, but a different project was on Jefferson's mind in 1813. That spring he updated his son-in-law on the project: "I have already resumed the inside finishing, which I had not before intended. I have engaged a workman to build offices."[55] It would be hard to take Jefferson at his word about not finishing the interior since he had just gone to so much trouble to get the grounds ready for plaster and trim. The other statement was partially true in concept. Jefferson now planned to replace the eastern row of trees connecting house and mound with a 24′ × 100′ service wing of "offices" that would contain a kitchen, laundry, smokehouse, and an unidentified space, possibly a spinning room.[56] Jefferson's note about the work that fall characteristically described the process of labor:

> 1813. Sep. In digging the foundation of offices at Pop. For. 4.f. deep of very hard clay, without stone 6. constant diggers, 2. fillers, 2. carters who help to fill, & 2 oxcarts with a yoke of oxen in each, dig 42. cub. yards of earth a day and carry it 100 yds. each cart carrying 1. cub. yard at a load.[57]

Fig. 67. Poplar Forest, exhibit showing how plaster grounds were first installed to make plaster plumb and level and then used for attachment of finished trim.

The extensive digging was necessary to accomplish several carefully thought-out aspects. Like the 100-foot service wings he had added to the President's House, and the Monticello service wings, the mass of the building would be sunk into the ground. This would allow the deck of the wing roof to match the level of the house floor for a seamless transition from indoors to out. As a consequence, the wing presented a lower and more pleasing height on the front of the house.

Jefferson's thirty-two-day visit in the spring of 1814 coincided with the wing work. Chisolm, who had finished the plaster in the house, had written to Jefferson stating that he had started the stonework on the wing and needed to know "the size of the building and the openings and whether I shall build the pillars with circular brick or with square bricks."[58] The fact that Chisolm asked for detailed instructions for the wing indicates that much of the instruction was now on-site and verbal. Jefferson's terse note described what he keenly observed that summer: "Chisolm & 2. Apprentices (one of them a new beginner) lay 1600 bricks a day."[59] Once again Jefferson fretted over his lumber order, so "important to the preservation of the work we have done," and gave instructions how the mill could overcome the limitations of sawing longer stocks.[60] That November Jefferson would see Reuben Perry constructing the complicated hidden roof of the wing. He updated his son-in-law in another letter: "I have built a most excellent house and . . . been doing much towards it's completion. . . . The inside work is mostly done, and I have this summer built a wing of offices 110 feet long, in the manner of those at Monticello, with a flat roof in the level of the floor of the house."[61]

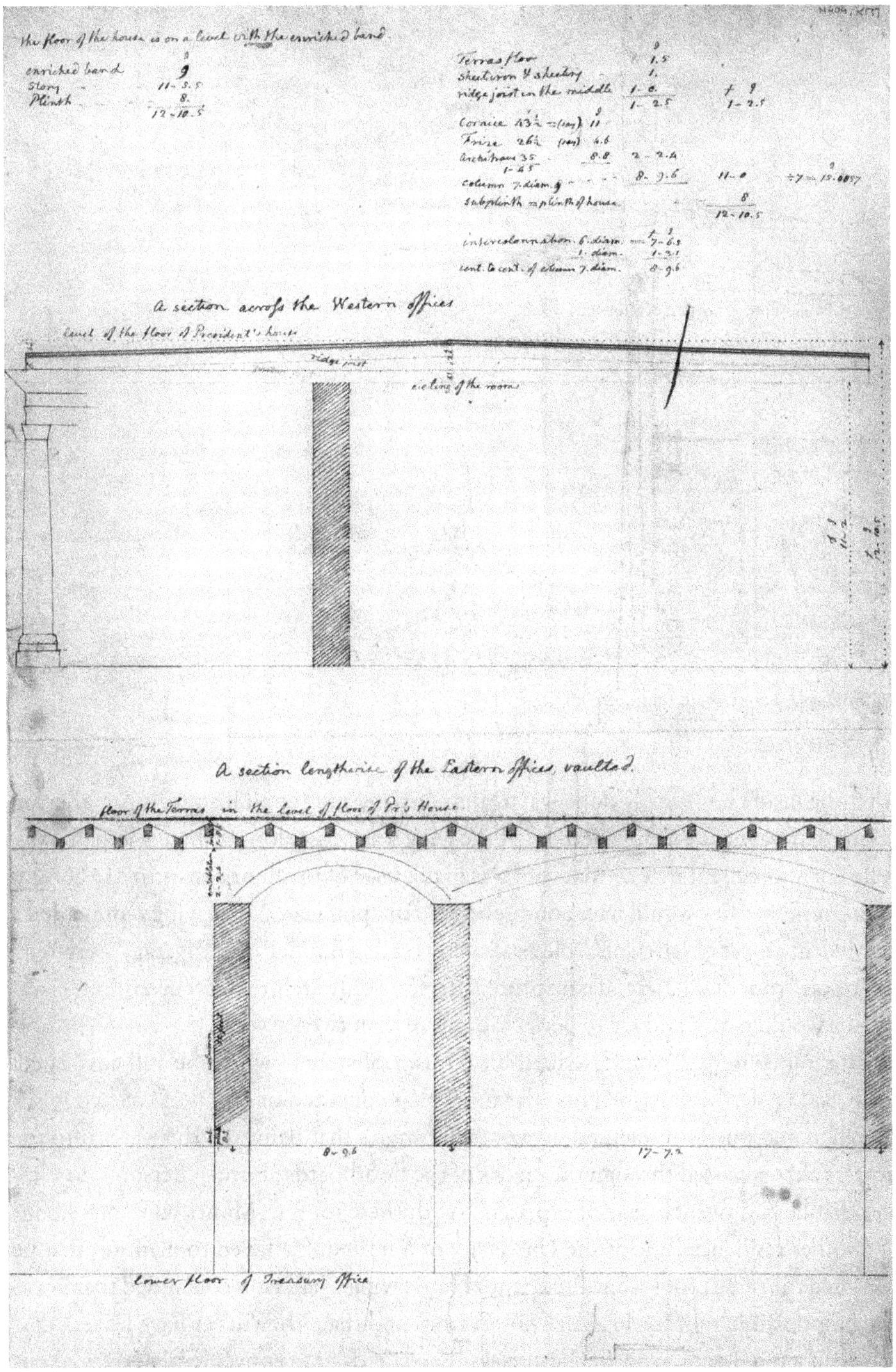

Fig. 68. Jefferson drawing of terras roof at President's House.

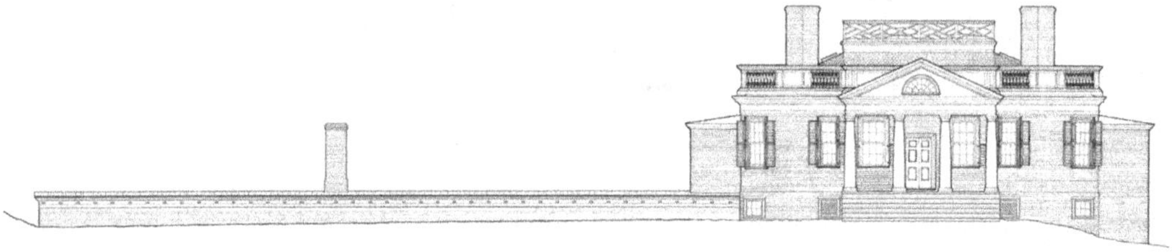

Fig. 69. Poplar Forest, north elevation with wing.

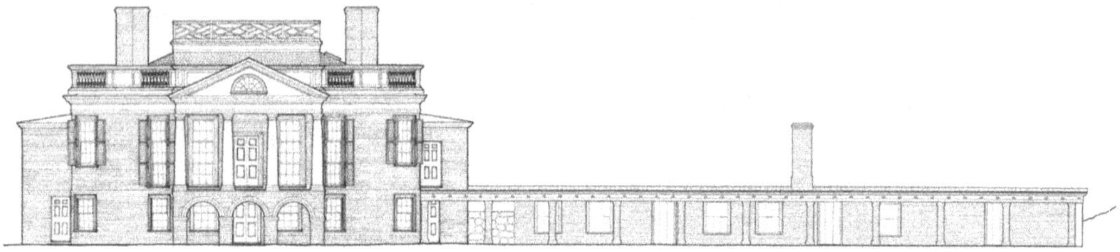

Fig. 70. Poplar Forest, south elevation with wing.

That the inside was mostly done was again not true, and for all his precision Jefferson seems to have inconceivably noted that the wing was 10 feet longer than it actually was. Jefferson's statement that the flat roof was in the level of the floor constituted a considerable task that few would have comprehended or appreciated. The wing represented a significant aspect of Jefferson's role as an architect and builder. The "zig-zag," "serrated," or "terras," roof design would constitute Jefferson's only architectural invention; it was one he would tweak and try to perfect for more than twenty years.

Late in his life Jefferson described his terras roof system, which he still advocated. To F. R. Hassler he described his "flat roof" that consisted of "rooflets" of two joists, one high and one low, spanned by wooden shingles that delivered the water into the gutters after it passed through the cracks of the floorboards above. Jefferson told Hassler that he had twenty years of experience with these roofs at Monticello, "one I built at another residence," and at the University of Virginia. He failed to mention that he had used the same roof for the President's House wings. Jefferson concluded that it was the best possible roof for Hassler's observatory and that "they never have leaked, cost less than a rafter roof," and were more easily repaired.[62] He conveniently forgot about the leaking dining room roof that Hemmings had repaired. Still, by the time Jefferson wrote this letter in 1825, he could speak with authority, having used his invention in several variations in several places for many years.

Jefferson had innovatively conceived a way to achieve the nearly impossible flat roof.[63] In reality it was a compressed hidden roof system with a flat deck on top. Benjamin Henry Latrobe, tasked with building Jefferson's service wings on the President's House in 1803, noted the originality of Jefferson's design.[64] Latrobe, who knew European methods of construction, referred to the "President's zig-zag roof of sheet iron uniting all the qualities of the pantile, without the bad ones."[65] The pantile comparison was not a bad one since Jefferson had experimented with placing sheet iron over the high and low joists.[66] Another letter from Latrobe mentioned building wings "of his [Jefferson's] own design."[67] The idea for this type of roof might have come from a flat roof on the fashionable suburban house of Jefferson's friend General Samuel Smith outside of Baltimore. In 1803 Jefferson asked Latrobe to stop and see Smith's Montebello, designed by William Birch, on his way between Philadelphia and Washington. Jefferson described it as having "the first and only example [of a flat roof] yet executed," noting that "it may furnish us, by the manner of its execution, information both as to what succeeds, and as to what may not succeed, and therefore is to be avoided, if anything about it does not succeed."[68] Alas, Latrobe's report was evidently given in person, and nothing about this flat roof on this now-demolished house is known.

Jefferson continued to be a great advocate for his terras roof system. He convinced John Hartwell Cocke to include a rooftop terras system on his house Bremo, which John Neilson designed. Jefferson argued successfully to James Madison that his new wings on Montpelier should have terras roofs and decks accessible from second-floor bed chambers. The largest use of the terras roof system was that at the University of Virginia, where it was used in slightly different ways for two pavilion roofs and over all the student rooms. Joseph C. Cabell, who was later vindicated, thought that the University roofs would leak, but he could not sway Jefferson. Cabell, as a Board of Visitors member, pleaded with Jefferson, saying his opinion was also "the prevailing opinion of the best workmen in the country."[69] John H. Cocke joined the chorus of opinions, stating that the "beauty and convenience" of the flat roofs "counterbalance some objections" and that Jefferson's "experiment had as yet stood the test of about 7 years." Cocke

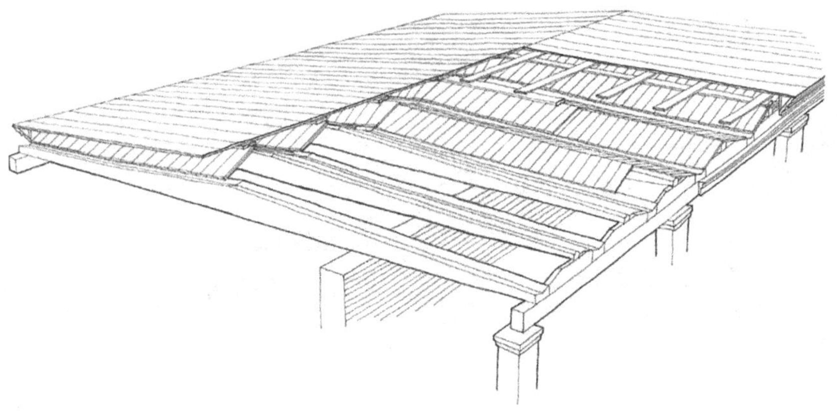

Fig. 71. Poplar Forest, drawing of service wing's terras roof.

felt that a low-pitched heart pine shingle roof trumped a flat one, where the "liability to decay increases."[70] If Cocke seemed adamant and somewhat bitter, it was because Jefferson had apparently cautioned Cocke about Bremo that "a gutter over a hall can never be safe."[71] Jefferson's caution would ironically be validated when the terras roof over his own dining room at Poplar Forest leaked. Cocke would also be vindicated. In 1836 he confided to his diary: "Commenced taking off Roof of the House to be replaced by a new one to get rid of the evils of flat roofing and spouts and gutters, or in other words to supersede the Jeffersonian by the common sense plan."[72] Still, Jefferson stubbornly continued to recommend his roof system. His 1822 design and specifications for the Buckingham County Court House included a terras roof that he advocated, stating, "I recommend this strongly, because they will be vastly handsomer and much cheaper than the common roof."[73] We do not know if his strong recommendation was carried out, since the courthouse burned. However, a house across the street, the Dr. Tucker House, had wings using a terras roof system, the only known example not connected to a Jefferson design.[74]

Jack McLaughlin considered the louvered blinds at Monticello as a metaphor for Jefferson's character.[75] At Poplar Forest the wing of offices could also stand as such a metaphor. It constitutes one of his most personal and tenacious ideas, starting with the dependency wings of service rooms that had been part of Monticello I. The idea came from the 1570 book of his Renaissance mentor Palladio (*The Four Books of Architecture*). Jefferson saw that the typical plantation outbuildings could be gathered in service wings in an orderly and economical manner, reserving the surrounding space for lawns and landscaped gardens. Figuring out how to use the roof of the wing spoke

Fig. 72. Poplar Forest, service wing, 2022.

to Jefferson's tendency to do things that were both ideal and practical. It presented a circumstantial challenge for him to solve. Walking or sitting upon the wing deck gave Jefferson another way to engage nature. Outdoor living on terraces and in gardens had been a strong memory from his French experience. The rooftop deck harkened back even further to sixteenth- and seventeenth-century roof platforms on English banqueting and country houses. The deck at Poplar Forest was entirely private and open without the need for the kind of louvered outdoor rooms built at Monticello. The wing deck further enforced a master/family separation from enslaved servants who worked in the rooms below, out of sight. Jefferson's changes to the roof design over many years reflected his undying optimism for better and more innovative solutions. When the roof needed rebuilding during his grandson's tenure, he came up with yet another new gutter detail that he said would make future repairs easier. The wing and its special roof represented historical precedent, precise design and specifications, modern concepts of outdoor living, innovative designs and materials, use of hired and enslaved workers, changes based on optimistic hopes for better performance and longevity, and the patience to experiment with one idea for many years. It was very Jeffersonian.

Third Era of Construction: 1815–23

Jefferson's dinner invitation to his Poplar Forest neighbor Charles Clay on August 25, 1815, portended the busy season to come and the last critical era of completing the retreat. Jefferson had cautioned Clay, "But you must come with your ears stuffed full of cotton to fortify them against the noise of hammers, saws, planes, etc. which assail us in every direction."[76] Jefferson's earlier letter to Poplar Forest overseer Joel Yancey had explained: "my workmen . . . will set out for Poplar Forest & myself the day after them. . . . [T]here will be one white (a brother of Mr. Goodman) and from 4 to 6 or 7 blacks."[77] The "white" workman coming from Monticello was resident carpenter Rolin Goodman (at Monticello from 1813 to 1817). The four to seven "blacks" accompanying him were critical for this accelerated pace of work. Jefferson's term "blacks" obliquely introduces into the Poplar Forest saga his own enslaved craftsmen, who would labor for more than ten years to complete Jefferson's masterpiece and, in so doing, create their own. Jefferson would now time most of his visits to Poplar Forest so that he could supervise the work there. Besides a stonemason, a plasterer, and the maker of frieze ornaments, most of the remaining work to finish the house would be executed by Monticello's enslaved craftsmen who came and went, by cart or on foot. The remote building site still posed challenges. Without a joinery shop at Poplar Forest, the lower level of the house became a makeshift shop as well as a dormitory for the workers. Most of the on-site work now depended upon lumber from the poplar forest that had to be cut, sent to the mill, and seasoned for scheduled work each year. The exception would be some final doors made in the Monticello joinery shop. English-made door hardware came from Richmond, and the ever-recurring order for the best replacement glass now came from Boston. The glass still came by ship to Richmond, then traveled upriver on bateaux to Lynchburg and, finally, on a risky ten-mile wagon ride, to the building site.

JOHN HEMMINGS AND HIS NEPHEWS

After 1815 the task of crafting the important interior and exterior classical details at Poplar Forest would be performed by the Hemings family of enslaved house joiners. Most notable was John Hemmings. Hemmings first appears in the records for Poplar Forest in 1810 as the maker of the four sets of sash doors for the dining room, but he would not work at the site until 1815. His first job at Poplar Forest was a major one. The group of Monticello "blacks" who journeyed to the site in the summer of 1815 would construct the classical balustrade at the edge of the roof. Coming with their uncle on this first trip were Beverly, age seventeen, and Madison, almost twelve. The other "blacks" coming to the site were other enslaved carpenters, most likely some of the younger tradesmen, aged nineteen to thirty-five: Lewis, Barnaby, Nace, James, Shepherd, Joe, or Davy.[78] At the end of August, Jefferson wrote his daughter, "It is rather evident we must have such another expedition the next year."[79] Lumber ordered for that 1816 expedition was for John Hemmings "and his two aids" (Beverly and Madison), who would work there from September into December. Jefferson focused their work on the exterior elements: finishing the balustrade and trim for the two pediments, and crafting the Tuscan entablature that wrapped around the upper walls of the house. By early December Jefferson wrote his daughter that "Johnny Hemings etc." would return home to Monticello. The sequence continued the following spring (1817), when Jefferson ordered more lumber "to employ John Hemings in the autumn."

The logistical task required harvested and mill-cut lumber that would be dry and stable for the scheduled work of the joiners each year. Lumber could certainly be pit-sawn by hand, but Jefferson preferred to send his poplar stock to a water-powered sawmill, even though it was more costly and almost always problematic. Jefferson's request for more stock to be milled in July 1815 was repeated ten times in the ensuing six years. It was important that the wood be "well seasoned," and several times Jefferson explained that the wood should be cut in the winter and "seasoned for the Fall's use," or sawed in December for "John Hemings and his assistants" to use in the spring.[80] The problem in central Virginia, where Poplar Forest is located, was a constant source of creek water to run the mills; Jefferson frequently feared that the "water may fail" and "we shall be obliged to get our stocks sawed by hand & to work them green & for outside work too."[81] This was yet another long-distance challenge.

Jerry's wagon was indispensable. Back and forth between Monticello and Poplar Forest it carried household or horticultural materials south and agricultural products north. If convenient, it also occasionally carried the workers and their tools. On-site, Jerry hauled lumber and other construction materials. Frequently Jefferson instructed that the wagon or the cart should not tarry because they were needed at one site or the other, especially "Jerry's wagon." For a man who had fine carriages made, it is inexplicable why Jefferson couldn't have made more wagons and carts. The 1826 Monticello

Fig. 73. Poplar Forest, tin-coated shingles, terras roof over dining room with skylight and Chinese railing.

inventory at Jefferson's death listed "1 road wagon" and "1 ox cart." Jerry's wagon brought tantalizingly vague things for the house: "articles," "other things," a "bundle," "baggage," or "boxes." More specific items heading south were doors, windows, window weights, sash pulleys, tools, nails, tin, lead, door locks, and entablature ornaments. The wagon also brought tables, books, food, a harpsichord, harnesses, a spinning jenny, and casks of beer, wine, and cider. For smaller loads and for "John Hemings and his staff" the smaller cart sufficed. Different enslaved men might drive the cart, but Jerry, born in 1777, seemed to be in command of the wagon. In one instance Jefferson wrote John Hemmings at Poplar Forest: "Lilburne has a hurt on his leg which will disable him from walking back. Eston must drive the cart therefore and Lilburne stay and come in the wagon."[82] This seems to be the first time Jefferson had referred in writing to his son Eston by name, except in the Farm Book rolls of the enslaved.

Cornelia and Ellen Randolph started accompanying their grandfather to Poplar Forest in 1816, sharing the east bed chamber. They were there that summer when Englishman George Flower visited. The following year Ellen wrote to her mother at Monticello: "Cornelia and myself are not comfortably fixed. Our room has been pulled down and it will be some time before we get in it, probably a fortnight—in the mean time we are in that little close, disagreeable room to the right as you enter the dining room, we are so crowded we can scarcely turn."[83] The "pulling down" referred to an alteration to close the south side of the east bed alcove for the young ladies' privacy. The granddaughters' correspondence fills in glimpses of life at Poplar Forest. Their letters to their mother at Monticello reveal a great deal about Jefferson; they mention Burwell Colbert and his uncle John Hemmings but fail to once mention Beverly, Madison, or Eston. This followed Jefferson's policy to not mention his sons by name but only as "assistants" to their uncle. Gordon-Reed feels that this was a way to avoid publicly acknowledging their parentage, similar to the absence of any written reference to their mother, Sally Hemings, in Jefferson's will or in any other places besides the rolls of the enslaved.

On November 22, 1817, Thomas Jefferson wrote from Poplar Forest to his daughter: "I arrived here, my dear daughter after a disagreeable journey, one day shut up at Warren by steady rain, the next travelling thro a good deal of drizzle & rain, and the last excessive cold, the road being full of ice, but all well in the end."[84] It was well in the end because the three-day trip, punishing even in good weather, led Jefferson to his most pleasurable sanctum, well worth the hardships getting there. Having settled in, he had "the leisure to attend to my absent friends," writing as many as five letters a day. Some of his letters described his new project, the University of Virginia: "I have only this single anxiety in this world. It is a bantling of 40 years birth & nursing, & if I can once see it on its legs, I will sing with sincerity & pleasure my nunc demittas."[85] Although he now had a new distraction, his immediate project was to finish his retreat. Just after arriving at Poplar Forest he had reported to his daughter that "Johnny Hemings had made great progress in his work."[86] In addition to closing the east alcove opening, Hemmings and his nephews worked on the interior trim such as the three-part architrave moldings for doors, windows, alcoves, and fireplaces. At the end of November Jefferson wrote to his daughter and called for the cart to be returned and estimated "Johnny Hemings" would not be finished until the middle of December.[87] On the same day Jefferson wrote to his Monticello overseer: "I send Bedford Billy down to be put to work with the Coopers under Barnaby, and Thrimston to leave Barnaby and work with the carpenters. I hope you will keep them all to their duty. Billy is found too ungovernable for Johnny Hemings."[88] Evidently Billy did not meet the high standards of John Hemmings and was shifted to the less exacting work of making barrels.

In 1819 Jefferson visited his retreat in the spring and in the summer. Early in the year the wagon brought doors from Monticello that Hemmings and his assistants had made that winter in the joinery shop. These interior doors with brass mortise locks would finally complete the bed chambers. In June a major hailstorm broke many windows in the house, including the dining room skylight, staining the oak floors. Jefferson immediately ordered more oversized glass and placed another lumber order for "Johnny Hemings and his assistants."[89] When he arrived in July, Jefferson wrote Monticello resident carpenter Edmund Meeks to "come with the three carpenters under you" to join the others: "It is so inconvenient for the house to spare the little mule and cart, and so few tools will be wanting here that they may bring them on their shoulders. . . . 2 hand saws, 2 jack planes, 2 pr chisels broad 1 narrow, some augers, foot adze & narrow adze. . . . These things divided among three will weigh little. Let them bring their own provision for the road."[90] This directive meant walking for three to four days in the middle of the summer, sleeping along the road, and carrying their tools. The tools were necessary for building a new terras roof and skylight that would replace the original

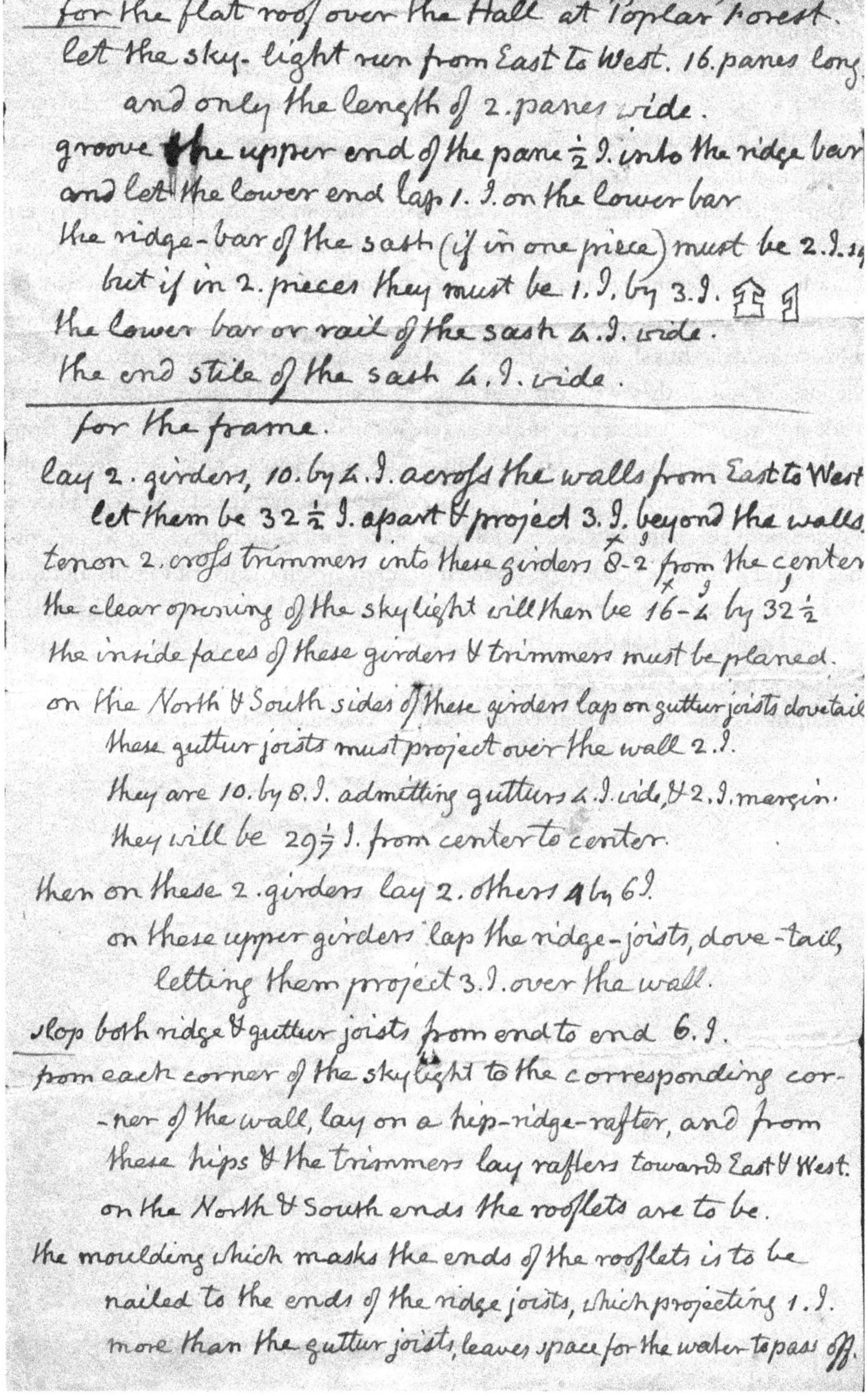

for the flat roof over the Hall at Poplar Forest.
let the sky-light run from East to West. 16. panes long
and only the length of 2. panes wide.
groove the upper end of the pane $\frac{1}{2}$ I. into the ridge bar
and let the lower end lap 1. I. on the lower bar
the ridge-bar of the sash (if in one piece) must be 2. I. sq
but if in 2. pieces they must be 1. I. by 3. I.
the lower bar or rail of the sash 4. I. wide.
the end stile of the sash 4. I. wide.

for the frame.
lay 2. girders, 10. by 4. I. across the walls from East to West
let them be 32 $\frac{1}{2}$ I. apart & project 3. I. beyond the walls.
tenon 2. cross trimmers into these girders 8f.-2I. from the center
the clear opening of the skylight will then be 16f.-4I. by 32 $\frac{1}{2}$
the inside faces of these girders & trimmers must be planed.
on the North & South sides of these girders lap on gutter joists dovetail
these gutter joists must project over the wall 2. I.
they are 10. by 8. I. admitting gutters 4. I. wide, & 2. I. margin.
they will be 29 $\frac{1}{7}$ I. from center to center.
then on these 2. girders lay 2. others 4 by 6 I.
on these upper girders lap the ridge-joists, dove-tail,
letting them project 3. I. over the wall.
slop both ridge & gutter joists from end to end 6. I.
from each corner of the skylight to the corresponding cor-
-ner of the wall, lay on a hip-ridge-rafter, and from
these hips & the trimmers lay rafters towards East & West.
on the North & South ends the rooflets are to be.
the moulding which masks the ends of the rooflets is to be
nailed to the ends of the ridge joists, which projecting 1. I.
more than the gutter joists, leaves space for the water to pass off.

Fig. 74. Jefferson roof specifications for new roof over dining room, 1819.

"rafter roof" and skylight over the dining room.[91] The new roof also featured a Chinese railing around its perimeter, a feature known only from a John Hemmings letter. Jefferson also noted at this time that John Gorman "has worked here under my eye about 3 weeks, dressing and laying some hearthstones and marble slabs."[92] This was yet another finished piece, permanent hearthstones that replaced the temporary brick hearths that had served ten long years.

During Jefferson's four trips to Poplar Forest in 1819 and 1820, he observed with great interest the joiners' work and engaged in conversation with his enslaved sons. Principal work for John Hemmings and his nephews, including Eston by this time, would be focused on interior trim. Jefferson would have come down from his chamber/cabinet suite to the makeshift shop in the lower level to see the joiners' progress. After hanging the interior doors, they were engaged forming the classically derived moldings that made up the bases, architraves, sur bases (chair rails), and entablatures, copied from books by James Gibbs and Andrea Palladio. The large Tuscan order wooden entablature graced the entrance passage and four chamber rooms. The classical entablature was composed of multiple wooden moldings making up its architrave, frieze, and cornice. John Hemmings would have directed his nephews in the use of various molding planes used to turn the raw planks from the mill into finished parts. They learned the grammar of classical architecture found in Jefferson's books: fillets, cavettos, astragals, fascias, cymas, and cyma rectas. The last happened to be a signature molding of John Hemmings's, used on things he constructed at Monticello and Poplar Forest.[93] The

Fig. 75. Poplar Forest, original varnished walnut door made by John Hemmings or his nephews.

precise moldings for walls doors, windows, and fireplaces were secured to the plaster ground boards serving in a second function for wall attachments. The Hemingses were privileged among Monticello's enslaved population by being literate in the first place, taught by Jefferson's grandchildren, and then, more uncommonly, literate in the elements of classical architecture. Both kinds of literacy, and practical joinery skills, would mean everything when these young men passed from slavery into freedom and could command a respected livelihood.

When Jefferson returned to Monticello in the fall of 1819, he left his workforce at Poplar Forest to finish their tasks for the year. This marks an important moment when Jefferson trusted John Hemmings to work there independently. Before Jefferson departed for Monticello, he sent a letter to University of Virginia proctor Arthur S. Brockenbrough describing his terras roof in great detail. Ironically, the first letter John Hemmings sent to Jefferson two weeks after his departure reported that his personal roof system was leaking. Before the year was out, Hemmings would send five more letters to Jefferson, receiving two in return. This rare correspondence between enslaver and enslaved details the story of what John Hemmings and his nephews were accomplishing at Jefferson's retreat.

CORRESPONDING MILESTONES

The eight letters John Hemmings wrote to Jefferson in 1819–21 reveal a great deal about his own work ethic and his diligent process to complete his master's special place. On September 26, 1819, John Hemmings wrote his first known letter from Poplar Forest to Jefferson at Monticello. Hemmings informed his master that the new terras roof over the dining room was leaking. This was one of Jefferson's most ideal elements, and it had failed in performance. Hemmings described the conditions of the leak, how long it had rained, and exact descriptions of how the terras roof parts performed, or, in this case, didn't perform. He suggested a fix, but, since it involved dismantling some roof trim, he said he would await Jefferson's visit. Hemmings wrote again on October 20, informing Jefferson that he had finished the "ballustrading" (Chinese rail of the upper roof?), had hung the doors of the "partitions" (alcove vestibules?), and was now working on "shutters" (louvered blinds).[94] He was "now giting the insid stuff ready," meaning that his apprentices would be planing the poplar plank into moldings. Hemmings wrote again on November 2 to say they were still working on the blinds, that he needed locks and hinges for the stair pavilion doors, and that the blinds will be "troublesome to git right if the [they] ant [ain't] made with much correctness."[95] Hemmings closed his letter by saying, "I have spent a great deal of dissatisfaction by you not being able to return but I hop you will soon get the better of it." Jefferson replied that the priority for the blinds "should be for the girls room which needs them most" and that hinges were coming on the cart.[96] The cart would also bring a firkin of butter, some dried fruit, and a map that must be "put into one of the closed rooms where the rats cannot get at it."[97] Damage from rats was a common occurrence and another reason why Jefferson preferred solid brick walls or wood walls filled with bricks.[98]

Hemmings's next letter described how one night around midnight "there came up a brisk rain and it woke me and I got up and lit a candle and went upstairs and it was leaking badly and I sat up until daylight and went on the roof of the house and took off the shutters and raised up the plank and examined for the water."[99] This letter speaks to Hemmings's conscientiousness. He described the problem in great detail, his method for solving it, his experiment to test it, and the anticipated results, "in hopes you will take this as an eye witness." Jefferson must have been proud of Hemmings's work and appreciative of his descriptions. At the end of November 1819, he wrote to Hemmings:

> Write to me every Wednesday and put your letter the same day into the post office of New London or Lynchburg and it will be sure to be in Charlottesville on Saturday evening. In these letters state to me exactly what work is done, and what you will still have to do, and endeavor to guess at a day by which you think it may all be finished, that I may be ready to send for you by that day. If after all is finished, you should have a little time to spare before the cart arrives, employ yourself on the 2 blinds of the North portico. These will need only half blinds, to wit, over the lower sash to prevent people seeing into the rooms.[100]

As instructed, Hemmings replied on December 2 to say he would finish in nine days and that on December 12, "I should be putting everything away & pacting [*sic*] up my things."[101] Hemmings instructed Jefferson to inquire of his wife, Pricilla, and to find some mule harnesses in his cabin for the two-mule wagon that would bring Hemmings, his assistants, and his tools home. They had been working there since June, and Hemmings was eager to get home to Monticello.

Early in 1820 Jefferson again ordered lumber for use in the fall. Jefferson's first visit for ten days in September coincided with another leaking roof, but this time it was not the terras roof but the principal shingle roof for which he ordered more chestnut shingles.[102] In an earlier letter that month Jefferson noted that "John Hemings and his people" would be coming with him, and in another he mentioned that "John Hemings and his gang will go about the same time." The Hemings "gang" would have been finishing interior trim at this time. At the end of his second visit that year, a thirty-four-day stay in the fall, Jefferson gave John Hemmings his annual "gratuity" of twenty dollars, which he usually presented while at Poplar Forest; Burwell Colbert also typically received his twenty-dollar annual gratuity while at Poplar Forest. Before departing, Jefferson had written his Monticello overseer, "Send a spare mule also if you please for Johnny Hemings who cannot perform the journey on foot." John Hemmings was forty-four years old and deserving of a ride. Two years later, in 1822, Jefferson paid one dollar for spectacles to aid Hemmings in his work and letter writing.[103]

Jefferson made four trips to Poplar Forest in 1821 for a total of fifty-nine days. This was the longest sojourn in the last two years. After returning from his fourth visit in November, John Hemmings, who had stayed behind, wrote to Jefferson to report on his progress: "I am at worck in the morning by the time I can see and the very same at

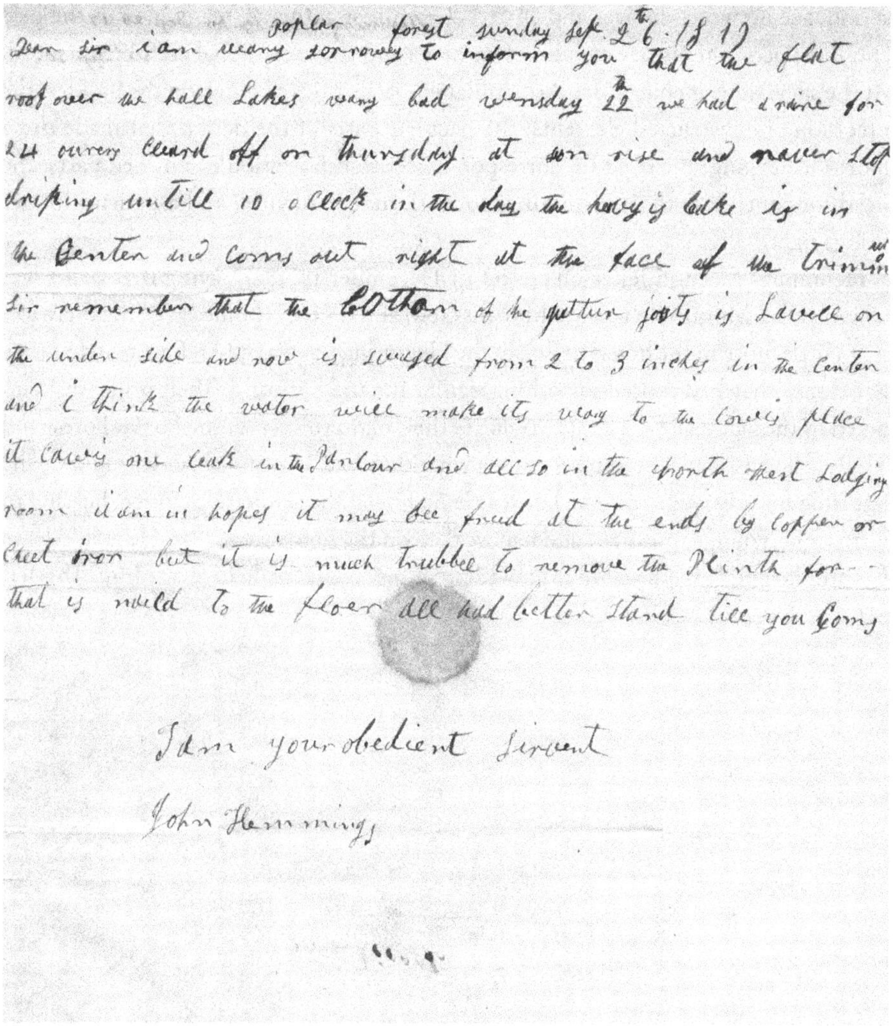

Poplar forest sunday sep 26. 1819

Dear sir i am veary sorrowey to inform you that the flat roof over the hall Lakes veary bad wensday 22th we had a raine for 24 ourers cleard off on thursday at son rise and never stop driping untill 10 oclock in the day the heavyis lake is in the center and coms out right at the face of the trimm[er] sir remember that the bottam of the gutter joists is Lavell on the under side and now is swaged from 2 to 3 inches in the Center and i think the water will make its way to the Lowes place it caus one leak in the Parlour and all so in the north west Lodging room i am in hopes it may bee fixed at the ends by copper or sheet iron but it is much trubbel to remove the Plinth for that is naild to the floor all had better stand till you Coms

I am your obedient servent

John Hemmings

Fig. 76. Letter from John Hemmings to Jefferson, 19 September 1826.

night. I have got the cornice nearly don. I am bout the tow last members dentil and quarter round. I should put an architrave on the skie light frame befour I take the Scaffold down. It will be 16 inchs leving the first face on the frame and planting on the twelve inches. This is ½ Inch thick and the ogee planted on it."[104] Hemmings's work ethic mimicked Jefferson's, who claimed the sun never caught him in bed. Hemmings typically went into great detail about the ogee molding and the other classical parts so that Jefferson would get a clear picture of what he had accomplished. The following month Hemmings reported with great pride that he had finished all of the interior moldings except the sur base (chair rail) that he was about to complete. He seemed especially proud of one item: "Putting the architrave on the skey light has made all the improvement imaginable."[105] The last big job was making the large dining room entablature; the parlor entablature would not be done for some years. This one-year correspondence between enslaver and enslaved, architect and craftsman, gives us the best and most personal history of John Hemmings and the exceptional craft he practiced. At the same time, it epitomizes the familiar characteristics of Jefferson the builder: the precision of constructed elements; the peculiar parts of the design that made them more challenging; the need for correspondence; transportation of finished parts; the need for control; faith in Hemmings to work independently; and a patience to get things right.

Hemmings received Jefferson's letter of December 18, 1821, saying that a cart was coming from Monticello to carry him, his crew, and his tools home.[106] While there was still a little more in the house to finish, the Hemmings crew could reflect on what they had done. They had crafted something significant and beautiful. Their pride was tempered by the fact that few people would see their masterpiece, yet the Poplar Forest and Monticello enslaved communities knew what they had accomplished. It would be the last time Beverly would see the house. He had been the senior apprentice, helping to instruct his younger brothers, and had worked on the house since 1815. He would leave Monticello and "disappear" in 1822, with no effort being made to locate him. This left

Fig. 77. Poplar Forest, base, surbase (chair rail), and door architrave moldings, 2021.

John with his other two nephew assistants. Beverly, Madison, and Eston had absorbed valuable professional and life lessons from their uncle—what they might have learned from working in close proximity to their father, and whether he expressed pride in their work, we will never know.

When Jefferson came for a short visit in the spring of 1822, he enjoyed an almost completed retreat house. It had been sixteen years in the making, and he would savor it for only one more year. Walking in the north portico door into the entrance passage, he saw above him the impressive Tuscan order entablature that commanded that narrow space. He could see through the house through the three sets of glass doors John Hemmings had made. It was the bright illumination from the skylight, however, that drew him ahead into the central room. His gaze immediately went upward to the large Doric order entablature that the Hemings men had labored over that surmounted the dining room's 20-foot-high walls. It was not yet finished, lacking its frieze ornaments, but the pleasure in seeing this element, in this special room, in his special house, had to have been one of his most memorable in recent years. These ornaments would be the subject of many letters in the next few years. Jefferson's life had been one associated with correct classical orders of architecture and this one, near the end of that life, had special meaning.

ORNAMENTAL DISTINCTION

An essential finishing touch at Poplar Forest was the work of English artist and sculptor William Coffee. He became known to Jefferson in March 1818 through Jefferson's friend Wilson Cary Nicholas. Coffee had come down from New York City to Richmond and had executed a terra cotta bust of Mrs. Nicholas. Nicholas suggested that Coffee sculpt a bust of Jefferson. Jefferson first cordially dismissed Nicholas's suggestion, due to a bad experience with a life mask years earlier. Nicholas ensured him that Coffee's method was safe, and Jefferson relented, saying he would be Coffee's "mannequin." Jefferson was immediately taken with Coffee, who modeled his bust and that of his daughter and a granddaughter. Coffee would go on to model terra cotta busts for some of the best-known Virginia families.

On March 16, 1820, Jefferson wrote his Poplar Forest overseer that Mr. Coffee, an "eminent artist in statuary and painting," would be stopping to see the house and could stay overnight if necessary, and that Hannah could accommodate him with "coffee, tea, sugar, wine, etc in the house."[107] Jefferson added, "I have a great regard for him."[108] This was the only instance in which Jefferson allowed someone to use Poplar Forest without his presence, and he obviously felt it was important to do so. The reason for Coffee's trip was to examine the dining room entablature that John Hemmings was constructing. Coffee made a third trip to see Jefferson at Monticello in February 1822. It was no doubt on this trip that Jefferson relayed to Coffee what he wanted at Poplar Forest and at the University of Virginia, relying both on his architectural books and examples on the Monticello walls. No other correspondence exists for the University ornaments regarding their sources except for an agreement between Coffee and the University in

March 1822 and a later invoice that did not go into specific sources.[109] Jefferson's letter to the sculptor that June stated: "When in Bedford [that May] I examined the Doric entablature for which I should want ornaments, on the model of that of the Thermae of Dioclesian, of which you took a note. My room will require 16 of the human busts, 20 oxsculls entire, and 4 other oxsculls cut in halves and mitered for the 4 corners, to be of composition. The spaces for the metopes are 15.I. high and 14. I. wide."[110] In his return letter to Jefferson, Coffee confessed he was suspicious of a misunderstanding about the Doric dining room ornaments.[111] The Roman Doric order from the Baths of Diocletian that was proposed for the Poplar Forest dining room, the exterior of Pavilion I and parlors of Pavilions VI and IX at the University, and used on the north portico at Monticello, should have the "human bust" (Apollo) alone and not mixed with skulls. Coffee stated that he had consulted his Nicholson book (*Principles of Architecture,* 1809) for the Baths of Diocletian order and saw no ox skulls. Nicholson's book, which Jefferson apparently did not own, was also referenced by Arthur Brockenbrough regarding the frieze ornaments of Pavilion II. Brockenbrough also suggested that the exterior trim of the pavilions would look better in a stone color rather than "perfectly white."[112]

Coffee could be excused for thinking he or Jefferson made a mistake as he consulted his sources for the Baths of Diocletian Doric order. Coffee was correct about what Jefferson had used at Monticello and had proposed for the University. His confusion stemmed from the difference with the Poplar Forest order. In one of the most important letters about Poplar Forest, Jefferson set Coffee straight:

> Your [*sic*] are right in what you have thought and done as to the metops of our Doric pavilion [at the University]. Those of the baths of Diocletian are all human faces, and so are to be those of our Doric pavilion. But in my middle room at Poplar Forest, I mean to mix the faces and ox-sculls, a fancy which I can indulge in my own case, altho, in a public work I feel bound to follow authority strictly. The mitred ox-sculls for my room are for it's inner angles.
>
> The other room in that house of which I meant to ornament the frize, is the Ionic of the temple of Fortuna virilis. My frize is 5. I. wide, very nearly, I believe, of the breadth of those of the Ionics you have to do for some of the rooms of the Pavilions. I will request you to make for me 80. Feet, running measure of that, of composition. . . . I shall be glad to receive the ornaments for my rooms early in September when my workman will go to Poplar Forest.[113]

Jefferson verified that the Poplar Forest parlor would have an Ionic order entablature based on the Temple of Fortuna Virilis. This was like the one Coffee was making for the exterior of Pavilion II and for the parlors of Pavilions I and VII at the University; it was also like the one in Jefferson's own bed chamber at Monticello. For the dining room, however, Jefferson explained he wanted to mix "ox-sculls" with the "faces."[114] He acknowledged departure from the "authority" of the classical prototype, saying it

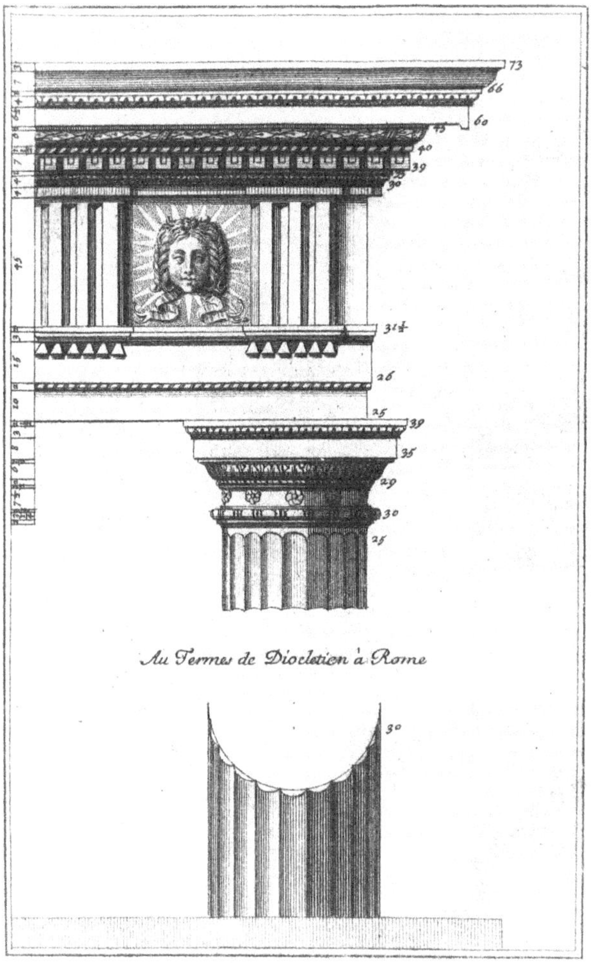

Fig. 78. Roman Doric order from Baths of Diocletian used for dining room entablature, from Freart de Chambray, *Parallèle de l'architecture antique avec la moderne* (1766).

was his "fancy," justified because of the private nature of the house. Jefferson's explanation sums up the very personal nature of Poplar Forest. The details were for Jefferson's eyes only. At Monticello and at the University, "authority" required that these more public examples (and we can consider Monticello public) be proper ornaments for educational reasons, like the different facades of each of the University pavilions. An entablature for Jefferson's fancy rested on the same rationale as building a near perfect work of architecture that was rarely shared or seen. It was intended for the owner's gratification and inspiration. Why Jefferson chose certain Roman entablatures and ornaments, whether for their symbolism or just personal preference for their design, he never says. It is tempting to think he chose the Baths of Diocletian because Emperor Diocletian was primarily remembered for peacefully retiring from public office to work in the garden of his retirement villa.

The ornaments for both the University and Poplar Forest were shipped from New York City in December 1822. Coffee's invoice for the Poplar Forest ornaments was for

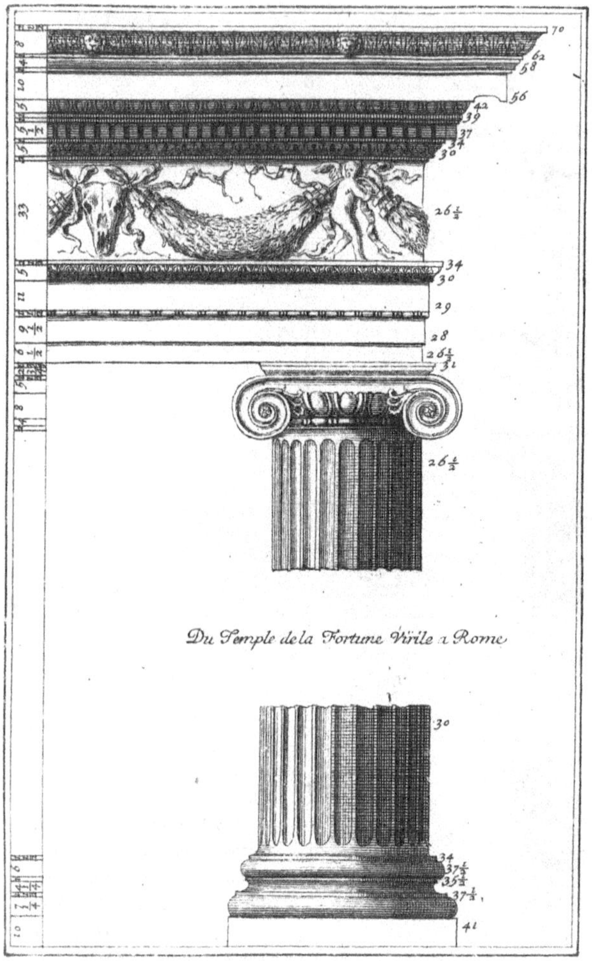

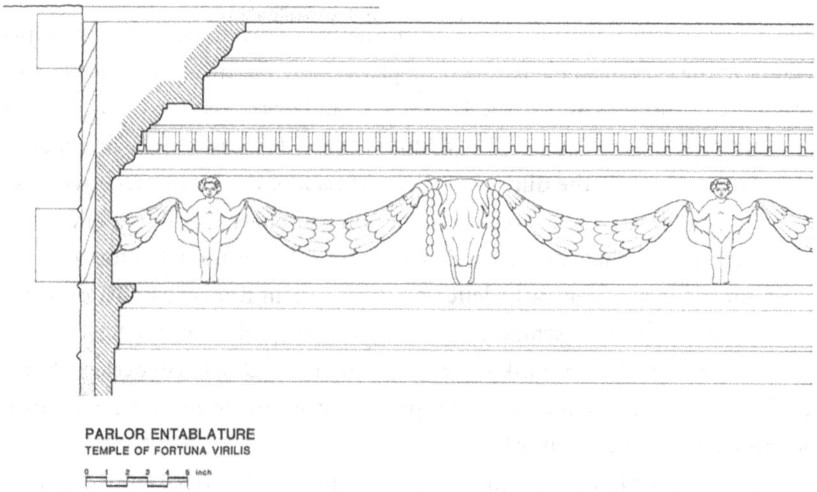

Fig. 79. Roman Ionic order from Temple of Fortuna Virilis for parlor entablature; illustration from Freart de Chambray, *Parallèle de l'architecture antique avec la moderne* (1766); and drawing by Mesick Cohen Wilson Baker Architects.

Fig. 80. Poplar Forest dining room entablature based on Baths of Diocletian as designed by Jefferson with added bucrania, 2022.

20 human masks in composition, 24 ox skulls in composition, and 80 feet of swag and boy frieze in composition.[115] In his letter of January 3, 1823, Coffee gave instructions for the installation of the ornaments. The very detailed instructions were for John Hemmings, mentioned by name, who would glue and screw the numbered pieces together on the entablature's wooden frieze board. Coffee had evidently met John Hemmings and knew that he could be entrusted to install the ornaments. Jefferson questioned Coffee as to whether the ornaments, referred to as composition, weren't "the nature of potter's ware." He offered that "if the ornaments of burnt clay succeed we may perhaps venture to call for those of the Rotunda in the same material, which I should expect to stand weather as well as lead."[116] Coffee replied that the "composition ornaments are not of the nature of Potters ware" but had been hardened by fire and would "stand any climate equal to marble."[117] Analysis of the Poplar Forest ornaments indicates that they were potter's ware, or terra cotta. The ribbons under Apollo's head were in lead owing to their thinness, Coffee noted. When ornaments for the University were found to be broken in shipment, Jefferson speculated that if they had been real composition they might have fared better.[118] The shipment proved to be a problem in other ways as well. Jefferson's Richmond merchant assumed Coffee had made a mistake and sent the Poplar Forest boxes to Monticello. Jefferson wrote, "I hope I may remedy by bedding my boxes in a good quantity of straw in the wagon."[119]

In May 1823 Jefferson made his last trip to Poplar Forest to settle his grandson there. It is likely that he did not see the dining room entablature ornaments in place when he arrived. Physical evidence confirms they were indeed installed, but a letter from Hemmings indicates they were put up later.[120] Still, seeing the completed wooden parts of the large Baths of Diocletian entablature was a fitting treat for Jefferson's last glimpse of his long-maturing personal retreat. Hemmings had yet to install the wooden parts for the parlor's Ionic order entablature, waiting once again for a lumber order. In 1825 William Coffee proposed a visit to see Jefferson at his "mansione of Hospitality" but

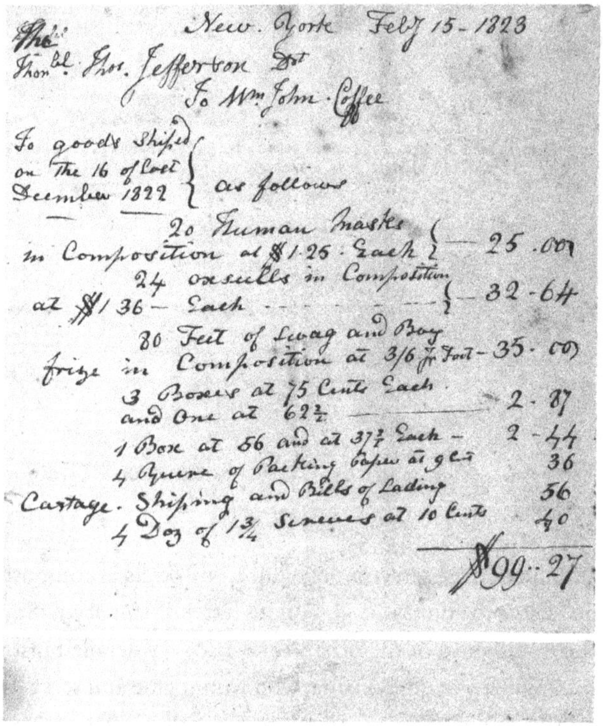

New York Feby 15-1823
The Honbl. Thos. Jefferson Dr
To Wm John Coffee

To goods Shiped on The 16 of Last December 1822 } as follows

20 Human Masks in Composition at $1.25 Each	25.00
24 Oxsculls in Composition at $1.36 Each	32.64
80 Feet of Swag and Bay frize in Composition at 3/6 pr Foot	35.00
3 Boxes at 75 Cents Each and One at 62½	2.87
1 Box at 56 and at 37½ Each	2.44
4 Quire of Packing Paper at 9 Cts	36
Cartage. Shipping and Bills of Lading	56
4 Doz of 1¾ Screws at 10 Cents	40
	$99.27

Fig. 81. William Coffee invoice for Poplar Forest entablature ornaments

never came. In his last letter that year Coffee offered his services to teach "the Arts" at the University of Virginia, for which he had made so many ornaments, and closed with, "I Paint Landscapes and Portraits tolerable well."[121] His entablature ornaments would have to suffice for his artistic contributions there.

The Final Era of Construction: 1824–26

The beginning of Francis Eppes's residency in 1823 and Jefferson's death in 1826 bookmark the final era of construction at Poplar Forest. Francis Eppes became a favored grandchild after his mother, Maria, died in 1804, when her son was three. Jefferson offered to provide a house and property for Francis since he had once promised one to Maria and her husband, John Wayles Eppes. Jefferson had even claimed that his Poplar Forest design had been intended for the Eppeses on his Pantops Mountain property near Monticello. It is hard to believe this claim since the Poplar Forest design so fit Jefferson's purpose and use as a retreat. Regardless, Jefferson promised that Poplar Forest would eventually be given over to Francis. Jefferson had directed Francis's education with the intention that he would enter the law, but in 1822, having turned twenty-one, Francis proposed marriage to Mary Elizabeth Cleland Randolph.[122] In an exchange of letters Jefferson and Francis's father both lamented the disruption in Francis's education, but, it "being a case not under the jurisdiction of reason, we must acquiesce and make the best of it."[123] Francis's father only insisted that he own property before his marriage. Jefferson reluctantly agreed that Poplar Forest would immediately become the couple's property after their marriage that November. Jefferson had no doubt looked forward to more years at his retreat just at the age when he craved even more peace and solitude. Nevertheless, Francis was given Poplar Forest with 1,000 acres, along with the enslaved population there. Jefferson planned one more trip to Poplar Forest. He had written to his Bedford neighbor William Radford: "The accident of a fractured arm is to confine me till Xmas day as my physician tells me. It will then be too cold for me to go to Bedford until the spring. In April I shall go to settle my grandson Fr. Eppes at the Pop. For.... He was married two days ago and his newly acquired spouse will add to your neighborhood a most amiable and valued member."[124] On May 14, 1823, Jefferson set off on his final trip to Poplar Forest to see the newlyweds settled in the retreat he had expended so much energy and experienced such happiness constructing. The travel party included Jefferson's daughter Martha and granddaughters Cornelia and Virginia, making for an unusually full house. Jefferson would have rejoiced at seeing the dining room entablature again, but ironically he was now a visitor in his own house and would have been forced to stay in one of the small bed chambers. He might have proudly explained some of the unusual features of the house to Mary Elizabeth, who would come to resent its isolation and even complain of some of its modern features. When the party returned to Monticello, Virginia wrote a friend, "what a pleasant visit we have had to Bedford, and that Grand Papa bore the fatigue of the journey was well as usual."[125] The friend from nearby Liberty (now the town of Bedford) wrote back, "I fear I shall never have the pleasure to see Mr. Jefferson again," which was true.[126] The fatigue of the return journey would have been the heavier, as was his heart, from seeing Poplar Forest for the last time.

Francis and Mary Elizabeth failed to appreciate the finished nature of Poplar Forest, much less the personal investment of ideas spent on its design. The newlyweds certainly did not enjoy the remoteness that Jefferson loved. Francis had written his cousin Nicholas Trist about a visit: "I can offer you what you have so long desired—solitude and books—uninterrupted solitude, if you wish it. We are not much pestered with company I can assure you."[127] When Francis learned that Jefferson's scheme to save Monticello through a legislative lottery had failed, he offered to return the property. Martha J. Randolph had confessed to her daughter Ellen that "Francis was so much dissatisfied with the house at Poplar Forest" that he had offered to sell it to his cousin.[128] Jefferson had painted the cozy picture of strolling with his granddaughters on the wing terras in the evening with the bats and the owls; Francis was said to be "heartily sick of: 'solitude and the screech owl.'"[129]

Francis Eppes unnaturally settled into his new life on the remote Poplar Forest plantation. Jefferson perhaps knew the nature of his grandson when he wrote him: "A Virginia estate requires skill and attention. Skill I had not, and attention I could not have. That was engrossed by more imperious calls, which after acceptance had a right of preference to all others. The wonder rather is that I should have been so long in years in arriving at the ultimate and unavoidable result."[130] Jefferson's frank admission was meant to convince Francis that a career in law would be a wise supplemental career not tied to the risks befalling a farmer. Francis did not follow this advice but eventually made good account of himself, albeit after Jefferson's death and outside of Virginia.

In the Eppeses' tenure, 1823–28, changes to the house were due to an accident, deterioration, and the last item of decoration. This is also the final era of correspondence between Jefferson and John Hemmings and the final work on the house over which Jefferson had any control. Of the five additional known letters written by John Hemmings, four to Jefferson discuss these changes to the house, and one more to Jefferson's granddaughter referred to his work there.

Two years after the Eppeses had been established at Poplar Forest, Jefferson wrote in February 1825 anxiously asking about the damage of a fire "indirectly & indistinctly" reported by friends. Jefferson waited "in hopes you would inform me of the particulars that I might know how far I could help you. I will spare J. Hem. To you & his two aids and he can repair everything of wood as well or perhaps better than any body there."[131] As in old times Jefferson went on to recommend stock be sent to Captain Martin's mill, "while his mill has water to spare. I used to cut & haul him stocks." Knowing Eppes was not a builder, Jefferson conveyed his knowledge of materials and recommended John Hemmings "& his two aids," who by this time were Madison, age twenty, and Eston, age seventeen. Eppes explained that a fire in the northwest chimney had burned about 2,000 shingles, portions of the balustrade, the terras deck above the dining room, and the Chinese railing. Jefferson would have been relieved to learn that the "cornice of the dining room was saved by the thickness of the plaistering."[132] In the same letter Francis reported, "Thinking your carpenters engaged, I had the roof repaired in a temporary manner with slabs, and had intended to make my carpenter tho' a rough hand, reshingle the whole if you think it desirable, but the balustrade and railing are I am afraid beyond his art." Whether this carpenter was one of the enslaved population we don't know, but the job was one for a joiner. Francis's letter gave more bad news: the terras roof joists and deck of the wing were "rotted completely, and nothing but an entire renewal can render the offices again habitable." Francis would have been much more concerned about the service functions below the deck than about strolling on top. He could not have had the same need and appreciation as his grandfather for the wing's unique roof system and all that it allowed. Jefferson replied: "John Hemings and his two aids have been engaged in covering this house with tin which is not yet finished. They shall repair to your assistance as soon as I can accompany them."[133] This was wishful thinking: Jefferson never set foot in Bedford County again. He offered his grandson advice for getting lumber milled to repair the wing roof and, in his patient, optimistic manner, said, "we can make the gutters in a different way which will for ever [*sic*] protect the joists from decay." He was tweaking his special roof design one final time. He had a plan for the main house roof as well: "I will desire Colo. Peyton to send up tin for covering the dwelling house."[134] Characteristically Jefferson was upgrading the roof covering from wood to a fireproof tin that he had opted for at Monticello and the University of Virginia. Jefferson's order for tin through his Richmond merchant

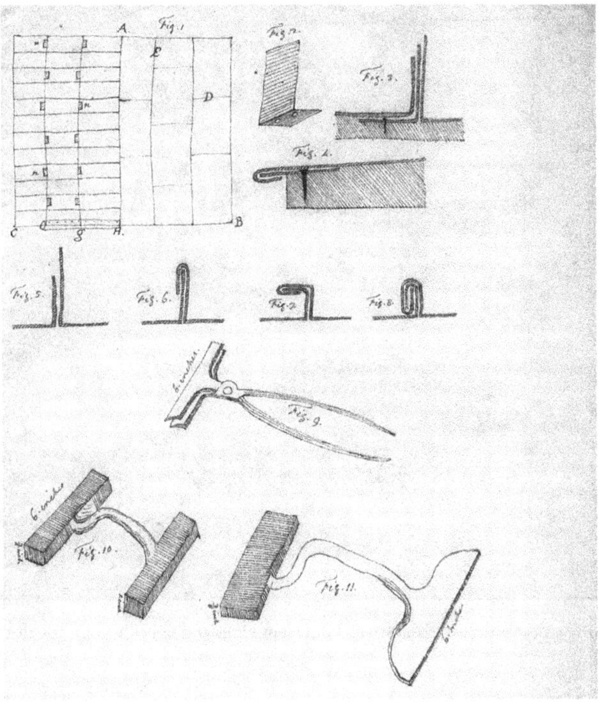

Fig. 82. Jefferson drawing, undated, for tin-coated shingles, tools, and directions for installation.

set into motion once again the distant movement of imported materials that had long been the custom for Poplar Forest.

That summer in 1825 John Hemmings found himself back at Poplar Forest and writing to Jefferson once again. He started his letter with: "Dear Sir I hope this few may find you well and in good health. we begin to tin the west side of the house . . . the rouft [roof] is so ruff that I am fost [forced] to imploy both of the boys."[135] The "boys" were young men now but still learning from their uncle, who was a forty-nine-year-old man wearing spectacles. Eppes faced the old persistent problem of getting a bill of lumber cut. Hemmings reported: "The owners of the saw mills wont agree to cut their timber trees at this seson for feare of the worms [killing] thee trees. Mr. Hiks tells me thars [*sic*] a man 25 miles off that says he will let him have it if he lets him have the haling and then says he wold deliver it for 5 dollars pay a hundred."[136] In his next letter, the following month, Hemmings reported that he had installed 15 boxes of tin but needed more. More wood was being hauled to the site, and he had had a conversation with Eppes about "tining the flat rouff [roof] over the hall."[137] More importantly, he said, "we should go about preparing the chines [Chinese] railing & putting up the ornaments of the hall."[138] Hemmings not only referred to the dining room as an old-fashioned hall, he confirmed the presence of a Chinese railing on the roof. His letter also indicated that the entablature ornaments were finally being installed.

Jefferson's last known letter to John Hemmings, on August 17, 1825 was in regard to his special terras roof. He responded to Hemmings's letter saying that using tin for

Fig. 83. Poplar Forest Chinese railing originally constructed in 1819 by John Hemmings and only known through a Hemings letter.

the terras roof would be a useless expense "because shingles will turn the water as well, and it would be no guard against fire as a plank floor is to be laid over them."[139] He mentioned the deck of the wing being of oak rather than "dear and distant heart pine" and said, "I believe you have the drawings." These were undoubtedly drawings used for the third or fourth time for the Monticello and Poplar Forest terras roof systems. This would be the last time they were needed. Jefferson also stated: "You will have to make up your mind to go once more to Bedford, to put up the entablature of the parlour. You know that the carved members are done, and the ornaments of the frieze ready. Before you come away examine the plank on hand of what we got for that cornice, and give Mr. Eppes a bill of what will be wanting to finish it, that it may be got at once and seasoned."[140] The "carved members" would have been the architrave and the cornice of the Ionic order entablature. The Temple of Fortuna Virilis ornaments would be the boy, swag, and bucrania pieces made several years before by William Coffee. Jefferson supposed that the lumber was on hand for the installation of the last finished portion of the interior.

Hemmings replied to Jefferson that there was oak and poplar "for the parlour cornice this fall. . . . I hope by the next to be able to let you no when I shall finich and when to send for me. Dear Sir I hope you well."[141] From this letter we can reasonably assume that the parlor entablature was installed, finishing the last member of the Roman classical details that mattered more to Jefferson than to his grandson. Francis and Elizabeth would have wanted their parlor finished after staring at the bare brick at the top of the wall for so long, but Jefferson's need was much greater. The entablature represented the final important piece in the most important room, and he still envisioned his family living there for many years to come. The next-to-last known letter from John Hemmings, written to Jefferson's granddaughter Septimia Randolph from Poplar Forest that August, inquired about Jefferson's health and that of the family. He reported: "I should gite don the house on Tuesday that is tining it. We have all the teeraste to do yet wich is one hundred feet Long and 22 feet 8 inches wide. Yesterday we just had one lode of the stuff brought home for the gutters and that is 25 miles off where it came from. I am in hope I shall be able to com home by the 25 of November. If life last."[142] It is remarkable that Hemmings would describe his work in such detail, but it speaks to the pride he still took in that work. By that fall in 1825 Hemmings was eager to return home to his wife, Pricilla, to his cabin on Mulberry Row, and to the Jefferson grandchildren with whom he had special relationships. In the last letter to Jefferson, John Hemmings wrote that he would be finished the first week in October and that the mules and the familiar cart should be sent from Monticello if "You please for me to ride" and for "the tools I shall bring home that have bin here some time."[143] John Hemmings deserved to ride back; it would be his last return trip of many that had started in 1815, when he was thirty-nine; he was now ten years older. Over those years he had been there he personally and proudly made most of the finished classical elements so important to Jefferson. Those which he hadn't made he had lovingly directed his nephews to make. Back at Monticello, Hemmings and his "aids" would still have plenty of maintenance work to do on a large house whose exterior elements were now decades old. Years earlier John Dix's description of Monticello in 1820 portrayed the architectural decline that Hemmings would have to keep up with: "The mansion of Mr. Jefferson, like its illustrative occupant, is rapidly hastening to decay. The effects of time are left unrepaired to grow into evidences of neglect and dilapidation. But in this state it harmonizes with the relations of its Sage. It holds a character of unique & solitary grandeur, elevated above the surface of ordinary things, but wasting into ruin under the attribution of years."[144] Nevertheless, the "faultless specimen of Italian architecture" that Dix described still showed the grandeur of John Hemmings's work, although it must have pained the craftsman to see it, and his master, slowly decay.

The final correspondence about an architectural element at Poplar Forest came at the very end of Jefferson's life and would have caused him great concern. A week before Jefferson died in 1826, a letter from Francis in late June bore unwelcome news. Francis wrote: "Knowing that all your pavilions at the University have tin coverings, I write to learn whether they have ever leaked, and if so what method of prevention has been used. Our roof here was perfectly close until about mid winter. It then began to leak not in one but a hundred places."[145] Eppes went on to describe his inspection of the roof that led to the conclusion that water was being drawn up under the edges of shingles:

> The plaistering of the parlour is so entirely wet every rain, that I begin to fear it will fall in. Large buckets of water pass through it. Your room is nearly as bad and the others leak more and more in every rain. The hall is in fact, the only dry room in the house. I have

been so completely baffled in every attempt to stop the leaking, that I really feel quite at a loss; we have had here, in the last four weeks, three of the most destructive rains every known in this neighborhood.[146]

Such a comprehensive roof failure threatened the entire house on which Jefferson had expended so much time, thought, and effort. Jefferson was too ill, and possibly too upset, to answer his grandson's letter. He died knowing that, although John Hemmings would be freed upon his death, he still had the assistance of Madison and Eston, who would be under their uncle's control. But they would never work at Poplar Forest again. Eppes wrote to his cousin that September: "I have just had workman here examining the roof of the house. there appears to be a radical fault in the putting on of the tin which can be remedied only, by removing and recutting it. He made an estimate of the expense including the loss at $185 and I have engaged him thereupon to recover the house. so much for J.H. god dam him!"[147] Eppes's Poplar Forest journal indeed documents that he engaged a "tinner" in 1826 and bought $80 worth of tin from "Warrick" for the job, which the tinner warranted for five years.[148] The fact that John Hemmings might have made a mistake, in putting on whole rather than half-size shingles, would have been a blow to Jefferson, who thought Hemmings could do no wrong. Word of the mistake must have gotten back to Hemmings, who would not have been pleased, especially knowing that Eppes had handed the job over to someone else. Jefferson's optimistic intention of covering the roof with an innovative material thus ended on a sad note.

Jefferson died still thinking his beloved Poplar Forest would remain in family hands, even if he knew that would not be the case with Monticello. He was spared the disappointment. The year after Jefferson's death Mary Elizabeth expressed her personal feelings about Poplar Forest and the Eppeses' economic prospects in a letter:

> These gullied worn out fields, and this unfinished leaking hull of a house . . . [has] become more than ever distasteful to both Francis and myself, and we needed little before to render them altogether odious. Tobacco is the only thing which can be made here, and after vast labour and expense, in raising and manufacturing the vile weed, and acquiring both skill and judgement in the business, to find still that no profit must be expected, is disheartening indeed, and Francis who began with sanguine hopes on the subject is now as much wearied and sickened with a planters life, as I who from the first abhorred it.[149]

Francis and Mary Elizabeth would stay there only two more years before leaving Virginia, like so many other young men at the time, for better economic horizons. Francis wrote to his cousin Nicholas Trist: "What say you to a general move to a more southern latitude. I want to go where I can make more money. . . . What say you to Florida, or Kentucki, or Tenessee, or Missouri? I will go any where so that we may all settle together: but from accounts lately received should greatly prefer E. Florida. I am told that money and health, are the spontaneous productions of that soil. . . . Here lies the road to wealth!"[150] Francis and family headed for the newest American frontier: Florida.[151] Francis would be one of the pioneers of Tallahassee, living in a log house before becoming more established in a proper mansion befitting his eventual role as governor of the state. He was one of the founders of the Episcopal Church in Florida and helped found a college (now Florida State). After the Civil War Francis and family were financially forced to leave Tallahassee to become pioneers once again, this time moving farther south to the Orlando area, where they started an orange grove. Jefferson had no idea that Francis wanted to bail out of economically depressed Virginia and leave his bespoke retreat home. Ironically, two months before Jefferson's death in 1826, A. B. Woodward sent him from Tallahassee "twelve seeds of the indigenous orange of Florida."[152]

5

LANDSCAPES OF USE AND ORNAMENT

In April 1813 Jefferson wrote his son-in-law, John Wayles Eppes, reporting on the status of Poplar Forest, since it was intended to be the future home of Eppes's son Francis. In that letter he stated he had "laid off a handsome curtilage connecting the house with the Tomahawk, have inclosed and divided it into suitable appendages to a Dwelling house, and have begun it's improvement by planting trees of use and ornament."[1] Like any subject he turned his mind to, Thomas Jefferson focused as much careful attention on plants of use as he did ones of ornament. Specifying the layout of his vegetable garden and the details of its perimeter fence was given no less planning than the location, size, and flower species of an ornamental bed. His need and desire to shape his environment at Poplar Forest can be seen on different levels, all mediating between the ideal and the circumstantial; between the aesthetic and the practical; between the natural landscape and Jefferson's desire to control it. The different aspects are: the natural environment and characteristics of the land; the man-made changes related to the plantation landscape and its enslaved population who worked it; the landscape gardening designs of beauty for the context of the house; and Jefferson's "culture of the earth" in his fruit and vegetable gardens. Understanding how these landscape features relate to Jefferson's practice at Monticello is no less important than perceiving his architectural precedents. For Thomas Jefferson architecture and its surrounding landscape were closely aligned aspects reflected in his holistic approach to conceiving and designing his dwellings, for either his principal home or his villa retreat. How did Jefferson's landscape improvements at Poplar Forest, concentrated in two periods, 1811–12 and 1815–16, reflect its nature and character?[2]

Having settled into a routine of visiting Poplar Forest from two to four times a year, Jefferson attended to his absent friends through letters. In 1811 he wrote from Poplar Forest to his good friend, the famous painter Charles Willson Peale, about their respective farming endeavors, saying, "Here, you know, we are all farmers."[3] At that time, and before his landscape improvements, Jefferson humbly told Peale that "we cannot give to our grounds that stile of beauty which satisfies the eye of the amateur." What he was giving to his grounds at Monticello was significantly beautiful, even if still evolving. At Poplar Forest he had not yet started significant improvements, but he conveyed to Peale his interest in a letter from there:

> I have often thought that if heaven had given me choice of my position and calling, it should have been on a rich spot of earth, well watered and near a good market for the productions of the garden. No occupation is so delightful to me as the culture of the earth, and no culture comparable to that of the garden. Such a variety of subjects, some are always coming to perfection, the failure of one thing repaired by the success of another, and instead of one harvest, a continued one through the year. Under a total want of demand except for our family table, I am still devoted to the garden, but tho an old man, I am but a young gardener.[4]

Jefferson's statement to Peale echoed one very similar from the ancient writer Columella describing his desire, "If Fortune would favor me," for the site of an ideal villa.[5] Jefferson's return to studying the classics at his own neoclassical villa retreat could have reinforced thoughts of rural virtues and shaping the Poplar Forest gardens.

Landscapes of Use

Jefferson euphemistically called himself a farmer in his letter to Peale. Neither spoken nor acknowledged, of course, was the southern economic system of essential cash crops made possible by enslaved workers. Poplar Forest had been a small tobacco plantation when Jefferson inherited it in 1773, and he had slowly increased its yield of crops and the number of enslaved men and women who labored for that income.[6] The culture of tobacco and wheat at Poplar Forest was no different from the seasonal cycles of those crops grown on the Monticello farms which required constant coordination and supervision.[7] Back in the bosom of his family at Monticello the retired president had actively turned to his neglected farms and gardens. He had admitted a number of times he was "unskillful" as a plantation manager and that it was not his inclination to be one, but he could say that "rural improvement" was "the least chequered by the way-ward occurrences of life."[8] He wrote several friends that "the occupations of the garden, the workshops, & the farms fill up the whole" of his days.[9] To another: "my garden & farms occupy me closely from breakfast to dinner, after which it is my habit to lounge, so that I read little."[10]

Jefferson's letter to Peale emphasized the "culture of the earth" and the culture of the garden. As Peter Hatch has written, Jefferson's vegetable garden at Monticello was his chief and revolutionary horticultural achievement, which was unrivaled in America for its rare and unusual species.[11] Vegetables were extremely important to Jefferson, who stated that he ate little animal food and used that "as a condiment for the vegetables which constitutes my principal diet."[12] Although not of the same scale as Monticello, the Poplar Forest garden reflected Jefferson's obsession with many types of vegetables. As Hatch has noted, Jefferson's vegetable garden was also an extension of his Enlightenment mind, which measured, counted, and recorded growth and produce. The garden also represented Jefferson's scientific mind through the numerous records in the Garden Book of time/labor studies and experiments with exposure, soils, and placement, as well as seasonal dates when fruits and vegetables were first brought to the table. Characteristically Jefferson created his own "Kalendar" of flowers, fruit, and vegetables with column headings of "what, where, sowed, transplanted, come to table, gone, seed gathered, and observations," which he freely shared with friends.[13]

Although Jefferson ranked his own gardening skills as a "zealous Amateur," he was a serious student and preferred a recommended system for garden design and planting advice.[14] He found this in Bernard McMahon's *The American Gardener's Calendar,* published in 1806. McMahon became Jefferson's "gardening mentor" and his book Jefferson's gardening "Bible."[15] The two men carried on a detailed correspondence for many years and shared plant seeds with each other. McMahon had taken Phillip Miller's *Gardener's Dictionary* and translated it for an American context. Jefferson would have appreciated the book's use of geometry for garden layouts that prescribed the size of squares, borders, and paths for large principal crops and border crops.

Jefferson's 1811 planting memorandum for Poplar Forest is a good example of his systematic organization of vegetables and berries in the area between two stables to the southeast of the main house.[16] In this memo he called out sections of the garden plot for gooseberries, grapes, rose bushes, bear grass, pinks, tomatoes, lettuce, raspberries, and asparagus, the last section being 80 feet long. As Hatch noted, Jefferson "fussed over his asparagus far more than any other vegetable" and "carefully amended [his] beds" because it was an investment that would yield results for up to twenty years.[17] Like any gardener anticipating future harvests, Jefferson directed his Poplar Forest overseer that if a "thimbleful of seed [lettuce] could be sowed every other Monday, on a bed of 4. f. wide & 6. Or 8. feet long it would be best, as I should then always find some fit for use when I come."[18] Jefferson generously shared his plants and gardening advice with his Poplar Forest neighbors. The leafy plant salsify, Jefferson told Charles Clay, remarkably could be fried in batter for a taste mimicking oysters.[19]

The retired president was particularly fond of fruit trees, which required greater patience. Some were planted at Poplar Forest as early as 1782, so that by 1809 peach, apple, and cherry trees were producing fruit. In 1815 Jefferson had written to his daughter that "we abound in the luxury of the peach."[20] Peaches were put up by Cate with the help of other enslaved laborers, who dried and preserved them for the family. Jefferson noted that it took 70 bushels of apples to make 120 gallons of cider, which was a staple table drink. Occasionally cider would be sent from Monticello to be stored along with the wine and beer in the house's deep cellar.

As he aged, Jefferson confided in friends that his physical limitations hampered the enjoyment he spent outdoors observing his gardens. As early as 1813 Jefferson wrote a friend from Poplar Forest, "I can walk no further than my garden."[21] Edible plants he would have inspected in the Poplar Forest kitchen gardens included tomatoes, lettuce, asparagus, carrots, salsify, spinach, haricots, kale, potatoes, peas, beans, squash, artichokes, gooseberries, raspberries, grapes, and two varieties of strawberries. The protection and laborious care of these large vegetable gardens, one 80 yards square, fell to enslaved garden workers. Nace, for instance, was instructed to plant artichoke roots sent from Monticello in the "locks of the fence within the large garden."[22] This might have been the "piquet fence" Jefferson specified in 1811 as being "7. feet high, & so close that a hare cannot get into it. It is 80 yards square, & will take, I suppose about 2400. rails 8. f. long, besides the running rails & stakes."[23] Curiously, Jefferson instructed in the same letter that "the sheep [are] to be folded in it every night."

A Shaped Landscape

Attention to "farm" operations yielded critical economic benefits, and that paid to gardens dietary benefits, but it was the oasis of landscaped pleasure gardens that most stimulated Jefferson. From his earliest days in Williamsburg he had acquired, and continued to acquire, important published works on landscape gardening, and he frequently corresponded with authors of the latest horticultural books. As remarkable and significant as Jefferson's ambitious academic architecture for Monticello I, his intended designs for its landscape were equally ambitious and are considered among the first reflections of picturesque English landscape gardening in America. He continued this education during his five years in France, through his English garden trip with John Adams, and was inspired by William Hamilton's Woodlands near Philadelphia. As Monticello had been Jefferson's "essay in architecture," so its landscape was a horticultural proving ground and reflected more mature ideas stemming from his European experience. Jefferson's ambitious designs for the President's House landscape got no further than his ideas to redesign the unfinished house's interior plan.[24] Because he was designing Poplar Forest from the President's House at this same time, some of his concepts for the Washington landscape were transferred into executed designs for the Bedford County site. The Poplar Forest landscape was a tabula rasa that offered Jefferson's fertile mind another landscape canvas on which to experiment.

Like the rich, lifelong fabric Jefferson wove in creating his own brand of neoclassicism, his developed taste for landscape gardening was equally rich with many threads. What William L. Beiswanger observed about Monticello's garden structures could easily stand for Jefferson's gardening designs: "the drawings and notes seem ample compensation for all that was unrealized or lost, for perhaps nowhere else in Jefferson's remarkable creative endeavors do we find such a wealth of ideas derived from architectural, historical, and literary sources."[25] In 1809 Jefferson's good friend Margaret Bayard Smith, upon visiting Monticello and hearing of his plans for Monticello II's landscaped gardens, thought Jefferson's abundant ideas would "require a whole life to carry into effect."[26] Young Jefferson's early concepts for the Monticello I landscape were certainly inspired by classical literature and the writings of Cicero, Horace, and

Pliny the Younger. It is also evident that as early as 1771 he was receptive to the natural style of English landscape gardening reflected in the writings of Alexander Pope, in William Shenstone's essay "Unconnected Thoughts on Gardening," and in Thomas Whately's published work *Observations on Modern Gardening*. Jefferson's serious study of landscape theory prior to his time in Europe established his "ideas on landscape gardening [that] were well established and were surprisingly little altered in succeeding years."[27] Although his fundamental concepts on landscape gardens might have already been formed, they were strongly reinforced by the many complex examples he keenly observed in both royal and private places. Most impactful was the relationship of architecture and landscape in private city and country houses where buildings opened to their surroundings. This concept would be significantly apparent in the designs of Monticello and Poplar Forest.[28]

Our knowledge of Jefferson's landscape designs for Poplar Forest comes from surviving landscape features, historic photographs, archaeology, and written documentation. Jefferson left many notes, drawings, and letters documenting his landscape designs and the flowers and trees he planted at Monticello and Poplar Forest.[29] Although there are comparative landscape clues for Monticello and the President's House, the nature of Poplar Forest and its site, its genius loci, resulted in a different type of landscape gardening. Thomas Whately, whose book Jefferson acquired in 1778, stressed the importance of respecting and using the character of each site:

> the business of a gardener is to select and to apply whatever is great, elegant, or characteristic in any of them [farm or park]; to discover and to show all the advantages of the place upon which he is employed; to supply its defects, to correct its faults, and to improve the beauties. . . . The style of every part must be accommodated to the character of the whole; for every piece of ground is distinguished by certain properties. . . . Whatever contributes to render the scenes of nature delightful, is amongst the subjects of gardening. . . . [N]othing is unworthy of the attention of a gardener, which can tend to improve his compositions. . . . The whole range of nature is open to him, from the parterre to the forest; and whatever is agreeable to the senses or the imagination, he may appropriate to the spot he is to improve.[30]

In 1786 Jefferson relied on Whately's book as his tour guide when seeing the English gardens with John Adams. The advice to use the genius loci, the spirit of the place, as a design template would already have been understood by Jefferson, who paid great attention to his surrounding environment and wrote descriptions of his native country in glowing terms, both its sublime as well as its beautiful scenes. As he once told his daughter, "There is not a sprig of grass that shoots uninteresting to me."[31] It is no surprise, then, that Jefferson would pay attention to the natural characteristics of his Bedford County environment and create a unique landscape at Poplar Forest that featured both formal as well as informal components, natural as well as created. He had observed French gardens that were composed of formal design elements mixed with naturalistic "jardin anglais" features. These seemingly incompatible ideas were not unlike the aesthetic shift from classicism and romanticism that Jefferson often bridged.[32]

Jefferson's final choice for his building site seems connected to a notable natural feature. The place name "Poplar Forest," established by the 1740s, referred to an actual forest of tulip poplar trees, a species described by Jefferson as the "junos of our groves."[33] The extent of this forest by the end of the eighteenth century is unknown but the prized old-growth lumber from the trees was being harvested for the house construction in 1806 and was still being harvested for the rebuilding in 1846. Jefferson marked out for bricklayer Hugh Chisolm the house site on a rise of land that had once been a tobacco field. To fill in this area north of the house within the circular road, Jefferson planted poplars to resemble a natural grove.[34] In addition to several instances of Jefferson ordering trees to be planted around the core and around the house, in undisclosed locations, an 1816 planting memorandum mentioned that 190 poplars had been planted "in the grounds" along with 5 Athenian poplars and 2 Kentucky locust trees "near house."[35] The planting of large specie trees near the house recalls Jefferson's description of his Gray's Ferry house on the Schuylkill River, where he lived and worked on the lawn under large shade trees. William Hamilton's Woodlands, near Gray's Ferry, Jefferson characterized as "the only rival [landscaped gardens] which I have known in America to what may be seen in England."[36] To Hamilton, Jefferson wrote his famous letter regarding the difference between natural European and American landscapes, apropos of his desire to improve the grounds of Monticello "in the style of the English gardens":

> Thither [to England] without doubt we are to go for models in this art. Their sunless climate has permitted them to adopt what is certainly a beauty of the very first order in landscape. Their canvas is of open ground, variegated with clumps of trees distributed with taste. They need more of wood than will serve to embrace a lawn or a glade. But under the beaming, constant and almost vertical sun of Virginia, shade is our Elysium. In the absence of this no beauty of the eye can be enjoyed. This organ must yield it's gratification to that of the other senses; without the hope of any equivalent to the beauty relinquished. The only substitute I have been able to imagine is this. Let your ground be covered with trees of the loftiest stature. Trim up their bodies as high as the constitution and form of the tree will bear, but so as their tops shall still unite and yield dense shade. A wood so open below will have nearly the appearance of open grounds. Then, when in the open ground you would plant a clump of trees, place a thicket of shrubs presenting a hemisphere the crown of which shall distinctly show itself under the branches of the trees. This may be affected by a due selection and arrangement of the shrubs, and will I think offer a group not much inferior to that of trees.[37]

This description suggests Jefferson's reason for planting so many large specie trees around the house, with a long view toward the mature results. Jefferson's planting of poplar trees in the ornamental core created a naturalistic and romantic aspect that was not incompatible with the more rational geometric plantings around the house.

Fig. 84. Old-growth poplar trees on north lawn of Poplar Forest seen ca. 1900, presumably planted by Jefferson ca. 1806.

The hilly Piedmont terrain of natural hills and cultivated fields within his vast Poplar Forest tract offered a "hill and dale" pastoral landscape. Without mentioning the enslaved people who worked it, Jefferson had expressed to Charles Willson Peale the beauty he saw even in plowed hillsides: "In point of beauty, nothing can exceed that of the waving line & rows winding along the face of the hills & vallies."[38] As Jefferson would have approached the house from the north, the road crossed the small Tomahawk Creek, which undoubtedly took its name from the time of indigenous people, just as nearby Bear Creek, Buffalo Creek, and Otter Creek referred to former indigenous fauna. Within sight of the house, the road came to a split-rail fence (a "Virginia fence") that enclosed a 61-acre curtilage (outer yard). Within this space it was apparent Jefferson had shaped the core landscape in geometrical forms. The house stood on a rise of land within a 10-acre-square yard and was encircled by a 540-yard round ring road (500-foot inner diameter, or about 5 acres) defined by inner and outer rows of paper mulberry trees planted on 20-foot centers.[39] On axis north of the house the ring road intersected with another geometric shape: the circular carriage turnaround paved with quartz cobblestones. The turnaround separated the existing poplar trees within the circular road and was itself bordered on its sides by two oval flower beds and a third anchoring its center. To either side of the front portico symmetrical "clumps" aligned with the blank chimney faces of the walls.[40] Clumps were a well-known English landscape feature described in all the significant publications, especially Whately, Miller, and McMahon. As archaeological excavations have revealed, each clump, of various trees and bushes, was meant to look natural but in fact had been designed and laid out by Jefferson in a geometrical spiral plan that equaled the length of a surveyor's chain.[41]

We can imagine the expansive scope and visual kaleidoscope of the trees, flowers, and shrubs that formed Jefferson's landscaped gardens at his villa retreat. Just the documented references from letters and memos provide a tantalizing array of species. Near the house Jefferson planted Athenian poplars, weeping willows, golden willows, Lombardy poplars, Balsam poplars, Monticello aspens, locusts (common and Kentucky), redbuds, dogwoods, calycanthus, liriodendrom (tulip poplars), paper mulberries, and Pride of China trees. Nonspecific locations for flower and shrub plantings fill out our imaginary picture with forms, fragrances, and color: roses (large and dwarf), Gelder roses, lilacs, altheas, daffodils, jonquils, narcissus, flags, lilies of "all kinds," hyacinths, tulips, white jessamine, and pyracantha. Some of these came from Monticello as seedlings and others as root stock. Some flowers came as bulbs. Some went into the plant nursery and some immediately into the ground. Archaeologists continue to discover the location and design of the many different trees, flowers, and shrubs that that formed Jefferson's colorful and variegated plantings around the house.

By this time in Thomas Jefferson's life, he was steeped in the history of classical villas and the poetry of English landscapes. He had acquired and studied the best landscape gardening books when still a college student; he collected ideas from visiting the best gardens in Europe; he corresponded with and received plant seeds from the leading horticulturalists of his day; and he had developed a sophisticated taste as a landscape architect and gardener that he first practiced at Monticello. All of this experience culminated in Jefferson's creation of his final and most personal landscape at Poplar Forest.

A Unique Marriage of Forms

In 1807 it occurred to Jefferson that dirt excavated from the south lawn could be used for an aesthetic design. Jefferson had directed that enslaved laborer Phil Hubbard and others excavate the south lawn so that the lower floor of the house was equal to grade on the south. Jefferson came up with a clever solution: to use the dirt nearby rather than carting it farther away. His idea called for the dirt to create symmetrical mounds east and west of the house. The mounds were then ready for treatment early in 1811.[42] In February of that year Jefferson directed that four weeping willows be planted on the top of each mound, making a 20-foot square of 20 feet apart; that golden willows be planted in a circle round the middle 15 feet apart; and that aspens be planted around the base 15 feet apart. This would have produced a "crown and hemisphere" shape that Jefferson had mentioned to William Hamilton in reference to the clump plantings. Six weeping willows were also to be planted around each of the octagonal privies, or "cloachinas," as Jefferson called them after the Roman goddess of sewers and following the nomenclature then common in England, and at William Byrd's Westover.[43] The following year, when the clumps were planted at the four chimney sides of the house, Jefferson directed that the mounds be connected to the house by a double row of paper mulberries. This connection meant that the mounds formed a symmetrical five-part

"Palladian plan," with the tall planted mounds standing in for architectural pavilions and the double row of trees as connecting hyphens. If the two privies are included, it would be a seven-part plan. This was Jefferson blending and blurring what was formal with classical allusions with something that was natural and more romantic. The symmetry would have harkened back to ancient or Renaissance villas, and for those who knew them, to medieval "mounts," as they were called, throughout Europe and especially England. When measuring the distance from the mounds to the house in 1812, Jefferson found that the east was 84 feet from the east stair pavilion and the west was 91 feet from the west pavilion. This discrepancy, possibly mitigated by the rows of trees, must have rankled a man known for precise measurements and reinforced his view that unsupervised projects produced imperfect results. Still, the architectural and landscape

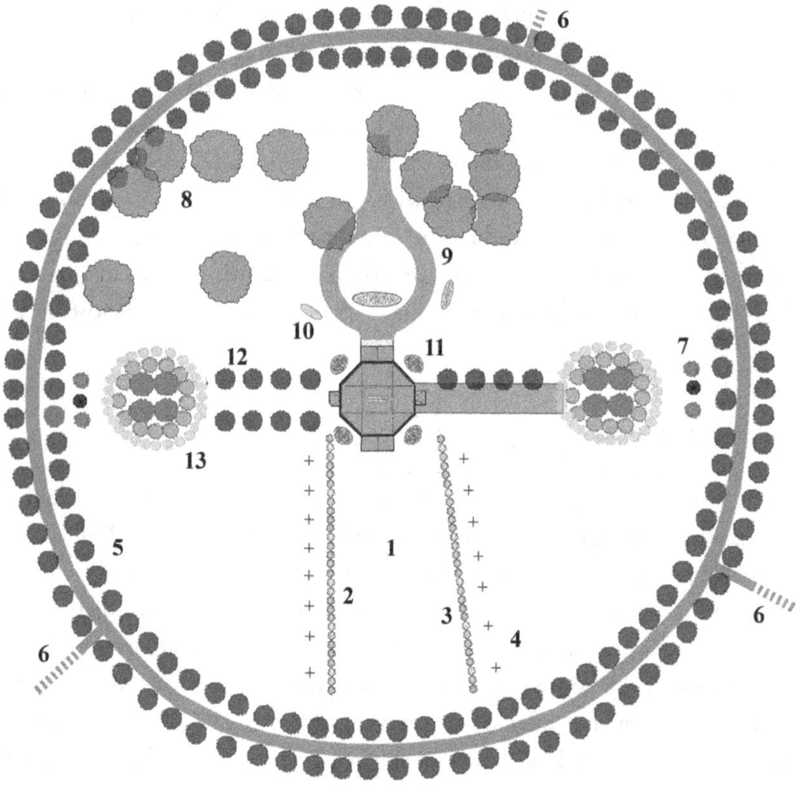

Fig. 85. Poplar Forest plan of planting in the five acres around the house.
Schematic of the core area showing major landscape features: 1) sunken lawn; 2) west bank planted with shrubs and flowers in 1812, including lilacs, Althaea, guelder roses, roses, and calycanthus; 3) east bank plantings canted outward with the addition of the Wing of Offices in 1814; 4) Kentucky coffee trees planted on the terrace above the sunken lawn; 5) circular road lined with paper mulberry trees; 6) axial roads leading away from the ornamental core; 7) octagonal privies initially surrounded by weeping willow trees with paper mulberry trees and privet later added; 8) north yard with grove of tulip poplar trees; 9) carriage turnaround; 10) oval beds planted with roses, dwarf roses, and bristly locust; 11) clumps of ornamental trees and shrubs, including Athenian and balsam poplars, black locust, Kentucky coffee trees, redbuds, dogwoods, calycanthus, and tulip poplars; 12) double rows of paper mulberry trees, partially removed on the east with the addition of the Wing of Offices; 13) earthen mounds initially planted with weeping and golden willows and ringed with aspen trees.

ensemble was unique and also served to divide the naturalistic features of the tree-filled area north and around the house from a more formal scene on the south.

Jefferson clearly had functional reasons for planting certain trees. In a letter to his neighbor Charles Clay accompanying some paper mulberry trees, he explained that they were "valuable for the regularity of their form, velvet leaf and for being fruitless. They are charming near a porch for densely shading it."[44] Paper mulberries were also given to James Barbour with the claim that they are "the most beautiful and best shading tree to be near the house, entirely clean, bearing no fruit, scarcely yet known in America."[45] Philip Miller's *The Gardener's Dictionary,* in recommending terraces connected to a house and extending into the landscape, stated that "the noblest Terrace is very deficient without shade . . . for no seat can be said to be complete where there is not an immediate shade almost as soon as out of the house."[46] Miller's caution about shade was not lost on Jefferson, who already valued it as part of nature's Elysium. His planting of double rows of paper mulberry trees from the house to the mounds might have anticipated later service wings that could slip between them. By 1815 a wing of service rooms replaced the southern row of trees connecting the house to the east mound. On the west, archaeological evidence confirmed the distance between each tree and the distance between the rows, which would have allowed for a service wing between them shaded by the trees had one been built.[47]

Mounds used as an architectural feature is one of the most unusual aspects of the Poplar Forest landscape. Jefferson's first mention of a mound comes from a note in his Building Notebook that is undated but most likely from the 1790s. He wrote: "the mound before Mr. Meredith's house rises 1. F. in 18 in. front & about 1. F. in 7. In the flank, from whence however it spreads wider, & consequently falls more gradually immediately."[48] If this note dates to Jefferson's time in Philadelphia, Mr. Meredith is most likely Samuel Meredith, Esq., who in the 1790s owned a country house called Green Hill just outside Philadelphia.[49] Mounds, or mounts, were not mysterious but were well-known garden features common to the best Elizabethan gardens in England and seen throughout Europe. Henry VIII's mount at Hampton Court Palace featured a banqueting house on top. As a college student Jefferson would have seen one in the Governor's Palace garden and probably the one in the Grissell Hay garden, each of which had a 20′ × 20′ viewing area on top.[50] Jefferson could also have seen the remains of an old one at the site of Greenspring Plantation that measured 15′ × 250′. On his English garden tour with John Adams Jefferson could have seen any number of "mounts," including four at Oxford University and perhaps some of the medieval castle "mottes" built for defense, or even the prehistoric mount of unknown purpose at Silbury Hill. Even though Jefferson noted on his English tour that Claremont had "Nothing remarkable," it did have a mound planted with trees.[51] Closer to home, mounds could be found in gardens from New England to South Carolina, the former having the architecturally distinguished Isaac Royal summer house on a mound. A distinguished octagonal summer house used as a library retreat and chapel was situated on a mound at John Burgwin's 1760s country house in North Carolina, the Hermitage. This was described in 1801 by Eliza Burgwin as "a small brick building called the study, on a high mound in the Big Garden, [with] a fine collection of books, writing desk and tables."[52] At Crowfield in South Carolina, a garden house surmounted on a mound was situated in the middle of a pond. The most obvious American prototype seen by Jefferson was George Washington's garden mounds planted with weeping willows and flanked by locusts.

The greensward that Phil's excavation established south of the house was not unlike a bowling green or parterre bordered on its banks with flowering shrubs (gelder roses, altheas, lilacs, calycanthus) in front of rows of Kentucky locust trees (Kentucky coffeetrees). This was the most formal and regular form on the site but with border plantings to introduce visual variety. The lawn itself, planted with grass seed gathered by enslaved children, did not have to have plantings but was plain like the "á l'anglaise" parterres in French gardens. From the south portico this created an enclosed allée on each side with a view toward the southern branch of Tomahawk Creek, presumably through an opening in the double row of mulberry trees that encased the circular road. Both Phillip Miller and Bernard McMahon recommended this type of lawn. McMahon, who sent Jefferson a copy of his book when it was published in 1806, had described "a grand and spacious open lawn of grass . . . contracted towards the habitation; widening gradually outwards, and having each side embellished with plantations of shrubbery, clumps, thickets, etc . . . with breaks or opens of grass spaces at intervals between the different plantations . . . winding under the shade of the trees."[53] This description and one by Miller for a similar lawn suggest a forced perspective when the banks of the lawn were splayed. The current condition of the east bank, and archaeological excavations, show that the initial parallel bank was splayed after the construction of the east wing; the west bank was not changed, perhaps because a west wing was never built.[54] Nevertheless, the trees, shrubs, splay and the triple square size (70′ × 210′) of the south lawn were right out of Jefferson's garden books. Photographs from the turn of the twentieth century show the Kentucky coffeetrees stretching south from the house and convey a romantic sense in their dense and dark maturity, even in a decaying state that mirrored that of the house by that time.

McMahon's gardening book provided everything Jefferson needed to shape his landscape. This included the site of a house, on an "elevated situation of some moderate rising ground," and instructions for creating and caring for a kitchen garden, a pleasure or flower garden, a plant nursery, and an orchard. McMahon recommended a variety of trees, shrubs, and flowers arranged in the "pleasure ground" so they revealed "new scenes" as one strolled through them. Although McMahon mentioned picturesque landscapes, he also said "we should not abolish entirely the appearance of art and uniformity" that "sets nature in the fairest and most beautiful point of view."[55] Jefferson's mounds certainly created such an appearance of art and uniformity. McMahon recommended that "new scenes" should be by "compartment" to reveal curious plantings, especially rising grounds and mounts with ornamental, curious, and shady trees. He also advocated that groves of stately trees be planted on grounds of grass "in which they will appear most rural and beautiful."[56] Clumps should be diversified by tree, shrub and

Fig. 86. Restored landscape features on the north side of the house showing carriage turnaround, and clumps of trees and bushes, 2021.

flower for variety of type and size and contrast. If large stately trees were found on the site, they could be "introduced into the design" and "preserved with the utmost care" due to their mature age and instant use. Instructions for the kitchen garden, "the most useful and consequential department of gardening," were just as proscriptive, deeming that garden useful not only for the "support of life and health" but also for its beauty of organization, and for the form of some of its plants and fruit trees. Jefferson's gardening Bible had provided him with the theory and rationale for every aspect of the landscape, but what he planted and how he thoughtfully arranged them was a personal choice.

Landscape Harmonies

If Jefferson's intentions for Monticello were significant for their concept rather than their full realization, the idealized order and geometric harmony for the Poplar Forest landscape was its compelling feature.[57] Enough evidence exists to show that Jefferson conceived of the Poplar Forest core landscape in an ideal geometric design. The round ring road encircled by trees was centered in the square 10-acre yard within the larger curtilage enclosure. According to C. Allan Brown, the basic dimensions of the core landscape were roughly devised by regular modules of 100 feet that could be inscribed within a regular octagonal shape within the round ring road. Geometrical plantings were supplemented with naturalistic plantings that blurred any of the strict harmonious geometries and provided great variety to the eye in this reduced-size core. It was a very artful milieu seen on foot in scenic sequence within the core, as befitting an aging man who could walk no farther than his garden. The landscape features were also meant to be seen from the house, from the large windows of the octagon walls, from the triple windows of the parlor, from the south portico, from the 100-foot wing terrace deck, and from the 20-foot-square rooftop deck that allowed distant views of the Blue Ridge Mountains. Rooftop decks and viewing platforms were an old tradition going back to Elizabethan houses in England, when country house owners were beginning to appreciate nature and using the rooftops of houses, hunting towers, or belvederes. On his travels to Germany Jefferson described a castle ruin that featured a circular room at the top with a viewing platform above that. One of the more famous views of a private nature was Verulum House, on Francis Bacon's Gorhambury estate, whose "very well leaded" flat roof provided "a lovely Prospect."[58] The landscaped grounds could be viewed from on high, as Lord Kames advocated, but more importantly one could be within them, like architecture. The groves of trees around Poplar Forest were like the "bosky groves" or "bosquets" in the French Sun King's garden at Versailles that served as outdoor rooms in which to engage nature, even if contrived. Planting new trees mattered in concept and imagination. To a friend Jefferson had explained late in life that he was "too old to plant trees for my own gratification, I shall do it for my posterity."[59] The Poplar Forest ornamental landscape was complex, but not expansive, and designed for the pleasure of an aging owner reduced to short strolls. In contrast to the openness of the Monticello mountaintop with its vistas to the eastern plain and the western mountains, the ornamental landscape at Poplar Forest was more closed and intimate where Jefferson retreated inside the perimeter fences, the circular road, and the octagonal house.

Nature

On August 23, 1767, a twenty-four-year-old Thomas Jefferson stopped in Rockbridge County to see the Natural Bridge. He wrote a characteristically lengthy description of it on the inside back cover of his Memorandum Book and drew a small sketch with the bridge's dimensions. Fourteen years later in Query V of his manuscript *Notes of the State of Virginia,* partially written at Poplar Forest, his remembered awe inspired him to call the bridge "the most sublime of Nature's works," and he would rank it along with the view from the heights of Harpers Ferry as the most impressive natural scenes in Virginia. Jefferson went beyond a scientist's description of the bridge: "It is impossible for the emotions arising from the sublime, to be felt beyond what they are here: so beautiful an arch, so elevated, so light, and springing as it were up to heaven, the rapture of the spectator is really indescribable!"[60] Small wonder then that the year after inheriting Poplar Forest in 1773, Thomas Jefferson bought the natural wonder and a tract of 157 acres surrounding it from the English Crown; he would own it for the rest of his life.[61] While it was not a contiguous part of the Poplar Forest land, the Natural Bridge was linked by proximity and by a conception that nature was still more unsettled in this part of the state. Charles Miller's book *Jefferson and Nature* made the point that theories of the Scottish Enlightenment were based on knowing nature by external senses, as Locke preached, or by the natural laws, as Newton proposed, or by knowing nature and knowledge through memory, reason, and imagination, as outlined by Bacon. This triumvirate of great men helped Jefferson understand concepts that all things came from, and led to, nature, leading to the discovery of any number of universal truths. As Miller wrote: "It was the raw nature of the New World and the opportunity to create new societies in America that most distinguished the American Enlightenment from the European. It was the blend of nature of western Virginia—near the frontier and prepared to oppose plantation society with small farms—and the learning of the Scottish Enlightenment that helped most to distinguish Jefferson's outlook from that of Americans elsewhere."[62] At Poplar Forest Jefferson could feel closer to both universal nature and to a particular landscape. In his book Jefferson also claimed the nearby Peaks of Otter to be among the highest mountains on the continent. Lewis and Clark would set that record straight, but in his seventies Jefferson and his good friend Jose Correa de Serra spent days with surveying equipment establishing their true elevation. The Peaks were visible from the rooftop deck on Poplar Forest and delineated on a plan Jefferson drew of the mountain ranges visible from seven windows on the north side of the house. The views were not as dramatic or obvious as those from Monticello, about which Jefferson waxed so eloquently to European friends, but in his mind's eye the view was expansive. Closer in were the remnants of the old-growth forest, a notable reminder of nature that had been honored since the 1740s with its place-name—Poplar Forest.

These scenes of nature, whether close or far, whether viewable or conceptual, whether sublime or picturesque, linked Poplar Forest to the classical writers and to the British poets and writers of the eighteenth century on whom Jefferson had bestowed honor when conceiving and writing about his earliest plans for Monticello. At his own villa retreat Jefferson could concentrate on his favorite ancient writers and historians. Of the roughly 1,000 books at Poplar Forest, the greatest number was poetry and literature (123 titles). Classical dreams eased the growing physical transition of aging in his artfully created house even if the artfully created landscape around might be in states of neglect. Feelings so emphatically stated in Jefferson's description of Virginia's natural wonders were the romantic threads that merged with the more rational ones forming and shaping Jefferson's concepts for the landscapes at Poplar Forest. The Poplar Forest landscape designs mirrored the contradictory and complex attitude of its creator and his deep-seated feelings and vision of Virginia nature and landscapes: it was settled and it was wild; it was shaped and it was natural; it was agricultural and it was ornamental; it was an enslaved landscape and it was an Enlightenment reflection. Whether it was incomplete and imperfect was less important than the perfected quality of its design and conception. For Jefferson the greater journey had always been the detailed process of conceiving, planning, and slowly putting plans into reality, and for this he had vision and unusual patience.

6

RETIRED LIFE AT POPLAR FOREST

Thomas Jefferson contemplated and discussed permanent retirement for years before it actually happened. He mentioned it in letters in 1779, 1789, and 1791. Staying at his rented Schuylkill River house in the summer of 1793 undoubtedly increased his daydreams about a permanent retreat. That fall he "desired nothing but rest & oblivion."[1] Late in 1793 Jefferson wrote of a premature retirement, saying, "I am then to be liberated from the hated occupations of politics, and to remain in the bosom of my family, my farm, and my books."[2] Official duties obviously weighed on him even before the presidency. In 1794 he had written, "I hope to spend the remainder of my days in occupations infinitely more pleasing than those to which I have sacrificed 18 years of the prime of my life."[3] He had written his daughter in 1797, "tranquility is now my object," even though public duties would not allow it for some time.[4]

Jefferson's two terms as president only increased his longing for retirement. When retirement was finally in sight, a crescendo of letters flowed to friends anticipating that goal. To his friend William Hamilton he wrote in 1806 that he had "made up my mind for retirement."[5] That same year he confided to two friends his plans to build Poplar Forest. To Levett Harris he remarked that a bust of Alexander "will constitute one of the most valued ornaments of the retreat I am preparing for myself at my native home."[6] To good friend Elizabeth Trist he said, "I am preparing an occasional retreat," to which Trist replied, "that you mean to pass your summers there . . . [is] a good plan to avoid being run down with company."[7] These letters in 1806 might be the first time he used the word "retreat" in conjunction with concrete plans for one. The following year, to a French friend, he wrote: "At the end of my present term, of which two years are yet to come, I propose to retire from public life, and to close my days on my patrimony of Monticello, in the bosom of my family. I have hitherto enjoyed uniform health; but the weight of public business begins to be too heavy for me, and I long for the enjoyments of rural life, among my books, my farms and my family."[8] In January 1809 he wrote James Madison, who would succeed him as president: "Five weeks more will relieve me from a drudgery to which I am no longer equal, and restore me to a scene of tranquility, amidst my family and friends, more congenial to my age and natural inclinations."[9] In March 1809, as the joyful day approached, his anticipation grew:

> Within a few days I retire to my family, my books and farms; and having gained the harbor myself, I shall look on my friends still buffeting the storm, with anxiety indeed, but not with envy. Never did a prisoner, released from his chains, feel such relief as I shall on shaking off the shakles [*sic*] of power. Nature intended me for the tranquil pursuits of science, by rendering them my supreme delight. But the enormities of the times in which I have lived, have forced me to take part in resisting them, and to commit myself on the boisterous ocean of political passions.[10]

Just before leaving Washington, the ex-president happily wrote to Madame de Corny: "At length I detach myself from public life, which I never loved, to retire to the bosom of my family, my friends, my farm and books, which I have always loved. I retire in hearty affection with the world, because indeed the world has been kinder to me than I claimed."[11] While he kept up by letter with family news, he longed for a more intimate daily connection in their "bosom." He certainly missed his great book collection at Monticello, and he couldn't wait to spend more time on intellectual, scientific, and domestic subjects that had eluded him for many years.

Tranquil Pursuits and Retirement Goals

Jefferson's object in retirement could not have been made clearer. The "object," he had written a friend in 1810, "at present is peace and tranquility."[12] To another he said he was "anxious in my retirement, to enjoy undisturbed repose."[13] Still to another he wrote, "in my present retirement, no duty forbids my wish for quiet."[14] Tranquility, quiet and repose were not completely found at Monticello, but he had known this and had prepared his retreat. After the third trip to Poplar Forest in 1810 he wrote Gideon Granger that September: "I am just returned from a place I possess in Bedford County near Lynchburg, and where I pass certain portions of the year. It is the most valuable of my possessions and will become the residence of the greater part of my family."[15] This had become his new idea, settling some of his family near Poplar Forest so as to enjoy the "bosom" of his family at his second residence.

Jefferson could experience some of his retirement pleasures at Monticello, but the peace and tranquility refrains centered on Poplar Forest. In 1812, when updating his son-in-law, John Wayles Eppes, on the improvements at Poplar Forest, Jefferson pronounced it "the best dwelling house in the state" and preferable to Monticello as "more proportioned to the faculties of a private citizen."[16] Indeed, it had been designed for the privacy of a private citizen, but Jefferson now thought it would also eventually suit his grandson as a primary residence. John Wayles Eppes understood Jefferson's use of the house and succinctly described it: "Mr. Jefferson has erected a very handsome Brick

Fig. 87. Ellen Randolph and Cornelia Randolph, Jefferson's granddaughters who accompanied him to Poplar Forest. The terra cotta bust is by William Coffee, who made the entablature ornaments for Poplar Forest.

house with eight rooms and passes much of his time there taking with him occasionally his granddaughters. For several years he has passed the months of August and September in Bedford."[17] Eppes associated Jefferson's retirement with the summer season even though he retreated outside of the normal season, which defines one of the principal distinctions of his retreat. He did time certain visits to supervise the harvest of crops, but his repeated linkage of the words "retirement" and "tranquility" left no doubt as to why he principally went there. To his former secretary in Paris, William Short, Jefferson wrote in 1816, "tranquility is the softest pillow for the head of old age."[18]

Jefferson's farms and gardens at Monticello had been severely neglected, and into those he would pour himself with great intensity once he permanently returned to the familiar mountaintop. The Poplar Forest plantation also needed attention, and its ornamental gardens had yet to be formed and would provide a pleasurable retirement project. To John Mason he wrote in 1810, "my garden & farms occupy me closely from breakfast to dinner (typically about 3pm), after which it is my habit to lounge."[19] The same year he had written another friend: "My occupations here are almost exclusively given to my farm and affairs. They furnish me exercise, health and amusement, and with the recreations of family and neighborly society, fill up most of my time, and give a tranquility necessary to my time of life."[20] He went into greater detail about a typical schedule when writing to his old friend Thaddeus Kosciusko: "I am retired to Monticello where, in the bosom of my family, and surrounded by books, I enjoy a repose to which I have been long a stranger. My mornings are devoted to correspondence. From breakfast to dinner, I am in my shops, my garden, or on horseback among my farms; from dinner to dark, I give to society and recreation with my neighbors and friends; and from candle light to early bed-time, I read. My health is perfect. . . . I talk of ploughs and harrows, of seeding and harvesting, with my neighbors."[21] The oft-mentioned tranquility, one of his fervent and fundamental goals, he would have to find at Poplar Forest, which was now, in 1809, ready to receive him, even in its incomplete state. Its completion was an obvious goal and would take some time, but it offered peace and quiet in the meantime.

Besides peace and tranquility, Jefferson's frequently expressed goal for retirement was family, friends, farms, and books. He pursued these retirement goals at both Monticello and at Poplar Forest, the difference being that Poplar Forest had been expressly conceived and built for retirement. Did Jefferson's design of Poplar Forest facilitate his stated retirement goals? The answer is found in examining Jefferson's use of the retreat and how well that aligned with his intended purpose.

FRIENDS

One of Jefferson's clearly expressed goals for retirement was connecting with friends. At Poplar Forest friends were of two types: local and distant. When he wrote that he could attend to his absent friends, he meant through letters. Many of these letters convey the pleasure he found at his retreat. After several trips to Poplar Forest, Jefferson wrote William Short in 1811, "I now make frequent journies to Bedford, and long stays, having a good house and accommodations there."[22] Even though the house was lacking most of its plaster and all of its interior trim, his joy in the solitude was unmistakable. A second letter to Short that year described the "health & happiness" to be found outside a city at a farm and added, "I experience this mere change of scene on my trips to Poplar Forest, distant as it is, and like this, in the country."[23] That same year Jefferson expressed his retirement bliss to his good friend Dr. Benjamin Rush: "I write to you from a place, 90. Miles from Monticello, near the New London of this state, which I visit three or four times a year & stay from a fortnight to a month at a time. I have fixed myself comfortably, keep some books here, bring others occasionally, am in the solitude of a hermit, and quite at leisure to attend my absent friends."[24] In an earlier letter to Rush in 1811 he complained of having to spend so much time writing to strangers who inquired of all manner of subjects and said, "My hope is that this obstacle to the delights of retirement, will wear away with the oblivion which follows that, and that I may at length be indulged in those studious pursuits, from which nothing but

Fig. 88. Poplar Forest, southwest elevation, 2022.

revolutionary duties would ever have called me."[25] Letters to strangers were primarily answered from Monticello, and letters to "my absent friends" were reserved for Poplar Forest, a decision even in letter writing that reinforced intimacy. By 1812 Jefferson had taken comfort in his freedom "to indulge the evening of my life with what have been the passions of every portion of it, books, science, my farms, my family & friends."[26]

Jefferson was not so much the complete hermit since he enjoyed getting together for dinner with Lynchburg friends and with neighbors of his choosing, as opposed to strangers who dropped in at Monticello. Strangers did not come to satisfy their curiosity at Poplar Forest as they did at Monticello; neighbors respected his solitude, and friends of friends were not directed there. Those few who stayed overnight came by invitation, like Englishman George Flower and the Portuguese scientist Abbé Joseph Francis Correa de Serra.

FAMILY

Jefferson's retirement goals importantly included family. Of that he had plenty at Monticello with Martha Jefferson Randolph's many children, but family played a significant role at Poplar Forest as well. Family members did occasionally accompany Jefferson to Poplar Forest, most frequently and significantly granddaughters Ellen and Cornelia Randolph. It is because these young women typically wrote to their mother, Martha, stuck as hostess at Monticello, that we know so much about Jefferson's daily life at Poplar Forest. Their correspondence and poignant reminiscences later in the mid-nineteenth century reveal the most about Jefferson's life in retirement at Poplar Forest, including his role as a grandfather. The granddaughters' letters from Poplar Forest also fill in the domestic picture at Poplar Forest with enthusiastic teenage and young adult observations. Unacknowledged was his "shadow family" of Beverly, Madison, and Eston Hemings. They form a fractured family bosom at Poplar Forest.

On June 24, 1816, Jefferson wrote to his son-in-law: "I am this moment arrived here with Ellen & Cornelia, and find Francis who arrived last night."[27] Thus began the periodic visits of these two young ladies, Ellen being nineteen at the time and Cornelia, sixteen. Grandson Francis, age fifteen, was at that time studying at an academy in Lynchburg and came for short visits. Ellen later recalled: "The first visit I ever paid with him to what afterwards became a favorite retreat, must have been I think in the summer of 1816. The house was then unfinished."[28] On that first visit they entered a house that now had full plaster on walls and ceilings but was lacking some interior doors and the interior moldings. The girls shared the east chamber, whose bed was in a center alcove like Jefferson's on the west. Francis would have stayed in the small northwest bed chamber off the front passage. Martha Jefferson Randolph paid her first visit to the site on Jefferson's quick thirteen-day visit that September. Along on that visit was granddaughter Virginia Randolph, age fifteen. In the last visit of the year Ellen and Cornelia again accompanied their grandfather to Poplar Forest. Cornelia wrote the first of many letters from Poplar Forest to sister Virginia at Monticello, commenting on the trip that was cold in the mornings and evenings, challenging on muddy roads, and in accommodations that were not too bad.[29] Cornelia asked her sister to send via the next cart a small English dictionary that she intended to give to "Daddy," the term the grandchildren used for John Hemmings, who was also beginning his many trips

Fig. 89. Dining room with restored entablature and doorway pediments, 2022. This was the last way Jefferson saw this room before the frieze ornaments were installed.

to Poplar Forest.[30] On this same trip Ellen wrote her first letter to her mother, saying, "[we] are making very good use of our time; I have got through the syntax. . . . Cornelia has been equally industrous—fortunately we have not been much interrupted by company. . . . Upon the whole, however, I like this place and neighborhood very much and should be well pleased to pass a part of my time here every year."[31]

The girls would indeed make many more trips, and their observant and regular letters back home would fill in important glimpses of how the family spent their time there. Jefferson's letter to Martha on that same late fall trip in 1816 mentioned that rain and snow had delayed their journey, but they were now in comfortable quarters, and "the girls have borne it wonderfully. They have been very close students, and I am never without enough to do to prevent me from ennui."[32] The term "ennui" and Poplar Forest could hardly be linked for Thomas Jefferson, with or without family members present. For most of his trips he came to his retreat with Burwell Colbert, his enslaved manservant, and any necessary workers, but time alone in the house was far from lonely: it was the long-sought goal.

Jefferson greatly enjoyed the companionship of his grandchildren at Poplar Forest, though he ensured that their time was far from idle. In a letter to their mother Jefferson proudly stated that Ellen and Cornelia were the "severest students I have ever met with. They never leave their room but to come to meals."[33] Ellen wrote her mother that she was able to accomplish four times more work than at Monticello. Ellen mentioned reading Virgil in Latin, making good use of syntax study, studying Spanish verbs, French, Greek, and being "very industrious." Ellen's description of typical days emphasized the life of books at Poplar Forest. Jefferson directed his granddaughters' studies and then discussed their comprehension and opinions. In a letter to her mother, Ellen noted, "Grand papa and myself are in the habit of sitting, some time after dinner, in conversation, upon different subjects."[34]

Cornelia also read and studied, but she also used her time at Poplar Forest to practice her drawing, mentioning essential elements of ink, crayons, pencils, and paper. Her subjects included a Shakespeare Desdemona, a beggar and dog, Ariadne, human figures, and flowers. Jefferson had even asked her to draw a Minerva figure when choosing the seal design for the University of Virginia. In a letter from Poplar Forest to her sister Virginia, Cornelia wrote:

> I wonder you do not persevere in attempting to draw human figures. It is so much more agreeable than flowers, since I have been here I have attempted several (times) an Ariadne, which I spoilt after completing the figure by trying to draw the rocks & failing in the attempt for landscapes are what I never could make anything like in my life. I am now drawing a Ferdinand & Miranda but they both have a great deal of expression in their countenances & I have not succeeded very well in that either.[35]

In separate letters to their mother describing the damage from the 1819 hailstorm, Ellen and Cornelia both lamented the fact that the dining room skylight was without glass and boarded up by temporary planking. Ellen described her sister's typical use of the space with its studio-like light:

> Cornelia does not appear to have remarked the additional gloom in the appearance of our dwelling, but has been fretting all the morning over the loss of the sky-light, which darkens the dining room so much that she cannot draw in it—and the glare of light which falls on her beggar and his dog shows the nose of the latter in so unseemly a place, that it shocks me to look at it. She hopes however with the aid of green baize curtains to get on pretty well with her work.[36]

Cornelia had also taken an interest in architecture, perhaps the only grandchild to do so. This is attested to by the fact that the John Neilson drawings of Poplar Forest, and even his drawings for the University of Virginia, were erroneously attributed to Cornelia. When she wrote her sister Virginia that a former tutor, Mr. Baldwin, had died, she regretted that Ellen had "a memorial" of him but she did not, except "knowledge of the distinguishing marks of the five orders of architecture, which I will never forget for his sake."[37] Her grandfather would have been the better tutor for things architectural, but he was not accomplished with freehand sketches.

BOOKS

Jefferson's litany of retirement goals always included his books, which for almost any other person would not have shared equal status with farms, family, and friends. In later years Ellen Randolph Coolidge portrayed her grandfather without a book only on horseback, at meals, or when writing letters. It is difficult to discuss Jefferson's life, especially his retired life, without mentioning the role books played. As Daniel Boorstin noted, "books were for him not ornaments but instruments for coming to terms with the world."[38] Sarah Randolph nicely characterized Jefferson and his relationship with books: "The books . . . in every change in the tide of his eventful life had ever remained to him as old friends with unchanged faces, and . . . their silent companionship had afforded him—next to the love of his friends—the sweetest and purest joys of life."[39] He commented to Benjamin Rush that at Poplar Forest he "kept some books there and bring others occasionally."[40] Books were carried back and forth between Monticello and Poplar Forest, but the 1,000-book library at his retreat furnished most of what Jefferson desired for retirement.[41] He had put together his retirement library while still president and could not foresee that it would become his principal library for a time. When he sold his principal library to replace the congressional library burned by the British army in 1814, the Poplar Forest library would constitute his largest collection until he slowly rebuilt one at Monticello. As Martha Jefferson Randolph and others noted, Jefferson received less than half of the library's fifty-thousand-dollar value from its sale to the government; many in Congress doubted its usefulness to begin with and complained it was too erudite. When the tenth and final wagonload of books left Monticello for Washington in 1815, Jefferson immediately left for Poplar Forest, where he could take comfort from his retirement library. With the money he received from the sale he began to replace his beloved books. In a gross understatement he wrote John Adams, "I cannot live without books."[42]

The importance of the Poplar Forest library, and one particular aspect, had been conveyed by Ellen Randolph Coolidge to Henry Randall and mentioned in his 1858 biography of Jefferson:

> In the above pictures of Poplar Forest there is one omission. In the drawing-room there was what Mr. Jefferson called his petit-format library, contained in four cases, each of which was perhaps between three and four feet in width and height. The books, to economize space, were generally of the smallest sized editions published. He had first made this collection for his convenience at Washington. It contained upwards of one hundred volumes of British, a considerable collection of Italian and French, and a few favorite Greek and Latin poets, and a larger number of prose writers of the same languages—all, it is unnecessary to say, in the original. These, with the last three or four new books and reviews, brought from Monticello, were the delights which, with the society of his granddaughters, and the occasional visits of neighbors who mixed the courtesy and simplicity of the old Virginia planter with the culture and self-respect of gentlemen, filled up that round of quiet enjoyments which contrasted, a portion of the time, so pleasantly with the hotel-like bustle and want of privacy at Monticello.[43]

Ellen had fondly remembered the special collection of 300 to 400 petite-size books that resided in the parlor in four small mahogany cases. When ordering a binding for "a small volume" in 1818, Jefferson explained to the bookbinder, "it is to be trimmed, as you will see, to fit my petit format shelves."[44] While still in Europe Jefferson mentioned that he liked books "of a handy size," especially after breaking his wrist.[45] Small books could also fit in a pocket of his waistcoat. The larger books in the 1,000-volume library were most likely housed in Jefferson's stacking "box" cases. He once described his "bookshelves" that could be "taken to pieces and put together again the whole of them in half an hour, as there is not a single nail, screw, nor glue used in putting them together."[46] The small mahogany cases probably sat on tables in the parlor.[47]

Jefferson based his organization of books on Francis Bacon's description of the faculties of the mind: Memory, Reason, and Imagination. Jefferson translated these fields into his own: History, Philosophy, and Fine Arts. Of the 336 titles now known to have been in the Poplar Forest library, equaling at least 961 individual volumes, the majority were poetry (50 titles, 257 volumes); literature (73 titles, 91 volumes); and history (62 titles, 152 volumes). Other categories include politics (19 titles, 50 volumes); ethics (31 titles, 72 volumes); mathematics (74 titles, 93 volumes); geography (18 titles, 29 volumes); language (22 titles, 32 volumes); astronomy (44 titles, 87 volumes); and religion (10 titles, 18 volumes). The rest spanned a dozen other subjects. Three of his largest title collections included the Comte de Buffon's 57-volume set of *Histoire naturelle,* the

Fig. 90. One of the petite volumes of the 108-volume *Poets of Great Britain* that was in the Poplar Forest library.

108-volume set of the *Poets of Great Britain,* and a 38-volume set of Shakespeare. Of the 336 titles, Jefferson ordered 50 specifically for Poplar Forest.[48]

Ellen Randolph Coolidge described Jefferson's favorite intellectual pursuits at Poplar Forest as reading, studying, and writing. She described Jefferson's retirement reading habits to Henry Randall:

> With regard to the tastes and wishes which he carried with him into the country, his love of reading alone would have made leisure and retirement delightful to him. Books were at all times his chosen companions, and his acquaintance with many languages gave him great power of selection. He read Homer, Virgil, Dante, Corneille, Cervantes, as he read Shakespeare and Milton. In his youth he had loved poetry, but by the time I was old enough to observe, he had lost his taste for it, except for Homer and the great Athenian tragics, which he continued to the last to enjoy. He went over the works of Aeschylus, Sophocles, and Euripides, not very long before I left him [1825]. Of history he was very fond, and this he studied in all languages, though always, I think, preferring the ancients. In fact, he derived more pleasure from his acquaintance with Greek and Latin than from any other resource of literature, and I have often heard him express his gratitude to his father causing him to receive a classical education. I saw him more frequently with a volume of the classics in his hands than with any other book.[49]

Ellen could not have been more correct about the classics. Jefferson had studied the classics with private tutors, through college, and thereafter, picking them up again as a "hard student" in his retirement. A classical scholar characterized Jefferson as "the most learned and dedicated classicist" of his generation in a time when every educated person was steeped in the classics.[50] Jefferson wrote to Nathaniel Macon from Poplar Forest in 1819: "I feel a much greater interest in knowing what passed two or three thousand years ago, than in what is now passing. I read nothing, therefore, but of the heroes of Troy, of the wars of Lacedaemon and Athens, of Pompey and Caesar, and of Augustus too. . . . I slumber without fear, and review in my dreams the visions of antiquity."[51] In a letter to John Adams about Poplar Forest in 1814, he wrote: "Having more leisure there than here [Monticello] for reading, I amused myself with reading seriously Plato's Republic. I am wrong however, in calling it amusement, for it was the heaviest task-work I ever went through."[52] His task was serious, for he had five different editions of Homer's *Iliad* and *Odyssey* at Poplar Forest and preferred to read Greek works in their original language. He wrote to a friend from Poplar Forest, "When the decays of age have enfeebled the useful energies of the mind, the classic pages fill up the vacuum of ennui, and become sweet composers to that rest of the grave into which we are all sooner or later to descend."[53] Ellen was mistaken, however, about the poetry. Given the number of volumes, 257, Jefferson had not lost his love of poetry, having sets of Italian, French, and British poets at Poplar Forest.

When he offered his library to Congress, Jefferson stated that the books he might keep were classical and mathematical.[54] His letter to William Short provided a glimpse of why he would keep these two subjects: "With one foot in the grave . . . [m]y business is to beguile the wearisomeness of declining life, as I endeavor to do, by the delights of classical reading and of mathematical truths."[55] Mathematics, seen in his precision for architecture, was more than mere numbers: it was a theory whose practice was truth. To Benjamin Rush he wrote in 1811: "Having to conduct my grandson through his course in mathematics, I have resumed that study with great avidity. It was ever my favorite one. We have no theories there, no uncertainties remain on the mind, all is demonstration and satisfaction."[56] The idealized nature of Poplar Forest represented geometric harmonies whose proportions and beauty had been established centuries before. Jefferson was surrounded by numeric calculations. He could sit in his perfect cube at the center of the house, surrounded by octagon rooms that were contained within the outer octagon shape, and encircled by a round ring road set within a square 10-acre yard.

FARMS

The "farms" part of Jefferson's retirement litany was undoubtedly about the economy of a successful plantation dependent upon the management and products of the enslaved. Jefferson was interested in innovative farming techniques, but he told his grandson, Francis Eppes, that he had not been the most successful farmer, laying blame on public duties that had kept him away for long periods. Now, in retirement, he would be on hand and would seriously turn his attention to his cash crops, especially since he was losing the considerable presidential salary he had enjoyed for eight years. Being honest, he would have admitted that it was the garden part of farming that interested him the most. Poplar Forest would occupy his interest with both, the needed income from tobacco and wheat, and a tabula rasa for landscape gardening.

When Jefferson inherited the property in 1773, long before he built his retreat house, Poplar Forest was a plantation worked by enslaved people, and it remained such. The Bedford County property consisted of three quarter farms: Tomahawk, Wingos, and Bear Creek. Tomahawk was the "old plantation" site that Jefferson's father-in-law had initially established and the site where Jefferson placed his retreat house. Jefferson slowly increased the number of enslaved workers, and thus the plantation's economic potential, from a handful to about one hundred. While we tend to focus on Jefferson in studious retreat, an essential part of his daily routine took him out of the house and beyond the ornamental grounds. Jefferson confided to a friend in 1818: "I shall pass the months of Aug. and Sep. in Bedford. I am still able to take that journey in an easy carriage. . . . I ride also on horse back 5 or 6 miles every day, but I cannot walk further than any garden, and weaken very fast: and not withstanding this increasing debility I enjoy perfect health."[57]

Jefferson typically rode for several hours at midday to inspect his three quarter farms, observing and interacting with the enslaved community. On his rides, with or without his overseers, Jefferson inspected the cultivated fields and seasonal crops: tobacco, wheat, corn, peas, oats, pumpkins, clover, timothy, cotton, hemp, and flax. Crops were rotated to prevent soil exhaustion. Jefferson instructed his overseer that the wheat and oat fields should "be turned out to rest" and sown in clover, with tobacco fields sown in timothy. Corn was ploughed over three times each winter, hemp was sown in March, and meadow grounds were planted with pumpkins or peas. The wheat, sown in the fall, was harvested in midsummer, when Jefferson would observe the process of cutting, gathering, binding, stacking, loading, storing, treading, and threshing. It was then transported 10 miles to the mills in Lynchburg. The 80,000 to 300,000 hillocks of tobacco required a great deal of labor and supervision, starting in the spring with transplanting seedlings, hoeing, and progressing to weeding, worming, topping, suckering, cutting, hanging, stemming, prizing, and transporting. Absent most of the time, Jefferson had that much more to inspect when he was on-site.

In the spring Jefferson would have ridden out to the far fields to inspect winter work conveyed to the overseers in his memos: moving fences, changing a road, mending cabins, preparing fields for crops, belting the poplars, clearing cut forests, splitting wood for fence rails, cutting wood for charcoal, and clearing and cleaning meadow grounds. While riding between these areas of plantation activities, Jefferson paid attention to nature and the natural resources of the land. In 1817 he mentioned in his notes the Poplar Forest boundary marker trees he rode past when surveying his property: red oak, post oak, white and Spanish oaks, hickory, locust, and "old," "large," and "great" poplars. Trees were an important resource. In an early Garden Book reference, Jefferson

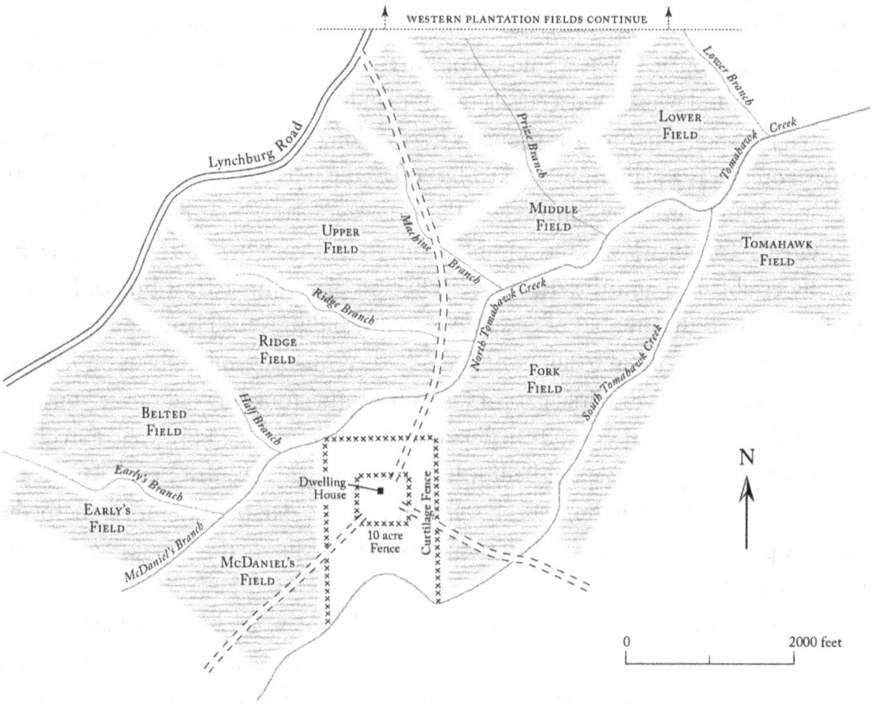

Fig. 91. Map of Poplar Forest showing plantation fields.

noted that one driver with a four-horse wagon could bring in 300 yards or five cords of firewood in one day, having made ten loads. The large quantities of wood used for fireplaces and stoves meant that the best trees were reserved for the best uses. Jefferson instructed his overseer in 1807 to "Use great economy in timber, never cutting down a tree for firewood or any other purpose as long as one can be found ready cut down & tolerably convenient."[58] In the kind of calculations for which he was famous, he praised his son-in-law at Monticello for an "experiment" with peach trees, which, planted 5 feet apart, will "furnish dead wood enough to supply a fireplace through the winter."[59] He had then calculated that ten fireplaces required 5,000 trees on 50 acres with a replacement of 700 trees per year. This undoubtedly was a consideration when planting the peach trees at Poplar Forest. In another calculation Jefferson noted that it took 27 cords of hardwood to make 605 bushels of charcoal used for heating and cooking. A tree of 18 inches diameter, he recorded, would yield 1 cord of wood, and an acre of "middling timbered land" would yield 30 cords of wood or "heaviest timbered" land, 100 cords.[60] Precise analytical calculations did not always equal an efficient outcome, but the mathematical effort seemed to soothe Jefferson's active mind.

Glimpses of Retired Life

There are only two general descriptions of Jefferson's retired life at Poplar Forest, one contemporary and one from memory. The contemporary snapshot came from Englishman George Flower, whom Jefferson invited to "become one of my family" at Poplar Forest in 1816. Flower's description perfectly captured the architectural effect Jefferson had created as well as the man himself:

> I found Mr. Jefferson at his Poplar Forest estate, in the western part of the State of Virginia. His house was built after the fashion of a French chateau, Octagon rooms, floors of polished oak, lofty ceilings, large mirrors betokened his French taste, acquired by his long residence in France. Mr. Jefferson's figure was rather majestic: tall (over six feet), thin, and rather high-shouldered: manners simple, kind, and courteous[.] His dress, in color and form, was quaint and old fashioned, plain and neat—a dark pepper-and-salt coat, cut in the old quaker fashion, with a single row of large metal buttons, knee-breeches, gray-worsted stockings, shoes fastened by large metal buckles—such was the appearance of Jefferson when I first made his acquaintance, in 1816. His two grand-daughters—Misses Randolph—well educated and accomplished young ladies, were staying with him at the time.[61]

Flower obviously contrasted Poplar Forest with other American houses he had visited and found it different. In a larger context this European found it more French than American.

The other description was more personal and nostalgic and emphasized Jefferson's family goal in retirement. Henry Randall's 1858 three-volume biography of Jefferson included an extraordinary description of his life at Poplar Forest. This came from Ellen Coolidge, who had readily responded to Randall in 1856 with great personal memories of her visits to Poplar Forest. The picture she paints is significant for understanding the family role of Thomas Jefferson, the grandfather, and the physical context of the architecture and furnishings at Poplar Forest. If ever there was a justification for the time, expense, and effort Jefferson put into creating his second home, it is found in Ellen's description. It is a rare glimpse of Thomas Jefferson and bears a full recitation:

> The house at Poplar Forest was very pretty and pleasant. It was of brick, one story in front, and, owing to the falling of the ground, two in the rear. It was an exact octagon, with a centre-hall twenty feet square, lighted from above. This was a beautiful room, and served as a dining-room. Round it were grouped a bright drawing-room looking south, my grandfather's own chamber, three other bedrooms, and a pantry. A terrace extended from one side of the house; there was a portico in front connected by a vestibule with the center room, and in the rear a verandah, on which the drawing-room opened, with its windows to the floor.... It was furnished in the simplest manner, but had a very tasty air; there was nothing common or second-rate about any part of the establishment, though there was no appearance of expense. As soon as the house was habitable, my grandfather began to take the ladies of his family, generally two at a time, with him, whenever he went. His first visit of a fortnight or three weeks was in the spring—the second, of about six weeks, in the early or late autumn. We have staid as much as two months at a time. My mother went occasionally—not very often—for she had too much to do at home. I . . . generally accompanied him with one of my younger sisters. Mr. Jefferson greatly enjoyed these visits. The crowd at Monticello of friends and strangers, of stationary or ever-varying guests, the coming and going, the incessant calls upon his own time and attention, the want of leisure that such a state of things entailed as a necessary consequence, the hustle and hurry of an almost perpetual round of company, wearied and harassed him in the end, whatever pleasure he may have taken, and it was sometimes great, in the society and conversation of his guests. At Poplar Forest he found in a pleasant home, rest, leisure, power to carry on his favorite pursuits—to think, to study, to read—whilst the presence of part of his family took away all character of solitude from his retreat. His young granddaughters were there to enliven it for him, to make his tea, preside over his dinner table, accompany him in his walks, in his occasional drives, and be with him at the time he most enjoyed society, from tea till bed time. The weather was generally fine (the autumn climate of this part of Virginia is delightful, and even the spring is pleasant), the neighbors, who were to a man exceedingly attached to him, were very friendly, without being oppressive in their attentions. There were some excellent people among those Bedford neighbors of ours, and something touching in their affection for their old friend, whose arrival they watched for with pleasant anticipation, and hailed with a sort of loyal satisfaction. It was no sooner known in the neighborhood that Mr. Jefferson had arrived, than our neighbors hastened to help our housekeeping with all kinds of fruit,

vegetables, poultry, game (I remember once a quarter of a bear's cub), the product of rich farms and an abundant country.

By and by the gentlemen came dropping in—the ladies soon followed—we were invited out to dine, and the neighbors came to dine with us—but not often enough to consume much time, or interrupt our home occupations. I remember among those neighbors a certain "Parson" Clay, as he was called, who must have been an Episcopal clergyman before the Revolution, to whose four sons my grandfather used to lend books, and who astonished me with their names of Cyrus, Odin, Julius and Paul.

My grandfather was very happy during these sojourns in a comparatively simple and secluded district—far from noise and news—of both of which he got too much at Monticello; and we, his grand-daughters, were very happy too. It was a pleasant change for us, a variety in life and manners. We saw, too, more of our dear grandfather at those times than at any other. He was most desirous that we should find congenial occupations, and we had books, drawing material, embroidery, and never felt time heavy on our hands. He interested himself in all we did, thought, or read. He would talk to us about his own youth and early friends, and tell us stories of former days. He seemed really to take as much pleasure in these conversations with us, as if we had been older and wiser people. Such was the influence of his affectionate, cheerful temper, that his grandchildren were as much at their ease with him, as if they had not loved and honored and revered him more than any other earthly being. I . . . not only listened with intense interest to all he said, but answered with perfect freedom, told my own opinions and impressions, gave him my own views of things, asked questions, made remarks, and, in short, felt as free and as happy as if I had been with companions of my own age. My grandfather missed my mother of course. Her company had become very necessary to him, but her absence seemed the only drawback on his unalloyed satisfaction during these short and highly prized intervals of rest and leisure.

Our days at Poplar Forest were cheerful and uneventful. We met in the morning for an early breakfast, which, like all his other meals, he took leisurely. Whilst sipping his coffee or tea he talked with us, and if there was anything unusual to be done, arranged our plans for the day. The forenoon, whilst we followed our own desires, he passed in the drawing room with his books. With the exception of an occasional visitor, he was seldom interrupted until the hour of his ride. We dined about three, and as he liked to sit over his wine (he never took more than three glasses, and these after, and not during dinner), I always remained at table till he rose. His conversation was at this time particularly pleasant—easy, flowing, and full of anecdote. . . . Sitting with my grandfather after dinner he would not infrequently speak to me of his early years and home and friends—of his favorite sister Jane, her rare talents, her wit, her musical powers—of my grandmother whose memory he cherished with deep and tender affection. He often quoted to us her sayings and opinions, and would preface his own advice with "your grandmother would have told you," "your grandmother always said." . . . After dinner he again retired for some hours, and later in the afternoon walked with us on the terrace, conversing in the same delightful manner, being sometimes animated, and sometimes earnest. . . . We did not leave him again til bed-time, but gave him his tea, and brought out our books or work. He would take his book from which he would occasionally look up to make a remark, to question us about what we were reading, or perhaps to read aloud to us from his own book, some passage which had struck him, and of which he wished to give us the benefit. About ten o'clock he rose to go, when we kissed him with warm, loving, grateful hearts, and went to our rest blessing God for such a friend. . . .

Our journeys to and from Bedford, were almost always pleasant. The weather at the season of our visit was good of course, though we were once or twice caught by an early winter. The roads were not bad for country roads. My grandfather travelled in his own carriage, with his own horses, his faithful Burwell on horseback by his side. It took us nearly three days to make the hundred miles. We always stopped at the same simple country inns, where the country-people were as much pleased to see the "Squire" as they always called Mr. Jefferson, as they could have been to meet their own best friends. They set out for him the best they had, gave him the nicest room, and seemed to hail his passage as an event most interesting to themselves. These were pleasant times, but I have dwelt on them long enough.[62]

George Flower's description set the overall architectural scene that Ellen completed and animated with emotional memories that stood out for her, and most likely for her sisters as well. These descriptions, together with letters back and forth from Poplar Forest and Monticello, let us piece together the appearance of the house and grounds; Jefferson's activities while there; the family's activities; interactions with the enslaved servants who came on the trip or were in residence; visits from neighbors and friends and to their homes; the sometimes eventful travel between the two sites; side trips to Natural Bridge; and the furnishings of the house as best we can understand them. Most of these glimpses are captured in the seamless history by Chambers so those that describe the house, its use, and its appearance will be the focus here.

Ellen's retrospective description of Poplar Forest was from a young adult's perspective that adeptly captured its unusual architectural character in addition to family vignettes. The north front did look like a one-story house and the south, two-story. This difference was owed to reducing the height of the main floor of a two-story house and excavating for a grade-level cellar on the rear. Ellen's description of "an exact" octagon was correct regarding the principal walls of the house that Jefferson had laboriously considered as an ideal shape. Ellen described the rear portico as a verandah, an elevated porch with no stairs that served as an outdoor room to engage the landscape. The "windows to the floor" description made reference to Jefferson's quest for maximum light and air. Ellen's clockwise (west to north to east) description of the perimeter rooms, starting with Jefferson's west side chamber suite, ended with "pantry," the southeastern room that allowed for public access to the wing roof and stair pavilion. Ellen described the "centre hall" as a 20-foot-square "bright" dining room and as a "beautiful room" "lighted from above." She failed to mention that the room was a cube, but, interestingly,

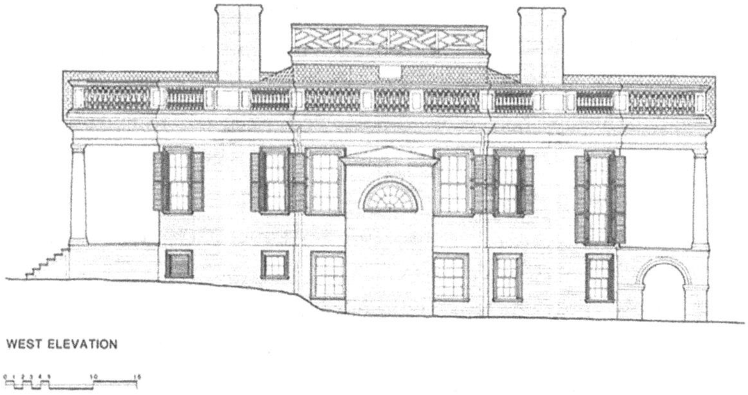

Fig. 92. Poplar Forest, west elevation.

she knew its size. Flower had also commented on the center room's "lofty ceilings." Ellen recalled that "the centre hall at Poplar Forest, its skylight shaded by Venetian blinds, and protected as it was from the Sun by the whole body of the house, was always deliciously cool."[63] She failed to mention the viewing deck of the center room's flat terras roof, where Jefferson undoubtedly took in the distant views of the mountains, but perhaps the climb over the roof and railing had not been appropriate for young ladies.

Ellen did not fail to mention her grandfather's important terras roof deck that extended from the east side of the house. This was the scene of delightful memories where, Jefferson remarked, "about twilight of the evening we sally out with the owls & bats and take our evening exercise on the terras."[64] Rooftop terraces, an English tradition, were uncommon in America. In his "Gardening and Architecture" essay, Lord Kames spoke of elevated English platform walks that were "airy" and "extend and vary the prospect, and elevate the mind."[65] The rooftop terrace above the dining room at Poplar Forest provided an even more elevated prospect of nature. Like that patrician placement of the wing terrace, it also provided another layer of privacy higher above the life of the enslaved workers below.

Jefferson's west-side suite contained two rooms divided by the bed alcove and received strong afternoon light from four windows. The alcove, like his own at Monticello, was open on both sides, unlike European prototypes and most of those at Monticello. This allowed for a cross-ventilation over his bed in the warmer months. In the colder months curtains on the alcove kept out drafts. Presumably one side of his suite served as a bed chamber and the other as a private cabinet or study, filled with books and writing materials. As in the chamber suites in Parisian houses, there were multiple means of egress and access. Three doors on the east side of the alcove formed a vestibule that connected to the dining room with a sash door. A doorway in the northwest diagonal wall led to the northwest chamber and from there to the entrance passage. On the alcove's west side three doors formed a vestibule that accessed the stair pavilion and the stair landing. In the west vestibule a ceiling hatch gave access to the cuddy (closet) over the alcove, and from there two ladders accessed the roof and the upper terras deck. The closet space above the bed received borrowed light via a transom from the stair pavilion's large lunette window. The stairs gave Jefferson access to three areas below: the cellar floor that was identical in plan to the upper floor; the exterior; and a retrofitted privy under the stairs. A greater measure of privacy was imparted to this wood-paneled privy by its being cleaned from the exterior.[66]

When not in his suite, Jefferson would have spent time reading or writing in the dining room, the parlor, or on the south portico. The south portico, or "verandah," as Ellen called it, served as a convenient outdoor reading room off the parlor.[67] The parlor, or drawing room, served as a social gathering space in addition to serving as the library. The great amount of light from the parlor's very transparent window wall was further enhanced by large mirrors on the opposite wall.[68] As the granddaughters testified, the skylight of the multipurpose dining room provided plenty of light even when louvered blinds covered it in the summer. Throughout the house were scattered 36 Windsor chairs of Jefferson's design that he had had made in Richmond.[69] These would also have been used on the south portico and on the wing deck. Life at Poplar Forest, as described by Jefferson's granddaughters, was reduced to the simple pleasures of the mind and of the family.

Privacy, by design, was enforced even when Jefferson was in residence alone. Jefferson's enslaved manservant Burwell Colbert accompanied him to Poplar Forest and took care of most of his needs, residing in the lower level. Compared to the Monticello's household staff of about thirty enslaved servants, a couple of people could serve Jefferson and family at Poplar Forest. Except for daily duties of serving food and

Fig. 93. Perspective drawing of Jefferson's west chamber suite showing alcove bed in the center of two rooms.

keeping fireplaces going in the winter, the few enslaved servants were mostly out of sight in the lower level and in the service wing. The presence of a dumb-waiter table at Poplar Forest implies that Jefferson's penchant for private dining, established in Paris, at the President's House, and at Monticello, was continued here to minimize the presence of servants. A call-bell system from the dining room out to the service wing meant that servants did not need to be stationed in the house.[70] When it came time for John Hemmings to install exterior louvered blinds on the windows, Jefferson instructed him that the north portico only needed a lower half-set, "to prevent people from seeing into the rooms."[71] The only people looking in the windows would have been enslaved workers.

When Jefferson was in residence, enslaved workers might be working in the wing, cooking, washing clothes, or tending the smokehouse. His terras roof deck meant he could sit or stroll above those who labored beneath him out of sight. The elevated south portico served the same function. The enslaved Hemings craftsmen finishing the interior of the house for many years were the significant exception to the privacy enjoyed on the upper level of the main house. The needs of one person at Poplar Forest skewed most conventional service requirements and reinforced the atmosphere of privacy. Even when Jefferson had been forced to bow to convenience in altering his original design—for instance, where to place the stairways—the solution was facilitated by the private nature of the house. Jefferson could retreat inside his private suite, inside the private house, and inside the private landscape; it was as private a world as he could make it.

Ellen's memory succinctly captured Jefferson's daily life at Poplar Forest. With or without grandchildren, his tranquil life revolved around his pleasures: reading, writing letters to friends, tending to his landscaped gardens, riding out to supervise plantation operations, and resting. Ellen described to her mother once that after arriving from the three-day, 93-mile journey, "Grandpa has been taking such a long nap."[72] He was, after all, seventy-five at the time. What Ellen, Cornelia, and everyone else consistently failed to mention was the presence of Jefferson's, and therefore their, "shadow family."

Retirement Taste

Ellen's memory that the house had "no appearance of expense" might have been true in regard to some of the furnishings. It certainly wasn't true of John Hemmings's fine woodwork, which surpassed that of most other houses.[73] Even the secondary spaces featuring large Tuscan order entablatures gave a "tasty air" in comparison with Governor Barbour's house (Barboursville), for instance, designed by Jefferson but executed without any interior entablatures or even simple cornices.[74] Ellen's memory that there was "nothing common or second rate" about the house was certainly true for anything Jefferson designed, not least his dream house. What stood out for George Flower were the uncommon parts: octagon rooms, polished oak floors, and large mirrors.[75] Other uncommon features were double-hung varnished walnut window sashes secured with

British spring locks, as well as fifteen Rumford-style fireplaces. Altogether the light-filled interior was uncommon in a polychromatic way: floors of golden oak; window sash and doors of varnished walnut; shiny brass hardware; creamy-white wood trim; white marble hearthstones; white Italian marble for two fireplace surrounds; iron fire-backs; and various shades of oil, pigmented lime wash, and distemper paints coloring the plaster walls. Jefferson's order of paint pigments Stone Ochre, Terra di Siena, and Prussian Blue could have been for the paints and washes that were shades of blue, gray, and tan.[76] The choice of materials and their finishes was uncommonly Jeffersonian. The two best rooms, the dining room and parlor, each had a special material as a fireplace surround, one imported and one native. The dining room, it is surmised, had the local white Virginia marble for its fireplace surround. The best room, the parlor, is believed to have had the imported Italian Carrara marble fireplace surround.[77] These choices represented an Old World and New World mixture that was also characteristically Jeffersonian.

Ellen's comment that Poplar Forest was furnished in the "simplest manner" came with the caveat that it had a "tasty air." What was "tasty" about the furnishings for such a unique and personal house? After all, Jefferson had carefully selected and brought back from France up-to-date neoclassical furnishings for Monticello. The incomplete picture of the furnishings at Poplar Forest comes from letters that mention what Jefferson sent down from Monticello on Jerry's wagon. This includes a chest of drawers made at Monticello (used by the granddaughters), a round table, four "other tables," three dozen Windsor chairs, one or two Campeachy "siesta" chairs, four Pembroke tea tables, two stoves, Maria Jefferson Eppes's harpsichord, at least one map, a "head of Christ" painting, books, and bookcases. In the 1815 Luxury Tax inventory, taxing mahogany furniture to help pay for Virginia's debts in the War of 1812, Jefferson listed furniture over the value of $200: four small mahogany book cases with mahogany sashes (to hold the petit format books), a three-part mahogany dining-room table, and four Pembroke tea tables. In 1819 Jefferson had a spell of rheumatism at Poplar Forest and wrote his daughter at Monticello: "I long for a Siesta chair which would have admitted the medium position. I must therefore pray you to send by Henry the one made by Johnny Hemings."[78] Jefferson later described the chair as having red Morocco leather with a green material across the back. Other furniture remains unknown since the estate inventory at Jefferson's death has never been found. Francis Eppes took most of the furnishings to Florida in 1828 and sold the rest. Nails and nail holes found in walls could be for Jefferson-era prints or paintings, if the busy walls at Monticello are any indication. Two dumbwaiters occupied their place next to the three-part dining room table with semi-octagon ends; the table could be made into a large octagon, a small octagon, or two side tables and a drop-leaf table. A drawing by Cornelia depicts a round revolving-top table and one of the Windsor chairs made for Poplar Forest. Another drawing shows a simple table, likely made by John Hemmings, with a round tray and a wine bottle.[79] One "tasty" purchase for the house was a set of china with scenes of Oxford and Cambridge depicted appropriately within octagonal borders. It seems that

Fig. 94. Jefferson used his south portico like an outdoor room where he could relax in his Campeachy chair.

simple and functional furniture sufficed for Jefferson's second home, which was never meant for entertaining and which saw few visitors.

The Labor of "My People"

We might imagine Jefferson in solitude, if he came to Poplar Forest without family members, but he was never alone. Since Poplar Forest was a satellite plantation, the enslaved workers were there primarily for plantation duties, not those associated with a full-time residence.[80] Still, some of the Poplar Forest enslaved community served Jefferson while he was in residence. Others he encountered as he rode around his property. The hired white workers also used their own enslaved craftsmen and laborers when building the house, but they also would have used the enslaved laborers living on one of the Poplar Forest quarter farms. Phil Hubbard, who excavated the south lawn, was good at making mortar and plaster. Others, like Jerry, drove a wagon from Monticello and hauled materials for the workers at Poplar Forest. Other examples of the connection between those living on these two plantations include Dick and Henry, who occasionally came with supplies from Monticello packed in a cart pulled by mules. A man named Harry transported goods from Monticello to Lynchburg on the James River. Gil and Israel Gillette accompanied Jefferson from Monticello as postilions for his carriage. Burwell Colbert, Jefferson's enslaved manservant who always accompanied him, came on horseback.

Colbert performed his typical duties as manservant and butler. He oversaw any enslaved people serving Jefferson, family, or guests, and he personally looked after Jefferson in his bed-chamber suite. Colbert and other enslaved workers made beds, laid fires, served meals, and fetched or carried various things. They served breakfast and dinner, brought tea and coffee, and lit the evening candles and lamps. Colbert might have supervised the cleaning of dishes and the polishing of silverware. Keeping the fireplaces going was not inconsiderable labor. Of the fifteen fireplaces in the house, nine were on the main level. Five of those, in the west chamber, dining room, and parlor, needed tending even when Jefferson was in residence alone. When others were there, an additional two to four fireplaces needed tending, not to mention the seven on the lower level where the workers lived and worked. There were also two stoves that would have been set into the most frequently used fireplaces. In his description of Virginia to a friend in 1815, Jefferson mentioned that constant fires were necessary five months of the year, and morning and evening fires for a month on either side of the season lasting from mid-October to mid-March.[81] In addition to household duties, Colbert attended to any painting or window reglazing and possibly polished the European-style oak floors. Colbert would have been in close proximity to Jefferson, but a servant-bell system reflected another means of calling those in the cellar or outside the house. Evidence showed that a bell wire connected the dining room with the east wing of offices where the kitchen was located, and possibly with the lower level.[82] Jefferson could have used the bell to announce when he was ready for food to be brought up from the kitchen to the east pantry, where it was received by Colbert and then served with refined earthenware ceramics onto the dumb waiters next to the dining room table. Enslaved workers might then be excused to the wing to await another bell call when the meal concluded. Service for Jefferson dining alone, or with two granddaughters, was simple and only slightly enhanced when neighbors were occasionally invited over.

Jefferson would have encountered the enslaved women who cleaned the house when he was in residence. Ellen wrote upon arriving after the 1819 hailstorm that "our room [was] clean and pretty well aired by Eugenia's care."[83] In a memo to his overseer in 1811, Jefferson mentioned that Edy or Aggy would be chosen to "clean the house and assist here part of the day when I am here."[84] Edy, Abby's daughter, was nineteen at that time. Dinah's daughter Aggy was twenty-two and later trained to use the spinning jenny. In the same memo Jefferson remarked that "Hannah cooks & washes for me." When writing to William Coffee about staying in the house by himself, Jefferson instructed the overseer that Hannah would accommodate Coffee's needs. An 1821 letter from

Jefferson to the overseer indicated that Hannah and Maria should "have the house in order."[85] In a unique instance Hannah, born in 1770, wrote to Jefferson in 1818, "Master I write you a few lines to let you know that your house and furniture are all safe as I expect you would be glad to know."[86] She went on to say she was sorry to hear of his illness and that he could not come that fall.

After 1815, John Hemmings and his nephews Beverly, Madison, and Eston frequently came to do skilled joinery work at Poplar Forest. Despite all the letters written by Ellen and Cornelia when visiting Poplar Forest, they never once mention the young Hemings "aids" who were their step-uncles as Jefferson's children through his relationship with Sally Hemings. John Hemmings was the exception. He was mentioned in a letter from Ellen to her sister Virginia Randolph:

> John Hemings begged it of me as a very particular favor to "give his news to Aunt Prisilla" to say he was doing well but mighty tired of the Forest and wished himself at home. Any message that she may send him it will give me great pleasure to receive from you—for Johnny is one of my favorites and more so, now than ever since I have witnessed his kind attentions to Burwell.[87]

What Ellen referred to was a serious illness that struck Burwell while at Poplar Forest. Cornelia's letter regarding Burwell's illness mentioned "Daddy who nursed him constantly with the greatest care and attention," a reference to John Hemmings.[88] Once Burwell regained his health, notwithstanding the care of a physician who bled and blistered him, he resumed his duties in the house as well as painting and glazing broken windows. The last known letter written by John Hemmings is one from Poplar Forest to his favorite Jefferson grandchild, Septimia Randolph, who lived at Monticello. In it he acknowledged a letter he had received from her and went on to describe in detail the work he was executing for Francis Eppes.[89]

On his daily rides around the property, Jefferson observed and conversed with white overseers and members of the enslaved community. Some handled livestock: oxen, horses, mules, cattle, hogs, and Merino sheep. Enslaved workers Jame Hubbard and Hal, among other duties, acted as hogkeepers for well over 100 hogs. Jefferson knew what to expect and inspect according to his Farm Book notes. He noted that a middle-size tree would make 17 bolts of wood that would produce 4 staves each; or the same tree would yield 20 cuts with each cut making 3 barrels; or two trees equaled about 50 barrels.[90] Barrels were needed for the processed tobacco and wheat that would make its way by down the James River by bateaux from Lynchburg to Richmond. Jefferson would have encountered Will and Hal, who produced charcoal when they were not working in the blacksmith shop. Jefferson would inspect the many plantation buildings and agricultural machines that constantly needed repair, like the spinning machine and wheat machine John Hemmings put in order.

Jefferson would have seen the enslaved women Edy, Aggy, Abby, Marie, Sally, Lucy, Nisy, and Cate occupied in spinning and weaving. They turned cotton, flax, hemp, and wool into plantation clothes and other useful items using the spinning jenny and the common loom. Jefferson's time / labor notes in the Farm Book indicated that 400 pounds of hemp would take three spinners twenty-six weeks to spin and that two weavers could make 60 yards of cloth per week.[91] The overseers were instructed that an acre of "the best ground" was to be kept for a permanent hemp patch. Other enslaved workers constantly processed food and material, some of which was sent to Monticello, like soap, lard, and butter, and even cattle and hogs, both on the hoof and as processed meats. In what little free time she had, Cate also raised turkeys and chickens to sell to Jefferson; other enslaved workers earned money by selling him watermelons and eggs.[92] On December 11, 1824, in a rare instance of using his enslaved children's names, Jefferson noted from Monticello, "Pd. Madison and Eston for 100. Cabbages 2.D."[93]

Besides his manservant, Burwell Colbert, Jefferson most frequently came in close daily contact with the enslaved Hemings men. From 1815 to 1823 Thomas Jefferson occupied his retreat at Poplar Forest as John Hemmings and his nephews—Jefferson's sons—Beverly, Madison, and Eston Hemings carefully crafted its finished parts. How much Jefferson engaged his sons is a mystery, but if written references are any indication, they were as invisible as most enslaved servants, even if their handiwork was greatly admired. Their work in the upper-floor rooms meant that, unlike other enslaved workers, they were in constant proximity. Their lives and their undocumented work at Poplar Forest are a historical silence both purposeful and poignant. While John Hemmings enjoyed certain privileges among the enslaved population, Jefferson's sons might have enjoyed a pride as skilled house joiners and any increased status accorded them as members of the Hemings family. They were consciously denied any privileges as members of the Jefferson family, although Madison recalled that he and his siblings "were permitted to stay about the 'great house,' and only required to do such light work as going on errands . . . and were measurably happy."[94] John is mentioned as a favorite of Jefferson's grandchildren, but they fail to mention John's nephews either in contemporary letters or in later histories. The obvious failure to call them by name served to deny their paternity and their identity. Besides their being listed in the rolls of the enslaved, and the reference to buying cabbages from them, there is only one other reference to Jefferson's sons—a note indicating that Eston drove a cart to Poplar Forest[95]

Fittingly, the last known joinery work executed by John Hemmings, in 1826, was for Jefferson's coffin with wood that he had been saving for that purpose. John Hemmings was among the few slaves given his freedom, to commence one year after Jefferson's death, along with the tools of his trade, and a "comfortable log-house" to be built on Monticello land with an accompanying curtilage of one acre. This location on home ground, Jefferson reasoned, would be "convenient to Charlottesville and the University where they [John Hemmings, Joe Fosset, and Burwell Colbert] will be mostly employed."[96] John Hemmings's health declined after his wife, Priscilla, died in 1830, and he slipped into depression and excessive drink. The interest in his trade also died. His legacy would be extended through his two remaining nephew apprentices. Beverly had been allowed to "disappear" in 1822 and was lost to history thereafter. Madison and Eston had been given a provisional freedom in Jefferson's will. Out of concern for his family's reputation, Jefferson did not directly free his two sons, which would have confirmed their special relationship, but gave their service to John Hemmings until they were twenty-one, making it seem like a favor to him. In an additional obscured reference to their relationship to Jefferson, his will requested that the Legislature of Virginia allow Madison and Eston to remain in the state when freed (freed slaves were required to leave the state unless granted special status to stay), "where their families and connections are, as an additional instance of the favor, of which I have received so many other manifestations, in the course of my life, and for which I now give them my last, solemn, and dutiful thanks."[97] This last statement of thanks is seemingly to the State of Virginia for the favor of granting his sons residency. It can perhaps be read as another veiled reference to his sons, finally thanking them for unacknowledged and excellent work for which Jefferson must have been proud. Jefferson had begun his will by giving Poplar Forest to his grandson Francis Eppes; ironically, he ended it with reference to his sons who had crafted his special retreat house.

Madison and Eston were freed in 1827, living with their mother, Sally, in Charlottesville until her death around 1835. In 1840 the brothers moved to Ohio, where Madison gainfully worked as a builder, identifying with the Black community and famously discussing his parentage in an 1873 newspaper article. Eston moved to Wisconsin, working as a musician, passing for white, and keeping his family secrets. As Annette Gordon-Reed has observed, Jefferson's sons had to leave behind their childhood as well as slavery. Jefferson "had a direct hand in shaping their progress through life and the way they viewed themselves."[98] Jefferson had given them an identity as skilled joiners, a trade he greatly valued, and one in which he could watch as they progressed under the loving direction of their uncle. They were denied much, but as Madison said, they were measurably happy in the life of slavery and left it while still young. They had a gray status of existence and identity in a black and white world, and as Gordon-Reed notes: "This intersection of bloodlines and slavery, and the way Jefferson chose to handle the intersection, was just one more way slavery distorted human relations."[99] Their lives were undoubtedly enriched through the professional tutelage and parental-like care of their uncle, and the years spent crafting their father's retreat. How different their lives might have been without that experience is impossible to know.

7

A RETIREMENT HOBBY

Jefferson's experience as an architect and builder, first gained at Monticello and then reinforced at Poplar Forest, was severely tested on a final magnum opus. On December 18, 1817, Thomas Jefferson wrote from Poplar Forest to his good friend Joseph C. Cabell, "I have only this single anxiety in this world, it is a bantling of 40 years birth & nursing, & if I can once see it on its legs, I will sing with sincerity & pleasure my nunc demittas."[1] Jefferson referred to "our University of Virginia, my present hobby."[2] The enormous scale and significant cost of the project would challenge Jefferson as never before for the familiar aspects of qualified workers, superior and innovative building materials, and quality control. Thomas Jefferson was not adept at, or even disposed to, explaining his architectural and institutional visions to those holding the purse strings. This would be his all-out risky gamble that, once begun, would require unusual patience and political fortitude despite complex circumstances that constantly threatened to negate his ambitious goals. Most significant was Jefferson's hand in everything from conception to completed construction, and everything in between that conveyed his experienced role as an architect, builder, and educator. His role in this final project is worth summarizing as the culmination of his experience with Poplar Forest.

The peace and quiet obtained at Poplar Forest facilitated Jefferson's design and planning for the University of Virginia. Jefferson confided to Benjamin Henry Latrobe in 1817 that he had conceived the idea for an academical village, rather than one large college building fifteen years before and that "2 or 3 years ago" he had drawn the "ichnography & elevations" for the buildings.[3] Typically Jefferson drew more than the elevations. His three-dimensional conception of every aspect of each building was reflected in precise specifications for every material down to the door hardware. Detailed drawings and careful planning allowed Jefferson to visualize the work and to instill some measure of control. The more critical aspect of control depended upon constant supervision. Jefferson knew all too well that workers were the wild card of quality construction. Jefferson confided to James Dinsmore at the beginning of the project, "I suppose the superintendence of the buildings will rest chiefly on myself as most convenient."[4] He warned another worker that "the constant inspection of a competent eye is necessary, with the power to dismiss the workman found incompetent or unfaithful."[5] Jefferson explained to John Adams that the University was four miles from Monticello and "gives me frequent exercise, and the oftener as I direct its architecture, its plan is unique, and it is becoming an object of curiosity for the traveler."[6] When walking became a burden for the elderly Jefferson, he would ride down from Monticello to inspect the University work from horseback. The inconvenience of supervising the work from Poplar Forest was another challenge, but it did not lessen Jefferson's responsibility. As he wrote Arthur Brockenbrough, the University proctor, "you can have an answer from here [Poplar Forest] to any letter in one week."[7] During one visit to Poplar Forest in 1819 Jefferson wrote nine letters about the University work, sometimes one every other day and even two in one day.

Quality control was never more important to Thomas Jefferson than when constructing his own major public project. The public facades of his University buildings had to display superior workmanship for which his designs would ultimately be judged. In a letter to Hugh Chisolm, who was constructing the first pavilion, Jefferson laid out his goal: "to have the work done in the best manner, is the first object," and more importantly, "I consider it as the interest of the College, the town, and neighborhood to introduce a reform of the barbarous workmanship hitherto practiced there, and to raise us to a level with the rest of the country. . . . I hope we shall take a higher stand."[8] Voluminous drawings, accounts, specifications, and letters demonstrate Jefferson's obsessive attention both to the smallest and most common component of construction, bricks and brickwork, and also to the largest and most uncommon design feature, correct architectural orders.[9] Jefferson's vision as an architect and builder, and his prowess as a builder, depended upon finding the right workers and keeping an eye on their work.

Construction materials and workers had been a consistent background affair during Jefferson's life, His idiosyncratic choices for quality materials and particular workmanship raised the ante for this public project. This was an enormous project, one of the largest in the country, employing up to two hundred workmen. Insisting on his own complex terras roof system over the student rooms and innovative tinned shingles on the pavilion roofs was not the easy or less expensive choice. Like the transportation challenges faced at Poplar Forest, most of the materials, besides lumber and brickwork, came through merchants in the nearest seaport, Richmond, and then to Charlottesville by wagon or upriver on bateaux. Imported goods included crown glass from Boston and Philadelphia; plaster from Nova Scotia; Franklin stoves from Philadelphia; sash cord, sheet iron, window weights, and Roman cement from New York; sheet iron from Baltimore; white pine lumber from Maine; the "best Russian hemp" rope and tinned shingles from Richmond; massive amounts of door and window hardware from England; and the special terra-cotta entablature ornaments from New York City.

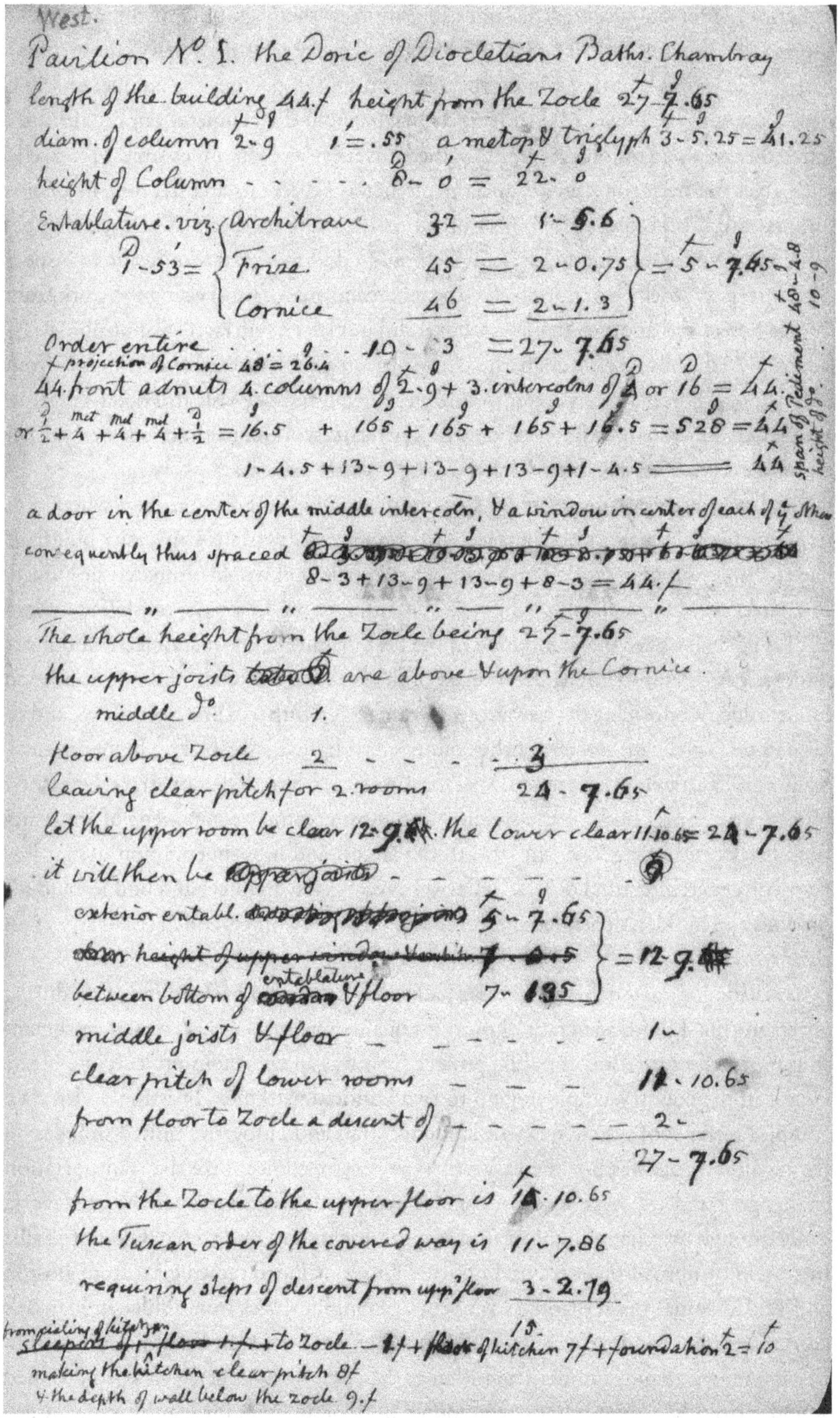

West.
Pavilion No. I. the Doric of Diocletians Baths. Chambray
length of the building 44.f height from the Zocle 27-7.65
diam. of column 2-9 1'=.55 a metop & triglyph 3-5.25 = 41.25
height of Column . . . . . . 8-0 = 22-0
Entablature. viz. Architrave 32 = 1-5.6
1-53 = Frize 45 = 2-0.75 = 5-7.65
Cornice 46 = 2-1.3
Order entire . . . . 10-3 = 27-7.65
+ projection of Cornice 48' = 26.4
44. front admits 4. columns of 2-9 + 3. intercolns of 4 or 16 = 44.
or 1/2 + 4 + 4 + 4 + 1/2 = 16.5 + 165 + 165 + 165 + 16.5 = 528 = 44
1-4.5 + 13-9 + 13-9 + 13-9 + 1-4.5 = 44
a door in the center of the middle intercoln, & a window in center of each of the others
consequently thus spaced
8-3 + 13-9 + 13-9 + 8-3 = 44.f
span of Pediment 48-4.8
height do. 10-9
The whole height from the Zocle being 27-7.65
the upper joists are above & upon the Cornice.
middle do. 1.
floor above Zocle 2 3
leaving clear pitch for 2. rooms 24-7.65
let the upper room be clear 12-9. the lower clear 11-10.65 = 24-7.65
it will then be
exterior entabl. 5-7.65
clear height of upper windows 7-0.5 = 12-9.
between bottom of entablature & floor 7-1.35
middle joists & floor 1-
clear pitch of lower rooms . . . 11-10.65
from floor to Zocle a descent of 2-
27-7.65
from the Zocle to the upper floor is 15-10.65
the Tuscan order of the covered way is 11-7.86
requiring steps of descent from upp. floor 3-2.79
from ceiling of kitchen to Zocle — 1f + floor of kitchen 7f + foundation 2 = 10
making the kitchen clear pitch 8f
& the depth of wall below the zocle 9.f

Fig. 95. Jefferson's calculation for bricks for the construction of a University pavilion.

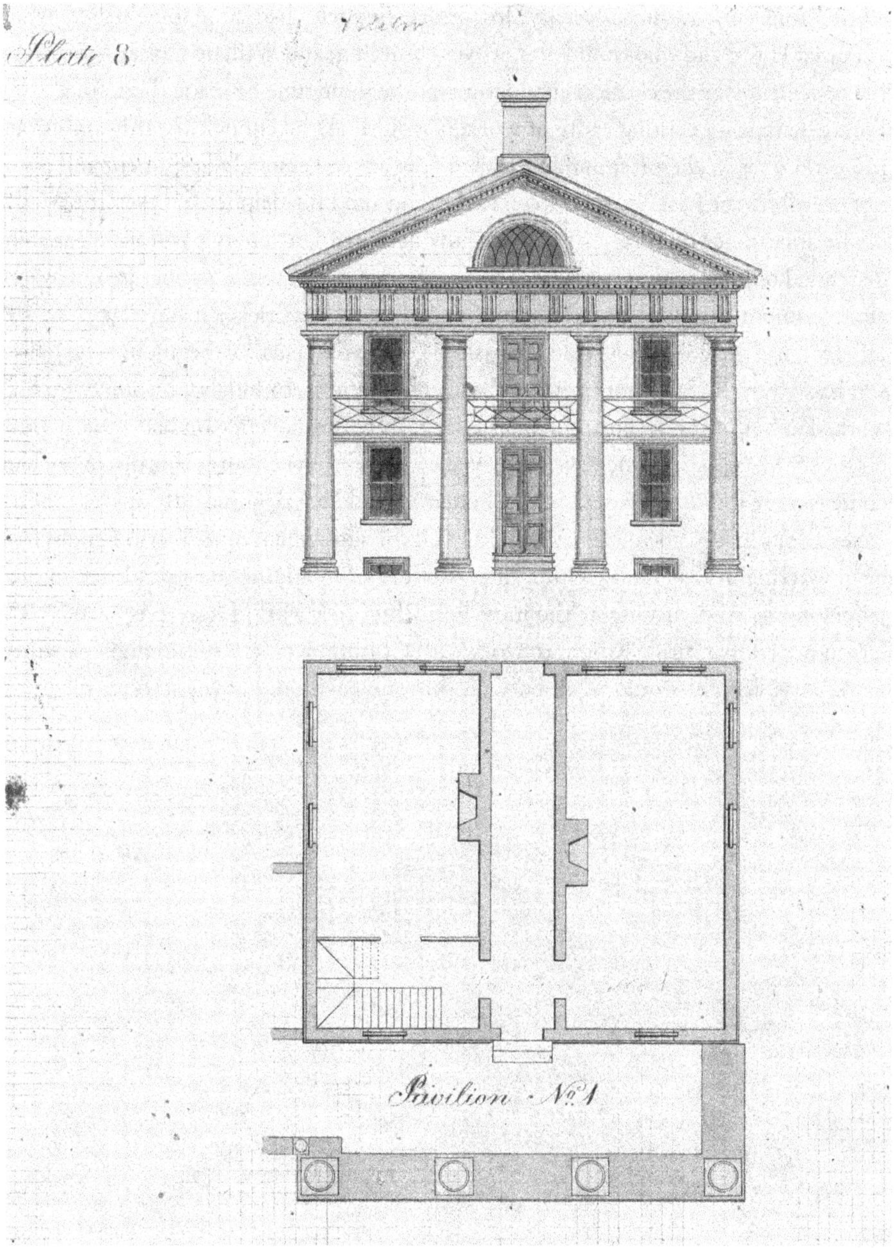

Fig. 96. John Neilson drawing for Pavilion I at the University.

Workers composed the other crucial part of the equation, whether they were local, recruited from outside Virginia, or imported from abroad. Jefferson started by hiring familiar workers who had proven their worth at Monticello and Poplar Forest: James Dinsmore, John Neilson, and James Oldham as finished trim joiners; Hugh Chisolm for bricklaying; John Perry, who would work as a general contractor overseeing several trades; John Gorman, who had laid the Poplar Forest hearthstones and who executed all the stonework at the University; Joseph Antrim, who had done some plaster work at Poplar Forest and who would plaster every building; and William Coffee, who made the ornaments for the classical entablatures at the same time he made those for Poplar Forest. Jefferson's existing cadre of workers would not be enough for this ambitious project. Other workers responded to newspaper ads or personal recruitment and came not only from the East Coast between Richmond and Philadelphia, but even from Italy.

The appearance of Jefferson's ten carefully designed University pavilions ultimately depended on the executed quality their facades presented to the public. In Tidewater and Piedmont Virginia the superior building material was brick, a material with which Jefferson had great experience. In his rush to get the first pavilion begun in 1817, Jefferson had given the brickwork contract, with reservations, to Hugh Chisolm, who had worked at both Monticello and Poplar Forest. By this time Jefferson had made a great discovery of a superior bricklayer and type of brick in Lynchburg; this discovery had come too late for Poplar Forest, but he hoped it would bear significantly on the appearance of "our first Academical pavilion," and all the subsequent ones. David Knight had been working in Lynchburg with a "new method of moulding the stock brick in oil," Jefferson reported, making it "the most beautiful brick work, I have ever seen."[10] Jefferson hoped that hiring Knight to work with Chisolm would result in higher-quality work. Alas, Knight would work only on this one pavilion, but his smooth oil-stock

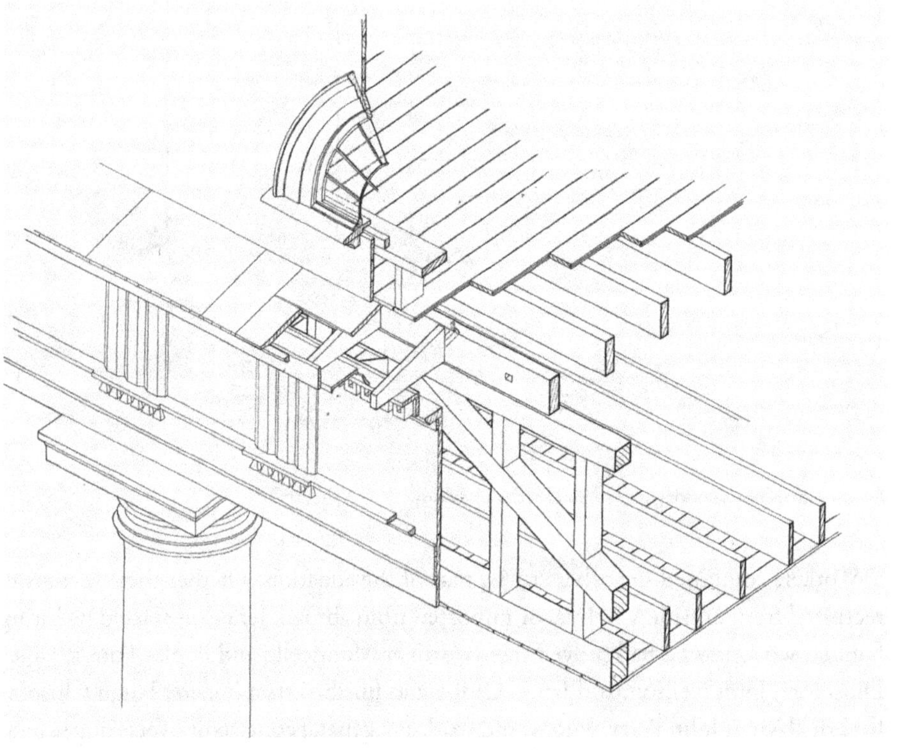

Fig. 97. Drawing of roof and entablature framing for Pavilion I.

brick would be used for all the pavilion facades along with a tight ribbon joint, a red wash, and a white penciled line equaling the most exquisite brickwork in the state. The brickwork of the student rooms was hierarchically lower in quality even though they were adjacent to the pavilion facades.[11] Despite the addition of Knight, Jefferson complained to James Madison as the first building season closed in the middle of November 1817 that "we fail in finishing our 1st pavilion this season by the sloth and discord of our workmen, who have given me much trouble."[12] Construction was off to a rocky start, and Jefferson might have wondered whether it portended ill luck for the rest of what would stretch out to become a nine-year project.

Jefferson hunted for bricklayers with the "1st degree of skill" in Richmond and as far away as Philadelphia, publishing ads in newspapers giving exacting specifications for the quality of brickwork he expected. The specifications revealed his understanding of the process, calling for three types of mortar (exterior, interior, and middle grout), mortar sand that contained no mould (dirt), for a minimum number of bats (partial bricks) in the Flemish Bond pattern, for clinkers (hard bricks) to be used for the exterior faces, and for no sammel (soft) bricks to be used on the exterior, with a fine levied for each one found. Jefferson would provide wall sizes, estimated number of bricks, distance from the site for materials (sand, lime, and wood), the finish for the joint, wash and penciling, and how the work would be measured for payment.[13] For the largest and most complicated building, the Rotunda, Jefferson calculated the exact number of bricks to be 1,087,740. His estimate included the costs for the different types of labor for making the bricks, the number that could be made each month, the quantity of cord wood needed to burn the bricks, and the cost of food and whiskey for each man.[14] Tight specifications up-front were essential for quality as well as for avoiding disputes of cost. A well-made and well-laid brick was just as important as a properly executed Corinthian column capital.

Jefferson's architectural vision mandated an effort to elegantly cloak the University buildings, showing "varieties of the finest examples." On Christmas Eve of 1819, he confided to a friend that the University "will form a unique and beautiful Academical Village, in which every Professor will have a distinct house, or pavilion, to himself. . . . These pavilions are of the best workmanship of street architecture, intended as regular and classical models for the lectures on that subject."[15] Without humility Jefferson proudly described his University project to his intimate friend Maria Cosway: "I have been myself the Architect of the plan of its buildings . . . and I assure you it would be thought a handsome & classical thing in Italy." He went on to explain that individual pavilions, rather than "a single, massive structure," would exhibit "varieties of the finest samples of architecture" and the whole "a model of beauty original and unique."[16] To other friends he variously referred to his designs as unique models; models of good taste and good architecture; the best variations of the Doric, Ionic, and Corinthian; a specimen strictly classical; unrivaled in this country; pure originality in the design; and a style of purely classical architecture.[17] To his architectural pupil Robert Mills, who would later design an addition to the Rotunda, Jefferson proudly wrote that the University buildings would be a "splendid establishment, would be thought so in Europe, and for the chastity of its architecture and classical taste leaves everything in America far behind it."[18] In another letter to Mills he called his designs, which were now a reality, a "specimen of every fine model of every order of Architecture, purely correct, and yet presenting a whole entirely new and unique."[19] Of the Rotunda Jefferson stated to a friend that it was a "specimen of classical architecture which would be remarked in Europe."[20] The Rotunda's exterior capitals, carved in Italy, were described by a Jefferson friend to be "equal in architectural perfection to any in the United States."[21]

If Jefferson displayed modesty as an architect up to this time, his boastful statements make it apparent that, second only to his conception of a new type of university, he was most proud of his architectural designs. He based his opinion on comparative models in America and Europe and remarked that the University buildings would be "worthy of attracting the curiosity" of visitors in addition to becoming a museum of classical orders for the students. Following his own precedents at Monticello and Poplar Forest, his designs were driven by the mathematical precision and codified proportions and precedents from antiquity. Jefferson's efforts to achieve the correct architectural models also mirrored his past experience—a tenacious conviction of what he wanted and an unusual patience for achieving an ideal outcome by overcoming challenges of materials and workmanship.

Those among the architecturally literate knew that the various architectural orders from antiquity could be distinguished not only by their distinct column capitals but also from the associated entablatures above that the columns supported. Some knew through architectural handbooks that there was a great variety within each of the classical orders. Jefferson's use of various Roman details at Monticello could be considered a private museum of his favorite orders and were primarily used as accurate copies. One at Poplar Forest he playfully altered to indulge his fancy. The orders Jefferson chose for the University, although frequently mentioned as models for public edification, displayed a variety of details and sources. Still, the commitment to using historically correct orders increased the challenge for special materials and proper workmanship.

Thomas Jefferson's previous experience with proper exterior columns had resulted in mixed results. For the front portico of Monticello he had first used stone shafts with a compromised result when they had to be taken down and reassembled. By the time he came to replace the temporary tree trunk "columns" on the rear portico of Monticello, he settled for a brick shaft coated with a lime render, but using real stone bases and capitals. At Poplar Forest he settled for even less with the entire Tuscan order column of base, shaft, and capital executed in brick and coated with render to resemble one large piece of carved stone. At the University Jefferson veered more toward the ideal, wanting stone bases and capitals attached to rendered brick column shafts. This posed an obvious and immediate dilemma because some of the capitals were of the elegant Ionic order and some were of the much more delicate and complex Corinthian order. After John Gorman tried his hand at carving local stone, Jefferson's solution was to import two Italian brothers to carve local stone with the sad realization that it was not

Fig. 98. Pavilion III, University of Virginia, with Corinthian capitals of Carrara marble.

suitable for finely carved work. Rather than compromising his design, Jefferson sent the Raggi brothers back to Italy to carve Ionic and Corinthian capitals in the superior Carrara marble, with the inevitable difficulty of shipping them to Virginia. The local stone was deemed good enough for all of the column bases, for the simpler Doric order capitals, and for the bases and capitals of the smaller Tuscan order columns connecting the pavilions. All of this stonework would be performed by John Gorman. Jefferson was constantly justifying the additional time, labor, and expense for his architectural vision. His less-than-convincing explanation was that he had considered putting different examples of architecture in a museum, but due to space requirements, it made more sense to put the specimens on the exterior of the ten pavilions.

The companion part of any Greek or Roman column was the entablature moldings and ornaments, and with these Jefferson had better luck. These large wooden exterior moldings constituted the most challenging work for the joiners responsible for finished woodwork. Jefferson had not only chosen his joiners wisely, using former workers James Dinsmore, John Neilson, and James Oldham, but his contracts also stated that finish work should be done in the "most perfect good manner . . . strictly according to the forms and orders of Architecture."[22] He even required his joiners to make their own construction drawings for his approval. In November 1817, after the first pavilion (today's number VII) was underway, Jefferson wrote to James Madison: "We are sadly at a loss here for a Palladio. I had three different editions but they are at Washington, and nobody in this part of the country has one unless you have. . . . [I need to] use it for a year to come."[23] A later letter from James Dinsmore to Jefferson made clear that he was using a Palladio book when he inquired, "whether you Intend using the Base and

Cap laid down in the twelfth plate of Palladios first Book (from which the entablature is taken) or from plate Eleven as there is considerable differences in the form & in the diminution of the Column between the two plates."[24] For interior entablatures Jefferson used Antoine Desgodetz's *Antiquities of Rome* (1682). His other critical source book for exterior orders was Roland Freart de Chambray's *Parallèle de l'architecture.* With the exception of the two northernmost pavilions on the Lawn (I and II), Jefferson based the variety of pavilion orders on the east side of the Lawn on Chambray and those on the west on Palladio. The odd-numbered pavilions on the west, according to Jefferson's notes, were based on the following, "No. 1 Doric of Diocletian's baths Chambray; No. 3 Corinthian Palladio; No. 5 Ionic with modillions Palladio; no. 7 Doric of Palladio with mutules Palladio; no. 9 Ionic with dentils. Temple of Fortuna Virilis. Palladio." The even-numbered pavilions on the east were, "No. 2 Ionic, with dentils from the Temple of Fortuna Virilis. Palladio; No. 4 Doric of Albans from Chambray; No. 6 Ionic of the Theatre of Marcellus, dentils. Chambray; No. 8 Corinthian of Diocletian's Baths from Chambray; No. 10 Doric of the Theatre of Marcellus. Chambray."[25] Jefferson's mention of specific sources from which the details came was important to the craftsmen executing those details, but the specific book from which the ornament details came was just as important due to different depictions of the antique orders and ornaments. With the exception of the two pavilions closest to the Rotunda (I and II), all of the exterior entablatures were without ornamental friezes. This was not true for the interior entablatures, unrelated to those on the building's exterior, which greatly expanded the specimens Jefferson wanted to display, albeit in the second-floor private parlors of the bachelor professors.

It could be argued that Jefferson splurged on this expensive trim and decoration for these second-floor parlors for his own personal architectural reasons. What put these entablatures over the top were the terra cotta and lead frieze ornaments made by William Coffee of New York City. Coffee made these pavilion entablature ornaments at the same time he made those for Poplar Forest, using two of Jefferson's favorite antique sources, the Doric Baths of Diocletian and the Ionic Temple of Fortuna Virilis.[26] It is odd that Jefferson's specific choices for Coffee's University ornaments are not found in any correspondence. Most likely they were discussed when the two men were together at Monticello.[27] Jefferson clearly used Antoine Desgodetz's (1779) book for some of these ornaments, but Coffee was also using Peter Nicholson's more recent *Principles of Architecture* (1819) for others.

It was almost universal on many large construction projects for builders in antebellum Virginia to use enslaved laborers and skilled enslaved craftsmen. Thomas Jefferson had relied on apprenticing his enslaved workers to his hired workers at Monticello, and his own enslaved craftsmen had finished Poplar Forest. The scope of the large University project called for the more common practice of enslaved workers who were either owned or leased by individual craftsmen, or leased by the University itself. When considered for the Rotunda job, John Neilson wrote to his former client John Hartwell Cocke, "our workmen are nearly all Africans Peck employs four of the Proctors carpenters his Old man Sam is an appendage to the university being a master of all Arts at one time a carpenter then tin man next painter."[28] With imperfect grammar, this note perfectly explains the common practice of using one's enslaved workers or hiring them from others. In this case the University proctor, Arthur Spicer Brockenbrough, charged for the use of his own enslaved workmen and was responsible for hiring more on behalf of the University.

University accounts are filled with references to Brockenbrough's hiring enslaved workers and their overseers between 1819 and 1826. A laborer might be hired for $60 per year, whereas a blacksmith brought $109 a year; the rate for boy laborers was as little as $35 per year. Jefferson wrote Brockenbrough, "I think we should hire as many hands for the next as we did for the current year, there is a great deal of work to be done yet on the grounds."[29] The annual balance sheet for the year 1822 included "Hand Hire $869.14" for general enslaved labor and a list of enslavers who were owed $773 "for the hire of negroes."[30] The following year fifteen laborers were hired for $65 a year, including one woman for $25 and overseers' wages of $150.[31] In 1825 fifteen enslaved men and boys were hired to make 900,000 bricks for the Rotunda in addition to other duties. Boys were typically hired for brickmaking. Richard Ware, the Philadelphia brickmaker, bricklayer, and carpenter, wrote to Brockenbrough in 1819: "You can send me one off bearer (one who carried the green bricks and stacked them to be dried and fired) a Boy & 4 good hands to work in my Brick Yard . . . James McCaig Stone cutter mentioned he could [send] me some hands if I Should want."[32] This was the case of white tradesmen from outside Virginia who did not own enslaved workers but needed to hire them to accomplish their contracts in an efficient and competitive way.

It was also common for trusted enslaved craftsmen to live independently and to hire themselves out for their enslaver's benefit. Jefferson's letter to Brockenbrough regarding the rat-proofing of meat houses at the University ended with these words: "I suppose Chisolm's Lewis is somewhere about the University. I have a room for him to plaister, and you will oblige me by sending him to me as I know not where to seek him."[33] This was one of Hugh Chisolm's enslaved men who had worked on waterproofing the cisterns at Monticello and might very well have worked at Poplar Forest. Free Blacks were also hired and are more likely to appear in the accounts with an associated last name.[34] One well-known newly freed person was mentioned in a letter from Cocke to Brockenbrough: "Burwell, the faithful Servant of our late lamented Rector is said to be a good painter—I wish you to offer him any job in his line at the University, that he would undertake."[35] This was Jefferson's longtime manservant Burwell Colbert, who was a skilled painter and glazier and who had been freed upon Jefferson's death. Burwell, who was well known to all of Jefferson's friends, received the offer of work just two weeks after Jefferson died.

Thomas Jefferson had always needed intellectual projects, and this one, fulfilling his fundamental belief in the value of education as the means to a better future, would be one of his greatest personal legacies. Upon hearing news that the state had taken out another loan to complete the final building, the Rotunda, Jefferson was said to "depict the joy of a father on the birth of a first and long-wished for son."[36] Jefferson had indeed created an outdoor museum of architectural orders unlike anything found in the United States, or even in Europe. Thus he was justifiably proud when describing his role as its father. He had managed, against all challenges of finance and execution, to achieve a large and complex institutional establishment that bore up to a close examination of its brickwork as well as its impressive overall compositional design. It was a fitting magnum opus for a talented architect and builder. Jefferson's accomplishment, one of three he wanted listed on his tombstone, was not without tremendous effort at a time when most others would have eased into their twilight years. After Jefferson's death, James Madison, one of the few who knew of Jefferson's personal role and effort, wrote to a friend summarizing the University project, "The University of Virginia, as a temple dedicated to science & Liberty, was after his [Jefferson's] retirement from the political sphere, the object nearest his heart, and so continued to the close of his life. His devotion to it was intense, and his exertions unceasing. It bears the stamp of his genius, and will be a noble monument to his fame."[37]

EPILOGUE

A restored Poplar Forest provides a new perspective on Thomas Jefferson, his retreat, and his life in retirement. The focus of this history has been on Jefferson's characteristic need for privacy and his role as architect and builder. Jefferson's history of using retreats and the features of privacy designed for Poplar Forest are perhaps the easier ones to comprehend regarding personality traits. Finding meaning in the design and construction of Poplar Forest is more challenging but no less relevant. If those who build their own houses replicate themselves in that endeavor, then we are tasked with trying to understand that personal meaning, especially in an intimate retreat. As one historian put it: "Jefferson's buildings still haunt our imagination, not simply as ingenious solutions to architectural problems but as the expression of deeper ideals."[1] This close examination of how Poplar Forest was designed and built, and how it was used, has sought those deeper meanings.

In the 1970s the ways in which architectural historians recorded and analyzed buildings began to change with disciplines that started to overlap regarding what could be learned from houses and their landscapes: vernacular architecture, material culture, social history, ethnology, historical archaeology, and cultural geography, to name the most relevant. Earlier two prominent architectural historians had suggested better ways of understanding complex buildings like Poplar Forest. In 1947 James Marston Fitch advocated for a holistic analysis of architecture in which the different users of a building, the "consumers of a building," were key to understanding the social functions of that building.[2] At that same time Vincent Scully approached the study of architecture that took a broader view that included social history, intellectual history, analysis of physical form, a building's relationship to nature and its site, and research methodologies that encompassed both behavior and aesthetics.[3] But it was in the 1970s that increased fieldwork surveys by state historic preservation offices slowly changed the direction of research and analysis beyond what had been taught in academic programs.[4] Since then, architectural historians typically look beyond stylistic heritage to analyze what buildings were intended to do and how they were actually used. Unraveling the influences that make up the design and use of Poplar Forest requires some research dexterity through several approaches and perspectives. At the same time, Poplar Forest also exudes clarity of purpose regarding the principal "consumers of a building." Jefferson's overriding concern with privacy describes the primary difference between his Bedford County retreat and Monticello, his famous home near Charlottesville. His lifelong goal of tranquility was much more fully realized at Poplar Forest—a place where he could escape the relentless tide of visitors to his primary residence and focus on cultivating his introverted personality.

Poplar Forest differed from other American second, seasonal homes. At his retreat Jefferson could enjoy the companionship of his granddaughters, correspond with old friends, and catch up with reading, particularly with his favorite classical authors. In retirement there he had the uninterrupted time to conceive and design his University of Virginia project. But the leisure and intellectual freedom his retreat afforded him was not without its own site-specific contradictions, shadowed as it was by the enslaved hands that crafted it. We might even say that Poplar Forest enabled enslaved craftsman John Hemmings and his three nephews, Beverly, Madison, and Eston Hemings to fashion their own sense of individual autonomy, however constrained. Working independently at times, and for long lengths of time, the Hemings men enjoyed a measure of privacy, living in the lower level of the house and focusing their talents on their great building project. Those measures of privacy at Poplar Forest meant many things to many people, some readily apparent, and some that remain elusive and are impossible to discern.

The Culture of Retirement

Some historians have said that Jefferson's greatest legacy was the quest for individual and personal freedom—the freedom of the human spirit.[5] Others have said that his quest for individual freedom translated personally into the freedom to be left alone.[6] Both of these ideas are represented at Poplar Forest in the culture of retirement. The culture of retirement had been well-established in England by the early eighteenth century and in America by the mid-eighteenth century. The ideas that fostered individual self-fashioning percolated in Jefferson's mind all his life. Jefferson had read the writings of John Locke, who outlined the intellectual basis for self-hood and an individual's relationship with society. By the mid-eighteenth century, bourgeois houses in England reflected their owner's character and occupations as well as rank and social standing.[7] A dwelling now articulated an individual's identity in its design, and that in turn could influence or shape an individual. Locke characterized the mind in architectural terms as being like cabinets or closets in a dwelling, with passages of knowledge and windows reflecting the bright light of understanding. His writings on knowledge as an individual pursuit that framed the basis for selfhood was then associated with an architecture reflecting personal choices, most notably in dedicated rooms for solitude and study.

Fig. 99. Perspective painting of the Poplar Forest ornamental core (L. Diane Johnson).

Jefferson's persona at Monticello constituted his self on wonderful display: in the entry hall's cabinet of native and natural curiosities; in the parlor's European furniture and artworks; in the numerous maps, in prints extolling European and American architecture, scenes, and wonders; in the tea room's busts of notable friends; and in his library and cabinet suite filled with books that reflected his intellectual pursuits and knowledge. On display at Poplar Forest, on the other hand, were privacy and the inner life of books and letters, not fashionable consumer goods and edifying artifacts. Using Locke's analogy, Poplar Forest was an entire cabinet of knowledge with its extreme quality of light reflecting wisdom.

Villa life and intellectual development were closely linked from ancient times forward and found receptive ground in Jefferson's imagination. His copy of Robert Castell's *Villas of the Ancients Illustrated* connected the virtues of the ancient villa retreat with Lockean ideas. Castell's description of Pliny the Younger's villa, as a simple place whose purpose was the intimate pursuit of study in retirement from society, helped form a consciousness of individual retirement, as did the poetry of Addison, Prior, and Pope in Jefferson's library. In the Earl of Shaftesbury's writings, Jefferson could read that dwellings were "instruments for solitary retirement for an active pursuit of a 'higher' state of mind."[8] The implications were obvious to anyone valuing privacy. Privacy was not only found in retreats; by the late eighteenth century, private spaces in American gentry houses became an important component of family relationships, intimacy, and domesticity.[9]

As a second home, Poplar Forest constituted a rare intellectual retreat primarily used by an individual and based on age-old models. Jefferson had used any number of retreats through his working life, but in retirement Poplar Forest would suit him as Pliny's villa suited him, for the pursuits of the mind. "Incantations of virtuous retirement to rural solitude after a career of public service," writes Joseph Ellis, "were familiar and even formulaic refrains within the leadership class of eighteenth-century Americans, none more so than within the Virginia dynasty. Everyone knew the classical models of latter-day seclusion represented by Cicero and Cincinnatus and the hymns to pastoral splendor in Virgil's *Georgics.*"[10]

Jefferson told a number of friends what he was retiring *to:* his family, his farms, and his books. What he was retiring *from* was public life, of which he had grown weary, and the bitter politics that was still evolving in the new republic. Jefferson's good friend Margaret Bayard Smith remarked in her journal that, like the Roman emperor Diocletian, Jefferson could retire from public life to his farm and enjoy as much pleasure working in his garden as leading a nation.[11] George Watterston also referenced Diocletian when describing his visit to Monticello in 1820, saying that Jefferson had "preserved [his] taste for the most innocent, as well as natural pleasures, and their hours, like those of that Roman emperor in retirement, are sufficiently employed in reading, planting and cultivating their farms, to exclude the miseries of indolence, and the horrors of *ennui.*"[12] Jefferson's use of the Doric order from the Baths of Diocletian for his dining room provided a fitting reference to that emperor's retirement pleasures. Boston elites had retreated from political concerns to rural hobbies as the British had done in "Opposition retirement."[13] In their retirement correspondence, John Adams and Thomas Jefferson both spoke of political concerns and of a moral and intellectual slippage in society. Adams wrote to Jefferson in 1815 that,

> according to the few lights that remain to us, We may say that the Eighteenth Century, notwithstanding all its Errors and Vices has been, of all that are past, the most honorable to human Nature. Knowledge and Virtue were increased and diffused, Arts, Sciences useful to Men, ameliorating their condition, were improved, more than in any former equal Period. But what are We to say now? Is the Nineteenth Century to be a Contrast to the Eighteenth? Is it to extinguish all the Lights of its Predecessor?[14]

Jefferson claimed that he preferred to read of the heroes of antiquity rather than current news.[15] As James Ackerman notes, the mythology of the villa retreat created a state that was impervious to reality. Poplar Forest allowed Jefferson to retreat not only from his own financial problems but from political and societal problems as well. The eighteenth-century notion of virtue, as Adams suggested, might be one of the past. In Jefferson's mind the aim of life—happiness—rested on a moral and civil virtuous life, both in the public and private spheres. In their pursuit of happiness enlightened people sought security and peace in retirement.[16] Although Jefferson and Adams questioned the political morality of a postrevolution society, they could retreat into the confines of their own inward enlightened reason. They expressed concern for a new generation's quest for societal happiness that was too often associated with a profit motive.[17] Near the end of his life Jefferson's republican faith for his country lay in its future.[18] He had done what he could to craft and manage the new nation and now others would have to carry on to refine its identity in political, social, cultural, and economic spheres. The slippery issue of slavery would have to be solved by a future generation.[19] Like his pursuit of architectural improvement, Jefferson fundamentally believed the principles articulated in the Bill of Rights would be tested and improved upon as the nation grew older.

Jefferson's retirement goal for "tranquility" was immediately realized at his retreat in 1809. John Stilgoe's introduction to the 1998 edition of Gaston Bachelard's *Poetics of Space* (1958) summarized the power of a house as "a nest for dreaming, a shelter for imagining."[20] Stilgoe further suggested that "out of the house spin worlds within worlds, the personal cosmoses." In his intimate autobiographical spaces at Monticello, Jefferson imagined an expanded personal cosmos on his remote Bedford County property. The spaces and forms that slowly took shape as finished rooms at Poplar Forest provided a shelter for happiness that would also become the place for happy family memories as well as an incubator for new ideas. Alain de Botton wrote that in creating an architecture of happiness "we require places where the values outside of us encourage and enforce the aspirations within us."[21] Poplar Forest was such a place for Jefferson, a sanctuary for imagining his final and most public University project. Jefferson's pursuit of happiness in retirement reflected the expansive individualism and architectural forms of privacy that had filtered into American culture from England.[22] Jefferson found himself faced, however, with the incompatible virtues of traditional Virginia hospitality and the increased need for personal privacy. His success at continuing to offer the former at Monticello compromised his goals for the latter and resulted in his necessary escape to Poplar Forest.[23] We can only begin to comprehend the satisfaction the introverted Jefferson derived from living at Poplar Forest.

Poplar Forest's design suggests that Jefferson was trying to create rational harmony in a lifetime that was seldom harmonious. But it also raises the question as to why he would design and build one of his most distinctive works and invite so few non–family members to see it. The answer is both simple and complex. The many complicated challenges that executing his plans entailed were a source of great satisfaction in his late-life pursuit of happiness. Unlike Monticello, Poplar Forest was not meant to make a cultural statement for social peers. Friends or neighbors who did get invited to Poplar Forest knew of Monticello's extravagant displays of architecture, art, and furnishings and understood Poplar Forest for what it was. With few visitors, Poplar Forest could have been a rustic and simple work, like seasonal second houses or hunting lodges, and not architecturally significant. The more complex answer is that the private milieu of

Fig. 100. Aerial photo of Poplar Forest with a view to the Blue Ridge Mountains, 2021.

Jefferson's very modern, unusual, and harmonious house and setting were perhaps too personal to share. It was his selfish indulgence.

A Work of Creative Genius

Jefferson's revolutionary designs for Monticello and the University of Virginia were recognized by the UNESCO World Heritage Convention for three criteria that represent value to all mankind. These criteria were a work of unique artistic achievement, a masterpiece of creative genius, and representing associations with ideas and beliefs of outstanding universal significance. Jefferson's various shades of humanism give him that universality in comparative ways, not the least in architecture.[24] Poplar Forest was deemed eligible for the same three criteria and completes our understanding as an important architectural middle piece.[25] At Poplar Forest, Jefferson put his creative genius to work designing a unique octagon house that expressed a geometric clarity and architectural ideals that stretched from Roman prototypes to modern European ones. It is the universality of Jefferson that puts his works in a special humanistic category.

Jefferson was confident enough as an architect to both follow the rules and to bend them where appropriate. Jefferson had an "antipathy to absolute systems" Karl Lehman concluded about his attitude in general, but the same could certainly be said of his attitude toward architecture. Though this seems at first to be a contradictory stance, it makes sense when we understand Jefferson's adoption of Vitruvius's and Palladio's admonishment that architects had to know monuments of the past, and the rules that formed them, in order to design good contemporary architecture. An often-cited quote is one in which Jefferson describes his book by Andrea Palladio as "his Bible" for architectural design. That is certainly true in the same way Jefferson used his Christian Bible in a cut-and-paste manner to make it his personal resource, leaving out the miracles of Jesus to emphasize his moral teachings. Historical precedent in architecture as well as law held great authority for Jefferson. Studying English law provided Jefferson with the fundamental concepts of traditional precedents that had to be interpreted by the circumstantial facts of a particular time and place.[26] Similarly, his self-education in classical architecture provided the foundation for his designs. The proportions of the Roman orders represented the rules of a language that were sacrosanct even though their syntax could vary. Renaissance books on architecture showed Jefferson the reasons why Sebastian Serlio, Leon Battista Alberti, Giacomo Vignola, and Andrea Palladio had simplified the Roman orders. The inventive Romans used so many details and orders in combination with each other, and even on the same building, that their architectural heritage had to be simplified for later designers and builders. This was the conclusion of the seventeenth-century French architect Claude Perrault, whose buildings Jefferson admired, when he argued that the proportion and the character of the orders, not their details, defined beauty. The classical system of design satisfied Jefferson's historical passion for authority and his penchant for precision, and at the same time allowed for flexibility. Jefferson's Virginia State Capitol is an example: the exterior form conformed to the correct proportions of an ancient Roman temple, but its function dictated something entirely different and modern for the interior. Jefferson followed the authoritative proportional formulas for the exterior orders and form of Monticello, Poplar Forest, and the University of Virginia, but he also bent the rules in the vocabulary of details. As an architectural scholar, Jefferson recognized the powerful idea that buildings could be both academically proper and yet uniquely different. We can characterize Jefferson's style as consistently eclectic.

Fig. 101. Poplar Forest, south elevation, 2020.

Jefferson's use of a flexible vocabulary of architectural elements, and how he followed the canonical rules, was analogous to his approach to languages in general. Jefferson's advocacy of "neology," meaning new words for new meanings, suited his philosophy on languages. The letters, pronunciation, syntax, and vocabulary of a language form the foundation of its use. Jefferson appreciated "subtle variations of idiom and style in Greek and Latin authors" and considered those languages "models of pure taste in writing" that had evolved into the "rational and chaste style(s) of modern composition."[27] Similarly Greek and Roman architecture formed the first rational styles of classical design, but classicism had evolved in the Renaissance and later with neoclassicism in the eighteenth century. Jefferson was interested in the original pronunciation of Greek and Latin, preferring to read those works in their original languages, but he also considered Greek as a living language that had evolved between its ancient and modern usages.[28] Language for Jefferson, notes H. M. Kallen, was "a living instrument of communication that the grammarian cannot cripple or the dictionary imprison. It undergoes a continual metamorphosis, in which old words die and new ones are born as circumstances require."[29] Jefferson's verbal preferences, Kallen explains, were based on a structure of space, order, and logic that came from antiquity. Joyce Appleby agrees that "in language, too, Jefferson felt the past's heavy hand" and "targeted the purist as the enemy of linguistic freedom."[30] Even as Jefferson extolled the purity of ancient languages, he fought the purism of those languages in modern form and usage, saying, "I consider purism as destroying the verve and beauty of the language," concluding, "while neology improves both and adds to its copiousness."[31] To prove the point, Jefferson even coined his own neologism: neologization.[32]

Jefferson believed that the practice of architecture reflected something like the neology of language—it should evolve in accord with contemporary realities. In yet another of his supposed contradictions, Jefferson followed authority without being constrained by it. This dialectic architectural tension had been shown at Monticello I when Jefferson cautiously mixed ideas from several source books. By the time he remodeled Monticello, he could confidently draw on and incorporate even more sources in a greater variety and mix of detail. That flexible practice continued and increased at Poplar Forest and the University of Virginia. It is not surprising, then, that in architecture, as in other aspects of his life and work, Jefferson was a great synthesizer.[33] Poplar Forest can thus be seen as an architectural neologism: a mixture of the ancient Roman retreats, Palladian Renaissance villas, eighteenth-century British Palladian octagons, and modern French conveniences. Jefferson's architectural composition is also analogous to a symphonic work in which familiar notes were colorfully and uniquely arranged yet canonically authentic.[34] Jefferson's elastic and eclectic use of classical details did not spring from a lack of imagination but from his confidence as an architect who had refined his work within one style. He had developed his own taste early on and thereafter refined it in what might be considered a narrow, yet highly developed, stylistic oeuvre we can call Jeffersonian classicism. While his design for Poplar Forest can be called modern in comparison with most Virginia and American houses of its time, it was on the cusp and out of step with the new styles of the Greek Revival—a more fashionable classicism that had swept the country by the time Jefferson died in 1826. What we know is that Thomas Jefferson was a "zealous amateur" in architecture, just as he had described himself with gardening.[35]

The criteria linking Jefferson's architecture with associated ideas of universal value are more abstract but significant. We might say that Poplar Forest represents in architecture what Arthur Bestor calls "the blueprint of his mind," when describing Jefferson's classification system for his library.[36] Jefferson divided his books into History, Philosophy, and Fine Arts, based on Francis Bacon's three faculties of the human mind: Memory, Reason, and Imagination. At Poplar Forest, Memory represents Jefferson's historical passion for the classical world and all of the favorite architectural ideas and elements he had studied and observed; Reason represents Jefferson's penchant for mathematical precision and the geometric formulation of his octagonal retreat; and Imagination represents the retreat's quiet power to stimulate Jefferson's rested mind. The essence of Jefferson's triumvirate of three great men in history—Sir Francis Bacon, John Locke, and Sir Isaac Newton—is reflected, albeit theoretically, in Poplar Forest's design. Bacon set his country houses in innovative gardens in order to promote reason and reflection; Locke fashioned the seventeenth-century concept of the self through associations with his own architecture; and Newton contemplated the higher purposes of mathematics and geometry in ways that resonated with Jefferson through his numerically supreme designs. In his own idiosyncratic way, Jefferson honored his heroes by his creating a retreat built on conceptions of individuality and self-expression.

Constructing Ideas

Transforming aesthetic ideas on paper into material reality, on the ground, was Jefferson's lifelong ambition. It seemed to have been his personal holy grail. His genius lay in creating architectural designs, patiently sustaining the creative tension of a process that could take many years before he ultimately arrived at a satisfactory solution. Much like Leonardo da Vinci, he used paper as a laboratory for visually thinking through myriad combinations to discover rational and intelligent results. Architecture is space enclosed by structure, but that structure is also a solution that rectifies form, proportions, materials, and details in a manner that is also comfortable and convenient as well as beautiful. It was a design and construction challenge that stimulated someone like Jefferson. He seems to have always been looking for a better solution and result, whether for political processes, innovative farming techniques, or correct classical columns. This is characteristic of Jefferson's concept of time in general, both his view of historical time and time projected into the future.[37] The first Monticello was a prime example, improved for privacy, convenience, and as an enlightened showcase of science, anthropology, and sophisticated European taste. He could patiently tolerate the "temporary" tree-trunk columns on the west portico of Monticello because of his abiding faith that they would eventually, at some distant date, be replaced by proper classical columns.

The seventeen years it took to complete Poplar Forest constituted another "long maturing project." Rebuilding the initial skylight and dining room roof was hardly necessary and certainly not easy, but it reflected his evolving vision of what would improve that room. Redesigning the gutters for the wing's terras roof anticipated its longevity and the inevitable need for future improvements. Improvement was important to Jefferson whether for the new nation or for his personal spaces where he could improve himself. Vision was never more necessary than in birthing his University, another experiment that he would barely see off the ground in hopeful anticipation of great future posthumous benefits. Poplar Forest's creation was not without difficulties, but Jefferson's vision of what it would be when completed was never compromised, only postponed. His optimism was especially evident in the landscape, combining a gardener's patience and a mind's-eye view of what his mature plantings would become. The grove of poplar trees Jefferson planted north of the house would become a romantic and majestic landscape feature by 1900, just as he had envisioned. Jefferson sought to create a special domestic context at his Poplar Forest retreat that would foster the very intellectual pursuits that were manifest in its long-protracted creation.

Poplar Forest Redivivus

Thomas Jefferson would have immediately recognized the late Latin word *redivivus.* He would have appreciated it as a neologism to the Latin language that came as late as the seventeenth century. It meant to be brought back or restored to life; reborn or renewed. The word seems perfectly appropriate to describe the restored Poplar Forest.[38] The knowledge compiled in this history, and the interpretation of its meaning, would not have been possible without the thirty-year process of restoring Jefferson's masterpiece. The ultimate question this work has attempted to answer is what new information Poplar Forest contributes toward an understanding of Thomas Jefferson. What truths have been revealed through the process of discovering restoration facts?

There are physical truths revealed in the historic fabric, and then there are the historical truths that come from new documentary evidence. In our own troubled times, telling the whole historical truth is paramount. That is a daunting challenge, for our project has revealed many complicated, sometimes apparently contradictory truths and a multiplicity of conflicting interpretations. "As we unearth the bones of the past," Caroline Winterer aptly writes, "we too debate how best to reassemble them. The people of the eighteenth century . . . walked a different earth from ours" and "in the end we are always visitors to their era."[39] To lift Jefferson out of his era into ours, quips Ellis, is like trying to plant cut flowers.[40] Still, through written history or museum restorations, professionals strive for more current honesty. That foreign country, the "real" past, constantly comes into a different focus depending upon the interpretive lens through which it is viewed. Facts are defined as things that were done, and as information having an objective reality. But we also know that objective historical facts are a moving target. The zeitgeist of any generation filters those facts of the past and renders an intelligent heritage for the present. The goal of good architectural restoration then, given the variable circumstances of each site, is to present an authentic historical "fact" based on objective research and analysis. It is then subject to interpretation as part of the viewable past, and in this case, it is a new view of the ever-scrutinized Thomas Jefferson. The controversial question ultimately focuses on who can successfully claim "the cultural authority to shape the memory of the American past," as constant revisions of Jefferson's image remind us.[41]

The restoration of museum houses as public history is no less a product of its generation than academic histories. The physical and restored truth of a restoration is a different kind of history, just as nuanced and just as complex. By restoring Poplar Forest to its original appearance, we have "put the object back on the shelf" for the general public to appreciate and for professionals to interpret. This project has given visitors a "value added" insight into a restoration process that in many ways resembles Jefferson's original construction campaign (though it has lasted much longer). The more intangible goal of an authentically restored house is to create a context in which visitors can connect with the intention of its creator, especially one whose character seems so elusive, especially in his private life at his private retreat. The "magic" of a historical place, in this case Jefferson's house, can be a distraction from its darker historical stories, a gap between aesthetics and moral content. Hannah Spahn explains that this "magic," a term from Jefferson's time that meant a mode of conveying historical information through the senses rather than reason, long served the public's view of seeing Jefferson's architecture strictly as a symbol of American democracy.[42] For some visitors, a restored house is architectural magic in and of itself; for others, the magic requires it to be peopled with associated stories. Poplar Forest *is* a magic place that now allows us to understand and appreciate a special and private aesthetic creation of Thomas Jefferson. It is also now incumbent on us to look beyond the aesthetics and to include the nuances of the Poplar Forest story—the drama of the extraordinary role played by John Hemmings and Jefferson's three biracial sons.

The impact of a restored Poplar Forest transcends the history and interpretation that can be expressed in any book. Visitors to Poplar Forest now see a house and site that have changed in fundamental ways from what they would have seen at the beginning of the restoration process. A visitor arrives at the ornamental core after driving through woods and fields that suggest the initial context of Jefferson's plantation. The house appears on a rise set against large poplar trees and nestled partway into the earth, fronted by a stone-paved carriage turnaround, symmetrical flower beds, and clumps of ornamental trees. Two unusual flanking earth mounds connect to the house by a service wing on the east and a double row of trees on the west. The exterior of the house betrays its Jeffersonian character: octagonal shape, large windows, columned porticos, Roman Tuscan entablature, classical balustrade, and a crowning Chinese railing. From the front public portico, one enters into the passage, where architectural differences are immediately apparent: polished oak floors, varnished walnut doors, and a large Tuscan entablature overhead. More dramatically, the eye is drawn ahead through three sets of glass doors through the house. The first room entered is the surprisingly large and cubistic central dining room, brightly lit by a rare domestic skylight. Crowning its commanding height is the large and impressive Doric entablature that Jefferson had playfully altered. A visitor then proceeds to the southern light-filled and airy octagonal parlor and library, which strongly conveys Jefferson's intention to open the walls of the room to the landscape through four triple-sash windows. A central glass door leads to the more private south portico, which served as an elevated outdoor room. Sitting outside on this very open portico or on the wing deck attests to the privacy of the retreat where Jefferson had the freedom to be undisturbed. Those who labored for his happiness could remain out of sight below, with the exception of the Hemings men as they crafted the interior finishes. To venture into the principal bed chambers on either side of the dining room is to penetrate into the most intimate spaces of the house. Jefferson's western chamber suite, his sanctum sanctorum, is divided in the center by his favored European bed alcove. To the outer side of the alcove lies the stair pavilion, its telling location a reminder that the house was not designed for public occupancy. It should be apparent that the shape of the house, its spatial volumes, the floors, the moldings, the skylight, the fireplaces, the beds, the amount of light and air, and even the colors and finishes all reveal the distinctly personal and highly uncommon choices Jefferson made for the design and decoration of his anciently inspired American villa retreat. It is a different kind of house, designed for a special purpose.

Poplar Forest now illuminates a long-obscured part of Jefferson's retirement. These were years in which the author of the Declaration of Independence continued to develop his skills as an architect and builder, and to further his intellectual and reflective quest for selfhood. Jefferson's design for his Bedford County retreat enhances our understanding of his many architectural works; construction of the house also sheds new light on the essential role played by the enslaved workers in fulfilling their owner's exacting and extraordinarily demanding vision. What we now know about Poplar Forest is of immense value to architectural historians who might have labeled it "Jeffersonian" without fully considering why that *is* an appropriate label. The restored aesthetic ambiance of the house and landscape is something to feel as much as to observe—a magical experience delivered by those rarest buildings we encounter, and with which we personally engage. Given the best authentic context of this intimate place, and hearing its stories, visitors will gain fresh insights into the elusive character of its owner and builder. The restored Poplar Forest offers us a new context for making sense of Thomas Jefferson.

AFTERWORD

Jefferson in Our Time

In this era of Jeffersonian reassessments, it is hard not to be self-conscious when writing about the man, even as an architect. Since his death in 1826, Thomas Jefferson has been one of the most written-about of Americans. He is, in some respects, a historical genre all his own. Historians have documented the ever-changing images of Jefferson in the last two hundred years and observe that he has been relevant to each generation and era, for one reason or another.[1] In 1960 Merrill Peterson published *The Jefferson Image in the American Mind,* outlining the challenges and fallacies faced by historians who must overcome the powerful and ingrained symbolic images created by Jefferson's "prodigious vigor and kaleidoscopic changeability."[2] Peterson recognized even then that there was "tremendous room for divided opinions" and that "the post-Bicentennial history of Jefferson's reputation will certainly be a very different character" than the view at that time. That was an understatement, given the proliferation of histories in the past thirty years that reassess Thomas Jefferson, in which era the Poplar Forest restoration significantly falls. A six-day symposium of Jefferson scholars assembled for the 250th anniversary of Jefferson's birth in 1993 focused on the relevant topics of race, cultural authority, and historical memory. Historians struggle with new perspectives that try to make sense of Jefferson's life and deeds that most acknowledge embody the nation's deepest contradictions.[3] Some have observed that the public and private Jefferson seem to have gone their separate and schizophrenic ways in the various histories written about him.[4] Poplar Forest certainly represents the private Jefferson, even when he is seen as the private citizen in retirement at Monticello.

Thomas Jefferson's role as an architect and builder might at first seem to have nothing to do with race, but this is not true. Architectural design reflects contemporary social, cultural, and economic signals. Jefferson's role as an enslaver is certainly apparent in the ways private and public interior spaces structured interactions with enslaved servants. This was true both at Monticello and at Poplar Forest.[5] Jefferson's role as a builder, at Monticello and at Poplar Forest, is more centrally related to the issue of slavery through the work of enslaved craftsmen, specifically Jefferson's mixed-race sons working at Poplar Forest. Thomas Jefferson was just as flawed and contradictory as an architect and builder as in other aspects of his life. How he resolved certain conflicts at Poplar Forest, whether architectural or human, conscious or subconscious, in simple ways or complex, is part of his character and legacy. The realities at Poplar Forest, as we know them, must inform our nuanced portrait of Jefferson if, as some historians suggest, we have to understand and hold opposing ideas in order to reach a complex truth.[6] How can Jefferson's idealistic intentions for his intellectual retreat be weighed against the reality of who constructed it and any compromises in how it was used? If we look hard at Ellen Randolph Coolidge's picture of familial bliss with her grandfather at Poplar Forest, it is a fractured one with figures who are out of focus in the shadows. If the psychological nature of the ages-old villa retreat is said to be impervious to reality, Thomas Jefferson might well have used Poplar Forest to ignore his late-life financial troubles. But the reality that he never acknowledged, but could not ignore, was the daily interaction with his biracial sons. That is the pregnant inner story and historical truth of Poplar Forest and one that has finally emerged. The story of the Hemings family at Monticello and their relationship with Thomas Jefferson has been skillfully researched and truthfully told by historians in the past few decades. The story of John Hemmings and Jefferson's sons Beverly, Madison, and Eston Hemings is only better placed in the history and construction narrative of Thomas Jefferson and Poplar Forest, giving them the acknowledgment and credit that is due for their extraordinary but unrecognized work.

APPENDIX A
CHRONOLOGY

1743 Thomas Jefferson born in Albemarle County, Virginia

1760 Attends the College of William and Mary in Williamsburg

1769 Begins building Monticello I

1784 Moves to Paris for five years

1800 Elected U.S. president for two four-year terms

1806 Hugh Chisolm starts making bricks at Poplar Forest
President Jefferson travels to Poplar Forest to help Chisolm lay out the foundation; alters design of house

1808 Brick walls and privies completed; John Perry frames roof and floors

1809 Retires from public life
Monticello II mostly complete
Poplar Forest ceilings plastered; exterior doors and windows made in Monticello joinery shop; Chisolm makes more bricks for stair pavilions and columns; Perry installs exterior doors and windows
Jefferson starts using the retreat

1810 John Hemmings makes four sets of sash doors for dining room

1812 Reuben Perry installs plaster grounds for interior trim

1814 Hugh Chisolm plasters walls; east wing constructed

1815 Exterior trim started by John Hemmings and apprentices
Granddaughters start coming to Poplar Forest

1816 Visit and description by George Flower

1817 Interior trim and doors by John Hemmings and apprentices
East room alcove alteration

1819 Central roof rebuilt as terras construction with skylight
Marble hearthstones laid
Major hailstorm breaks many windows in house
More interior doors installed along with louvered blinds

1821 Dining room entablature constructed

1823 William Coffee ornaments received for dining room and parlor
Last visit by Jefferson
Francis Eppes begins living at Poplar Forest

1824	Dining room ornaments installed in entablature
1825	Roof fire; tin shingles installed
1826	Parlor ornaments installed in entablature
	Thomas Jefferson dies
1827	John Hemmings freed
1828	Frances Eppes sells Poplar Forest to William Cobbs
1833	John Hemmings dies
1845	House largely destroyed by fire
1846	House rebuilt by Cobbs/Hutter family
1947	Watts family modernizes the house
1979	Last year of Watts family's residency
1983	Poplar Forest purchased for museum property
1989	Architectural restoration process begins
2022	Restoration largely completed

APPENDIX B
JEFFERSONIAN ELEMENTS AND MATERIALS

Alcove Beds

Jefferson wrote to James Madison about bed alcoves: "alcove bedrooms to which I am much attached" (*Papers,* 19 May 1793). He used them in Paris and saw many other examples there. He used one in the house he rented in Philadelphia from James Leiper and measured it for his Building Notebook. Two other Philadelphia houses he knew had them: the Woodlands and Solitude. The only contemporary house in Virginia to have one was John Wickham's in Richmond. Besides his own at Monticello, all the alcoves there were one-sided like those in Paris. His designs for various projects featured them, like his 1800 townhouse and some early Poplar Forest designs. At Poplar Forest he used two open-sided alcoves for his own west chamber and the east, although the latter was later closed on one side for privacy. Putting the beds in alcoves reserved the walls for a door, window, or fireplace. The Poplar Forest alcoves seen on the Neilson plan were confirmed by ghost marks on the brick walls. A "cuddy," or storage space, was above each bed, accessed by a trap door in the outer vestibule ceiling. A vestibule on each side of the alcoves had three doorways.

Architraves

Architrave moldings were specified by Jefferson for the Palladian one-sixth the size of the window or door opening. These moldings were taken out of the Leoni edition of Palladio's book. Similar architraves were used at Monticello and the University of Virginia. They were typically made of pine for exterior and sometimes poplar for the interior. The interior moldings were painted white like all the rest of the exterior and interior wood trim. Architrave moldings were also used for each fireplace, helping to frame the opening or to hold the stone surrounds.

Balustrade

At Monticello "old Abram" was making balusters out of locust, and James Dinsmore was making and installing the other parts based on James Gibbs's *Rules for Drawing Architecture.* At Poplar Forest Jefferson specified that the balusters should be made out of heart poplar. It is assumed that the Doric plinth shown in Gibbs's book was also the source for the Poplar Forest balustrade, shown in the Neilson elevation drawing, and made and installed by John Hemmings and his nephews. One large iron spike survived on the southwest chimney to show how the balustrade fastened to the chimneys. The Monticello practice of holding up the balustrade above the roof on iron rods to let water run underneath was adopted for the Poplar Forest restored balustrade. Physical evidence on the chimney faces indicates a panel was used in those locations.

Base

Jefferson's design for a baseboard was taken out of James Gibbs's *Rules for Drawing Architecture* and used at Monticello and the University of Virginia. The Poplar Forest base was modeled on the same. At Monticello it was most often painted a dark blue/gray.

Bells

Jefferson ordered "Chinese bells brass with wire and cranks" from London for Monticello I in 1769 (*MB,* 29). In 1808 he installed call bells with "thumb levers" in Monticello II. The use of enslaved servant bells at Poplar Forest is based on archaeological artifacts and physical evidence. A small nailing block in the dining room installed near the chair rail was associated with a hole through two brick walls that aligned with the exterior south wall of the service wing.

Blinds

Jefferson used the term "blinds" or "louvered blinds" for those on the outside and "shutters" for those on the interior. Monticello had folding shutters, but Poplar Forest only had fixed panels in each interior window jamb. Monticello had a variety of blinds made in Paris, Philadelphia, New York, and Washington. The Poplar Forest blinds were made on-site by John Hemmings and his nephews. Physical evidence of shutter dogs shows that the blinds were done in stages that corresponded with the window sash for a variety of uses. The grass-green color of the Poplar Forest blinds is based on an original blind louver found in the Monticello attic. It was typical for blinds on most houses to be a grass-green color. The blinds for the north portico were specified only for the lower sash for privacy reasons, not to shelter from the sun.

Brick

Jefferson was very particular about brick specifications for any of his buildings. He was known to produce full-scale drawings for brick molds and details. He calculated the number of bricks for most of his realized and unrealized projects, using a standard brick and mortar joint size to calculate the sizes of walls. At Monticello and the University of Virginia he used a common practice of painting the walls a brick red with lime wash to blend the various colors of the bricks. At the University he also used a special ribbon joint that was then painted with a "pencil" white stripe to make the brickwork look more refined. At Poplar Forest he used the typical eighteenth-century "grape vine" joint that helped make the irregular bricks look more regular. The Poplar Forest bricks, approximately a quarter million, were made on-site by the enslaved brickmakers of Hugh Chisolm and laid by Chisolm and his brother John. The special-shaped bricks were the octagon corner squint bricks, the beveled bricks for the rear of fireplaces, and the molded base, shaft, and capital of the columns.

Chair Rails

The chair rails, or "sur bases," were based on the typical ones Jefferson used at Monticello and the University of Virginia, taken out of James Gibbs's *Book of Architecture.* Plaster ground ghost marks confirmed the size.

Chimney

Poplar Forest has four symmetrical chimneys with four flues each that served fifteen fireplaces on both floors. The dining room fireplace had a diagonal flue that ran through the northwest diagonal wall to the northwest chimney. Physical evidence showed that this fireplace mass in the northwest corner of the dining room had been originally constructed to the ceiling and then demolished down to a shelf within the first five years (based on plaster evidence). It is hard to believe that Jefferson would have designed a fifth nonsymmetrical chimney for this fireplace. The conclusion is that the bricklayer made a mistake. Jefferson had also used diagonal flues at Monticello. The northeast chimney had one unused flue due to the north basement room having no fireplaces. Physical evidence on the sides of the chimneys shows that lead or sheet metal flashings were attached to their sides. Paint ghosts and nailing blocks on each chimney face indicate that a panel was used there for the balustrade. All four chimneys survived the 1845 fire.

Chinese Railing

The Chinese railing around the top terras deck was only known from a John Hemmings letter in which he describes repairing it after a fire; it was not shown on the Neilson drawing. Jefferson used a similar railing around the top deck on Monticello and above the student rooms at the University of Virginia. The restored Poplar Forest design is conjectural based on other Jefferson Chinese railings. Jefferson's remodeling of Farmington in Charlottesville also featured a Chinese railing on the roof.

Columns

At Monticello I Jefferson used real stone column shafts, bases, and capitals for the front portico. At Poplar Forest the Tuscan order columns are made of brick for the shafts with molded brick bases and capitals, all made by Hugh Chisolm. These were proportioned from Roman/Palladian dimensions according to the Tuscan order, although Hugh Chisolm got the diameter slightly wrong. This was all was covered in a thin lime render coat to resemble monolithic stone columns. When he eventually erected the final columns on the west portico of Monticello, he also used brick shafts covered with render but with real stone bases and capitals, similar to what was done at Barboursville. At the University of Virginia, the shafts were brick, covered with render, and the bases and capitals were stone. The Ionic and Corinthian capitals there were made in Italy of marble; the rest of the bases and capitals were a local stone carved by John Gorman, who had installed the hearthstones at Poplar Forest. All of these examples used entasis, the Greek and Roman practice of diminishing the top diameter portions of each column shaft to correct for visual distortion. For the Poplar Forest wing Jefferson relied on square brick piers (archaeological evidence) like those used for the wings at Monticello. The portico columns survived the 1845 fire, but the capitals were altered in the 1846 rebuilding.

Countersealing

Jefferson used "countersealing" as a fireproofing means between the floor joists at Monticello, filling the spaces with brick resting on ledger boards. It is assumed he used the same technique at Poplar Forest. This same method is also found at Jefferson's remodeling of Farmington in Virginia. At the University of Virginia, he used a thick bed of plaster held up on ledger boards between the floor joists. He claimed that this method saved Monticello from burning down. Jefferson referenced "Lord Stanhope's method" for this system.

Cube Room

The 20-foot cubistic dining room at Poplar Forest had a prototype in the 18-foot cubistic dining room at Monticello. Cube rooms were a common European design but usually of much larger scale. At Poplar Forest the center cube room was in effect Jefferson's rotunda space, designed after Andrea Palladio's famous Villa Rotonda. Its placement and skylight also had precedent in Parisian house examples. The one fireplace in the dining room is a corner fireplace using a diagonal flue.

Door Hardware

Jefferson used door hardware he had accumulated at Monticello and also ordered the best brass mortise locks for other doors. Hardware came from Richmond merchants, who received it from England.

The physical evidence on the Hemmings doors and archaeological evidence show that round and oval knobs, night latches, and escutcheons were used. Edge bolts were also ordered and used for the bivalve doors of the stair pavilions, the north and south doors, and the sash doors. The earliest hardware for the exterior doors might have had an earlier type of hardware since the rest of the hardware came over a long period. Iron rim locks are thought to have been used for the lower-level doors. The original privy door hardware consisted of H-L hinges and a Suffolk latch. It is assumed similar lower hierarchy hardware was used for the service wing doors.

Doors

Most of the Poplar Forest doors were made in the Monticello joinery shop and sent down on wagons. Some of the last doors were made on-site by John Hemmings and his nephews. These were similar in design to those made for Monticello by James Oldham. Two of the original Hemmings doors survived the 1845 fire and were reused in the house. The conservation of these doors showed that they were varnished walnut and featured a cyma recta molding that was peculiar to things John Hemmings made at Monticello. The restored Poplar Forest doors, made of Virginia walnut, are based on these original doors. The physical evidence on the original doors showed what type of brass mortise locks and hardware Jefferson used. Archaeological evidence shows that different-style door hardware was also used on some doors. The faux-grained north and south doors are based on the fact that these original doors were being made at Monticello at the time Richard Barry grained all of the doors there; Barry was glazing the Poplar Forest window sash at the same time. Jefferson also had a tradition of faux-graining the exterior pavilion doors at the University of Virginia.

Entablature Ornaments

English sculptor and painter William Coffee made the frieze ornaments for the dining room and parlor entablatures out of a terra cotta material with lead used for the ribbons below Apollo's face. He made similar ornaments for the University of Virginia pavilions at the same time, mostly for the second-floor parlors of each pavilion, and for the exterior entablatures of Pavilion I and II. At Monticello Jefferson use composition and lead ornaments for his entablatures. These numbered pieces for Poplar Forest were screwed and glued to the wood of the frieze boards.

Entablatures

On the exterior Jefferson used the Roman Tuscan order with a large entablature that wrapped around the building and its two portico pediments. This was confirmed by physical evidence on the exterior walls. For the interior, physical evidence showed that entablatures were used in all rooms. The Tuscan was used for the front passage and the bed chambers as was the practice at Monticello and the University of Virginia. The central dining room had a Roman Doric order from the Baths of Diocletian but with added bucrania. The parlor had a Roman Ionic order from the Temple of Fortuna Virilis. Both of these examples had been used at Monticello, and both would be used at the University of Virginia, but were unlike the customized choice for the dining room.

Firebacks

Seven iron firebacks were ordered from the Oxford Iron Furnace just east of Lynchburg. Physical evidence in several fireplaces show that these two-piece backs were held by iron pins. A large piece of one fireback was found on the property and used as a model for having reproductions made. The dining room fireplace was the only one that was different, with sides as well as back, like those at Monticello. The purpose of the firebacks was to prevent the brickwork from deteriorating.

Fireplaces

There are fifteen fireplaces in Poplar Forest, nine on the upper floor and six on the lower floor. Each of these was an innovative Rumford design based on the book by Count Rumford that Jefferson used. This design included a shallow back, splayed sides, a narrow throat, and a smoke shelf. Physical evidence shows that the back and sides were parged with mortar and that some of the upper-level fireplaces had firebacks. Each fireplace opening had two jack arches supported by iron lintels. Evidence shows that rather than mantels each fireplace had a stone or wood surround. The corner fireplace of the dining room used a diagonal flue to the northwest chimney. This fireplace had a shelf that might have been a Rumford design for radiant heat purposes. Paint evidence around some of the openings indicate that a brick red paint was used to mitigate soot stains when the parging material fell off. The corner fireplace of the dining room was held up by a squinch arch in the wine cellar.

Floors

Jefferson mentioned to his workers that he wanted oak floors because the best houses in Europe had them. What made his floors European was the fact that they were oiled, waxed, and polished. A piece of the original floor was found during investigations, and it confirmed the presence of oil, as did the walls where some oil slopped on the brick during treatment. The oak floorboards were tongue-and-grooved on their sides and ends. Jefferson's letter mentioned that a herringbone pattern like Monticello's entry hall was to be used, and it was conjectured that this would have only been used in the dining room. John Perry, who laid the Poplar Forest floors, had laid some of those in Monticello in 1804. At Monticello the pine floors, and the parlor's parquet floors, were oiled, waxed, and polished. In Paris a "frotteur" servant polished the floors daily.

Foundations

The Poplar Forest brick walls were laid directly upon the ground without spread footings or stone footings, except for the north portico wall, where a stone foundation was used. The lack of footings was in contradiction to a Jefferson note specifying that underpinning should be one-fourth the height of the first story. The shorter brick walls of the later east wing were laid on stone foundations. There was a 2.5-degree shift in the lower brick walls of the main house during construction that might be related to Jefferson helping Hugh Chisolm lay out the foundation in 1806.

Framing

The structural framing in the house for floors and roof was old-growth poplar and similar to sizes Jefferson used for Monticello and the University of Virginia. The floor and ceiling joists were 4″ × 10″. Without a source for old-growth poplar, the restored framing members in the house were made of white oak and those of the central terras roof old-growth pine. John Perry was the carpenter who, with his enslaved workers, constructed the principal framing. His brother Reuben Perry was a joiner in Lynchburg and did some of the more exacting work.

Glass

Jefferson used large-size glass panes that he imported from Europe. He specified Bohemian crown glass, and later crown glass made in Boston. All of this had to be shipped to Richmond and then sent on boats upriver to Lynchburg. In 1768 he was importing the best crown glass from England for Monticello I. For the upper sash windows at Poplar Forest, the size was 12″ × 18″. For the lower sash, it was 12″ × 12″ and for the sash doors 18″ × 18″. The many glass orders were a mixture of crown glass and cylinder glass. These were sizes similar to those Jefferson used at Monticello and the University of Virginia.

Grout

As was his practice, Jefferson used a very liquid mortar to pour into the inner cavities of the brick wall. Physical evidence of this was found during investigation. Jefferson specified this for the University of Virginia buildings.

Gutters

It is conjectured that the Poplar Forest roof had the built-in gutter trough like that of Monticello. An iron rod protruded out of this gutter to hold the balustrade up above the surface of the roof.

Hearthstones

Stonemason John Gorman spent three weeks in 1819 laying and polishing marble hearthstones and "slabs" for the fireplaces. Before the marble Jefferson must have had temporary hearths of brick. The hearths were supported by a brick arch that was in turn supported by arched iron bands, like the hearths of Monticello. The ironwork was a redundant system but typical of Jefferson's overbuilding for permanence. For the restored hearthstones a similar vein of local marble was located just east of Lynchburg.

Kitchen

The original kitchen was mentioned in 1808 and would have been a stand-alone building. Nothing is known about this kitchen or its location. In 1815 one of the four rooms in the service wing of "offices" was a kitchen. This kitchen was up-to-date with a hearth, bake oven, set kettle, and stew stove range. A stew stone grate was found archaeologically and the other features determined through archaeology since the wing was demolished in the mid-1840s. The kitchen was reconstructed as part of the wing complex. Physical evidence compared with the Montpelier kitchen that Hugh Chisolm had built just before the Poplar Forest kitchen helped identify the bake oven location. The original wrought-iron cooking crane was found on the property and had been used in the 1840s kitchen building.

Laundry

One room in the wing, adjacent to the kitchen, was the laundry, or washhouse, with a fireplace as big as that in the kitchen. This room later became the 1840s kitchen space when the wing was partially demolished and its two eastern rooms converted into stand-alone buildings.

Lead

Leftover sheet lead was carried on a wagon from Monticello to Poplar Forest to flash the sides of the chimneys where the wooden shingles ended. The lead gutter downspouts (leaders) in restoration are conjectural, based on lead leader pipes used at Monticello.

Lumber

Jefferson preferred to have his old-growth poplar lumber taken to water-powered sawmills. In some instances, the mills were not running due to low water, and the stock had to be sawn by hand using pit saws. Enslaved workers cut and processed the lumber. Old-growth poplar trees were "banded," or girdled, to die and left standing until they were needed for lumber stock. Old-growth heart poplar was as prized as old-growth heart pine for exterior and interior use.

Lunette Windows

Four lunette, or "fan," windows were used at Poplar Forest. One each was used in the north and south porticos and the east and west stair pavilions. It was customary for these pediment windows to be opened in the summer to exhaust the hot air from the attic spaces. The pavilion lunettes served to light the staircases. The west stair pavilion lunette window also threw borrowed light into a transom that lighted the storage space above Jefferson's bed alcove. The Poplar Forest lunette windows were made by James Oldham in Richmond in 1806. The lunette windows were hinged on their bottom and opened inward on the top.

Marble

There are two types of marble used at Poplar Forest, a local type and an Italian type. The local type came from quarries near downtown Lynchburg. John Gorman spent three weeks at Poplar Forest in 1819 preparing, laying, and polishing this material for the fireplace hearthstones and surrounds. The front door sill had already been installed using the local marble. The same geologic vein east of Lynchburg was used for the restored hearthstones. The other marble piece found on the site has been identified as a Carrara marble from Italy that was part of a fireplace surround. Jefferson ordered Carrara marble for Monticello surrounds in 1824 but was also getting various pieces before then. It is not known how much Italian marble Jefferson used at Poplar Forest, but it is believed it would have been used in the best room, the parlor.

Moldings

Jefferson's moldings for Poplar Forest, inside and out, were Roman derived, as they were for Monticello and the University of Virginia. He seldom varied those for bases, sur bases (chair rails), or door and window architraves. The architrave, based on the Palladian one-sixth of the opening, was from an Ionic order. Most of these he took out of James Gibbs's *Rules for Drawing Architecture.* The large Tuscan entablature moldings were taken from Palladio, whereas the Doric and Ionic moldings of the dining room and parlor entablatures were taken from Freart de Chambray's *Parallèle de l'architecture antique avec la modern.* Both Palladio and Chambray were used at Monticello and the University of Virginia. All of the finished moldings were made on-site by John Hemmings and his three nephew apprentices, Beverly, Madison, and Eston Hemings.

Mortar

Mortar was made on-site by burning limestone. It was then slaked with water and mixed with good river sand before being used to lay brick in a "hot mix." The same material was used for the column rendering and for the plaster. For the University of Virginia, Jefferson specified a one-lime to two-sands mixture for interior mortar and a one-to-one ratio for a stronger exterior mix. The inner grout would be a watered-down version of the inner mix. Enslaved men and boys would make the mortar. Hugh Chisolm and his brother John were the bricklayers, stonemasons, and plasterers. Enslaved worker Phil Hubbard was also used for mortar making.

Nails

The initial nails for the house framing were those hand-wrought in the nailery at Monticello. Small cut or machine nails for the plaster lath were also made there. In about 1815 large cut nails became available and were used for the exterior and interior trim. Monticello was constructed with all wrought nails and the University of Virginia with all cut nails. Poplar Forest, with both, was the transitional site in between those two.

Nogging

In addition to the countersealing method of filling the floors and ceiling spaces with brick Jefferson also used a nogging method to fill in between the vertical studs of a wood wall with brick. This was considered a fireproofing measure and could also have acted as insulation, soundproofing, and ratproofing. It is conjectured that Jefferson used wall nogging for the passage walls. A written reference is to nogging the bed alcove walls; at Monticello it is known he used wall nogging.

Orders

Jefferson used three Roman architectural orders: Tuscan (exterior, passage, and bed chambers), Doric (dining room), and Ionic (parlor). This was a hierarchy of higher orders as one moved through the house. These large wooden moldings were crafted by John Hemmings and his nephews. The sequence of Tuscan-Doric-Ionic was a standard one from classical times. Jefferson once told a friend that the Tuscan was something used for barns and outbuildings, but he nevertheless used it for the exterior of Poplar Forest and Barboursville. For the exterior of Monticello Jefferson used the Doric. For the exterior of the University of Virginia buildings he used Doric, Ionic, and Corinthian.

Paint

Physical evidence tells us that Jefferson used the same linseed oil white finish paint for his wooden moldings both exterior and interior. The only interior wooden parts that were not painted this color were the varnished walnut window sash and the varnished walnut doors on the upper level. The plaster walls were colored with pigmented lime washes and distempers in blue/gray colors; a light tan oil was also used on plaster walls. Surviving pieces of finished plaster were found out of context so the colors can be confirmed but not which room had which color. Surviving material in the upper east stair pavilion shows that it had the blue-gray distemper finish whereas the west pavilion only had the white coat of plaster with no other finish. The restoration paint finishes in the house are based on surviving evidence and preferences for room finishes at Monticello. The lower-level stone and brick walls were originally painted with a Spanish brown paint, most likely to blend the two materials together. The east privy had a pinkish lime wash on its plaster, and the west privy had only a white coat with no other finish.

Passage

The north entrance passage was defined by ghost marks of its original partition walls on the south side brickwork. This passage was widened in the 1846 rebuilding in order to accommodate sidelights (the doorway also received a transom). It is assumed that the stud walls of the passage, the only other wood walls besides the alcoves, received a brick nogging fill like those of the alcoves. The passage received the same Tuscan order entablature as that of the bed chambers (based on physical evidence).

Pediments

The north and south portico pediments are typical of those Jefferson designed for any of his full-size porticos. The Neilson south elevation drawing shows a full Tuscan entablature above its columns, although the same drawing only shows a cornice rather than a full entablature wrapping around the rest of the building. The same drawing shows the typical Doric plinths on the pediment roof. The absence of a pediment lunette window in the Neilson drawing was, like the other irregularities, thought to be incorrect based on Jefferson's precedents of always placing a window in each pediment tympanum. The pediments over the four dining room and parlor door frames is conjectural and based on Monticello and Montpelier.

Plaster

The house received a typical three-coat plaster finish on the interior walls and ceiling consisting of a scratch coat, a brown or levelling coat, and a thin white coat. The ceilings were by Richard Richardson and the walls by Hugh Chisolm. Plaster was applied directly to the brick walls and on riven lath for the ceilings, the bed alcove walls, and the north passage walls. Plaster on the lower-level brick and stone walls was the third period after a Spanish brown paint and a white wash; it is unclear in which period the plaster came, most likely in the Cobbs period. Jefferson mentioned that a high-quality sand should be brought to the site from Blackwater Creek for the plaster. The analyzed plaster was composed of slaked lime and a pinkish sand with an added brick dust in some cases. Plaster for the ceiling might also have had animal hair to help secure it. The upper-level plaster was colored in most cases by pigmented lime washes and distemper paints, as was the east privy. After the fire of 1845 the Jefferson plaster was removed for an entirely new plaster.

Plaster Grounds

Reuben Perry and his enslaved workers installed plaster grounds throughout the house. This was an extra method of installing boards to small nailing blocks in the brickwork wherever wood trim would be attached. The purpose of the grounds was to have the plaster plumb on the uneven walls and level on the ceilings. The typical method was to install the finished trim and to plaster to it. The finished trim would then be nailed to the grounds.

Portico

The Neilson elevation and plan drawings show the intended porticos on the north and south. These were added to the design after Jefferson visited the site in 1806, having started with a pure octagon shape. The four-column tetra-style portico was proportioned from Palladian dimensions. The arcade on the lower level of the south portico is a feature, combined with the columns and pediment, that comes from the British Palladian designs rather than from a Palladian prototype. The porticos had no railings. For the restoration a Jefferson-designed bench was placed on the sides of the north portico for a safety feature. The south portico was used like an outdoor room without stairs.

Privy

The two domed octagonal privies were placed on the far side of the east and west mounds. In effect they form a seven-part Palladian scheme along with the mounds and the hyphens of trees that originally connected the mounds to the house. Each domed privy has an exterior cornice that is proportioned accordingly to Roman / Palladian dimensions. On the interior a seat is on the outermost wall and situated over an arched clean-out hole below the water table. Two small lunette windows served to light each privy. Each privy had plaster on brick walls, the east having a pinkish tint lime wash, and the west having only a white coat finish. Neither privy had a plaster ceiling. Evidence on the original roof sheathing shows that they were originally covered with wood chestnut shingles with a lead cap on the apex. Fragments of original shingles have evidence that they were coated with a tar pitch material to help prolong their life. The original door survives on the east privy with H-L hinges and a Suffolk latch. The original seat survives in the west privy. Jefferson also retrofitted a privy under the west stairs off of his bed chamber. Physical evidence indicates that it had wood paneling on the walls and was cleaned by access via an arched opening on the north pavilion wall. Jefferson had used indoor water closets in Paris and had two installed in the President's House. He had indoor privies at Monticello in addition to those in the service wings.

Render

The brick columns of the north and south porticos were originally coated with a lime render, or stucco, the color of stone. This treatment was an old Roman one that made the columns mimic monolithic stone. This treatment was also used in the Renaissance by Andrea Palladio and described in his 1570 book. Analysis of the very thin render shows that it was later coated with lime wash, most likely after the 1845 fire. Analysis of the render revealed that it had a hard-fired brick dust that acted as a strengthening agent. This was also an ancient Roman practice. All of the columns on the University of Virginia Lawn were treated in the same manner with unpainted lime render. This was also true of the west portico columns on Monticello, at Montpelier (on Jefferson's remodeling for Madison), and at Barboursville (a Jefferson design).

Roof

The hipped roof was originally covered with square-butt chestnut shingles. These were replaced after a chimney roof fire in 1825 with tin-coated metal shingles that Jefferson had just installed on Monticello and on pavilions at the University of Virginia. John Hemmings incorrectly installed whole-size shingle sheets that had to be redone in 1826, when Francis Eppes was living in the house. The initial center part of the roof over the dining room had a "rafter roof" with a skylight that was replaced with Jefferson's terras roof and skylight in 1819. Jefferson would have accessed the flat deck of the terras roof by going through a trap door in the ceiling of his outer alcove vestibule, up over his alcove bed, and then up ladders to another trap door in the roof. Enslaved servants would have accessed the terras roof in the same way to open or close the skylight blinds. The roof was covered with seamed tin sheets after the 1845 fire. The privy roofs were covered with wood shingles and then tin shingles before being covered with seamed metal sheets in 1846.

Sash Doors

The first known feature John Hemmings made for Poplar Forest in the Monticello joinery shop in 1810 were four sets of bivalve "sash doors" (glass doors) for the dining room. He presumably made the south sash door of the parlor under James Dinsmore's direction. Monticello had three sets of sash doors on axis from the front door through the parlor. At Poplar Forest these three sets of glass doors on axis allowed one to see through the house from the entrance passage. The east and west sash doors of the dining room allowed light from the skylight to light the otherwise dark alcove vestibules. Sash doors were common in Parisian houses, and Jefferson used them in his designs after his time there. The Monticello parlor has an inner sash door and an outer solid door in the same jamb. This was the prototype for the south parlor door at Poplar Forest since the Neilson south elevation drawing shows a solid door in a wall Jefferson wanted as open as possible.

Sheet Iron

Leftover sheets of roofing iron were sent from Monticello to Poplar Forest to line the gutters of the porticos' hipped roof valleys. These sheets were typically too large to be coated in tin, so they would have to be painted for preservation. At the University of Virginia, Jefferson also used sheet iron to line the ridges and valleys of his terras roofs, as he had done at the President's House wings.

Shingles

The original roof covering was square-butt chestnut shingles. The initial roof for Monticello II was chestnut shingles. The two layers of shingles for the terras roof were pine with water grooves on each side of the top face. Based on fragments found for the privy roofs, the main house shingles were probably also coated with a tar pitch material for longevity. These wooden shingles caught fire from a northwest chimney in 1825, when Francis Eppes was living at Poplar Forest. Jefferson sent John Hemmings to install tin shingles when he finished installing them on Monticello. The privies were recovered with the same shingles. What was not understood was the capillary action that drew water under the shingles and caused the roof to leak. Jefferson used the same tined shingles at the University of Virginia that had the same problem; these were later replaced there with slate roof coverings.

Skylight

The original "rafter roof" over the central dining room had some type of skylight. In 1819 Jefferson replaced this whole roof with his terras design that allowed for a flat deck above. This second roof system, described in letters, had the 16-foot-long skylight that was restored. A granddaughter remarked that louvered blinds were closed over the skylight in the summer to make the house cooler. An archaeological artifact revealed what is thought to be the hinge for these blinds.

Smokehouse

One of the four rooms in the wing of "offices" was a smokehouse. What was unusual about this smokehouse was the flat roof of the terras. Typically smokehouses had a high-pitched roof for hanging meat, like the rebuilt Hutter smokehouse of the 1840s. Jefferson had configured a similar flat roof smokehouse in the wing at Monticello, using a vestibule with a fireplace so that one did not have to be in the smoke-filled room to keep a fire going. Archaeology revealed the same type of stone vestibule for the Poplar Forest smokehouse. He designed a similar flat roof smokehouse for the President's House service wing.

Stairs

Jefferson struggled with where to place the staircases in his initial pure octagon design. He resolved the issue by putting them into external pavilions. He followed Palladio's advice that you should not waste space or expense on large showy staircases. These stairs allowed one to travel from the east and west bed chambers down to the lower level or to the exterior. Jefferson retrofitted a privy under the stairs on the west off of his chamber suite. Food from the wing would come up the east stairs to the dining room, and later, to the pantry in the southeast room. The house was placed partially in the ground so that the front north stairs were minimized in height to access the north portico and front door. There were no stairs for the south portico, making it a raised outdoor "verandah," as a granddaughter described it.

Stone

Jefferson used stone for the foundation of the north portico front wall, for the deep cellar walls, and for the internal walls of the wing of offices. It was not used for the principal walls of the main house. Stone was used in the wing where it was not visible on the exterior; brick being the better material to see. All of this was local fieldstone. The hearthstones and the front door sill were a local white marble. The imported stone found during investigation was an Italian marble for the fireplace surrounds.

Stoves

There is a reference that Jefferson brought two stoves from Monticello for use at Poplar Forest. He bought and used a variety of stoves at Monticello. Those used at Poplar Forest were probably placed in front of one of the frequently used fireplaces, with the stove flue connected to the fireplace opening.

Terras Roof

Jefferson's only architectural invention was his terras roof. He also called this a serrated and zigzag roof. This compressed roof system of ridges and valleys was a hidden system that allowed for a flat usable deck above, through which the rain water passed and exited via the gutter scuppers. The laborious construction of such a unique system was all so Jefferson could use the deck above to sit, walk, and engage the outdoors. Jefferson's terras decks at the President's House and at Poplar Forest had no railing. A partial picket railing is seen for Monticello's deck. Jefferson designed a terras system for the President's House wings at about the same time that he converted the wing roofs at Monticello. At Poplar Forest, after the President's House example, this roof system was on the wing of offices and, after 1819, above the dining room on the main roof. At Monticello and the President's House, the gutters collected water. At the University of Virginia, over the student rooms on the Lawn, and at Poplar Forest, the gutters dumped their water on the ground. Jefferson tweaked his design for more than twenty years, sometimes lining the ridges and gutters with sheet metal. He influenced James Madison to install terras roofs over the wings at Montpelier and Jefferson's worker John Neilson constructed a terras roof at Bremo. The anatomical theater at the University of Virginia had a terras roof with skylight, not unlike that of the main house roof at Poplar Forest.

Tin Shingles

Jefferson was always looking for innovative building materials. In 1825 he replaced the wood shingle roof at Monticello with tin shingles. This was a lightweight and fireproof material he had seen. In 1825, during Francis Eppes's tenure, at Poplar Forest a chimney fire burned a great number of the wooden shingles. Jefferson sent John Hemmings to Poplar Forest to install a tin shingle roof. Jefferson also used the same covering for some of the pavilions on the University of Virginia Lawn. The inherent failing of this system was the short 2-inch lap between courses that allowed capillary action to draw up water, making the roof leak in many places. Francis Eppes had to redo the tin shingle roof at Poplar Forest in 1826 due to this problem.

Tuscan Order

Although Jefferson mentioned to a friend that the Tuscan order should not be used for a dwelling house, he designed it for the exterior of Poplar Forest. He also used it for two courthouses, a church, and at least four other house designs. The exterior of the Poplar Forest order was from the Leoni edition of Palladio's book.

Walls

Poplar Forest was constructed with brick walls using a standard-size common brick in a Flemish Bond pattern. The cellar walls were 18 inches thick. The walls reduced to 12-inch thickness above the water table where the main floor joists rested. The exception in material was the fieldstone walls of the central wine cellar. The 45-degree corners of the outer octagon walls were made with oversized squint bricks that had the wall angle on either side of a header or stretcher face. These two faces were necessary for the Flemish Bond system of alternating headers and stretchers. Squint bricks were also used for the octagonal corners of the two privies. The tall 20-foot-high dining room walls were buttressed on their four corners by the large triangular chimney masses. The weight-relieving device for the windows and doors was a segmental arch. Jefferson left the wooden lintel forms under each arch after it was built, possibly as a backup if the arches ever failed.

Windows

After living in Paris Jefferson tried to put as much light in his buildings as possible. The Poplar Forest window sash was made in the Monticello joinery shop under the direction of James Dinsmore. They came in their frames and were inserted in the walls by Hugh Chisolm. They were glazed at Monticello by Richard Barry. Replacement glass was installed over many years by Burwell Colbert, who had been trained as a painter and glazier. Jefferson's sash windows, 3′ 3″ × 3′ 3″, had the thinnest muntins (5/8″) that held the largest glass he could use, 12″ × 18″ for the six-over-six upper sash. His window sashes were modern by being hung on weights, and even more modern by having the top sash weighted and useable. English brass pulleys for the sash cord and weights were purchased in Richmond. For the parlor, Jefferson used three sashes together, all hung, opening up the south brick wall to a great degree. The sashes were secured closed by English brass spring locks, which Jefferson also used at Monticello and the University of Virginia. The sash cord was hemp rope; for the restoration custom hemp rope was made in Holland. Jefferson specified that the upper sash be walnut and varnished for a "richer look." The lower sash, with 12″ × 12″ panes, was painted pine. The upper sash architraves were within the opening, whereas the lower sash architraves were planted on the brick surface. The facets of the exterior octagon walls allowed for more windows than in a conventional house design.

Wing

The eastern "wing of offices," or service rooms, had a lineage dating back to Andrea Palladio's book of 1570, in which he showed villas with attached agricultural wings. Jefferson used this idea for Monticello I. By grouping all the plantation activities in wings, the lawn could be reserved for landscape gardening. The Poplar Forest wing had four rooms: an unheated room that might have served as a spinning room; a kitchen; a laundry; and a smokehouse. After Jefferson put two 100-foot service wings on the President's House, he added the 100-foot Poplar Forest wing on the east side of the house, replacing the hyphen of mulberry trees that connected the house to the mound. He never built a balanced west service wing. The roof of the wing had his signature terras roof system with deck that he could access via a retro-opened doorway in the upper wall of the east stair pavilion. The wing was partially in the ground when seen from the north, just as the house itself was set into the ground. This reduced the mass of the wing from the front of the house, but the principal reason was to have the wing deck level with the main floor of the house and for the wing's floor to be level with the cellar floor of the house. The southern elevation of the wing showed its full size with doors, windows, and square piers supporting the extended roof over a covered walkway. The northern below grade retaining wall and the internal walls of the wing were fieldstone, whereas all walls seen on the exterior were brick. One chimney in the center of the wing served the fireplaces of the kitchen and the adjacent laundry. Jefferson's design for remodeling Farmington in Charlottesville featured a service wing but one of two stories with no terras roof. The Poplar Forest wing fell into disrepair during Francis Eppes's tenure and might not have been put in order, even though Jefferson stated he had a new, improved design for the gutters. In the mid-1840s, after the house was rebuilt after the 1845 fire, the two rooms closest to the house were demolished and the other two rooms converted into a stand-alone kitchen and smokehouse with conventional roofs. The gable-roof attic above the kitchen was used as living quarters for the enslaved kitchen workers. In the 1940s the wing was converted into guest quarters with the addition of a bathroom.

Wood

In Jefferson's time different species of wood were used for features and locations that emphasized its characteristics. The principal structural members of the house were made of old-growth poplar since the house stood near a forest of those trees. The heartwood of this old-growth wood was also prized for exterior trim, and Jefferson specified that the balusters of the balustrade be made of this material. Poplar wood was also good for the classical trim moldings of the interior. Pine could also be used for interior plaster grounds, framing, and trim. Jefferson specified that the floors be made of oak. These were oiled and waxed for a high polish like European examples. Jefferson mentioned that the upper window sash should be made of varnished walnut, whereas the cellar windows could be made of painted pine. The exterior doors were made of pine in the Monticello joinery shop and either faux-painted or painted the trim color. Later interior doors were made on-site by John Hemmings and his nephews out of walnut and varnished. The carved wooden lintels used to create the segmental window and door arches were pine. Jefferson mentioned that the window sills might be made of locust, like the door sills of the two privies. The doors, seats, lunette windows, and roof sheathing of the privies were made of pine, whereas the roof rafters were of oak. The structural members of the wing terras roof were poplar, and the two layers of shingles in the terras roof were pine.

APPENDIX C
THOMAS JEFFERSON'S TYPOLOGY OF OCTAGON DESIGNS

Thomas Jefferson's use of the octagon shape throughout his architectural career displays an amazing comprehensive variety. Most of these were for domestic works, and most were never executed. Nevertheless, they show the tenacious ways in which that shape could be used in plan designs. The ones shown here are the unique combinations and are not by any means all of the designs with that shape. Almost all of these plans, most of which are unidentified, can be found in Fiske Kimball's 1916 work *Thomas Jefferson, Architect,* from which these have been taken. The numbers refer to those in Kimball's book. Two exceptions are the first ca. 1781 plan for Poplar Forest, which has a Nichols number from the University of Virginia collection, and the plan for Monticello II. These designs have been divided into three categories of domestic plans and one of some public designs.

Full Octagon Plans

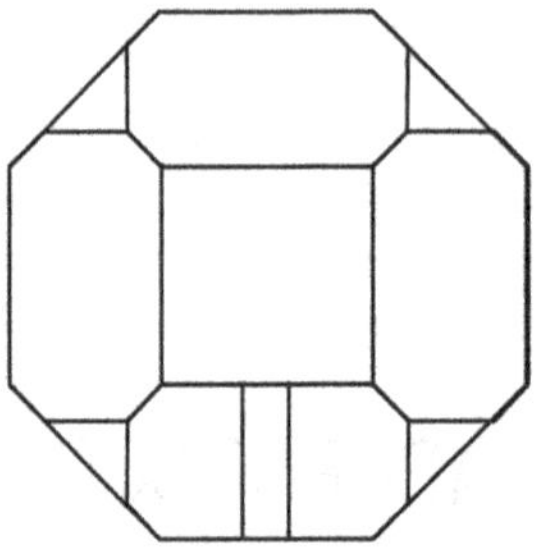

193

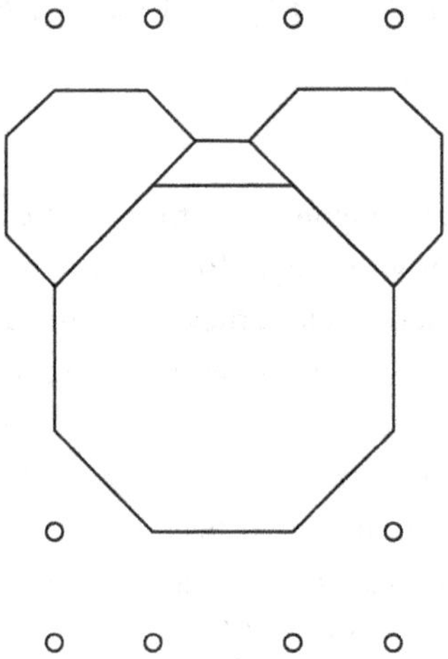

217 B

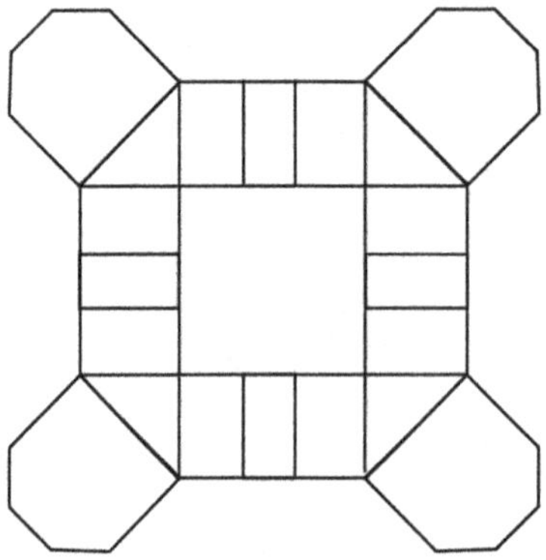

220 B

Semi-Octagon Bays

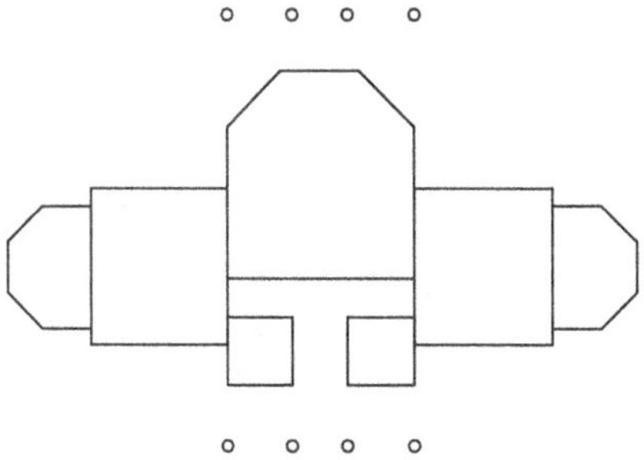

32

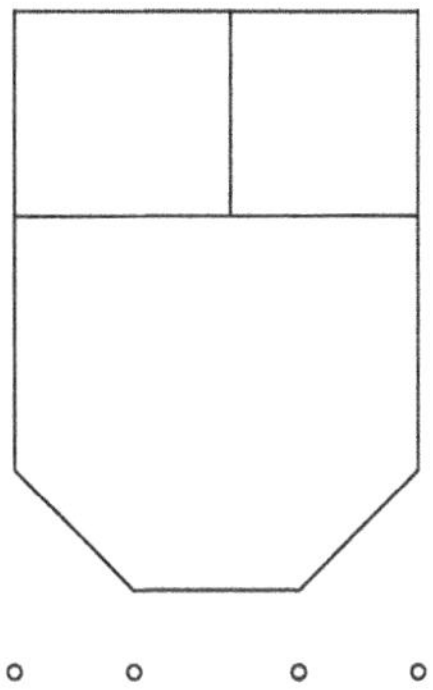

58

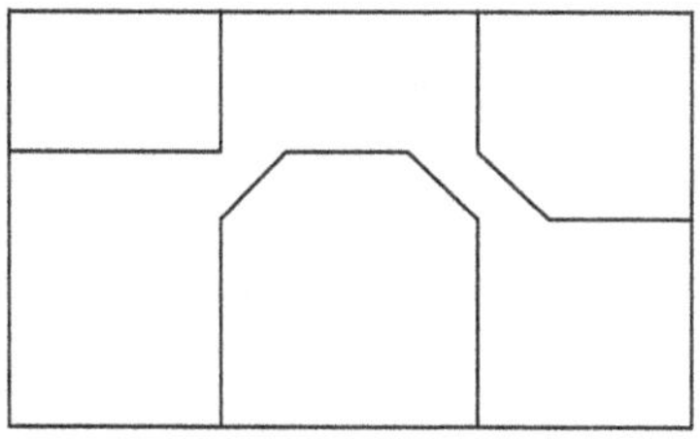

202

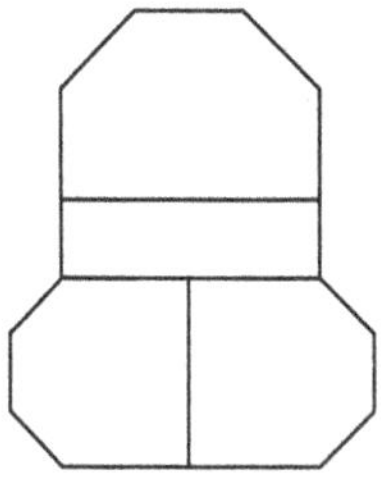

217 C

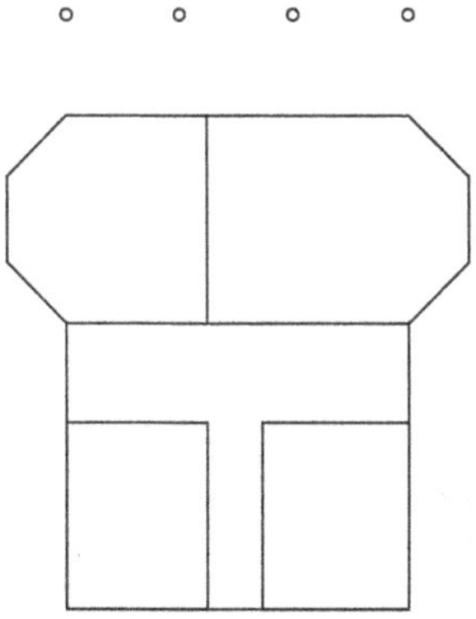

183

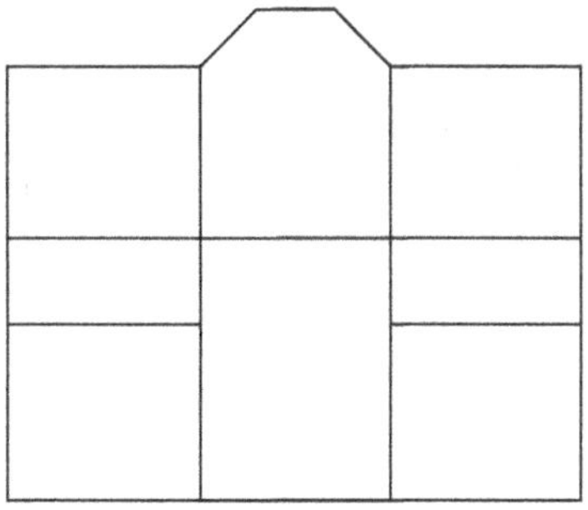

172

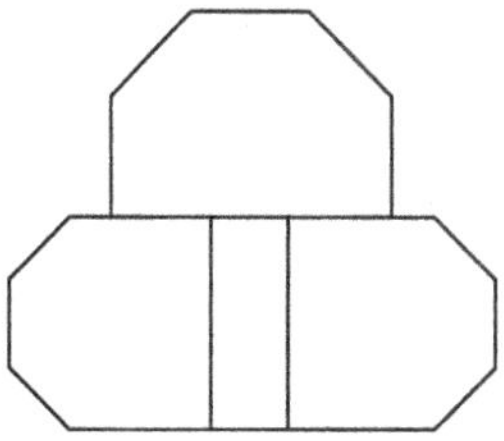

217 D

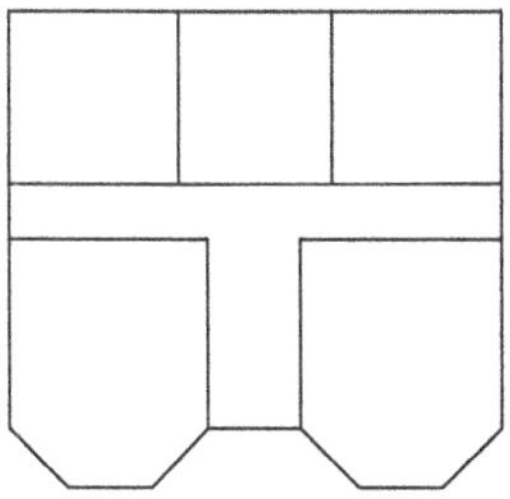

201 A

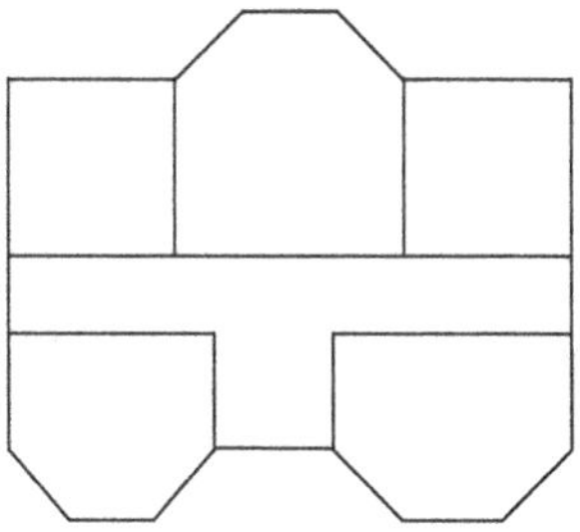

201 B

Full Octagon Rooms

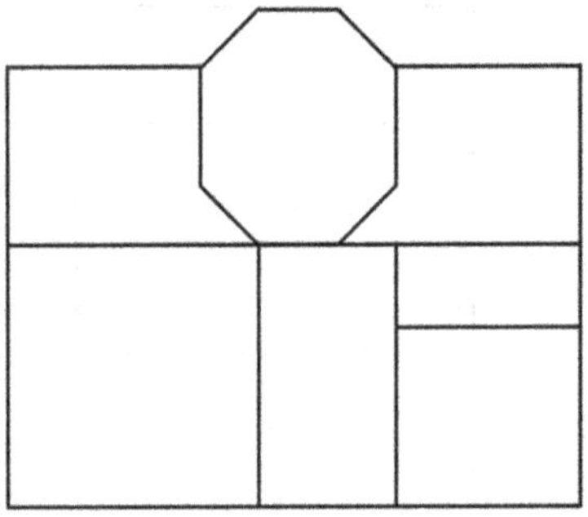

101

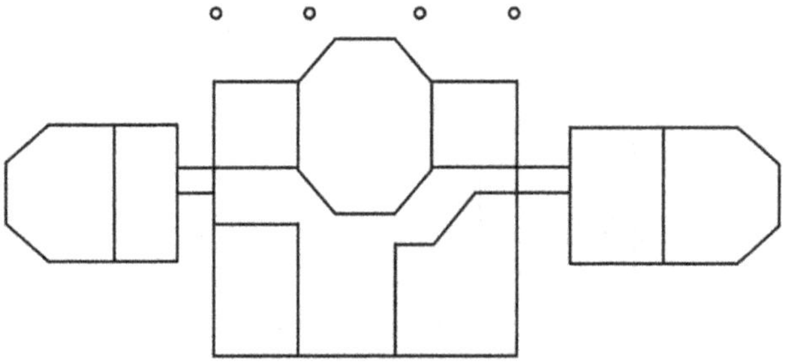

First Poplar Forest plan N-255

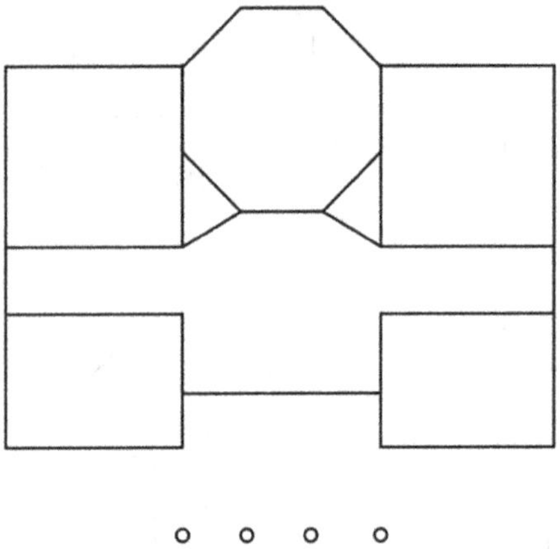

206

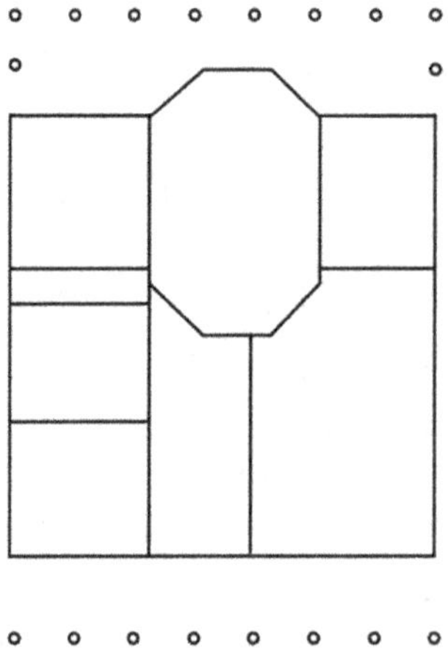

99

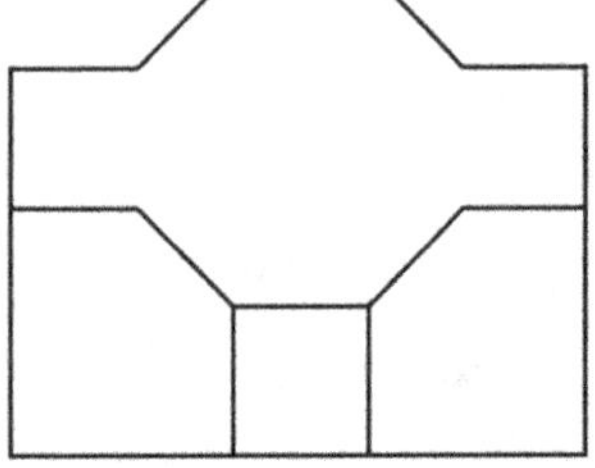

104

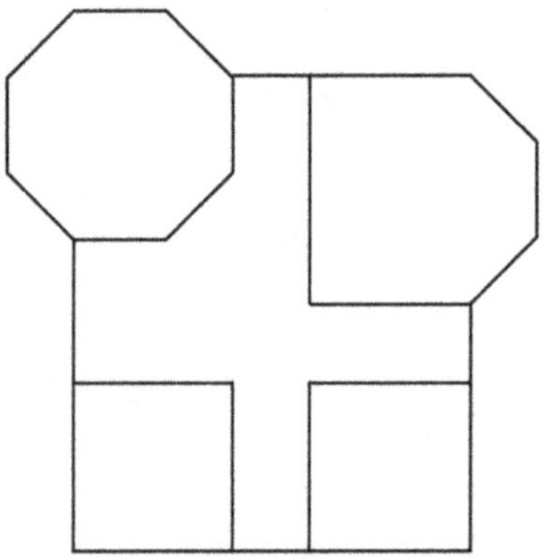

184

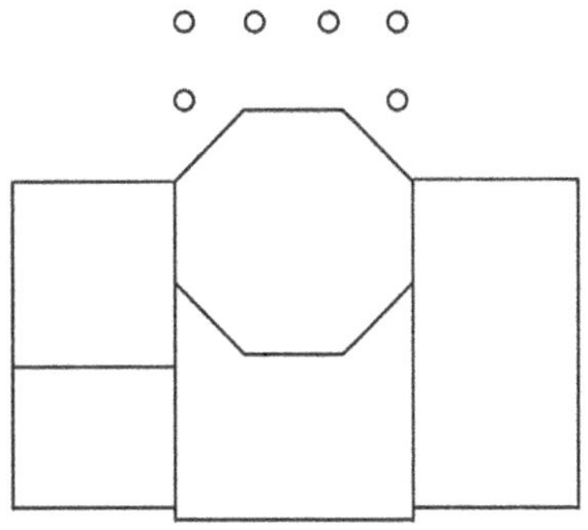

186

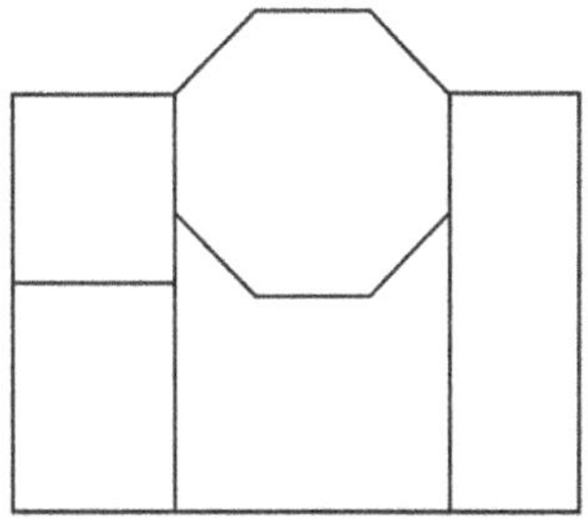

189A

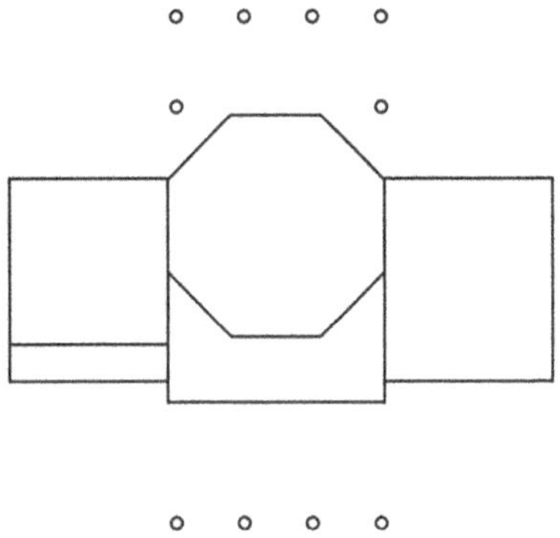

186

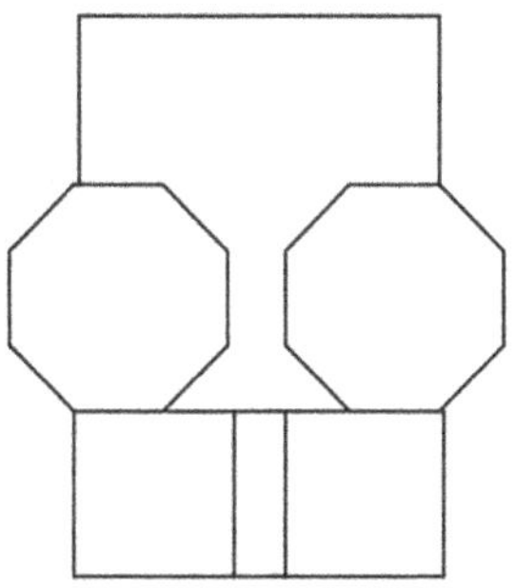

189B

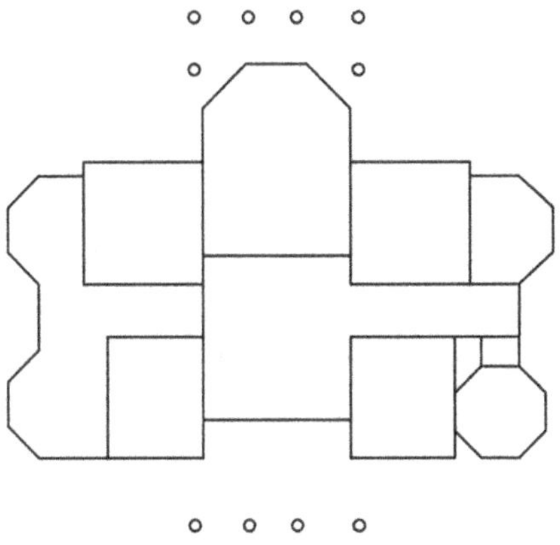

Monticello II

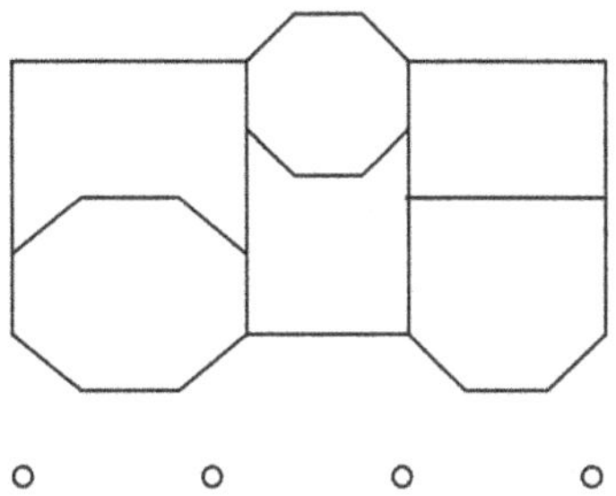

191

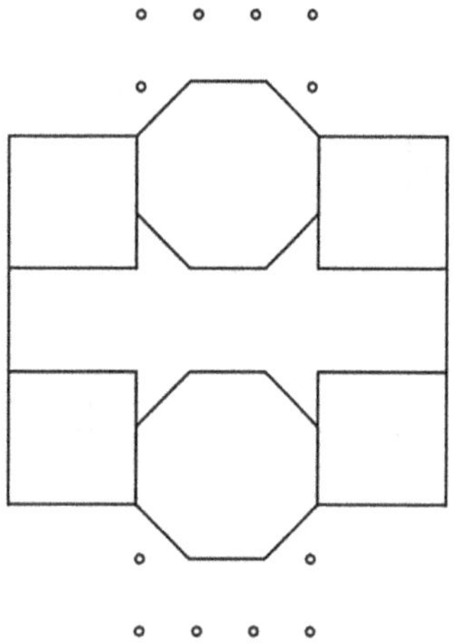

191

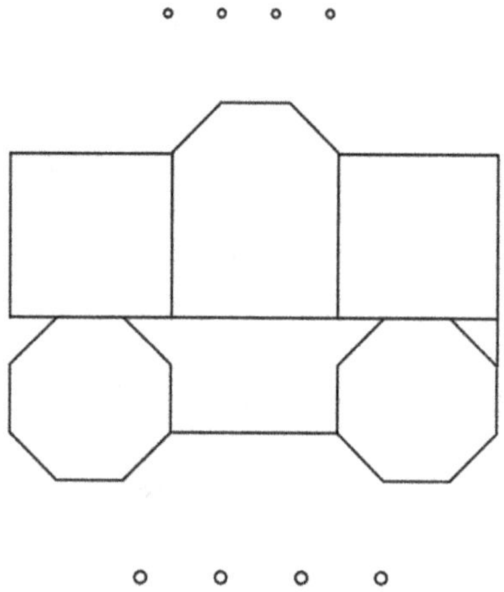

199

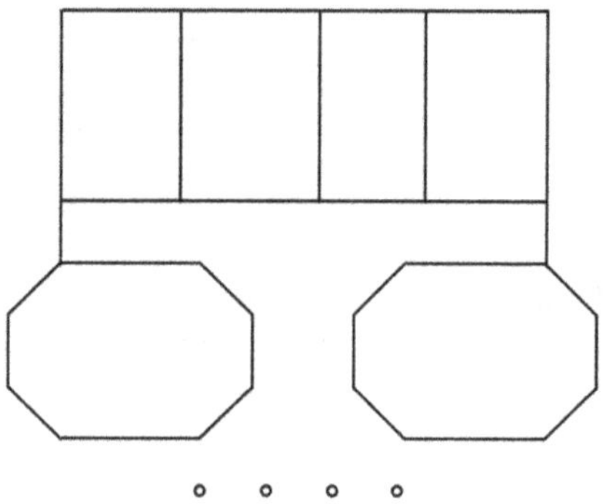

203

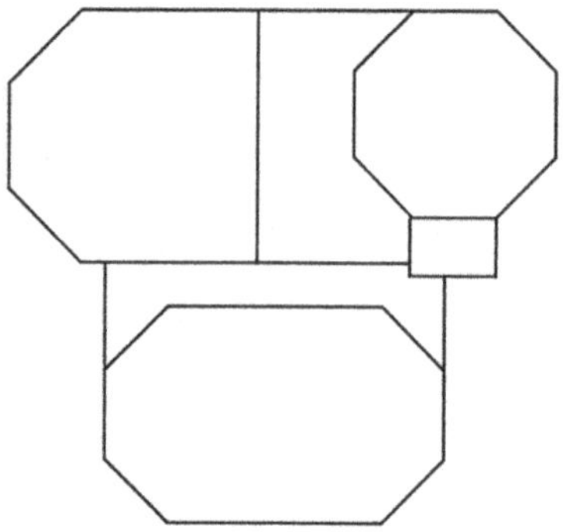

216

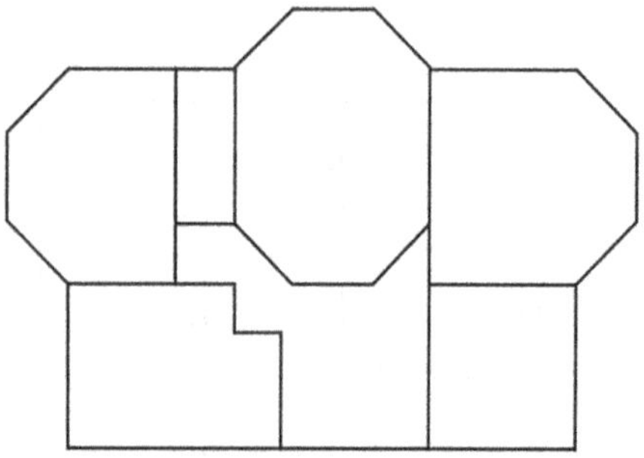

219

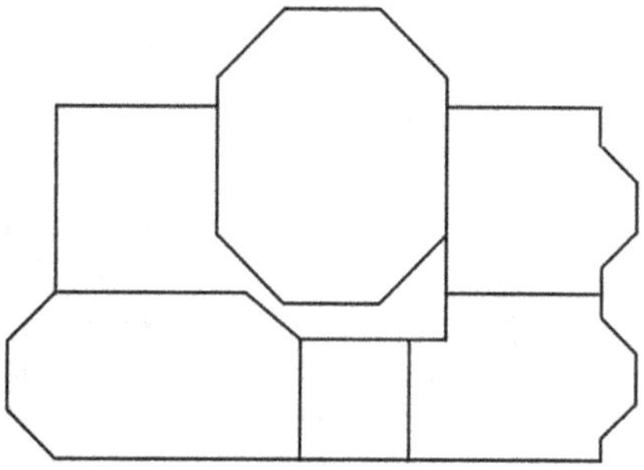

220

Public Designs

Three of Jefferson's public designs using the octagon shape are worth depicting.

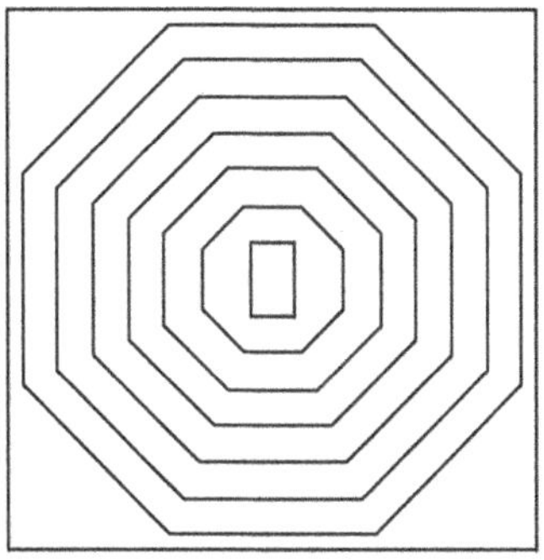

Anatomical Theater, University of Virginia

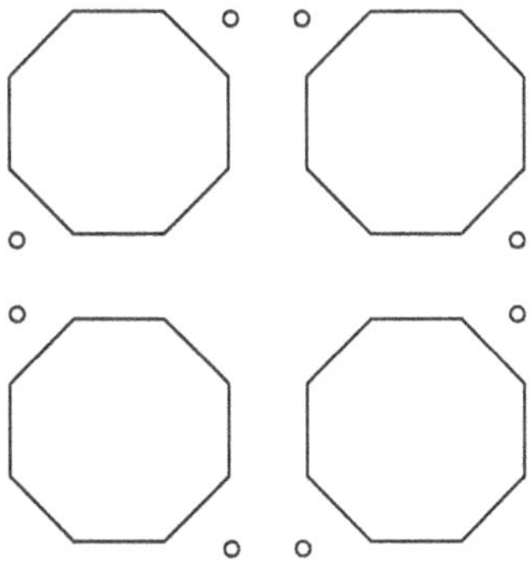

Unexecuted observatory for the University of Virginia

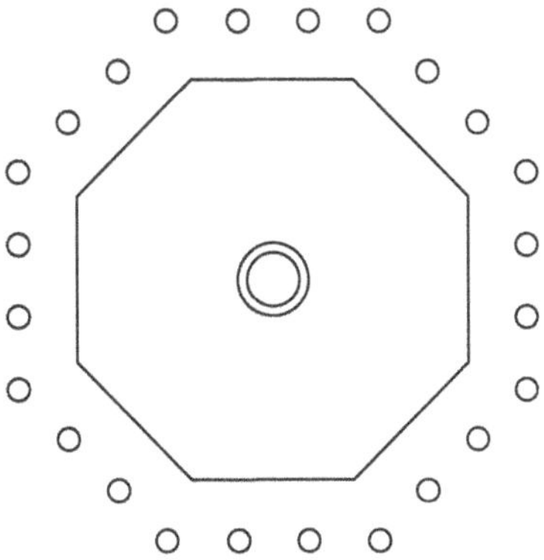

Unexecuted chapel in Williamsburg

NOTES

PREFACE

1. S. Allen Chambers Jr., *Poplar Forest and Thomas Jefferson* (Forest, VA: Corporation for Jefferson's Poplar Forest, 1993).

2. See Camille Wells, "The Multi-Storied House: Twentieth-Century Encounters with the Domestic Architecture of Colonial Virginia," in *Material Witnesses: Domestic Architecture and Plantation Landscapes in Early Virginia,* by Wells, 188–235 (Charlottesville: University of Virginia Press, 2018). See Cary Carson and Carl R. Lounsbury, eds., *The Chesapeake House* (Chapel Hill: Colonial Williamsburg Foundation and University of North Carolina, 2013).

INTRODUCTION

1. Thomas Jefferson (hereafter cited as TJ) to J. W. Eppes, 18 September 1812, in *The Papers of Thomas Jefferson,* ed. Julian Boyd et al., 43 vols. to date (Princeton, NJ: Princeton University Press, 1950–). Thomas Jefferson, *The Papers of Thomas Jefferson, Retirement Series,* ed. J. Jefferson Looney, 17 vols. to date (Charlottesville, VA: Thomas Jefferson Foundation, 2004–). The Princeton Papers project starts with Jefferson's earliest papers and concludes with Jefferson's retirement; it is cited hereafter as *Papers.* The Retirement Papers project (Monticello) starts with Jefferson's retirement in 1809; it is cited hereafter as *Papers, Retirement.*

2. Edwin Morris Betts, ed., *Thomas Jefferson's Farm Book* (Philadelphia: American Philosophical Society, 1953).

3. I refer to Wikipedia, Jon Meacham (*Art of Power*), Kenneth Hayes (*Road to Monticello*), Andrew Burstein (*Inner Jefferson*), and Joseph Ellis (*American Sphinx*).

4. Chambers, *Poplar Forest.*

5. Wendell Garrett, *Thomas Jefferson Redivivus* (Barre, MA: Barre Publishing, 1971).

6. Garrett, *Redivivus,* 10

7. Cited in Chambers, *Poplar Forest,* 185

8. Karl Lehman, *Thomas Jefferson, American Humanist* (Charlottesville: University Press of Virginia, 1985), 19.

9. The initial investigations were under the direction of William Kelso, who was on leave from Monticello for two years in 1988–90, and thereafter under the direction of Barbara Heath, who had also been at Monticello.

10. This was architects John Mesick and Jeff Baker of Mesick Cohen Wilson Baker Architects from Albany, New York. William L. Beiswenger, director of restoration at Monticello, was the indispensable oracle at that site.

11. Lynn Beebe was hired as the first executive director in 1986. She sought initial advice from Nicholas A. Pappas, formerly chief historical architect for Colonial Williamsburg, and Hugh C. Miller, formerly chief historical architect for the National Park Service. A 1988 restoration planning meeting included Pappas, Miller, William Beiswanger, and Henry Chambers. Members of the Architectural Advisory Panel included William Beiswanger, Robert Burley, Nicholas Pappas, Lee Nelson, and Orlando Ridout. Later members included Hugh Miller, Edward Chappell, Robert Self, and John Larson. Travis McDonald was hired in 1989 as the restoration coordinator and Andrew Ladygo in 1990 as the architectural conservator. Consulting architects Mesick Cohen Wilson Baker (formerly Mesick Cohen Waite) were chosen in 1990 with John Mesick and Jeff Baker being the principal architects for the project.

12. Even though Jefferson used Poplar Forest from 1809 to 1823, coming from two to four times each year, he was still directing its completion after his grandson Francis Eppes started living there in 1823, and continued to do so until his death in 1826. Poplar Forest passed out of the Jefferson family and history when Francis sold the property in 1828.

13. Barbara J. Heath and Jack Gary, eds., *Jefferson's Poplar Forest: Unearthing a Virginia Plantation* (Gainesville: University Press of Florida, 2012).

14. Mark R. Wenger, "Two Aspects of Jefferson's Domestic Architecture," typescript copy, 1991; Dell Upton, *Architecture in the United States* (Oxford: Oxford University Press, 1998); Camille Wells, "Virginia by Design: The Making of Tuckahoe and the Remaking of Monticello," in *Material Witnesses: Domestic Architecture and Plantation Landscapes in Early Virginia,* by Wells, 147–75 (Charlottesville: University of Virginia Press, 2018).

15. Upton, *Architecture,* 30–31.

16. See Carl R. Lounsbury, "The Building Process in Ante-Bellum North Carolina," *North Carolina Historical Review* 60, no. 4 (October 1983): 431–56. See also chapters by Carl R. Lounsbury and Catherine W. Bishir in *Architects and Builders in North Carolina: A History of the Practice of Building* (Chapel Hill: University of North Carolina Press, 1990).

17. Jack McLaughlin, *Jefferson and Monticello: The Biography of a Builder* (New York: Henry Holt, 1988). One published article on the construction of Poplar Forest is Travis C. McDonald Jr., "Constructing Optimism," in *People, Power, Places* (Knoxville: University of Tennessee, 2000).

18. McLaughlin, *Jefferson and Monticello,* vii.

1. THE RETREAT

1. Anna Maria Thornton Diary, September 18–22, 1802, Papers of Mrs. William Thornton, Library of Congress, quoted in Merrill D. Peterson, ed., *Visitors to Monticello* (Charlottesville: University Press of Virginia, 1989), 33–35.

2. Henry S. Randall, *The Life of Thomas Jefferson,* 3 vols. (1858; repr., Freeport, NY: Books for Libraries Press, 1970), 3:331.

3. Cited in James A. Bear, ed., *Jefferson at Monticello* (Charlottesville: University Press of Virginia, 1967), 114–15.

4. Randall, *Life,* 3:334

5. Garrett, *Redivivus,* 10

6. Barbara J. Heath, *Hidden Lives: The Archaeology of Slave Life at Thomas Jefferson's Poplar Forest* (Charlottesville: University Press of Virginia, 1999).

7. Martha Jefferson Randolph quoted in Margaret Bayard Smith, *The First Forty Years of Washington*

Society, ed. Gaillard Hunt (New York: Scribners, 1906), 387. This was first called to my attention by Ann Lucas.

8. Quoted in Edwin Morris Betts, ed., *Thomas Jefferson's Garden Book* (Philadelphia: American Philosophical Society, 1944), 21. In his Memorandum Book for March 1, 1770, Jefferson crossed out the word "Hermitage" and wrote "Monticello," although he had referred to the site as "Monticello" in a transaction of 31 July 1769; Thomas Jefferson, *Jefferson's Memorandum Books,* ed. James A. Bear Jr. and Lucia Stanton (Princeton, NJ: Princeton University Press, 1997), 30–31; hereafter cited as *MB.*

9. Quoted in Susan R. Stein, *The Worlds of Thomas Jefferson at Monticello* (New York: Harry N. Abrams, 1993), 13.

10. Quoted in Bear, *Jefferson at Monticello,* 17.

11. Randall, *Life,* 3:341.

12. Randall, *Life,* 3:341. A visit to Poplar Forest in the fall of 1800 is cited by biographer Henry Randall as another possible impetus for considering a future retreat there.

13. Quoted in Howard Rice, *Thomas Jefferson's Paris* (Princeton, NJ: Princeton University Press, 1976), 105.

14. Sarah N. Randolph, *The Domestic Life of Thomas Jefferson* (1871; repr., New York: Harper, 1978), 73.

15. Quoted in Howard Rice, *Thomas Jefferson's Paris,* 105.

16. TJ to Alexander Donald, 7 February 1788, quoted in Douglas L. Wilson and Lucia Stanton, eds., *Jefferson Abroad* (New York: Modern Library, 1999), 214.

17. TJ to Thomas Leiper, 16 December 1792, in *Papers.*

18. TJ to Thomas Leiper, 16 December 1792, in *Papers.*

19. TJ to James Brown, 7 April 1793, in *Papers.*

20. The date assigned to the drawing is defined by dated water marks on the paper and by the fact that Jefferson's labels in French are accompanied by notes by French architect Stephen Hallet, whom Jefferson had hired to supervise the construction of the United States Capitol in 1793. Jefferson, who conversed and corresponded with Hallet in French, would have seen him last in 1794.

21. Fiske Kimball, *Thomas Jefferson, Architect* (New York: Da Capo, 1968), 159.

22. About this same time Jefferson had submitted an anonymous design in a round shape with oval rooms for the 1792 United States Capitol competition. A similar shape would appear only once more in Jefferson's designs: for the Rotunda of the University of Virginia.

23. Kimball, *Architect,* 195, K-216–218. Drawings in Kimball, *Architect,* are hereafter cited as *K,* followed by the drawing number.

24. K-216, K-217, K-220 (N-496). Jefferson drawing numbers might also have a Nichols catalogue number from Frederick D. Nichols, *Thomas Jefferson's Architectural Drawings* (Charlottesville: University Press of Virginia, 1961) and are hereafter cited as *N,* followed by the drawing number. Nichols renumbered the Kimball numbers in his compilation, so different numbers from each might refer to the same drawing.

25. One design Kimball labeled as a study for a Poplar Forest retreat was later identified as a ca. 1800 townhouse (K-187, K-188). Notes on this drawing are from William L. Beiswanger, Monticello Research Library Files.

26. TJ to Hugh Chisolm, 23 February 1808, quoted in William L. Beiswanger, *Monticello in Measured Drawings* (Charlottesville, VA: Thomas Jefferson Foundation, 1998), 69. The "scholar" room was described by Isaac Jefferson as a schoolroom for grandchildren, and a study for a Charles Bankhead, but Jefferson also could have used it as a study space.

27. Beiswanger, *Monticello,* 69.

28. See William L. Beiswanger, "The Temple in the Garden: Thomas Jefferson's Vision of the Monti-

cello Landscape," in *British and American Gardens in the Eighteenth Century,* ed. Robert P. Maccubbin and Peter Martin (Williamsburg, VA: Colonial Williamsburg Foundation, 1984), 179, 182.

29. Beiswanger, "Temple," 184.

30. James S. Ackerman, *The Villa: Form and Ideology of Country Houses* (Princeton, NJ: Princeton University Press, 1990).

31. See Meyer Reinhold, ed., *The Classic Pages: Classical Readings of Eighteenth-Century Americans* (University Park: Pennsylvania State University Press, 1975); Meyer Reinhold, "The Classical World," in *Thomas Jefferson: A Reference Biography,* ed. Merrill D. Peterson, 135–56 (New York: Charles Scribner's Sons, 1986); Peter S. Onuf and Nicholas P. Cole, eds., *Thomas Jefferson, the Classical World, and Early America* (Charlottesville: University of Virginia Press, 2011); and Louis B. Wright, "Thomas Jefferson and the Classics," *Proceedings of the American Philosophical Society* 87, no. 3 (1943).

32. See Ann M. Lucas, "Ordering His Environment: Thomas Jefferson's Architecture from Monticello to the University of Virginia" (master's thesis, University of Virginia, 1989).

33. Ackerman, *Villa,* chap. 2, "The Ancient Roman Villa."

34. Quoted in John Archer, *Architecture and Suburbia: From English Villa to American Dream House, 1690–2000* (Minneapolis: University of Minnesota Press, 2005), 35.

35. Quoted in Archer, *Architecture,* 35.

36. Quoted in Archer, *Architecture,* 46.

37. Quoted in Archer, *Architecture,* 46. Jefferson had purchased a 1565 edition of Alberti's *The Ten Books of Architecture,* originally published in 1452.

38. See Archer, *Architecture;* Mark Reinberger and Elizabeth McLean, *The Philadelphia Country House: Architecture and Landscape in Colonial America* (Baltimore, MD: Johns Hopkins University Press, 2015); Mark Girourad, *Robert Smythson and the Elizabethan Country House* (New Haven, CT: Yale University Press, 1983); and Paula Henderson, "Secret Houses and Garden Lodges," *Apollo,* July 1997, 29–35.

39. Girourad, *Robert Smythson,* 107.

40. Quoted in Henderson, "Secret Houses," 31.

41. Quoted in Henderson, "Secret Houses," 29.

42. Henderson, "Secret Houses," 74.

43. Quoted in Gervase Jackson-Stops, George Mott, and Sally Sample Aall, *Follies and Pleasure Pavilions* (New York: Harry N. Abrams, 1989), 29. Jackson-Stops, Mott, and Aall, *Follies and Pleasure Pavilions,* 25.

44. Henderson, "Secret Houses," 29.

45. See Henderson, "Secret Houses."

46. See Archer, *Architecture.* See especially Archer's chapter 3, "The Apparatus of Selfhood," 93–170.

47. Archer, *Architecture,* 8.

48. Quoted in Archer, *Architecture,* 68.

49. See Clay Lancaster, "Jefferson's Architectural Indebtedness to Robert Morris," *Journal of the Society of Architectural Historians* 10, no. 1 (March 1951): 3–10.

50. Quoted in Archer, *Architecture,* 49.

51. Ackerman, *Villa,* 159.

52. TJ to John Page, 31 May 1791, in *Papers.*

53. For a discussion of opposition retirement, see Tamara Plakins Thornton, *Cultivating Gentlemen: The Meaning of Country Life among the Boston Elite, 1785–1860* (New Haven, CT: Yale University Press, 1989). "To stroll through Stowe was to hear the Opposition argue its case, to see Pope's satire writ large in the landscape" (50).

54. See Henry F. May, *The Enlightenment in America* (Oxford: Oxford University Press, 1976); and Caroline Winterer, *American Enlightenment* (New Haven, CT: Yale University Press, 2016).

55. Ackerman, *Villa,* 9.

56. See Philip Vickers Fithian, *The Journal of Philip Vickers Fithian: A Plantation Tutor of the Old Dominion,* ed. Hunter Dickenson Farish (Williamsburg, VA: Colonial Williamsburg Foundation, 1943), xxxi. The Tayloes of Mount Airy owned a house in Williamsburg and later built the Octagon House in the new city of Washington, DC, as their city place. Some elites moved into the Virginia capital of Williamsburg for the political season, renting houses. Wealthy planters in South Carolina who principally lived on their river plantations would escape to their Charleston houses for cooler summer breezes.

57. Ackerman, *Villa,* 10.

58. Bill O'Donovan, "A Secret American Historic Site," *Colonial Williamsburg,* winter 2014, 69–74.

59. Cary Carson, "Banqueting Houses and the 'Need of Society' among Slave-Owning Planters in the Chesapeake Colonies," *William and Mary Quarterly* 70, no. 4 (October 2013): 725–80.

60. Quoted in Carson, "Banqueting Houses," 747.

61. Wikipedia's "White Hall, Maryland" entry.

62. Susanne Williams Massie and Frances Archer Christian, *Houses and Gardens of Old Virginia* (Richmond, VA: J. W. Ferguson and Sons, 1930), 357.

63. Massie and Christian, *Houses,* 381.

64. Fairfax County website, fairfaxcounty.gov.

65. See Reinberger and McLean, *Philadelphia;* and Martin and Maccubbin, *British and American Gardens.*

66. Harold Donaldson Eberlein and Cortlandt VanDyke Hubbard, *Portrait of a Colonial City: Philadelphia 1670–1838* (Philadelphia: Lippincott, 1939), 547.

67. Beiswanger, "Temple," 182.

68. See William L. Beiswanger, "Designs for Garden Structures at Monticello" (master's thesis, University of Virginia, 1977); and Beiswanger, "Temple."

69. Rebecca Yancey Williams, *The Vanishing Virginian* (New York: Dutton, 1942), 41.

70. Quoted in W. Barksdale Maynard, *Architecture in the United States, 1800–1850* (New Haven, CT: Yale University Press, 2002), 132.

71. Quoted in Maynard, *Architecture,* 129.

72. Harold D. Eberlein and Courtlandt Van Dyke Hubbard, *Historic Houses of Georgetown and Washington City* (Richmond, VA: Diety, 1958), 143.

73. Roger G. Kennedy, *Orders from France: The Americans and the French in a Revolutionary World, 1780–1820* (New York: Knopf, 1989), 253.

74. Massie and Christian, *Houses,* 155.

75. Kennedy, *Orders,* 119.

76. William Strickland, quoted in Maynard, *Architecture,* 130.

77. Cooper, *Notions of the Americans Picked up by a Travelling Bachelor,* quoted in Maynard, *Architecture,* 130.

78. For a good discussion of this development, see Maynard, *Architecture;* and Archer, *Architecture.*

79. Tamara Plakins Thornton, *Cultivating Gentlemen: The Meaning of Country Life among the Boston Elite, 1785–1860* (New Haven, CT: Yale University Press, 1989), 27.

80. George Cabot to Oliver Wolcott, 26 March 1798, quoted in Thornton, *Cultivating,* 48.

81. Archer, *Architecture.*

82. Fisher Ames to Oliver Wolcott, 4 April 1803, quoted in Thornton, *Cultivating,* 48–49.

83. See Peter J. Hatch, *A Rich Spot of Earth: Thomas Jefferson's Revolutionary Garden at Monticello* (New Haven, CT: Yale University Press, 2012).

84. Reinberger and McLean, *Philadelphia.*

85. Reinberger and McLean, *Philadelphia,* 77.

86. William Russell Birch, *The Country Seats of the United States,* edited by Emily T. Cooperman (1808; Philadelphia: University of Pennsylvania Press, 2009), introduction.

87. Reinberger and McLean, *Philadelphia,* 236.

88. Reinberger and McLean, *Philadelphia,* 236.

89. Quoted in Reinberger and McLean, *Philadelphia,* 327.

90. Quoted in Reinberger and McLean, *Philadelphia,* 81n22.

91. TJ to Moses Cox, 17 September 1793, *Papers.*

92. Quoted in Bear, *Jefferson at Monticello,* 113–14.

93. Quoted in Bear, *Jefferson at Monticello,* 113–14.

94. TJ to Martha J. Randolph, 7 July 1793, *Papers.*

95. This house is shown in Steve Currall's *Jefferson's Monticello on the Schuylkill,* in *Hidden City Philadelphia* (9 December 2011). The original watercolor is in the collection of the Historical Society of Pennsylvania.

96. Richard J. Betts, "The Woodlands," *Winterthur Portfolio* 14, no. 3 (autumn 1979): 213–34.

97. TJ to William Hamilton, July 1806, quoted in Betts, *Garden Book,* 189.

98. George Cabot to Oliver Wolcott, 26 March 1798, quoted in Thornton, *Cultivating,* 48.

99. Lee Langston-Harrison, *A Presidential Legacy: The Monroe Collection* (Fredericksburg, VA: James Monroe Museum, 1997).

100. Reinberger and McLean, *Philadelphia,* 309–11.

101. Worthington P. Peare to Travis McDonald, 1 May 2007.

102. A good discussion of Solitude is found in Roger W. Moss, *The American Country House* (New York: Henry Holt, 1990), 85–97.

103. Eberlein and Hubbard, *Portrait,* 434. Most of this information comes from this work.

104. Carl Eugene, Duke of Württemberg, was known for his botanical gardens, love of opera, and extensive library. The Castle Solitude was designed by Johann F. Weyhing and Philippe de la Guepiere in the Baden-Württemberg area near the town of Gerlingen (Wikipedia entry).

105. Eberlein and Van Dyke, *Portrait,* 435.

106. Eberlein and Van Dyke, *Portrait,* 435.

107. Quoted in Chambers, *Poplar Forest,* x.

108. Chambers, *Poplar Forest,* 177.

109. Chambers, *Poplar Forest,* xii.

110. Williams, *Vanishing,* 21.

111. Quoted in Chambers, *Poplar Forest,* 200.

2. THOMAS JEFFERSON'S EDUCATION AS ARCHITECT AND BUILDER

1. Anna Maria Thornton, *Papers,* quoted in McLaughlin, *Jefferson and Monticello,* 15.

2. Kimball's 1916 book *Thomas Jefferson, Architect* came out first in a very limited edition of 350. It was not until Da Capo Press reprinted the work in 1968 that the general public and most architectural historians knew the work and Jefferson's output.

3. Jefferson's granddaughter Ellen Randolph married into the Coolidge family, and later family members rescued Jefferson drawings from other Jefferson family members still in Charlottesville.

4. Kimball, *Architect,* 81–83.

5. A. Hyatt Mayor, "Jefferson's Enjoyment of the Arts," *Metropolitan Museum of Art Bulletin* 2, no. 4 (December 1943): 144.

6. Wenger, "Two Aspects." The most prolific and astute published architectural historian writing about Thomas Jefferson's architecture is Mark R. Wenger.

7. Thomas Jefferson, *Notes on the State of Virginia,* in *Thomas Jefferson: Writings,* ed. Merrill Peterson, Library of America 17 (New York: Literary Classics of the United States, 1984), 279.

8. William Howard Adams, *The Eye of Thomas Jefferson* (Charlottesville: University Press of Virginia, 1976). This book accompanied the major Bicentennial exhibition Adams curated at the National Gallery of Art in 1976.

9. See Kennedy, *Orders from France;* Mary Ellen Hayward and Frank R. Shivers Jr., *The Architecture of Baltimore* (Baltimore: Johns Hopkins University Press, 2004).

10. Some of the best interpretations of Jefferson's architectural works in general, and in their largest scope of meaning, still comes from Fiske Kimball's *Thomas Jefferson, Architect,* which was the first and still truest crack at interpretation; William Pierson's more traditional views of Jefferson's works within the four American phases of neoclassicism (*American Buildings and Their Architects: The Colonial and Neo-Classical Styles*); William Howard Adams in *Eye of Thomas Jefferson* and *Thomas Jefferson's Monticello;* Dell Upton's *Architecture in the United States;* and Charles Brownell in *Making Virginia Architecture.* More focused views of Jefferson's architecture are William Ackerman's *The Villa;* insightful yet quirky views in Roger G. Kennedy's *Orders from France;* Robert Tavernor's *Palladio and Palladianism;* Jack McLaughlin's *Jefferson and Monticello;* Richard Guy Wilson and Joseph Lasala in *Thomas Jefferson's Academical Village;* and Mark R. Wenger's articles placing Jefferson's works in the traditions of Virginia architecture.

11. Thomas Jefferson, *Autobiography,* in *Thomas Jefferson: Writings,* 4.

12. Jefferson, *Autobiography,* 4.

13. From 1762 to 1767, while living with and studying law under George Wythe, Jefferson might easily have encountered Wythe's father-in-law, Richard Taliaferro, a well-known gentleman architect. Fauquier was familiar with the famous British Palladian architect James Gibbs, whose house he had rented in London. Two of Gibbs's books would serve Jefferson in his design of Monticello and throughout his life.

14. TJ to Thomas Turpin, 5 February 1769, quoted in Seymour Howard, "Thomas Jefferson's Art Gallery for Monticello," *Art Bulletin* 59, no. 4 (December 1977): 583.

15. Daniel Boorstin quoted in Douglas L. Wilson, *Jefferson's Books* (Charlottesville, VA: Thomas Jefferson Foundation, 1966), 7.

16. "When it is remembered that Jefferson's architectural achievements are second only to his political contributions to the United States, the importance of the group of books dealt with here can be appreciated. Without these books it is impossible to understand fully either Jefferson's philosophy of architecture or his sources for the visual forms with which he gave objective life to that philosophy" (William B. O'Neal, *A Fine Arts Library: Jefferson's Selections for the University of Virginia Together with His Architectural Books at Monticello,* catalogue for *An Exhibition Sponsored by the Alderman Library & the Committee on the Bicentennial, February-May 1976* [Charlottesville: University of Virginia], 3). This catalogue was later expanded and published as William Bainter O'Neal, *Jefferson's Fine Arts Library: His Selections for the University of Virginia Together with His Own Architectural Books* (Charlottesville: University Press of Virginia, 1976).

17. Jefferson, *MB,* 213.

18. Jefferson, *MB,* 206. Waller was the bookseller in London.

19. For a general history of Jefferson's libraries, see Douglas L. Wilson, *Jefferson's Books* (Charlottesville, VA: Thomas Jefferson Foundation, 1996).

20. Bennie Brown, "The Ownership of Architectural Books in Colonial Virginia," in *American Architects and Their Books to 1848,* ed. Kenneth Hafertepe and James F. O'Gorman, 17–34 (Amherst: University of Massachusetts Press, 2001).

21. D. Wilson, *Jefferson's Books,* 22.

22. Eleanor D. Berman, *Thomas Jefferson among the Arts* (New York: Philosophical Library, 1947), 114.

23. Thomas Whately's *Observations of Modern Gardening* (1770; acquired by 1783); William Chambers's *Chinese Designs* (1763; acquired by 1771); Claude Perrault's translation of *Vitruvius* (1684; acquired by 1775); William Halfpenny's *Practical Architecture* (1724; acquired by 1778); William Kent's *Designs of Inigo Jones* (1727; acquired by 1778); Vicenzo Scamozzi's *Five Orders of Architecture* (1764; acquired by 1778); Batty Langley's *Practical Geometry* (1729; acquired by 1781); and *The Builder's Dictionary* (1734; acquired by 1780).

24. TJ to John Page, quoted in McLaughlin, *Jefferson and Monticello,* 51.

25. Several historians have speculated that Jefferson might have seen important European works of art, sculpture, and books on architecture at the home of Dr. John Morgan in Philadelphia on his 1766 trip to be vaccinated for small pox (see Fiske Kimball, "Jefferson and the Arts," *Proceedings of the American Philosophical Society* 87, no. 3 [July 1943]: 238–45; and Howard, "Art Gallery").

26. Jefferson, *MB,* xix.

27. Kimball, *Architect,* 26.

28. See Kimball, *Architect;* Frederick Nichols, "Jefferson: The Making of an Architect," in *Jefferson and the Arts: An Extended View,* ed. William Howard Adams, 159–86 (Washington, DC: National Gallery of Art, 1976); Adams, *Eye;* Beiswanger, *Measured Drawings;* Buford Pickens, "Mr. Jefferson as Revolutionary Architect," *Journal of the Society of Architectural Historians* 34, no. 4 (December 1975): 257–79; Wells, "Virginia by Design"; McLaughlin, *Jefferson and Monticello;* Wenger, "Two Aspects"; Lancaster, "Architectural Indebtedness"; Gene Waddell, "The First Monticello," *Journal of the Society of Architectural Historians* 46, no. 1 (March 1987): 5–29; D. Wilson, "Dating Jefferson's Early Architectural Drawings," *Virginia Magazine of History and Biography* 101, no. 1 (January 1993): 53–76; and Mesick Cohen Wilson Baker, *Historic Structures Reports,* Monticello Research Files.

29. Kimball, *Architect,* 13.

30. See William M. S. Rasmussen, "Drafting the Plans," and William M. S. Rasmussen and Charles E. Brownell, "Idea, Toll, Evidence," both in *The Making of Virginia Architecture,* ed. Brownell et al. (Charlottesville: University Press of Virginia for Virginia Museum of Fine Arts, 1993); and David Gebhard and Deborah Nevins *200 Years of American Architectural Drawings* (New York: Whitney Library of Design, 1977).

31. Gebhard and Nevins, *200 Years,* 32

32. Brownell et al., *Making,* 156.

33. Brownell et al., *Making,* 212.

34. Isaac Coles to John Coles, 23 February 1816, Cocke Papers, Special Collections, University of Virginia.

35. James Ackerman remarked that Jefferson's "approach to design was less committed to observing precedents and rules of vocabulary and composition and less deferential to Palladian models" (Ackerman, *Villa,* 186).

36. Brownell et al., *Making,* 46.

37. Giles Worsley, *Classical Architecture in Britain: The Heroic Age* (London: Yale University Press, 1995), 285.

38. Mills Lane, *Architecture of the Old South: Virginia* (Savannah, GA: Beehive, 1987), 126.

39. Quoted in Lane, *Virginia,* 126.

40. Quoted in John M. Bryan, ed., *Robert Mills, Architect* (Washington, DC: American Institute of Architects, 1989), 4.

41. Quoted in Bryan, *Mills,* 2n5.

42. Benjamin Latrobe's statement that Jefferson "loves the taste of Queen Elisabeth best," was in reference to the latter era of the monarch's reign with its English Renaissance style (Travis McDonald, "The East and West Wings of the White House: History in Architecture and Building," *White House History* 29 [summer 2011]: 65n49). Latrobe would have been more correct to refer to Jefferson's tie to the British Palladian movement of the eighteenth century. Still, Latrobe saw Jefferson's tenacious love of Roman classicism as out-of-date and soon to be replaced by the ascendant Greek Revival movement.

43. See Susan Kern, *The Jeffersons at Shadwell* (New Haven, CT: Yale University Press, 2010).

44. McLaughlin, *Jefferson and Monticello,* 39.

45. Travis McDonald research for Poplar Forest in Central Virginia regarding antebellum builders and enslaved craftsmen.

46. Jefferson, *MB,* 29: "note: hinges, pulleys and mortise locks got from Thomas Nelson in March 1770."

47. Jefferson, *MB,* 25.

48. Cited in McLaughlin, *Jefferson and Monticello,* 163.

49. TJ to John Harvie, 29 December 1777; 15 September 1778, in *Papers.*

50. Quoted in McLaughlin, *Jefferson and Monticello,* 78; and Randall, *Life,* 3:673.

51. Robert C. Baron, ed., *The Garden and Farm Books of Thomas Jefferson* (Golden, CO: Fulcrum, 1987), 53.

52. Jefferson, *MB,* 145.

53. In the fall of 1769 Jefferson asked his friend James Ogilie, who was headed to England, to procure special materials and to gather estimates on the cost of British stonecutters who would produce the exterior moldings of the house in stone. One of these was not for Monticello but for George Wythe. Entitled "Estimate sent to G. Wythe from London of some expenses of building such a house as that at Monticello," it included an itemized list for a well-designed and -appointed house done in Portland stone with all of the correct carved Doric and Ionic order moldings as well as wallpaper, and the most fashionable hardware. The other two are for Jefferson, entitled "Valuation of masonry by Thomas Patti, mason in Bristol" in which was listed all of the carved stone elements for a compete Doric order. Another report was "Valuation of Masonry by William Gates Mason at the Old Swan, London Bridge, London," which appears to be a second comparative estimate like that given Patti for itemized Doric elements in "A range of smooth looking stone that will stand the weather to go round a house with the moldings." Stonemasons could be found in the Piedmont or valley regions of Virginia but not in the Tidewater (Jefferson, *MB,* 24, 29n12).

54. Betts, *Garden Book,* 55

55. Betts, *Garden Book,* 55.

56. Betts, *Garden Book,* 57.

57. Betts, *Garden Book,* 352.

58. Jefferson, *MB,* 368.

59. Edwin Morris Betts, ed., *Thomas Jefferson's Farm Book* (Charlottesville: University Press of Virginia, 1987).

60. Lucia Stanton file notes, Monticello Research Library.

61. This is also emphasized by one of the most knowledgeable historians of Jeffersonian architecture, architect John I. Mesick, who with his partner, Jeffrey Baker, has been studying and restoring Jefferson buildings at the University of Virginia, Monticello, and Poplar Forest since the 1980s.

62. Cited in Peterson, *Visitors,* 8.

63. Chastelleux, *Travels in North America,* published 1786 in Paris and 1787 in English, quoted in Peterson, *Visitors,* 10–17.

64. See Howard, "Art Gallery"; O'Neal, *Fine Arts Library;* Mayor, "Jefferson's Enjoyment"; H. M. Kallen, "The Arts and Thomas Jefferson," *Ethics,* 53, no. 4 (July 1943): 269–83; Berman, *Thomas Jefferson;* and Kimball, "Jefferson and the Arts."

65. Beiswanger, "Designs," 20.

66. Isaac Weld Jr., *Travels through the States of North America, 1799,* quoted in Peterson, *Visitors,* 18.

67. TJ to Carlo Bellini, 30 September 1785, quoted in Wilson and Staunton, *Jefferson Abroad,* 42.

68. William Howard Adams, *The Paris Years of Thomas Jefferson* (New Haven, CT: Yale University Press, 1997), 77.

69. Annette Gordon-Reed and Peter S. Onuf, *"Most Blessed of the Patriarchs": Thomas Jefferson and the Empire of the Imagination* (New York: Norton, 2016), 138, 109. This observation was previously noted by Charles Brownell, Williams Beiswanger, and William H. Adams.

70. Gordon-Reed and Onuf, *Most Blessed,* 109.

71. See Adams, *Paris Years;* Adams, *Eye;* Rice, *Jefferson's Paris;* Dumas Malone, *Jefferson and the Rights of Man* (Boston: Little, Brown, 1951); James C. Thompson *Thomas Jefferson's Enlightenment* (Alexandria, VA: James C. Thompson, 2013).

72. Daniel Boorstin, *The Lost World of Thomas Jefferson* (Chicago: University of Chicago Press, 1993), xii.

73. Quoted in Adams, *Eye,* xxxiv.

74. TJ to James Madison, 20 September 1785, quoted in Wilson and Stanton, *Jefferson Abroad,* 33

75. TJ to Mme. De Brehan, 14 March 1789, *Papers.*

76. For the history of French architecture of the eighteenth century, see Anthony Sutcliffe, *Paris: An Architectural History* (New Haven, CT: Yale University Press, 1993); Allan Braham, *The Architecture of the French Enlightenment* (Los Angeles: University of California Press, 1980); Wend Von Kalnein, *Architecture in France in the Eighteenth Century* (New Haven, CT: Yale University Press, 1995); Michel Gallet, *Stately Mansions: Eighteenth Century Paris Architecture* (New York: Praeger, 1972); Richard A. Etlin, *Symbolic Space: French Enlightenment Architecture and Its Legacy* (Chicago: University of Chicago Press, 1994); Mark Girouard, *Life in the French Country House* (New York: Knopf, 2000); and Michael Dennis, *Court & Garden: From the French Hotel to the City of Modern Architecture* (Cambridge, MA: MIT Press, 1988).

77. Adams, *Eye,* xxxix.

78. TJ to Maria Cosway, 12 October 1786, in Wilson and Stanton, *Jefferson Abroad,* 96.

79. Dora Wiebenson mentioned some of these omissions by Jefferson in her review of *Thomas Jefferson's Paris,* by Howard Rice, *Journal of the Society of Architectural Historians* (December 1977): 271–72.

80. A discussion of this system of interior planning, also used by Benjamin Henry Latrobe, is found in Dennis, *Court & Garden;* and Michael W. Fazio and Patrick A. Snadon, *The Domestic Architecture of Benjamin Henry Latrobe* (Baltimore, MD: Johns Hopkins University Press, 2006), 187.

81. For a history of garden pavilions, see Eleanor P. DeLorme, *Garden Pavilions and the 18th Century French Court* (UK: Antique Collectors' Club, 1996); Jerome Zerbe and Cyril Connolly, *Les Pavillons: French Pavilions of the Eighteenth Century* (New York: Macmillan, 1962); Ian Thompson, *In the Sun King's Garden* (New York: Bloomsbury, 2006); and Jackson-Stops, Mott, and Aall, *Follies and Pleasure Pavilions,* 25.

82. Architect Henry's 1788 round house for M. Vassale in Paris, with its oval and octagonal rooms, was another prototype.

83. The great number of interior octagon rooms, and especially the sequence of vestibule/dining room/salon, can be seen in Kraft and Ransonnette's two volumes, the first of which Jefferson owned. Jefferson would have seen many of these new hotels in person.

84. Gondoin's new building replaced Chalgrin's earlier anatomical theater that Jefferson could have seen. The earlier building featured concentric octagonal seating like that Jefferson designed for the University of Virginia building.

85. "Notes of a Tour of English Gardens," in Wilson and Stanton, *Jefferson Abroad,* 65.

86. TJ to John Page, 4 May 1786, in Wilson and Stanton, *Jefferson Abroad,* 71.

87. TJ to John Page, 4 May 1786, in Wilson and Stanton, *Jefferson Abroad,* 71.

88. TJ to Mme de Tesse, 20 March 1787, in Wilson and Stanton, *Jefferson Abroad,* 131.

89. TJ to Mme de Tesse, 20 March 1787, in Wilson and Stanton, *Jefferson Abroad,* 131. These ruins included the amphitheater and triumphal arch in Orange; the cenotaph, arch, and remains of the town of Glanum in St-Rémy; the arena in Arles; and the Pont du Gard, Maison Carrée, amphitheater, and Temple of Diana in Nîmes.

90. TJ to Mme de Tesse, 20 March 1787, in Wilson and Stanton, *Jefferson Abroad,* 131.

91. TJ to James Madison, 20 September 1785, in Wilson and Stanton, *Jefferson Abroad,* 33.

92. TJ to Mme de Tesse, 20 March 1787, in Wilson and Stanton, *Jefferson Abroad,* 131.

93. TJ to George Wythe, 16 September 1787, quoted in Edward Dumbauld, *Thomas Jefferson American Tourist* (Norman: University of Oklahoma Press, 1946), 102.

94. Clérisseau was one of the most influential architects bringing back details of classical remains that he examined with Robert Adam, Giovanni Battista Piranesi, and Johann Joachim Winckelmann in the 1750s. Clérisseau studied Roman remains in Italy from 1749 to 1767, producing extraordinary drawings and paintings that Jefferson would have seen in his studio in Paris. Clérisseau was also said to have the finest library of any architect of his time in Paris. Jefferson bought Clérisseau's book on the antiquities of Nîmes and could have also perused his library. Clérisseau's significant role in introducing the archaeological interest in neoclassicism in England and France is covered in Thomas J. McCormick, *Charles-Louis Clerisseau and the Genesis of Neo-Classicism* (London: MIT Press, 1990).

95. The best detailed account of the design and construction of Monticello, both I and II, is found in a series of *Historic Structure Reports* by Mesick Cohen Wilson Baker Architects from 1991 to 1993, as well as Monticello staff reports by William L. Beiswanger (Mesick Cohen Wilson Baker Architects, *Historic Structure Reports,* various volumes, Monticello Research Library; William L. Beiswanger files, Monticello).

96. See Amy Facca, abstracts of Jefferson letters regarding architecture and construction for Mesick Cohen Wilson Baker, Monticello Research Library; hereafter cited as Abstracts.

97. TJ to Francois D'Ivernois, 6 February 1795, in Library of America, *Thomas Jefferson, Writings,* 1023.

98. TJ to George Wythe, 23 October 1794, in *Papers.*

99. Peterson, *Reference Biography,* 167.

100. TJ to Benj. Hawkins, 22 March 1796, in *Papers.*

101. TJ to Thomas Mann Randolph, 11 April 1796, in *Papers.*

102. TJ to Volney 10 April 1796, in *Papers.*

103. TJ to Nicholas Lewis, 26 June 1791, in *Papers.*

104. TJ to Count Constantin Francois de Volney, 3 April 1797, in *Papers.*

105. Quoted in Peterson, *Visitors,* 21–22.

106. Quoted in McLaughlin, *Jefferson and Monticello,* 250.

107. Beiswanger, *Measured Drawings,* 11.

108. Charles Errard and Roland Freart de Chambray, *Parallele de l'architecture* (1766); Antoine Babuty Desgodetz, *Les edifices antiques de Rome* (1779).

109. Brownell et al., *Making,* 212.

110. Quoted in Peterson, *Visitors,* 67.

111. Jefferson, Abstracts, "Building Notebook," N-143, p. 10.

112. In the Renaissance, Alberti had called this harmonic synthesis of numbers and proportions "concinnitas."

113. Betts, *Farm Book,* "Building/Brick" section, 352. His notes from 1796 calculated: "one ld. Mortar takes 3 hhds water to the 1000. bricks; an acre of ground yields a million of bricks for every foot depth; 10. Bushels of limestone make 15 bushels of lime, & lay 1000 bricks, the inside mortar being half lime & half sand, & the outside mortar 2/3 lime, & the walls grouted. From my own experience; 1796 Aug. 26 32 cords of wood burnt a kiln of 9 eyes & 42 M. bricks."

114. TJ Instructions, November 1792, in *Papers;* TJ to TMR, 21 January 1793, in *Papers.*

115. Thomas Mann Randolph to TJ, 8 May 1793, in *Papers.*

116. Betts, *Farm Book,* 1794, "Roll of Negros," 245.

117. B. L. Rayner, *Sketches of the Life, Writings, and Opinions of Thomas Jefferson* (New York: A. Francis and W. Boardman, 1832), 524.

118. Bear, *Jefferson at Monticello,* 70.

119. Jefferson, *MB,* 1032.

120. Jefferson, *MB,* 1098.

121. Betts, *Farm Book,* 304–5.

122. TJ to Thomas Mann Randolph, 3 February 1793, in *Papers;* Betts, *Farm Book,* 244.

123. TJ to Thomas Mann Randolph, 19 May 1793, in *Papers.*

124. TJ to Thomas Mann Randolph, 15 February 1798, in *Papers.*

125. TJ to Martha Jefferson Randolph, 5 April 1798, in *Papers.*

126. On June 13, 1798, Jefferson recorded in his Memorandum Book: "Gave James Dinsmore order on Barnes for 64.55 D. This is for tools purchased of him & sent on to Monticello" (Jefferson, *MB,* 985; James Dinsmore, list of tools 15 April 1809, in *Papers*).

127. TJ to Thomas Mann Randolph, 20 December 1798, in *Papers.*

128. Jefferson's overseer, Edmund Bacon, who served from 1806 to 1822, commented on Dinsmore: "Dinsmore, who lived with him a good many years, was the most ingenious hand to work with wood I ever knew. He could make anything. He made a great deal of nice mahogany furniture, helped make the carriage, worked on the University, and could do any kind of fine work that was wanted" (Rev. Hamilton Wilcox Pierson, *Jefferson at Monticello: The Private Life of Thomas Jefferson* [Charles Scribner, 1862], quoted in Bear, *Jefferson at Monticello,* 70).

129. McLaughlin, *Jefferson and Monticello,* 86, 87.

130. McDonald, "East and West Wings."

131. Jefferson, *MB,* 1067.

132. See Robert L. Self and Susan R. Stein, "The Collaboration of Thomas Jefferson and John Hemings: Furniture Attributed to the Monticello Joinery," *Winterthur Portfolio* 33, no. 4 (1998): 231–48. See also Emilie Johnson, "John Hemmings: Enslaved Craftsman of Classical Architecture," *Classicist* 13 (2016): 9–15.

133. Jefferson, *MB,* 390.

134. Madison Hemings's autobiography states that his uncle John was born of Joseph Neilson. Jefferson variously listed John's birth year as 1775 and 1776. Published in Annette Gordon-Reed, *Thomas Jefferson and Sally Hemings: An American Controversy* (Charlottesville: University Press of Virginia, 1997), 245.

135. "Memorandum with respect to Watson," 25 October 1793, in *Papers.*

136. TJ to Thomas Mann Randolph, 3 February 1793, in *Papers.*

137. Thomas Mann Randolph to TJ, 8 May 1793, in *Papers.*

138. TJ to Thomas Mann Randolph, 19 May 1793, in *Papers.*

139. "Sep. & Oct. 1799" memorandum; *Farm Book* addenda, Monticello Research Library file on James Dinsmore.

140. N-147-l-n, 147-u.

141. Betts, *Farm Book,* 258.

142. Jefferson, Abstracts, 42–43, N-147l recto, n.d.

143. TJ to Thomas Mann Randolph, 20 December 1793, in *Papers.*

144. Bear, *Jefferson at Monticello;* 69.

145. Betts, *Farm Book,* 369.

146. TJ to Thomas Mann Randolph; 1 June 1797, in *Papers.*

147. Bear, *Jefferson at Monticello,* 68.

148. Stated in Madison's autobiography, published in Gordon-Reed, *Thomas Jefferson and Sally Hemings,* 245.

149. Annette Gordon-Reed, *The Hemingses of Monticello: An American Family* (New York: Norton, 2008), 610.

150. See Lucia Stanton, *Free Some Day: The African-American Families of Monticello* (Charlottesville, VA: Thomas Jefferson Foundation, 2000); Lucia Stanton, *Those Who Labor for My Happiness: Slavery*

at Thomas Jefferson's Monticello (Charlottesville: University Press of Virginia, 2012); and Gordon-Reed, *The Hemingses.*

151. Kimball, *Architect,* 81–83.

3. DESIGNING A RETREAT

1. Edge Hill was enlarged in 1828 by Thomas Jefferson Randolph. It burned in 1916 and was rebuilt.

2. The Nicholas house design is mentioned in a letter from Jefferson of 19 August 1796. Jefferson designed a plan based on the owner's requirement that the entry be through a cross passage. Jefferson feared that the middle octagon rooms would encroach upon the passage too much and would make them oblong octagons that "would injure their shape and sacrifice the passages" (ViU 4; Jefferson, Abstracts, 42). The town house is the most documented of these, having two plans, an elevation, a section, and two pages of specifications. Kimball and Nichols misidentified the elevation of this town house (K-205, N-4) as Barboursville, and Kimball misidentified the two plans (K-187 and K-188) as studies for Poplar Forest rather than the town house. William Beiswanger attributed the town house date of about 1800 based on the statement in the specifications that Jefferson was currently building a DeLorme-style dome. The Higginbotham design consists of a plan and specifications (N-17). The Farmington design was altered and constructed by local workers that resulted in a more Kentucky Federal style. Barboursville is the second-most-documented house design for a friend with drawings and specifications. Its execution fell short, however, without the dome and interior entablatures.

3. Edgemont is "Jeffersonian," but the attribution is far from clear. Jefferson did a design for Ampthill in 1817, but the house was not completed until about 1835.

4. The addition to Eppington that included an octagon is known only from correspondence (Maria Jefferson Eppes to TJ, 20 March 1798, in *Papers*).

5. Nichols, *Architectural Drawings.* For example, some drawings Kimball thought were Poplar Forest studies (K-185–92) Nichols assigned to Farmington, Kentucky (K-189–92). Kimball's 187 and 188 were not Poplar Forest but for a circa 1800 town house. Those Kimball thought were for rebuilding Shadwell (K-171–174) were reassigned to Edgemont.

6. TJ to Benjamin Henry Latrobe, 10 October 1809, in *Papers, Retirement.*

7. The first work to seriously discuss Jefferson's use of octagons, and Poplar Forest, was a University of Virginia master's thesis in 1988 (Amy E. Facca, "Thomas Jefferson's Poplar Forest" [master's thesis, University of Virginia, 1988]). This was written under the direction of her thesis advisor, Charles E. Brownell. The principal challenge, Amy Facca noted, was a lack of scholarly information on Poplar Forest. Facca, like all other architectural historians up to that time, had to guess at what Jefferson had actually designed, a synthesis of a few drawings, his correspondence, and the existing house that had been so altered after a 1845 fire and 1940s modernization. Facca benefited from another thesis by C. Allan Brown, "Poplar Forest: Thomas Jefferson and the Ideal Villa" (master's thesis, University of Virginia, 1987). William M. Kelso, archaeologist at Monticello, also shared information from a preliminary project at Poplar Forest in 1986. Kelso was on leave from Monticello to Poplar Forest from 1988 to 1990 to ground-truth some hypotheses put forth in Brown's academic study. The most important outcome of Facca's work was her chronological narrative of Jefferson's long and consistent use of the octagon form. Fiske Kimball's 1916 book on Jefferson's drawings did not reach the general public until its reprint in 1968, when it offered the obvious visual realization that the octagon shape was used repeatedly in Jefferson's designs.

8. Isaac A. Coles to John Hartwell Cocke, 23 February 1816, in *Papers.*

9. TJ to William Giles, 19 March 1796, in *Papers.*

10. See Michael Olmert, "Of Garden Mounts," *Colonial Williamsburg Magazine,* summer 2014, 28–34.

11. Worsley, *Classical,* 113; Archer, *Architecture,* 102.

12. James W. Tottis to Travis McDonald, personal correspondence, 1 April 2019. The wing is believed to be original and not an addition. Tottis refers to a 1785 newspaper ad mentioning the room when the house was used as a tavern.

13. Carol Ward, "Beyond George Washington," *Antiques Magazine,* January/ February 2017, 188–95.

14. The Tayloes wanted a winter home in a more cosmopolitan location than their family's Palladian style Mount Airy in the northern neck of Virginia. Interestingly, Tayloe married Ann Ogle of Ogle Hall in Annapolis, whose family house from the 1770s featured semi-octagonal wings like the Hammond-Harwood House. Having first considered building a city house in Philadelphia by Latrobe, the Tayloes were convinced to build in the new capital city with a neoclassical Federal-style house that might inspire others still unconvinced of the capital's potential. Their house, and the Van Ness house by Latrobe, just to the southwest of the President's House, was clearly more fashionable than Hoban's presidential mansion, which Jefferson would occupy in 1801. The odd shape was primarily dictated by the shape of the site at the intersection of New York Avenue and Eighteenth Street.

15. Reinberger and McLean, *Philadelphia,* 321–22.

16. Reinberger and McLean, *Philadelphia,* 321–22.

17. Letter from Mrs. H. Clay Brown of Chestertown, Maryland, 8 April 1938, University of Virginia No. 6478–6. In a letter from Milton L. Grigg to Morley J. Williams regarding the sale of the document, Grigg states that the sketches are "without a doubt, from Jefferson's hand" (UVA No. 6478–6).

18. Documents and evidence exist for two other early octagon houses that Jefferson did not see. William McKimmey built a small tabby-wall octagon house on the May River in South Carolina by 1796. An 1802 Charleston newspaper called it "Octagon Plantation." The foundations of this house were discovered by archaeologist Mary Socci in 2009. It is thought to have been destroyed in an 1804 hurricane (Mary C. Socci to Travis McDonald, personal correspondence, 23 February 2010). Another small (24′ × 24′) frame octagon building, called The Little Lodge, was located on an estate called The Caves outside of Baltimore and used by widow Margaret Tilghman Carroll as a summer retreat in the early nineteenth century. (Michael Trostel and Worthington P. Peare to Travis McDonald, personal correspondence).

19. The two University of Virginia octagons were Jefferson's unexecuted design for an observatory with four octagonal corners and the Anatomical Theater, which had octagonal bleachers. One mysterious full octagon building that has been attributed to Jefferson is the Botetourt County Courthouse in Fincastle, Virginia. The assertion stems from an 1818 letter to James Breckinridge in which Jefferson referred to drawings and specifications. Delos D. Hughes concluded in 1997 that the building was designed and constructed under the direction of Breckinridge in 1822 with a central octagonal form covered by a dome (Hughes, "Building a Courthouse in Fincastle: A Footnote to Jefferson Studies," *Arris* 8 [1997]: 41–53). No drawings or photographs exist for the building, which was demolished in 1845, but we can say with confidence that it was inspired by Jefferson's use of octagons and domes.

20. Worsley, *Classical,* 234–42.

21. Beginning in the 1770s the canted bay started to appear on wings or pavilions on American houses. The five-part Hammond-Harwood House (1774) in Annapolis, which Jefferson sketched, is a prominent early example. Other examples of canted bay wings are Mount Clare (1767) and Montpelier (1770s) in Maryland; Walnut Grove outside Philadelphia (1787 wings); and The Hill (1797) in New York. What became more common by the 1790s was a canted bay that extended from a rear semi-octagonal center room, usually a drawing room. Examples are Lansdowne (1770s) near Philadelphia; Bolton (1786) and Willowbrook (1797) in Maryland; and the Moses Myers House (1795) in Virginia. One variation of this type, with semi-octagon bays forming the sides of a projecting rear room, was Mount Athos near Lynchburg, Virginia. The projecting rear bay could also result from a regular-size octagon room. Examples are the Perez Morton House in Boston (1796), Oatlands (1798) in Virginia, and the Jacob Rutsen Van Rensselaer house (1798) in New York. The more unusual example of this

type was a house Jefferson designed for John Speed in Louisville, Kentucky (1810) that featured two octagonal rooms centered in the house that projected to each side. Oval parlor rooms could also project as canted bays, such as in the Russell House (1808) in Charleston, South Carolina; and Willowbrook (1796) in Maryland. Two houses in New York featured octagon rooms that did not project: the John R. Livingston House, Massena (1795); and Alexander Hamilton's Hamilton Grange (1799), with its two octagon rooms.

22. These houses are documented in Mary Wingfield Scott's 1941 architectural history of Richmond (Scott, *Houses of Old Richmond* [Richmond, VA: Valentine Museum, 1941]). John P. Little commented on these distinctive house designs in his 1850 *History of Richmond.* Fiske Kimball attributed Richmond's Alexander MacRae House design to Jefferson based on a similar sequence of unidentified plans, but this is doubtful and has never been verified.

23. Some of Jefferson's preliminary designs did not always show porticos that might have been intended.

24. This was Monticello II, the ca. 1800 town house, and Barboursville. The town house was not built and the dome was left off of Barboursville.

25. The octagonal seating is similar to Chalgrin's early anatomical theater in Paris whereas the one that replaced it from the 1770s by Gondoin featured a skylight. Jefferson combined both of these features, most likely having seen them in Paris. Gondoin's design also featured round occuli windows around the exterior that might have inspired Jefferson to use lunette windows in the same locations.

26. This was by Claude Perrault and featured two octagons as its corner towers. The cover page illustration of Claude Perrault's 1684 translation of Vitruvius featured three of his own buildings. Two of these were admired by Jefferson: the new wing of the Louvre and on the hill, and the observatory. Jefferson owned this edition by 1775 and saw both buildings in Paris.

27. N-255, reverse. Mark R. Wenger confirmed this supposition in Mark R. Wenger, "Jefferson's Designs for Remodeling the Governor's Palace," *Winterthur Portfolio* 32, no. 4 (winter 1997): 223–42.

28. TJ to Mr. Carmichael, 26 December 1786, in *Papers.*

29. K-133. Jefferson would also design a round scheme for the U.S. Capitol with oval rooms. His final round building shape with oval rooms would be his last: the Rotunda of the University of Virginia.

30. K-216, K-217.

31. Monticello, the Governor's Palace, the Governor's House, Edgemont, the ca. 1800 "town house," and the "retreat" designs. He would continue to use it for designs related to Farmington, Kentucky, the McRae House, Barboursville, "urban dwellings," and the Higginbotham House.

32. Kimball attributed six other plans (K-187–92) to Poplar Forest studies, but it is now known that only three of those are possible in this sequence (K-186, K-192). K-187–88 are the town house; K-189–91 are Farmington, although 189 and 190 might be something else.

33. K-186, K-192

34. The Huntington drawing was coded by Nichols N-12–2.

35. General shape: 33′ × 60′ K-186; 36′ × 58′ K-185; and 37′ × 62′ Trist; entry hall: 16–20′ × 22′ K-186; 20′ × 22′ K-185; 20′ × 24′ Trist; parlor: 22′ K-186; 22′ K-187; 24′ Trist.

36. TJ to John W. Eppes, 4 June 1804, in *Papers.*

37. C. Allan Brown, "Thomas Jefferson's Poplar Forest: The Mathematics of an Ideal Villa," *Journal of Garden History* 10, no. 2 (1990): 117–39.

38. N-496. In between each of the projecting arms was a porch. On the same sheet Jefferson drew a structural reflected ceiling plan showing brick and wood walls and beams, the location and span of floor joists, and even the floorboards of the porches. Rachel Fletcher analyzed this drawing and concluded that it, too, was based on a root-two ratio, "a medley of root-two rectangles and sides and diagonals of squares" (Rachel Fletcher to Travis McDonald, 23 April 2019).

39. The hospital plan is shown in Anthony Blunt, *Art and Architecture in France 1500–1700* (New

York: Penguin, 1953). A similar octagon plan with radiating corner rooms is found in Androuet du Cerceau's *Livre d'architecture,* 1559, number 44, scale plans of projects 26–50. Jefferson did not own this work but might very well have seen it in Paris.

40. K-193.

41. K-194.

42. Chambers, *Poplar Forest,* 16.

43. Quoted in Chambers, *Poplar Forest,* 16.

44. K-196.

45. K-196.

46. Two Jefferson examples of this arrangement would be the 1781 Poplar Forest design (N-255) and the rotunda-style Governor's House design of ca. 1780 (N-281). In the former plan, one pavilion was devoted to bed chambers and the other to a washhouse and kitchen. In the latter example one pavilion was a kitchen/pantry and the other a laundry (washhouse). Both examples show the pavilions connected to the house with arches (N-255) or columns (N-281).

47. The Governor's House pavilions were 24 feet from the 60-foot-wide house, and if we assume an average 60-foot size of the "mature" Poplar Forest designs, the pavilions would be about 20 feet away.

48. The only Jefferson design similar regarding size, windows, fireplace, and doors is a preliminary scheme for one of Monticello's pavilions at the ends of the wings (K-15).

49. See McDonald, *Wings.* The fact that the house was suppressed into the ground was more for keeping the front lower to access the main floor than for an anticipated service wing that would also be partially in the ground.

50. For Jefferson as a synthesizer, see Joyce Appleby, "Jefferson and His Complex Legacy," in *Jeffersonian Legacies,* ed. Peter S. Onuf (Charlottesville: University Press of Virginia, 1993), 1–16.

51. Perhaps less so compared with designs by émigré architects practicing in cities or suburbs along the eastern seaboard. A good example is William Jay's design for the Owens House in Savannah in a British Regency style.

52. Brownell et al., *Making,* 50.

53. Kimball, *Architect,* 82.

54. Kimball, *Architect,* 81.

55. Kimball, *Architect,* 82.

56. See Travis McDonald, "Poplar Forest: A Most Palladian Villa," *Arris* 28 (2017): 6–29.

57. Isaac Coles to John H. Cocke, 23 February 1816, Cocke Papers, Special Collections Library, University of Virginia.

58. Kimball, *Architect,* 71. Kimball's 1916 landmark publication not only documented Jefferson's lifelong role as an architect but established insights of his development that still stand.

59. There is a proliferation of books interpreting Palladio and showing his works. Classics like James S. Ackerman's *Palladio* (1966) and Robert Tavernor's *Palladio and Palladianism* (London: Thames and Hudson, 1999) have been joined by many excellent works, especially the translation of the *Four Books* and essay by Robert Tavernor and Richard Schofield (1997). I am also indebted to Guido Beltamini, director of the Palladio Museum, and Howard Burns, who taught me many things at the Palladio Museum Study Course in Vicenza, Italy, in 2016. These two authorities have defined the field of Palladian scholarship with publications like Burns, *Andrea Palladio 1508–1580* (1975); Burns and Beltramini, *The Complete Illustrated Works;* Beltramini and Burns, eds., *Palladio* (London: Royal Academy of Arts, 2008); Beltramini, *The Private Palladio* (2012); Beltramini et al., *Palladio and His Legacy: A Transatlantic Journey* (2010); Beltramini et al., *Jefferson and Palladio: Constructing a New World* (2015). Other notable works are Bruce Boucher's *Andrea Palladio: The Architect and His Time* (1998); *Palladian Design: The Good, The Bad, and the Unexpected* (2016); Tracey Cooper's *Palladio's Venice* (2005); Vincent Scully et al. *The Villas of Palladio* (1992); Joseph Rykwert's *The Palladian Ideal* (1999); Mandred/Wndram/

Thomas/Pape, *Andrea Palladio: Architect between the Renaissance and Baroque* (n.d.); and Douglas Lewis's *The Drawings of Andrea Palladio* (2000).

60. Beltramini and Burns, *Palladio,* 276.

61. Fiske Kimball commented on this as a "rotunda" house (*Architect,* 106) as did Thomas Waterman, *The Mansions of Virginia* (Chapel Hill: University of North Carolina Press, 1945): 14. It is interesting that Kimball shows a plan copied from James Gibbs's *Architecture,* Plate 67 (K-35) and a sketch of the same (K-37) that featured a square symmetrical building with identical Doric order columns fronting pedimented "lodges" (recessed) on each side that led into an octagonal center space, 26 feet high, with "circular lights in the attic" and surmounted by a dome or cupola.

62. Rachel Fletcher, *Infinite Measure* (Staunton, VA: George F. Thompson, 2013).

63. Two works that described Jefferson's geometries at Poplar Forest, but both done before the restoration, are E. Kurt Albaugh, "Thomas Jefferson's Poplar Forest: Symmetry and Proportionality in a Palladian Summer House," *Fine Homebuilding* 42 (October/November 1987): 74–79 and Alvin Holm, "Poplar Forest: Jefferson's Solar Calendar," *NEARA Journal* 30, no. 1 and 2 (1996): 1–5.

64. John Mesick believes that Jefferson's geometry and proportional use of the orders resulted in the octagons-within-octagon plan with the center square (John Mesick to Travis McDonald, personal correspondence, 11 April 2017).

65. Fletcher noted that on the "Neilson" plan of Poplar Forest there is a line inscribed inside the thickness of the outer walls, providing for a 22-foot sided octagon and a 20-foot side for the cube room (Fletcher to McDonald, 13 April 2017).

66. This was a practice that went back to the Romans. It is our modern sensibility that believes the material of the column should match that of the base and capital. There are many examples where the contrasting material and color was common in the Renaissance and in Palladio's work, such as the Carita Convent in Venice, and remnants of red wash on interior columns at Saint Giorgio Maggoire in Venice, on exterior columns at Malcontenta, and on the Capitaniato Loggia columns in Vicenza. The rendered brick columns of tan color at the University of Virginia did not match the white marble Corinthian capitals used on some pavilions. The local Virginia stone for simple bases and capitals on The Lawn was more of a match. At Barboursville, local stone bases and capitals are a perfect match for the rendered shaft, or vice versa. Kristen Fetzer wrote a master's thesis at University of Pennsylvania in architectural conservation in the 1990s that compared the column render at Poplar Forest with that at UVA (Pavilion 8) and Barboursville and concluded that the "stone color" was intentional and that the render contained a pozzolanic agent brick dust, another Roman technique for strengthening the material. This column render treatment was done also at Montpelier. At Poplar Forest even the base and capital were made in shaped brick. For a discussion of brickwork at Poplar Forest, see Travis C. McDonald Jr., "The Brickwork at Poplar Forest: Mr. Jefferson Builds His Dream House," *Association for Preservation Technology Bulletin* 27, no. 1–2 (1996): 36–46.

67. Cited in O'Neal, *Fine Arts Library,* 119.

68. Brownell et al., *Making,* 38.

69. Seen from the north, the house appears to sit on a hilltop, but this elevated land stretches to the south, making it more of a rise.

70. TJ to Madame de Tesse, 26 October 1805, cited in Betts, *Garden Book,* 305. The name "Poplar Forest" went back before Jefferson's 1773 ownership to at least the 1740s and referred to this old-growth stand of tulip poplar trees. When people of Jefferson's time and afterward referred to "the Forest," it was understood which one.

71. For a discussion of Jefferson's engagement of nature at Monticello see Beiswanger, "Art of Living Outdoors."

72. Brown, "Mathematics," 117–39. See McDonald, "East and West Wings," for the similar landscape plan Jefferson proposed for the President's House. See also Nichols and Griswold, *Thomas Jefferson,*

Landscape Architect. Allan Brown first pointed out how the core area landscape and its features at Poplar Forest were proportionally designed and related to both classical and European traditions.

73. See McDonald, "East and West Wings."

74. The various designs for Jefferson's serrated roof system are found in Mesick Cohen Wilson Baker Architects, Historic Structure Reports for Monticello, Poplar Forest, and the University of Virginia.

75. Certainly there were other Renaissance architects who designed gardens with their villas as well as many example of French, European, and English garden landscapes, the latter of which Jefferson famously toured with John Adams.

76. Ingrid D. Rowland and Thomas Noble Howe, *Vitruvius: Ten Books on Architecture,* trans. Ronald Taylor (Cambridge: Cambridge University Press, 1999).

77. Worsley, *Classical;* Hanno-Walter Kruft, *Architectural Theory from Vitruvius to the Present* (London: Zwemmer; New York: Princeton Architectural Press, 1994), 346.

78. See Wenger, "Two Aspects."

79. See Mark R. Wenger, "Town House and Country House," in *The Chesapeake House,* ed. Carson and Lounsbury, 120–55 (Chapel Hill: Colonial Williamsburg Foundation and University of North Carolina, 2013).

80. Marlene E. Heck, "Palladian Architecture and Social Change in Post-Revolutionary Virginia" (PhD diss., University of Pennsylvania, 1988).

81. TJ to Benjamin Henry Latrobe, 10 October 1809, in *Papers.*

82. See Denis, *Court and Garden.*

83. Indoor privies or water closets were not common in American houses in 1800. Unless a new house had been designed to include an indoor privy, adding one to an existing house posed a challenge as to where it would be located. The leftover space under a staircase proved to be the solution Jefferson used at Poplar Forest. Physical evidence shows that it was not intended when the stair pavilions were built but added later. In three other unidentified "urban dwelling" house designs Jefferson located the privy, designated by a small circle, under a staircase (K-220, K-225, K-228). At the University of Virginia, professors and students followed general custom and used privies in the rear yards of pavilions.

84. McDonald, "East and West Wings," 66n51. At Poplar Forest Jefferson cautioned the builder that the deck be "in the level of the floor of the house" (McDonald, "East and West Wings," 66, 52).

85. Only Jefferson's own bed alcove at Monticello was open on both sides like those he designed for Poplar Forest. Bed alcoves open on both sides might have been Jefferson's innovation and more important for cross-ventilation in hot Virginia weather than the European models with only one opening.

86. Randall, *Life,* 342–44. In contemporary terms this was not where food was stored but where food from the kitchen could be put on china and where the china and silver were washed and kept secure.

87. Dining rooms were convertible spaces where the tables could be broken down and pushed against the walls. The three-part octagonal dining room table Jefferson designed for Poplar Forest lent itself to this practice by being a drop-leaf table with two semi-octagonal ends.

88. TJ notes regarding William Coffee's ornaments for "hall and parlor," Jefferson Papers, James Monroe Library; John Hemings to TJ, regarding installing "ornaments of the hall" 11 August 25, Jefferson Papers, James Monroe Library; "the hall is the only dry room in the house," Frances Eppes to TJ, 23 June 26; a "centre-hall," Ellen Wayles Randolph Coolidge to Henry Randall, 1856, Ellen Coolidge Letter Book, University of Virginia.

89. Ellen Randolph Coolidge to Henry Randall, 27 February 1856, Ellen Coolidge Letter Book, University of Virginia.

90. This tradition was pointed out to me by William Seale (William Seale to Travis McDonald, personal correspondence, 10 June 2005).

91. John Mesick first brought this similar sequence to my attention in the dozen or so plans shown

in Kraft and Ransonnette's *Les plus belles maisons de Paris* of 1802; Jefferson bought volume 1 in December 1804.

92. Cited in McDonald, "East and West Wing," 56n19.

93. TJ to Benjamin Henry Latrobe, May 1807, in *Papers.*

94. Quoted in Chambers, *Poplar Forest,* 106n28.

95. Quoted in Chambers, *Poplar Forest,* 46n10.

96. Jefferson, *MB,* 2 November 1784, n. 13. At Monticello Jefferson achieved the same effect by oiling and waxing his parquet and pine floors.

97. Cited in Beiswanger, *Measured Drawings,* 29.

98. Joel Yancey to TJ, 13 June 1819, in *Papers.*

99. Mary Elizabeth Eppes to Virginia Randolph, 2 January 1825, Randolph Papers, Virginia Historical Society.

100. The fact that the entire southern brick wall was rebuilt from chimney to chimney after the 1845 fire might be due to the collapse of the slender piers between windows and door.

101. Beiswanger, "Art of Living Outdoors."

4. THE CONSTRUCTION SAGA

1. Jefferson, *MB,* 1160.

2. Jefferson, *MB,* 1163.

3. Jefferson, *MB,* 1163.

4. The story of Jefferson building Poplar Forest is found in Chambers, *Poplar Forest;* and McDonald, "Constructing."

5. Most of the entries in the Farm Book section under "Building" are not dated, but the few that are give an approximate chronological sequence. The 1814 reference is to Hugh Chisolm and laying bricks, possibly for the Poplar Forest wing.

6. Critically important for understanding any type of evidence was the knowledge gained by consulting architects John Mesick and Jeff Baker, who were simultaneously investigating Monticello and the University of Virginia.

7. For a much more detailed description of the brickwork at Poplar Forest, see McDonald, "Brickwork."

8. Jefferson, *MB,* 258.

9. TJ to Hugh Chisolm, 15 December 1807, in *Papers.* The sand-molded bricks made for Poplar Forest averaged 8 ½″ × 3 ½″ × 2 ¾″. For calculating the number of bricks needed for a project, Jefferson typically used the size of 2″ × 3″ × 8″, together with the calculated mortar joint size.

10. TJ to Martha Jefferson Randolph, 16 June 1806, in *Papers.*

11. TJ to Hugh Chisolm, 6 September 1806, in *Papers.*

12. See John J. Zaborney, *Slaves for Hire: Renting Enslaved Labor in Antebellum Virginia* (Baton Rouge: Louisiana State University Press, 2012).

13. Hugh Chisolm to TJ, 17 November 1807, in *Papers.*

14. Jefferson, *MB,* 1811 Memo (after June?).

15. Hugh Chisolm to TJ, 15 June 1807, in *Papers.*

16. Jefferson, Abstracts, "Building Notebook," N-139, p. 6.

17. Hugh Chisolm to TJ, 1 June 1807, in *Papers.*

18. TJ to Hugh Chisolm, 5 June 1807, in *Papers.*

19. TJ to Hugh Chisolm, 5 August 1807, in *Papers.*

20. There is no reference to making shingles for the initial roof covering, but this would have been a responsibility of Perry's and his enslaved workers.

21. The old-growth Poplar Forest, a place-name going back to the 1740s, was still the source for lumber, still pit-sawn by enslaved workers, as late as 1846, when the house was rebuilt after a fire. Julius Curle rebuilt the house and owned a large number of enslaved building craftspeople as the largest contractor in the area.

22. TJ to Thomas Mann Randolph, 21 January 1793, in *Papers.*

23. John Perry to TJ, 11 December 1807, in *Papers.*

24. TJ to John Perry, 29 March 1808, in *Papers.*

25. Hugh Chisolm to TJ, 22 July 1808, in *Papers.*

26. Hugh Chisolm to TJ, 4 September 1808, in *Papers.* Wood seems like an inadequate choice for a builder fixed on permanency. Jefferson had specified unexecuted wood capitals for the upper Ionic columns for the first Monticello, and there are two drawings of his that show how wood should be split out of a tree trunk for a wooden column shaft. The only other wood capitals Jefferson used were those for the interior dome room of the Rotunda in the 1820s, a more appropriate place for wood capitals with intricate Corinthian details.

27. TJ to Benjamin Henry Latrobe, 28 February 1804, in *Papers.* "Would it not be best to make the internal columns of well-burnt brick, moulded in portions of circles adapted to the diminution of the columns? Burlington, in his notes on Palladio, tells us that he found most of the buildings erected under Palladio's direction, and described in his architecture, to have their columns made of brick in this way and covered with stucco. I know an instance of a range of six or eight columns in Virginia, twenty feet high, well proportioned and properly diminished, executed by a common bricklayer. The bases and capitals would of course be of hewn stone."

28. These solid stone pieces for the front lower portico of Monticello had been taken down for the rebuilding but put back up with the incorrect sequence for the classical entasis. They had been chipped so badly that Jefferson had to coat them with sanded paint to hide the damage.

29. John Perry would have made special wood molds for the capital and base shapes, along with the ones for the column shaft with proper radii for classical entasis, the Greek and Roman method of tapering the upper third of a column to correct for optical distortion. Jefferson had made full-size drawings for brick molds for Monticello and most likely did the same for Poplar Forest. The size of the wooden molds was critical since the brick would shrink during firing. Jefferson as well as Chisolm would know this.

30. Hugh Chisolm to TJ, 22 July 1808, in *Papers.*

31. The process for shingle-making was very standard, but Jefferson called out the steps in a 1793 memo for Monticello: "In rainy weather the carpenters are to be employed in splitting, planning, jointing and rounding shingles." The only specific reference to Poplar Forest shingles is a Jefferson letter of 1820 in which he is making roof repairs. He specifies chestnut shingles that were not to be rounded. Fragments from the privy shingles confirm that material and shape. In one of his typical Farm Book memoranda that recorded time and labor processes Jefferson recorded that three men would make five hundred rough shingles in a day and join, or finish, three thousand per day.

32. Lynchburg legal records for Reuben Perry mention he "owned" enslaved carpenters Reuben, Billy, Phil, David, James and Patrick, all of whom might have anonymously worked at Poplar Forest in addition to other local projects.

33. TJ to James Dinsmore, 28 December 1806, in *Papers.*

34. TJ to James Dinsmore, 25 October 1807, in *Papers.*

35. TJ to James Dinsmore, 9 October 1807, in *Papers.*

36. The fact that Barry was faux-graining all of Monticello doors at this time and was installing the glass in the Poplar Forest window sashes leads to the conjectural conclusion that Jefferson would have had him paint the upper exterior doors for Poplar Forest at the same time. Knowing that Barry painted

even the door to the attic on the third floor of Monticello, and that Jefferson directed exterior doors to the pavilions at the University of Virginia to be faux-painted, supports this conjecture.

37. I am indebted to Al Chambers for this fact mentioned in Chambers, *Poplar Forest,* 37.

38. Edmund Bacon to TJ, 29 December 1809, in *Papers, Retirement.*

39. TJ to John Perry, 7 May 1809, in *Papers, Retirement.*

40. Jefferson, *MB,* 980. Richardson must have been related to bricklayer Richard Richardson, who worked at Monticello from 1796 to 1801 since Jefferson mentioned both, along with John Chisolm, in a Memorandum Book entry for 1798.

41. Burgess Griffin to TJ, 27 December 1809, in *Papers.*

42. TJ to Madame de Corny, March 2, 1809, in *Papers.*

43. TJ to Pierre Samuel du Pont de Nemours, March 2, 1809, in *Papers, Retirement.*

44. TJ to Benjamin Rush, 17 August 1811, in *Papers, Retirement.*

45. TJ to James Dinsmore, 26 September 1810, in *Papers, Retirement.*

46. James Dinsmore, "Memdm. Of Carpenters tools belonging to Mr. Jefferson," 15 April 1809, "ref. Henry Ingle accounts."

47. TJ to Reuben Perry, 10 May 1811, in *Papers, Retirement.*

48. James Oldham made the lunette windows in Richmond following Jefferson's "model of circular sash" but using English crown glass when Bohemian glass could not be found.

49. TJ to Gideon Grander, 20 September 1810, in *Papers, Retirement.*

50. TJ to John W. Eppes, 18 September 1812, in *Papers, Retirement.*

51. TJ to Reuben Perry, 9 August 1812, in *Papers, Retirement.*

52. TJ to Reuben Perry, 10 December 1812, in *Papers, Retirement.*

53. TJ to Jeremiah Goodman, 18 October 1812, in *Papers, Retirement.*

54. TJ to Jeremiah Goodman, 18 October 1812, in *Papers, Retirement.*

55. TJ to John W. Eppes, 18 April 1813, in *Papers, Retirement.*

56. What Jefferson did for a kitchen before the wing is a mystery. Chisolm stated in 1808 that he was ready to build a kitchen, but nothing of this building or its location is known.

57. Thomas Jefferson, Weather Record 1776–1818, Jefferson Papers, series 7, vol. 2, Library of Congress.

58. Hugh Chisolm to TJ, 22 May 1814, in *Papers, Retirement.*

59. Quoted Baron, *Garden and Farm Books,* 353.

60. TJ to Jeremiah Goodman, 11 July 1814, in *Papers, Retirement.*

61. TJ to John W. Eppes, 16 July 1814, in *Papers, Retirement.*

62. TJ to F. R. Hassler, 3 December 1825, in *Papers, Retirement.*

63. Eighteenth-century examples of flat roofs in America included seamed lead coverings, tarred canvas, and *M-* or *W*-shaped roofs with platforms. The former was practical for smaller areas and not decks, and the latter hidden behind parapets. European roof platforms were either of masonry construction or built up over conventional roofs and placed behind parapets or balustrades.

64. For an extensive article on the President's House wings, see McDonald, "East and West Wings."

65. Benjamin Henry Latrobe to John Lenthall, 26 September 1803, microfilm, fn. 38, Papers of Benjamin Henry Latrobe.

66. At the President's House, with government money and materials, lapping sheet iron that covered the tops of the ridge joists and the valleys of the gutter joists. Jefferson would adopt the same metal-covered shingles and joists at Monticello and in some places at the University of Virginia. For a discussion of these roofs at Monticello and the University, see *Historic Structure Reports* at those places by Mesick Cohen Wilson Baker Architects.

67. Benjamin Henry Latrobe to Christian I. Latrobe, 5 June 1805, microfiche, Papers of Benjamin Henry Latrobe.

68. TJ to Benjamin Henry Latrobe, 23 May 1803, microfiche, Papers of Benjamin Henry Latrobe.

69. Joseph C. Cabell to TJ, 17 April 1819, in *Papers, Retirement.*

70. John H. Cocke to TJ, 3 May 1819, in *Papers, Retirement.*

71. Isaac Coles to John H. Cocke, 23 February 1816, cited in Fiske Kimball, "The Building of Bremo," *Virginia Magazine of History and Biography* 57, no. 1 (January 1949): 1–13.

72. John H. Cocke, Diary, 19 September 1836, quoted in Kimball, "Bremo," 13.

73. TJ to Charles Yancey, 12 July 1822, in *Papers, Retirement.*

74. Travis McDonald investigation of the Dr. Tucker House.

75. McLaughlin, *Jefferson and Monticello,* 322.

76. TJ to Charles Clay, 25 August 1815, in *Papers, Retirement.*

77. TJ to Joel Yancey, 18 July 1815, in *Papers, Retirement.*

78. Betts, *Farm Book,* "Slave Rolls," 1810.

79. TJ to Martha Jefferson Randolph, 31 August 1815, in *Papers, Retirement.*

80. TJ to Joel Yancey, 10 November 1818, in *Papers, Retirement.*

81. TJ to Joel Yancey, 11 February 1820, in *Papers, Retirement.*

82. TJ to John Hemings, 18 December 1821, in *Papers, Retirement.*

83. Ellen Randolph to Martha J. Randolph, 18 August 1817, in *Papers, Retirement.*

84. TJ to Martha J. Randolph, 22 November 1822, in *Papers, Retirement.*

85. TJ to George C. Cabell, 19 December 1817, in *Papers, Retirement.*

86. TJ to Martha Jefferson Randolph, 22 November 1817, in *Papers, Retirement.*

87. TJ to Martha Jefferson Randolph, 29 November 1817, in *Papers, Retirement.*

88. TJ to Edmund Bacon, 29 November 1817, in *Papers, Retirement.*

89. TJ to Joel Yancey, 25 June 1819, in *Papers, Retirement.*

90. TJ to E. Meeks, 19 July 1819, in *Papers, Retirement.*

91. Nothing is known about this first skylight other than it was in a "rafter roof."

92. TJ to Arthur Spicer Brockenbrough, 17 August 1819, in *Papers, Retirement.*

93. This detail was noticed by Robert Self, architectural conservator at Monticello.

94. John Hemmings to TJ, 20 October 1819, in *Papers, Retirement.*

95. John Hemings to TJ, 2 November 1819, in *Papers, Retirement.*

96. TJ to John Hemings, 14 November 1819, in *Papers, Retirement.*

97. TJ to John Hemings, 14 November 1819, in *Papers, Retirement.*

98. Jefferson provided round holes in his third-floor attic access doors at Monticello so that cats could control the rat population. The evidence of rats' nests in the Poplar Forest house spanned 1846, when the house was rebuilt, to the 1970s (see Travis McDonald, "Rat Housing in Middle Virginia," *Building Environments: Perspectives in Vernacular Architecture,* vol. 10, 169–84 [Knoxville: University of Tennessee Press, 2005]).

99. John Hemings to TJ, 18 November 1819, in *Papers, Retirement.*

100. TJ to John Hemings, 27 November 1819, in *Papers, Retirement.*

101. John Hemings to TJ, 2 December 1819, in *Papers, Retirement.*

102. TJ to Joel Yancey, 28 October 1820, in *Papers, Retirement.* He wrote to his Richmond merchant, "I am here in a leaky house which cannot be remedied but by sheet iron and tin." Jefferson ordered five hundred or one thousand chestnut shingles "got and ready drawn for it. They must be of the length of those we used before, and are not to be rounded. I presume you can get some workman there to do *it immediately.*"

103. Jefferson, *MB,* 1391.

104. John Hemmings to TJ, 29 November 1821, in *Papers, Retirement.*

105. John Hemings to TJ, 11 December 1821, in *Papers, Retirement.*

106. TJ to John Hemings, 18 December 1821, in *Papers, Retirement.*

107. TJ to Joel Yancey, 16 March 1820, in *Papers, Retirement.*

108. Jefferson would later pay for Coffee's trip down from New York in March 1822 in exchange for Coffee cleaning and revarnishing Jefferson's collection of paintings.

109. Coffee would make lead entablature ornaments for the exterior of Pavilion I and II and terra cotta and lead ornaments for the parlor ornaments for all ten of the pavilions.

110. TJ to William Coffee, 14 June 1822, in *Papers, Retirement.* An undated Jefferson note labelled "D Hall and Parlour" had been thought by Fiske Kimball to be for the University but was for Poplar Forest. The note mentioned "36 Metops 14 I. wide 15 I. high 4. Do. Angular, Mitred. The two moieties equal to one whole. June 14: wrote to Coffee for the above. Parlour 74.8 f. of frieze but say 80. F= 28. D 80 C running measure." James Monroe Memorial Foundation, quoted in Frank E. Grizzard Jr., "Documentary History of the Construction of the Buildings of the University of Virginia, 1817–1828" (PhD diss., University of Virginia, 1996), 821.

111. William Coffee to TJ, 25 June 1822, in *Papers, Retirement.*

112. Arthur S. Brockenbrough to TJ, 7 June 1820, in *Papers, Retirement.* The rendered brick column shafts of the buildings on the Lawn were originally just the color of the lime coating, a tan color. Painting the wood trim a similar color would make it all seem like stonework in more of a European manner. Recent paint analysis at the University has revealed that a tan "stone color" was used on some, if not all, of the pavilions, but eventually the wood trim, and the columns, were painted white.

113. TJ to William Coffee, 10 July 1822, in *Papers, Retirement.*

114. The bucrania ox skull that Coffee made for the Poplar Forest dining room was most likely similar to those he made for the University in the parlors of Pavilions II and V.

115. Coffee's ornaments for the parlors of Pavilion I and VII were the Ionic Temple of Fortuna Virilis and identical to the parlor ornaments at Poplar Forest. The face of Apollo in the dining room at Poplar Forest would have been the same as that in the parlors of Pavilion VI and IX. The added ox skull or bucrania in the Poplar Forest dining room entablature was most likely the same as the bucrania in Pavilions II and V. Coffee most likely used as his sources Palladio, Nicholson, Chambray, and Desgodetz. The designs for the Temple of Fortuna Virilis and the bucrania were unlike any sources and resulting in Coffee's sculptor's artistic license. The exterior entablatures of Pavilion I and II were different since they were in lead and not terra cotta.

116. TJ to William Coffee, 22 March 1823, in *Papers, Retirement.*

117. William Coffee to TJ, 27 March 1823, in *Papers, Retirement.*

118. Composition was a combination of whiting and hide glue.

119. TJ to William Coffee, 30 April 1823, in *Papers, Retirement.*

120. One piece of ornament found during investigation was the chin of Apollo with a white lead paint, a screw hole, and "No 1" inscribed on the back, indicating that the faces were in numbered parts. Another piece was part of a bucrania mitred for one of the corners.

121. William Coffee to TJ, 1 December 1825, in *Papers, Retirement.*

122. She was the daughter of Thomas Eston Randolph, brother-in-law of Jefferson's daughter Martha.

123. TJ to John Wayles Eppes, 28 July 1822, in *Papers, Retirement.*

124. TJ to William Radford, 30 November 1822, in *Papers, Retirement.*

125. Virginia Randolph to Nicholas Trist, 13 May 1823, in *Papers, Retirement.*

126. Elizabeth Trist to Virginia Randolph, 29 May 1823, in *Papers, Retirement.*

127. Frances Eppes to Nicholas Trist, 7 November 1826, Nicholas Trist Papers, North Carolina University, quoted in Chambers, *Poplar Forest,* 169.

128. Martha Jefferson Randolph to Ellen Randolph Coolidge, 5 April 1826, Coolidge Collection, University of Virginia.

129. Virginia R. to Nicholas Trist, 9 January 1824, Nicholas Trist Family Papers, University of North Carolina.

130. TJ to Francis Eppes, 9 March 1826, Jefferson Family Papers, Group 10, University of Virginia.

131. TJ to Francis Eppes, 17 February 1825, Jefferson Family Papers, Group 10, University of Virginia.

132. Francis Eppes to TJ, 25 February 1825, Jefferson Papers, Massachusetts Historical Society (hereafter MHS).

133. TJ to Francis Eppes, 6 April 1825, cited in Betts, *Garden Book,* 616.

134. TJ to Francis Eppes, 6 April 1825, cited in Betts, *Garden Book,* 616.

135. John Hemings to TJ, 23 July 1825, Jefferson Papers, MHS.

136. John Hemings to TJ, 23 July 1825, Jefferson Papers, MHS.

137. John Hemings to TJ, 7 Aug 1825, Jefferson Papers, MHS.

138. John Hemings to TJ, 7 Aug 1825, Jefferson Papers, MHS.

139. TJ to John Hemings, 17 August 1825, Jefferson Papers, MHS.

140. TJ to John Hemings, 17 August 1825, Jefferson Papers, MHS.

141. John Hemings to TJ, 18 September 1825, Jefferson Papers, MHS.

142. John Hemings to Septimia Randolph, 28 August 1825, Special Collections, 4726-A, University of Virginia.

143. John Hemings to TJ, 28 September 1825, Jefferson Papers, MHS.

144. John A. Dix, after 19 February 1820, in *Papers, Retirement,* 15, 404.

145. Francis Eppes to TJ, 23 June 1826, Jefferson Papers, MHS.

146. Francis Eppes to TJ, 23 June 1826, Jefferson Papers, MHS.

147. Francis Eppes to Thomas Jefferson Randolph, 21 September 1826, Jefferson, MHS.

148. Poplar Forest journal of Francis Eppes, Corporation for Jefferson's Poplar Forest.

149. M. E. R. Eppes to Jane Randolph, 1 April 1827, Edgehill-Randolph Papers, University of Virginia.

150. Francis Eppes to Nicholas Trist, 7 November 1826, Trist Papers, University of North Carolina.

151. See Chambers, *Poplar Forest,* for the story of Eppes's journey and life in Florida.

152. A. B. Woodward to TJ, 21 April 1826, cited in Betts, *Garden Book,* 619.

5. LANDSCAPES OF USE AND ORNAMENT

1. TJ to John W. Eppes, 18 April 1813, in *Papers, Retirement.*

2. The ongoing archaeological investigations at Poplar Forest continue to explore Jefferson's ornamental and plantation landscapes and the enslaved communities that lived there. Archaeological staff reports and published articles by Barbara Heath, Jack Gary, Eric Proebsting, Lori Lee, and Timothy Trussell are found in the Poplar Forest on-site archives.

3. TJ to Charles Willson Peale, 20 August 1811, in *Papers, Retirement.*

4. TJ to Charles Willson Peale, 20 August 1811, in *Papers, Retirement.*

5. Brown, "Poplar Forest," 17. This was cited from Castell's *Villas of the Ancients Illustrated.*

6. See Heath and Gary, *Unearthing.*

7. Ron Giese has written extensively about the various agricultural crops that Jefferson grew at Poplar Forest (see Giese research reports in the Poplar Forest research library).

8. TJ to Reibelt, 22 December 1807, in *Papers.*

9. TJ to Honore Jullien, 8 January 1810, in *Papers, Retirement.*

10. TJ to John Mason, 22 June 1810, in *Papers, Retirement.*

11. See Hatch, *A Rich Spot.*

12. TJ to Vine Utley, 1819; cited in Hatch, *Rich Spot,* 5.

13. Hatch, *Rich Spot,* 34.

14. Quoted in Hatch, *Rich Spot,* 13.

15. Hatch, *Rich Spot,* 76.

16. "Planting Memorandum for Poplar Forest," 27 February 1811, cited in Betts, *Garden Book,* 464.

An ornamental plant nursery was located southeast of the main house based on archaeology as documented in file reports from 2010 by Jack Gary, Eric Proebsting, and Lori Lee.

17. Hatch, *Rich Spot,* 200.

18. TJ to J. Goodman, 13 December 1812, in *Papers, Retirement.*

19. TJ to Charles Clay, 14 December 1812, in *Papers, Retirement.*

20. TJ to Martha Jefferson Randolph, 31 August 1815, in *Papers, Retirement.*

21. TJ to Mrs. Trist, 10 May 1813, in *Papers, Retirement.*

22. TJ to J. Goodman, 6 March 1817, in *Papers, Retirement.*

23. "Instructions for Poplar Forest Management," December 1811, in *Papers, Retirement.*

24. See McDonald, "East and West Wings."

25. Beiswanger, "Temple," 170.

26. Quoted in Beiswangaer, "Temple," 170.

27. Beiswanger, "Designs," 20.

28. See Beiswanger, "Temple"' Beiswanger, "Art of Living Outdoors"; Nichols and Griswold, *Thomas Jefferson: Landscape Architect;* Claus Daufenbach, "Jefferson's Monticello and the Poetics of Landscape Gardening," *Soundings: An Interdisciplinary Journal* 78, no. 3–4 (fall/winter 1995); Brown, *Mathematics.*

29. Archaeological investigations of the grounds and landscape around the ornamental core, and the plantation landscape beyond, has been directed since 1988 by William Kelso, Barbara Heath, Jack Gary, and Eric Proebsting.

30. Thomas Whately, *Observations on Modern Gardening* (1770), quoted in Nichols and Griswold, *Landscape,* 83.

31. TJ to Martha J. Randolph, 23 December 1790, in *Papers.*

32. A. Hyatt Mayor remarked about Jefferson's enjoyment of the arts: "As one might expect in a man who was born before David and died after Byron, Jefferson was by turns a classicist and a romantic. It might even be said that he could be both at once" (Mayor, "Jefferson's Enjoyment," 145). Dell Upton points out that this dichotomy is also seen at Monticello where its rational neoclassical architecture is combined with the romantic spirit in which Jefferson described its setting in the natural world (Upton, *Architecture,* 113).

33. Quoted in Betts, *Garden Book,* 305. Photographs from around 1900 show about a dozen large poplar trees on the north lawn, of which five were surviving in 2020.

34. Evidence that the house site was already cleared for tobacco fields is based on archaeological investigations and maps that indicate a late eighteenth-century clearing. Dendrochronology dated one of the surviving poplars to 1806 and regression analysis indicates that the others are about the same age (see reports in the Poplar Forest archives for these studies).

35. Planting Memorandum, 22 November 1816, Monticello Research Library.

36. TJ to William Hamilton, July 1806, in *Papers.*

37. TJ to William Hamilton, July 1806, in *Papers.*

38. TJ to Charles Willson Peale, 17 April 1813, in *Papers, Retirement.*

39. This road was confirmed through archaeology (see Barbara Heath, "Thomas Jefferson's Landscape of Retirement," in *Estate Landscapes: Design, Improvement and Power in the Post-Medieval Landscapes,* ed. Jonathan Finch and Kate Files, 129–47 [Woodbridge, UK: Boydell and Brewer, 2007]).

40. The northeast and northwest clumps have been restored, but the two on the southeast and southwest sides of the house have not been restored.

41. Jack Gary, "Paper Mulberry Trees, Clumps, and Oval Beds: The First Phase of Landscape Restoration at Thomas Jefferson's Poplar Forest," *Magnolia: Publication of the Southern Garden History Society* 25, no. 4 (2012): 1–7; Eric Proebsting, Jack Gary, and Barbara Heath. "The Other End of the Chain: Viewing the Poplar Forest Landscape from an Enslaved Perspective," paper presented at the An-

nual Meeting of the Society for Historical Archaeology, 2014; Will Rieley, "Garden Club of Virginia's Newly Minted Restorations," *Garden Club of Virginia Journal* 66, no. 1 (2021): 16–19.

42. The dirt from the south lawn, and later from the east wing area, was also used to level an area to the southeast of the main house, possibly a work area related to the old plantation landscape.

43. The privies at Wrest were named "Temple of Cloacina."

44. TJ to Charles Clay, 18 November 1815, in *Papers, Retirement.*

45. TJ to James Barbour, 5 March 1816, in *Papers, Retirement.*

46. Philip Miller, "Terraces" (London 1768), quoted in Brown, "Poplar Forest."

47. Archaeological evidence for the west row of trees was confirmed as was evidence for the northern row on the east side; the southern row of the east side would have been disturbed when the wing was built. Archaeologists discovered that the spacing of the east rows would have allowed a future west wing to have been built. But, if a second wing was added, it too would have lost its southern row due to the grade change that would have taken place. Drawings and memos from Monticello also show that Jefferson planted these shade trees very close to the service wings flanking the house. This evidence is documented in Gary, "Paper Mulberry Trees."

48. Building Notebook, N-149–19, undated

49. Cited in Reinberger and McLean, *Philadelphia.*

50. Michael Olmert, "Of Garden Mounts," *Colonial Williamsburg Magazine,* summer 2014, 28–34.

51. An account of this trip is found in Wilson and Stanton, *Jefferson Abroad, 65–69.*

52. Maccubbin and Martin, *British and American Gardens,* 126.

53. Bernard McMahon, *The American Gardener's Calendar,* 62, quoted in Brown "Poplar Forest," 32.

54. See Trussell in Heath and Gary, *Unearthing.*

55. Bernard McMahon, *The American Gardener's Calendar,* 62, quoted in Brown "Poplar Forest," 56.

56. Bernard McMahon, *The American Gardener's Calendar,* 62, quoted in Brown "Poplar Forest," 62.

57. This was mentioned in Beiswanger, "Temple"; and Brown, "Mathematics."

58. Henderson, "Secret Houses."

59. TJ to Constantine Samuel Rafinesque, 9 October 1822, quoted in Charles Miller, *Jefferson and Nature* (Baltimore, MD: Johns Hopkins University Press, 1988), 279.

60. Jefferson, "Notes," 148.

61. The property was sold in 1833 as part of Jefferson's estate.

62. Miller, *Jefferson and Nature,* 252.

6. RETIRED LIFE AT POPLAR FOREST

1. September 1793, cited in Garrett, *Redivivus,* 139.

2. TJ to Angelica Church, 27 November 1793, cited in Betts, *Farm Book,* xiii.

3. Quoted in Joseph Ellis, *American Sphinx* (New York: Knopf, 1997), 118.

4. TJ to Martha Jefferson Randolph, 8 June 1797, in *Papers.*

5. Cited in Betts, *Garden Book,* 189.

6. TJ to Levett Harris, 18 April 1806, in *Papers.*

7. TJ to Elizabeth Trist, 27 April 1806; Elizabeth Trist to TJ; 19 May 1806, in *Papers.*

8. TJ to Monsieur Le Comte Diodati, 29 March 1807, in *Papers.*

9. TJ to James Madison, 28 January 1809, in *Papers.*

10. TJ to P.S. Dupont de Nemours, 2 March 1809, in *Papers, Retirement.*

11. TJ to Madame de Coggay, 2 March 1809, in *Papers, Retirement.*

12. TJ to D. Howell, 15 December 1810, in *Papers, Retirement.*

13. TJ to Willian Duane, 12 August 1810, in *Papers, Retirement.*

14. TJ to John B. Colvin, 20 September 1810, in *Papers, Retirement.*

15. TJ to Gideon Granger, 20 September 1810, in *Papers, Retirement.*

16. TJ to John Wayles Eppes, 18 September 1812, in *Papers, Retirement.*

17. John Wayles Eppes to Cesar Rodney, 7 October 1818, in *Papers, Retirement.*

18. TJ to William Short, 5 May 1816, in *Papers, Retirement.*

19. TJ to John Mason, 22 June 1810, in *Papers, Retirement.*

20. TJ to William Lambert, 16 July 1810, in *Papers, Retirement.*

21. TJ to Thaddeus Kosciusko, 26 February 1810, in *Papers, Retirement.*

22. TJ to William Short, 8 March 1811, in *Papers, Retirement.*

23. TJ to William Short, 17 May 1811, in *Papers, Retirement.*

24. TJ to Benjamin Rush, 17 August 1811, in *Papers, Retirement.*

25. TJ to Benjamin Rush, 16 January 1811, in *Papers, Retirement.*

26. TJ to James Maury, 5 April 1812, in *Papers, Retirement.*

27. TJ to John Wayles Eppes, 24, June 1816, in *Papers, Retirement.*

28. Ellen R. Coolidge to Henry Randall, 18 February 1856, in Randall, *Life,* 3:342.

29. Cornelia Randolph to Virginia Randolph, 25 October 1816, Nicholas Trist Papers, University of North Carolina.

30. Cornelia Randolph to Virginia Randolph, 25 October 1816, Nicholas Trist Papers, University of North Carolina.

31. Ellen Randolph to Martha J. Randolph, November 1816, Coolidge Collection, 9090, University of Virginia.

32. TJ to Martha J. Randolph, 3 December 1816, in *Papers, Retirement.*

33. TJ to Martha Jefferson Randolph, 31 August 1817, in *Papers, Retirement.*

34. Ellen Randolph to Martha Jefferson Randolph, 28 July 1819, Coolidge Collection, University of Virginia.

35. Cornelia Randolph to Virginia Randolph, 17 August 1817, Nicholas Trist Family Papers, University of North Carolina.

36. Ellen Randolph to Martha Jefferson Randolph, 18 July 1819; Coolidge Collection, 9090, University of Virginia.

37. Cornelia Randolph to Virginia Randolph, 28 July 1819, Nicholas Trist Family Papers, University of North Carolina.

38. Quoted in D. Wilson, *Jefferson's Books,* 8.

39. Randolph, *Domestic Life,* 405.

40. TJ to Benjamin Rush, 17 August 1811, in *Papers, Retirement.*

41. About seven hundred Poplar Forest volumes are documented in an auction catalogue from 1873, when Francis Eppes sent the Poplar Forest library, which had been taken to the wilds of Florida in 1828, to New York City. The other volumes are known from a small code Jefferson put in his large master book list when selling his library to Congress.

42. TJ to John Adams, 10 June 1815, in *Papers, Retirement.*

43. Randall, *Life,* 3:341–44.

44. TJ to Joseph Milligan, 9 December 1818, in *Papers, Retirement.*

45. Quoted in Wilson and Stanton, *Jefferson Abroad,* 264.

46. TJ to Mr. Wilson, 17 April 1793, in *Papers, Retirement.*

47. One of these small cases is now in the Winterthur Museum collection. Although these cases could have been hung on walls, there was no physical evidence to support that placement. Small cases with petite-size books can be seen resting on tables in English country houses.

48. The Poplar Forest library is known fully through the research of Thomas Baughn when he was working on the Jefferson library project at Monticello.

49. Ellen Randolph Coolidge to Henry S. Randall, Randall, in Randall, *Life,* 342–44.

50. Reinhold, "The Classical World," 155.

51. TJ to Nathaniel Macon, 12 January 1819, in *Papers, Retirement.*

52. TJ to John Adams, 5 July 1814, in *Papers, Retirement.*

53. TJ to John Brazier, 24 August 1819, in *Papers, Retirement.*

54. TJ to Samuel H. Smith, 21 September 1814, in *Papers, Retirement.*

55. TJ to William Short, 31 October 1819, in *Papers, Retirement.*

56. TJ to Benjamin Rush, 17 August 1811, in *Papers, Retirement.*

57. TJ to William Short, 29 May 1818, in *Papers, Retirement.*

58. TJ to Edmund Bacon, 13 May 1807, in *Papers, Retirement.*

59. TJ to Thomas Mann Randolph, 1 January 1792, in *Papers.*

60. Baron, *Garden and Farm Books,* 371.

61. Quoted in Mrs. E. A. Watson, "Thomas Jefferson's Other Home," *Antiques,* April 1957; F. Nichols "Thomas Jefferson's Poplar Forest," *Iron Worker,* spring 1974.

62. Randall, *Life,* 3:341–44.

63. Ellen R. Coolidge to Henry S. Randall, Coolidge Letter Book, University of Virginia.

64. TJ to Martha Jefferson Randolph, 31 August 1817, in *Papers, Retirement.*

65. Cited in Beiswanger, *Measured Drawings,* 22. Beiswanger has described the terras decks as the most universally satisfying aspect of Jefferson's design for Monticello.

66. An arch in the stair pavilion's north wall facilitated the clean-out, just as the arches under the seats of the two octagonal privies. Several of Jefferson's domestic designs showed privies under staircases because this indoor facility was still unusual for American houses and required innovative locations when being retrofitted. At Monticello Jefferson had squeezed a "public" and a private privy space in the widened wall between the south passage and his bed chamber.

67. For a discussion of the portico/piazza/verandah in American architecture, see John E. Crowley, *The Invention of Comfort: Sensibilities & Design in Early Modern Britain & Early America* (Baltimore, MD: Johns Hopkins University Press, 2001); and Maynard, *Architecture.*

68. Evidence for the location of the "large French Mirrors" described by Flower was found on the parlor walls opposite the windows where attachment holes indicated large heavy items hung symmetrically on either side of the doorway. It was common for mirrors to be situated opposite a window wall for reflected light.

69. These were black with gold bands representing a bamboo-like design. Cornelia's drawing of one of the chairs next to the round revolving top table has always been a puzzle. It shows a stretcher connecting the bottom of the back legs. Jefferson's sketch and specifications for these chairs show no stretchers, nor would it have been typical. The conclusion from furniture experts is that it represents a repair.

70. Physical evidence found during the investigation confirmed the presence and location of a bell system.

71. TJ to J Hemings 27 November 1819, in *Papers, Retirement.*

72. Ellen Randolph to Martha Jefferson Randolph, 14 April 1818, Coolidge Collection, 9090, University of Virginia.

73. The premise that a culture's ideology is reflected in their material culture can certainly be fully demonstrated through Jefferson's design and furnishings at Monticello. This same lens through which to evaluate Jefferson and Poplar Forest does not work in any conventional manner due to the incomplete documentation of furnishings and also the very private nature of the house. Although the house was architecturally distinguished, its furnishings were simple, not reflective of expensive consumerism but more in keeping with its private nature as a retreat. It did not seem to have any of the French furniture and decorative arts Jefferson acquired in Paris. There was very little "public" to impress.

74. Travis McDonald investigation.

75. The source of the mirrors or their travel to the site is not documented, but they were probably

brought back from France; no other mention is made for them in Jefferson's account book. Physical evidence for their location opposite the windows in the parlor was found during investigation.

76. Paint was ordered in 1805 and 1807, but it was not indicated whether it was for Monticello or Poplar Forest. Hundreds of fragments of plaster found during the investigation reveal finishes that were tan oil paints and gray lime washes and gray distemper paints. Gray was one of Jefferson's favorite colors at Monticello, as was a blue-gray baseboard color. The creamy-white linseed oil finish for interior and exterior woodwork was a Jefferson tradition at Monticello and the University of Virginia.

77. Pieces of each of these were found during the investigation, as was the local white marble for the hearthstones and the front door sill.

78. TJ to Martha Jefferson Randolph, 24 August 1819, in *Papers, Retirement.*

79. Francis Eppes bought a mahogany wall bracket at the Monticello estate sale after Jefferson's death.

80. See Heath, *Hidden Lives.* The slaves at Poplar Forest, as had the land, been part of Martha Wayles Jefferson's inheritance whereas most of the enslaved people at Monticello came from Jefferson's inheritance. Enslaved people were frequently moved from one plantation to another.

81. TJ to Jean Baptiste Say, 2 March 1815, in *Papers, Retirement.*

82. It is also possible this wire connected to a bell in the east cellar.

83. Ellen Randolph to Martha J. Randolph, 18 July 1819, Coolidge Collection, 9090, University of Virginia.

84. TJ to Jeremiah Goodman, Memo, December 1811, in *Papers, Retirement.*

85. TJ to Joel Yancey, 15 August 1821, in *Papers, Retirement.*

86. Hannah to TJ, 15 November 1818, in *Papers, Retirement.*

87. Ellen Randolph to Virginia Randolph, 4 August 1819, Coolidge Collection, 9090, University of Virginia.

88. Cornelia Randolph to Virginia Randolph, 28 July 1819, Trist Collection, University of North Carolina.

89. John Hemings to Septimia Randolph, 28 November 1825, Coolidge Collection, 4726-A, University of Virginia.

90. Baron, *Garden and Farm Books,* 369.

91. Baron, *Garden and Farm Books,* 480.

92. The Poplar Forest slave quarters revealed garden crops of corn, beans, cow peas, and black-eyed peas. Diets were also supplemented by natural foods: blueberries, sumac, grapes, hickory nuts, and black walnuts.

93. Jefferson, *MB,* 1408.

94. Madison Hemings, "Life among the Lowly," *Pike County (OH) Republican,* March 13, 1873, in Annette Gordon-Reed, *American Controversy,* 245–48.

95. For the full history of the Hemings family, see Stanton, *Those Who Labor;* and Gordon-Reed, *The Hemingses.*

96. Jefferson's will is found in Saul K. Padover, ed., *The Complete Jefferson* (New York: Duell, Sloan and Pearch, 1943), 1297–99.

97. Padover, *Complete Jefferson.*

98. Gordon-Reed, *The Hemingses,* 598.

99. Gordon-Reed, *The Hemingses,* 638.

7. A RETIREMENT HOBBY

1. TJ to Joseph C. Cabell, 18 December 1817, in *Papers, Retirement.*

2. TJ to Albert Gallatin, 29 October 1822; TJ to Henry A. S. Dearborne, 31 October 1822, in *Papers, Retirement.*

3. TJ to Benjamin Henry Latrobe, 3 August 1817, quoted in Grizzard, "Construction," 82.

4. TJ to James Dinsmore, 13 April 1817, in *Papers, Retirement.*

5. TJ to John Perry, 3 June 1817, in *Papers, Retirement.*

6. TJ to John Adams, 15 August 1820, in *Papers, Retirement.*

7. TJ to Arthur S. Brockenbrough, 29 July 1819, in *Papers, Retirement.*

8. TJ to Hugh Chisolm, 31 August 1817, in *Papers, Retirement.*

9. Frank Grizzard's electronic dissertation on the construction of the university represents a heroic effort of transcribing one of the best documented early American construction projects outside of federal buildings.

10. TJ to Benjamin Henry Latrobe, 16 July 1817, in *Papers, Retirement.* David Knight was a Maryland brickmaker and bricklayer who had apprenticed in Baltimore before coming to Lynchburg. Knight had just constructed the Franklin Hotel in Lynchburg, owned by Jefferson's friend Samuel J. Harrison and completed in 1817. Jefferson would also hire Matthew Brown from Lynchburg to work at the University.

11. Hierarchically the ten pavilions and the Rotunda had the best-quality work: smooth oil stock rubbed for an even greater smoothness that was laid in a Flemish Bond pattern with tight ribbon joints and the whole painted in a brick-red wash with painted "penciling" lines over each joint to make the appearance even more exquisite. The adjacent student rooms, fitting their status, had a sand stock brick in Flemish Bond with typical joints and red wash. The sides and backs of the pavilions had the lowest status and were laid with a sand stock brick in a typical five-course common bond pattern with wash and standard joints but no penciling. The exception would be where a pavilion's side faced a public space, like the north side of Pavilion I. The sides of the first pavilion, No. VII, also have Flemish Bond sides as befitting the first stand-alone pavilion. The six hotels, intended for dining halls on the Ranges, show a hierarchy for their location of Flemish Bond with regular struck joints and wash but no penciling. While Jefferson sought to keep a consistent quality on the Lawn, the hotels and student rooms on the ranges have a variety of bonds and details that probably resulted from the many different men from different places working at different times.

12. TJ to James Madison, 15 November 1817, in *Papers, Retirement.*

13. TJ to Joseph C. Cabell, 19 December 1817, in *Papers, Retirement;* "Advertisement for Brickwork," 7 December 1817, in *Papers, Retirement.*

14. "Estimate for Brickmaking Costs for the Rotunda," 1823, cited in Grizzard, "Construction," 1862.

15. TJ to George Ticknor, 24 December 1819, in *Papers.*

16. TJ to Maria Cosway, 24 October 1822, in *Papers.*

17. All of these references are found in the transcribed letters in Frank Grizzard's documentation of the university construction.

18. TJ to Robert Mills, 24 November 1821, in *Papers, Retirement.*

19. TJ to Robert Mills, 3 March 1826, in *Papers, Retirement.*

20. TJ to Wm. Short, 19 October 1822, in *Papers, Retirement.*

21. Henry Dearborn to TJ, 6 September 1825, in *Papers, Retirement.*

22. Contract with John Perrry, 23 June 1817, in *Papers, Retirement.*

23. TJ to James Madison, 15 November 1817, in *Papers, Retirement.*

24. James Dinsmore to TJ, 1 July 1819, in *Papers, Retirement.*

25. TJ Notes, post 1817, quoted in Grizzard, "Construction," appendix A.

26. William Coffee cites two of his architectural source books in a letter regarding the Poplar Forest ornaments: Peter Nicholson's *Principles of Architecture,* and Andrea Palladio (unknown edition). It is clear the Nicholson is one source for the university ornaments in addition to Antoine Desgodetz's *Antiquities of Rome* and Freart de Chambray's *Parallele de l'architecture.* Coffee took artistic liberties with the Temple of Foruna Virilis and the Doric bucrania to the point they are hard to source.

27. Coffee visited Monticello for the second time on 16 March 1820; this is the same trip during

which he visited Poplar Forest. His third trip to Monticello was in February 1823 where he and Jefferson went to see the University construction. These are the likely times, especially the latter, when verbal instructions would have been given for ornaments, details, and their sources. No other correspondence mentions this (see Travis McDonald memo of August 5, 2020, "William Coffee and Poplar Forest Entablature Ornaments;" and Travis McDonald memo of August 7, 2020, "William Coffee Ornaments at UVA," in Poplar Forest Restoration Files).

28. John Neilson to John Hartwell Cocke, 22 February 1823, quoted in Grizzard, "Construction," 1623.

29. TJ to Arthur Spicer Brockenbrough, 28 December 1823, quoted in Grizzard, "Construction," 1854.

30. Balance Sheet, 23 November 1922, quoted in Grizzard, "Construction," 1526.

31. Arthur Spicer Brockenbrough to TJ, 28 November 1823, quoted in Grizzard, "Construction," 1844.

32. Richard Ware to Arthur Spicer Brockenbrough, 22 August 1819, quoted in Grizzard, "Construction," 596.

33. TJ to Arthur Spicer Brockenbrough, 15 November 1825, quoted in Grizzard, "Construction," 2422.

34. After most of the initial University work was completed, a faculty resolution in 1828 stated that "faculty disapprove of Free negroes being located within the University." The reason was not given.

35. John Hartwell Cocke to Arthur Spicer Brockenbrough, 17 July 1826, quoted in Grizzard, "Construction," 2592. Colbert was known to be a trained glazier who could replace glass in sash windows. This is most likely the reference to "pointer," referring to the points used in holding glass to their muntins.

36. Alexander Garrett to John Hartwell Cocke, 18 February 1823, quoted in Grizzard, "Construction," 1616

37. James Madison to Samuel Harrison Smith, 4 November 1826, quoted in Grizzard, "Construction," 2635.

EPILOGUE

1. Henry Adams, "The Architectural Jefferson," in *The Private Jefferson* (Boston: Massachusetts Historical Society, 2016), 27.

2. James Marston Fitch, *American Building: The Historical Forces That Shaped It* (1947; Boston: Riverside, 1966).

3. Vincent Scully, "American Houses: Thomas Jefferson to Frank Lloyd Wright," in *The Rise of an American Architecture,* ed. Edgar Kaufman Jr. (New York: Praeger Publishers in Association with the Metropolitan Museum of Art, 1970). Scully's article actually came from his 1949 dissertation "The Cottage Style" that appeared in print in 1953 and 1955.

4. For a good history of these changes in fieldwork recording, see Thomas Carter and Elizabeth Collins Cromley. *Invitation to Vernacular Architecture: A Guide to the Study of Ordinary Buildings and Landscapes* (Knoxville: University of Tennessee Press, 2005). See also Dell Upton, "New Views of the Virginia Landscape," *Virginia Magazine of History and Biography* 96, no. 4 (October 1988): 403–70; and Wells, "Multi-Storied House," in *Material Witnesses,* by Wells. For the tradition of fieldwork in Virginia, see Travis McDonald, "The Fundamental Practice of Fieldwork at Colonial Williamsburg," in *Perspectives in Vernacular Architecture Journal,* ed. Warren Hofstra and Camille Wells, vol. 13, no. 2 (2006–7): 35–53.

5. Appleby, "Jefferson and His Complex Legacy."

6. Ellis, *American Sphinx.*

7. Archer, *Architecture,* xvi–xix.

8. Archer, *Architecture,* 48.

9. See Wenger, "Town House."

10. Ellis, *American Sphinx,* 119.

11. Margaret Bayard Smith to Miss Susan B. Smith, March 1809, in Smith, *Forty Years,* 64.

12. George Watterston (attributed), "Account of a Visit to Monticello and Montpelier by 'W.,'" before 15 August 1820, in *Papers, Retirement,* 16, 198.

13. See T. Thornton, *Cultivating.*

14. Adams to Jefferson, 13 November 1815, quoted in May, *Enlightenment,* 336

15. TJ to N. Macon, 12 January 1819, in *Papers, Retirement.*

16. Winterer, *American Enlightenments,* 175.

17. Jack P. Greene, *Pursuits of Happiness: The Social Development of Early Modern British Colonies and the Formation of American Culture* (Chapel Hill: University of North Carolina Press, 1988), 196.

18. Peter Onuf, "The State of the World," in *The Private Jefferson* (Boston: Massachusetts Historical Society, 2016), 15.

19. See Hannah Spahn, *Thomas Jefferson, Time, and History* (Charlottesville: University Press of Virginia, 2011) for a discussion of Jefferson's concept of temporality as it relates to his views on slavery. The same views can be seen in his personality trait to have the patience to make something better, especially his building projects.

20. John Stillgoe, introduction to Gaston Bachelard, *The Poetics of Space: The Classic Look at How We Experience Intimate Places* (1969; Boston: Beacon, 1998), viii.

21. Alain de Botton, *The Architecture of Happiness* (New York: Vintage, 2006).

22. See Archer, *Architecture;* and Virginia C. Kenny, *The Country-House Ethos in English Literature 1688–1750: Themes of Personal Retreat and National Expansion* (New York: St. Martin's, 1984).

23. For a discussion of privacy, see Wells, *Virginia by Design;* Upton *Architecture;* Carson and Lounsbury *Chesapeake House;* Peter Ward, *A History of Domestic Space: Privacy and the Canadian Home* (Toronto: UBC, 1999); and Crowley, *Comfort.*

24. These large humanist themes are found in Lehman, *American Humanist.*

25. Poplar Forest is on the Tentative List to join the thematic Jefferson listing. The National Park Service declared Poplar Forest eligible for these three criteria.

26. This has been pointed out by Herbert Mayor, William Howard Adams, and Jack McLaughlin.

27. Wright, "Thomas Jefferson," 226, 231.

28. Wright, "Thomas Jefferson," 230.

29. Kallen, "The Arts," 270.

30. Appleby, "Jefferson and His Complex Legacy," 6.

31. Joyce Appleby, "Jefferson and His Complex Legacy," 6.

32. Cited in Appleby, "Jefferson and His Complex Legacy," 6.

33. This general characterization was from Joyce Appleby, "Jefferson and His Complex Legacy," 6: "Jefferson's great gift was as a synthesizer. He took several strands of liberal theory and braided them into a coherent rope on which to hang his reforms." In 1994, having worked at Poplar Forest for only five years, I wrote an article entitled "Poplar Forest: Synthesis of a Lifetime." This more traditional architectural history summarized the more obvious and well-known influences on Jefferson's architecture as reflected in his Poplar Forest design, only recently confirmed through investigation. I concluded that Poplar Forest was "the personal epiphany of Thomas Jefferson's architectural life." While one might argue that the University of Virginia is more appropriate for this title, Poplar Forest was certainly his domestic epiphany. However, what strikes me about this article with twenty-seven years hindsight is the word *synthesis,* which still seems very true.

34. Karl Lehman first mentioned Jefferson's architecture as being like a symphony (Lehman, *Humanist,* 168).

35. Hatch, *Rich Spot,* 13.

36. D. Wilson, *Jefferson's Books,* 35.

37. See Spahn, *Time.*

38. My use of the term came from an excellent 1971 book by Wendell D. Garrett, *Thomas Jefferson Redivivus.*

39. Winterer, *American Enlightenments,* 256.

40. Ellis, *American Sphinx,* 291. This analogy was first offered by Daniel Boorstin.

41. Scott A. French and Edward L. Ayers, "The Strange Career of Thomas Jefferson: Race and Slavery in American Memory, 1943–1993," in *Jeffersonian Legacies,* ed. Peter S. Onuf, 418–56 (Charlottesville: University Press of Virginia Press, 1993), 419.

42. Spahn, *Time,* 211.

AFTERWORD

1. Merrill D. Peterson, *The Jefferson Image in the American Mind* (New York: Oxford University Press, 1960).

2. Peterson, *Image,* 444.

3. Gordon-Reed and Onuf, *Most Blessed;* Annette Gordon-Reed, "Thomas Jefferson and the Boundaries of American Civilization," in *Thomas Jefferson: Genius of Liberty,* ed. Gary Wills (New York: Viking Studios in association with the Library of Congress, 2000), 83–138.

4. French and Ayers, "The Strange Career of Thomas Jefferson."

5. In particular, see Wells, "Virginia by Design"; and Upton, *Architecture.*

6. Richard Gard, "The Jefferson Progression," *Virginia Magazine,* winter 2019, 36–45.

BIBLIOGRAPHY

Ackerman, James S. *The Villa: Form and Ideology of Country Houses.* Princeton, NJ: Princeton University Press, 1990.

Adams, Henry. "The Architectural Jefferson." In *The Private Jefferson,* 27–54. Boston: Massachusetts Historical Society, 2016.

Adams, William Howard. *The Eye of Thomas Jefferson.* Charlottesville: University Press of Virginia, 1976.

———. "The Fine Arts." In *Thomas Jefferson: A Reference Biography,* edited by Merrill D. Peterson, 199–214. New York: Charles Scribner's Sons, 1986.

———, ed. *Jefferson and the Arts: An Extended View.* Washington, DC: National Gallery of Art, 1976.

———. *Jefferson's Monticello.* New York: Abbeville, 1983.

———. *The Paris Years of Thomas Jefferson.* New Haven, CT: Yale University Press, 1997.

Appleby, Joyce. "Jefferson and His Complex Legacy." In *Jeffersonian Legacies,* edited by Peter S. Onuf, 1–16. Charlottesville: University Press of Virginia, 1993.

Archer, John. *Architecture and Suburbia: From English Villa to American Dream House, 1690–2000.* Minneapolis: University of Minnesota Press, 2005.

Bachelard, Gaston. *The Poetics of Space: The Classic Look at How We Experience Intimate Places.* 1969. Boston: Beacon, 1994.

Baron, Robert C., ed. *The Garden and Farm Books of Thomas Jefferson.* Golden, CO: Fulcrum, 1987.

Bear, James A., ed. *Jefferson at Monticello.* Charlottesville: University Press of Virginia, 1967.

Beiswanger, William L. "Designs for Garden Structures at Monticello." Master's thesis, University of Virginia, 1977.

———. *Monticello in Measured Drawings.* Charlottesville, VA: Thomas Jefferson Foundation, 1998.

———. "The Temple in the Garden: Thomas Jefferson's Vision of the Monticello Landscape." In *British and American Gardens in the Eighteenth Century,* edited by Robert P. Maccubbin and Peter Martin, 179–82. Williamsburg, VA: Colonial Williamsburg Foundation, 1984.

———. "Thomas Jefferson and the Art of Living Outdoors." *Antiques Magazine,* April 2000, 594–605.

———. "Thomas Jefferson's Essay in Architecture." *Thomas Jefferson's Monticello.* Charlottesville, VA: Thomas Jefferson Foundation, Inc., 2002.

Beltramini, Guido, and Howard Burns, eds. *Palladio.* London: Royal Academy of Arts; and Vicenza, Italy: Centre Internazionale di Studi di Architettura, 2008.

Berman, Eleanor D. *Thomas Jefferson among the Arts.* New York: Philosophical Library, 1947.

Betts, Edwin Morris, ed. *Thomas Jefferson's Farm Book.* Charlottesville: University Press of Virginia, 1987.

———, ed. *Thomas Jefferson's Garden Book.* Philadelphia: American Philosophical Society, 1944.

Betts, Richard J. "The Woodlands." *Winterthur Portfolio* 14, no. 3 (autumn 1979): 213–34.

Birch, William Russell. *The Country Seats of the United States.* 1808. Edited by Emily T. Cooperman. Philadelphia: University of Pennsylvania Press, 2008.

Bishir, Catherine W. "Black Builders in Antebellum North Carolina." In *Southern Built: American Architecture, Regional Practice.* Charlottesville: University of Virginia Press, 2006.

Boorstin, Daniel. *The Lost World of Thomas Jefferson.* Chicago: University of Chicago Press, 1993.

Boucher, Bruce. *Andrea Palladio: The Architect and His Time.* New York: Abbeville, 1998.

Braham, Allan. *The Architecture of the French Enlightenment.* Los Angeles: University of California Press, 1980.

Brown, C. Allan. "Poplar Forest: Thomas Jefferson and the Ideal Villa." Master's thesis, University of Virginia, 1987.

———. "Thomas Jefferson's Poplar Forest: The Mathematics of an Ideal Villa." *Journal of Garden History* 10, no. 2 (1990): 117–39.

Brownell, Charles, Calder Loth, William M. S. Rasmussen, and Richard Guy Wilson. *The Making of Virginia Architecture.* Charlottesville: University Press of Virginia for Virginia Museum of Fine Arts, 1993.

Brugger, Robert J., ed. *Our Selves/Our Past: Psychological Approaches to American History.* Baltimore, MD: Johns Hopkins University Press, 1981.

Bryan, John M., ed. *Robert Mills, Architect.* Washington, DC: American Institute of Architects, 1989.

Bushman, Richard L. *The Refinement of America: Person, Houses, Cities.* New York: Random House, 1993.

Carson, Cary. "Banqueting Houses and the "Need of Society" among Slave-Owning Planters in the Chesapeake Colonies." *William and Mary Quarterly* 70, no. 4 (October 2013): 725–80.

———. *Face Value: The Consumer Revolution and the Colonizing of America.* Charlottesville: University Press of Virginia, 2017.

Carson, Cary, and Carl R. Lounsbury, eds. *The Chesapeake House.* Chapel Hill: Colonial Williamsburg Foundation and University of North Carolina, 2013. (Other authors in this indispensable work are Edward A. Chappell, Lorena S. Welsh, Mark R. Wenger, Orlando Ridout V, Willie Graham, Susan Buck, and Margaret Beck Pritchard.)

Chambers, S. Allen, Jr. *Poplar Forest and Thomas Jefferson.* Forest, VA: Corporation for Jefferson's Poplar Forest, 1993.

Cote, Richard Charles, "The Architectural Workmen of Thomas Jefferson in Virginia." PhD diss., Boston University, 1986.

Crowley, John E. *The Invention of Comfort: Sensibilities & Design in Early Modern Britain & Early America.* Baltimore, MD: Johns Hopkins University Press, 2001.

Daufenbach, Claus. "Jefferson's Monticello and the Poetics of Landscape Gardening." *Soundings: An Interdisciplinary Journal* 78, no. 3–4 (fall/winter 1995): 399–415.

De Botton, Alain. *The Architecture of Happiness.* New York: Vintage, 2006.

DeLorme, Eleanor P. *Garden Pavilions and the 18th Century French Court.* UK: Antique Collectors' Club, 1996.

Dennis, Michael. *Court & Garden: From the French Hotel to the City of Modern Architecture.* Cambridge, MA: MIT Press, 1988.

DeWitt, Lloyd, and Corey Piper, eds. *Thomas Jefferson, Architect.* Norfolk, VA: Chrysler Museum of Art, 2019.

Dumbauld, Edward. *Thomas Jefferson, American Tourist.* Norman: University of Oklahoma Press, 1946.

Eberlein, Harold Donaldson, and Cortlandt Van Dyke Hubbard. *Historic Houses of Georgetown and Washington City.* Richmond, VA: Diety, 1958.

———. *Portrait of a Colonial City: Philadelphia 1670–1838.* Philadelphia: Lippincott, 1939.

Ellis, Joseph. *American Sphinx: The Character of Thomas Jefferson.* New York: Knopf, 1997.

Etlin, Richard A. *Symbolic Space: French Enlightenment Architecture and Its Legacy.* Chicago: University of Chicago Press, 1994.

Facca, Amy E. Abstracts of Jefferson letters regarding architecture and construction for Mesick Cohen Wilson Baker. Monticello Research Library. Cited in notes as Abstracts.

———. "Thomas Jefferson's Poplar Forest." Master's thesis, University of Virginia, 1988.

Fazio, Michael W., and Patrick A. Snadon. *The Domestic Architecture of Benjamin Henry Latrobe.* Baltimore, MD: Johns Hopkins University Press, 2006.

Fithian, Philip Vickers. *The Journal of Philip Vickers Fithian: A Plantation Tutor of the Old Dominion.* Edited by Hunter Dickenson Farish. Williamsburg, VA: Colonial Williamsburg Foundation, 1943.

Fletcher, Rachel. *Infinite Measure.* Staunton, VA: George F. Thompson, 2013.

French, Scott A., and Edward L. Ayers. "The Strange Career of Thomas Jefferson: Race and Slavery in American Memory, 1943–1993." In *Jeffersonian Legacies,* edited by Peter S. Onuf, 418–56. Charlottesville: University Press of Virginia, 1993.

Gallet, Michel. *Stately Mansions: Eighteenth Century Paris Architecture.* New York: Praeger, 1972.

Garrett, Wendell. *Thomas Jefferson Redivivus.* Barre, MA: Barre Publishing, 1971.

Gary, Jack. "Paper Mulberry Trees, Clumps, and Oval Beds: The First Phase of Landscape Restoration at Thomas Jefferson's Poplar Forest." *Magnolia: Publication of the Southern Garden History Society* 25, no. 4 (2012).

Gary, Jack, and Eric Proebsting. "The Multiple Landscapes of Thomas Jefferson's Poplar Forest." *Historical Archaeology* 50, no. 1 (2016): 61–79.

Gebhard, David, and Deborah Nevins. *200 Years of American Architectural Drawings.* New York: Whitney Library of Design, 1977.

Giordano, Ralph G. *The Architectural Ideology of Thomas Jefferson.* Jefferson, NC: McFarland, 2012.

Girouard, Mark. *Life in the French Country House.* New York: Knopf, 2000.

———. *Robert Smythson and the Elizabethan Country House.* New Haven, CT: Yale University Press, 1983.

Gordon-Reed, Annette. *The Hemingses of Monticello: An American Family.* New York: Norton, 2008.

———. *Thomas Jefferson and Sally Hemings: An American Controversy.* Charlottesville: University Press of Virginia, 1997.

———. "Thomas Jefferson and the Boundaries of American Civilization." In *Thomas Jefferson: Genius of Liberty,* edited by Gary Wills, 83–137. New York: Viking Studio, 2000.

Gordon-Reed, Annette, and Peter S. Onuf. *"Most Blessed of the Patriarchs": Thomas Jefferson and the Empire of the Imagination.* New York: Norton, 2016.

Greene, Jack P. *Pursuits of Happiness: The Social Development of Early Modern British Colonies and the Formation of American Culture.* Chapel Hill: University of North Carolina Press, 1988.

Grizzard, Frank E., Jr. "Documentary History of the Construction of the Buildings of the University of Virginia, 1817–1828." PhD diss., University of Virginia, 1996.

Hafertepe, Kenneth, and James F. O'Gorman, eds. *American Architects and Their Books to 1848.* Amherst: University of Massachusetts Press, 2001.

Hatch, Peter J. *A Rich Spot of Earth: Thomas Jefferson's Revolutionary Garden at Monticello.* New Haven, CT: Yale University Press, 2012.

Heath, Barbara J. *Hidden Lives: The Archaeology of Slave Life at Thomas Jefferson's Poplar Forest.* Charlottesville: University Press of Virginia, 1999.

———. "Thomas Jefferson's Landscape of Retirement." In *Estate Landscapes: Design, Improvement and*

Power in the Post-Medieval Landscapes, edited by Jonathan Finch and Kate Giles, 129–47. Woodbridge, UK: Boydell and Brewer, 2007.

Heath, Barbara J., and Jack Gary, eds. *Jefferson's Poplar Forest: Unearthing a Virginia Plantation.* Gainesville: University Press of Florida, 2012.

Heck, Marlene Elizabeth. "Palladian Architecture and Social Change in Post-Revolutionary Virginia." PhD diss., University of Pennsylvania, 1988.

Henderson, Paula. "Secret Houses and Garden Lodges." *Apollo,* July 1997, 29–35.

Howard, Seymour. "Thomas Jefferson's Art Gallery for Monticello." *Art Bulletin* 59, no. 4 (December 1977): 583–600.

Hunt, John Dixon. *Gardens and the Picturesque.* Cambridge, MA: MIT Press, 1997.

Hunt, John Dixon, and Peter Willis, eds. *The Genius of the Place: The English Landscape Garden 1620–1820.* Cambridge, MA: MIT Press, 1988.

Isaac, Rhys. *The Transformation of Virginia: 1740–1790.* Williamsburg, VA: Institute of Early American History and Culture, 1982.

Jackson-Stops, Gervase, George Mott, and Sally Sample Aall. *Follies and Pleasure Pavilions.* New York: Harry Abrams, 1989.

Jefferson, Thomas. Abstracts of Jefferson letters by Amy Facca for Mesick Cohen Wilson Baker. Thomas Jefferson Libraries, Monticello. Cited in notes as Abstracts.

———. *Autobiography,* in *Thomas Jefferson: Writings,* 1–102.

———. Building Notebooks. Boston: Coolidge Collection of the Massachusetts Historical Society.

———. *Jefferson's Memorandum Books: Accounts, with Legal Records and Miscellany, 1767–1826.* Edited by James Adam Bear Jr. and Lucia C. Stanton. Princeton, NJ: Princeton University Press, 1997. Cited in notes as *MB.*

———. *Notes on the State of Virginia.* In *Thomas Jefferson: Writings,* 123–326.

———. *The Papers of Thomas Jefferson.* Edited by Julian Boyd et al. 43 vols. to date. Princeton, NJ: Princeton University Press, 1950–.

———. *The Papers of Thomas Jefferson, Retirement Series.* Edited by J. Jefferson Looney. 17 vols. to date. Princeton, NJ: Princeton University Press, 2004–.

———. *Thomas Jefferson, Architect: Original Designs in the Coolidge Collection of the Massachusetts Historical Society.* With an essay and notes by Fiske Kimball, and a new introduction by F. D. Nichols. New York: Da Capo, 1968.

———. *Thomas Jefferson's Farm Book: With Commentary and Relevant Extracts from Other Writings.* Edited by Edwin Morris Betts. Chapel Hill: University of North Carolina Press, 2002.

———. *Thomas Jefferson's Garden Book, 1766–1824: With Relevant Extracts from His Other Writings.* Annotated by Edwin Morris Betts. Charlottesville, VA: Thomas Jefferson Memorial Foundation. 1999.

———. *Thomas Jefferson: Writings.* Edited by Merrill Peterson. Library of America 17. New York: Literary Classics of the United States, 1984.

Johnson, Emilie. "John Hemmings: Enslaved Craftsman of Classical Architecture." *Classicist* 13 (2016): 9–15.

Kallen, H. M. "The Arts and Thomas Jefferson." *Ethics* 53, no. 4 (July 1943): 269–83.

Kelso, William M., and Rachel Most, eds. *Earth Patterns: Essays in Landscape Archaeology.* Charlottesville: University Press of Virginia, 1990.

Kennedy, Roger G. *Orders from France: The Americans and the French in a Revolutionary World, 1780–1820.* New York: Knopf, 1989.

Kenny, Virginia C. *The Country-House Ethos in English Literature, 1688–1750: Themes of Personal Retreat and National Expansion.* New York: St. Martin's, 1984.

Kern, Susan. *The Jeffersons at Shadwell.* New Haven, CT: Yale University Press, 2010.

Kimball, Fiske. "The Building of Bremo." *Virginia Magazine of History and Biography* 57, no. 1 (January 1949): 1–13.

———. "Jefferson and the Arts." *Proceedings of the American Philosophical Society* 87, no. 3 (July 1943): 238–45.

———. *Thomas Jefferson, Architect.* New York: Da Capo, 1968.

Kovarsky, Joel. *The True Geography of Our Country: Jefferson's Cartographic Vision.* Charlottesville: University of Virginia Press, 2014.

Kruft, Hanno-Walter. *A History of Architectural Theory from Vitruvius to the Present.* London: Zwemmer. Translated by Ronald Taylor, Elsie Callander, and Antony Wood. New York: Princeton Architectural Press, 1994.

Lancaster, Clay. "Jefferson's Architectural Indebtedness to Robert Morris." *Journal of the Society of Architectural Historians* 10, no. 1 (March 1951): 3–10.

Lane, Mills. *Architecture of the Old South: Virginia.* Savannah, GA: Beehive, 1987.

Langston-Harrison, Lee. *A Presidential Legacy: The Monroe Collection.* Fredericksburg, VA: James Monroe Museum, 1997.

Lehman, Karl. *Thomas Jefferson, American Humanist.* Charlottesville: University Press of Virginia, 1985.

Lounsbury, Carl R. "The Building Process in Ante-Bellum North Carolina." *North Carolina Historical Review* 60, no. 4 (October 1983): 431–56.

Lounsbury, Carl R., and Catherine W. Bishir, eds. *Architects and Builders in North Carolina: A History of the Practice of Building.* Chapel Hill: University of North Carolina Press, 1990.

Lucas, Ann M. "Ordering His Environment: Thomas Jefferson's Architecture from Monticello to the University of Virginia." Master's thesis, University of Virginia, 1989.

Maccubbin, Robert P., and Peter Martin, eds. *British and American Gardens in the Eighteenth Century.* Williamsburg, VA: Colonial Williamsburg Foundation, 1984.

Malone, Dumas. *Jefferson and the Rights of Man.* Boston: Little, Brown, 1951.

Marley, Anna O. "Landscapes of the New Republic at Thomas Jefferson's Monticello." In *Building the British Atlantic World,* edited by Daniel Maudlin and Bernard Herman. Chapel Hill: University of North Carolina Press, 2016.

Massie, Susanne Williams, and Frances Archer Christian. *Houses and Gardens of Old Virginia.* Richmond, VA: J. W. Ferguson and Sons, 1930.

May, Henry E. "The Enlightenment." In *Thomas Jefferson: A Reference Biography,* edited by Merrill D. Peterson, 47–58. New York: Charles Scribner's Sons, 1986.

———. *The Enlightenment in America.* New York: Oxford University Press, 1976.

Maynard, W. Barksdale. *Architecture in the United States, 1800–1850.* New Haven, CT: Yale University Press, 2002.

Mayor, A. Hyatt. "Jefferson's Enjoyment of the Arts." *Metropolitan Museum of Art Bulletin* 2, no. 4 (December 1943).

McCormick, Thomas J. *Charles-Louis Clérisseau and the Genesis of Neo-Classicism.* London: MIT Press, 1990.

McDonald, Travis C., Jr. "The Brickwork at Poplar Forest: Mr. Jefferson Builds His Dream House." *Association for Preservation Technology Bulletin* 27, no. 1–2 (1996): 36–46.

———. "Constructing Optimism." In *People, Power, Places,* edited by Sally McMurry and Annmarie Adams. Knoxville: University of Tennessee, 2000.

———. "The East and West Wings of the White House: History in Architecture and Building." *White House History* 29 (summer 2011): 44–87.

———. "The Fundamental Practice of Fieldwork at Colonial Williamsburg." In *Perspectives in Vernacular Architecture,* ed. Warren Hofstra and Camille Wells, vol. 13, no. 2 (2006–7): 35–53.

———. "Jefferson: Builder." In *Jefferson and Palladio,* edited by Guido Beltramini and Fulvio Lenzo. Vicenza, Italy: Centro Internazionale di Studi di Architettura Andrea Palladio, 2015.

———. "Poplar Forest: A Most Palladian Villa." *Arris* 28 (2017): 6–29.

———. "Poplar Forest: Synthesis of a Lifetime." In *Notes on the State of Poplar Forest,* vol. 2. Lynchburg, VA: Corporation for Jefferson's Poplar Forest, 1994.

———. "Rat Housing in Middle Virginia." In *Building Environments, Perspectives in Vernacular Architecture,* vol. 10, 169–84. Knoxville: University of Tennessee Press, 2005.

McLaughlin, Jack. *Jefferson and Monticello: The Biography of a Builder.* New York: Henry Holt, 1988.

Meacham, Jon. *Thomas Jefferson: The Art of Power.* New York: Random House, 2012.

Mesick, John I, Partner in Charge, Mesick Cohen Waite Architects. *Historic Structure Reports, I–IV.* Charlottesville, VA: Thomas Jefferson Foundation, 1991–93.

Mesick, John I, and M. Jeffrey Baker, Mesick Cohen Waite Architects. *Report on Investigations, 1990–1993.* Thomas Jefferson's Poplar Forest Library. Forest, VA: Corporation for Jefferson's Poplar Forest, 1993.

Mesick Cohen Waite Architects and Mesick Cohen Wilson Baker Architects and John G. Waite and Associates. *Historic Structures Reports.* Charlottesville: University of Virginia. 1988–2017.

Miller, Charles A. *Jefferson and Nature: An Interpretation.* Baltimore, MD: Johns Hopkins University Press, 1988.

Miller, Philip, *The Gardeners Dictionary.* London, 1735.

Moss, Roger W. *The American Country House.* New York: Henry Holt, 1990.

Nichols, Frederick D. "Architecture." In *Thomas Jefferson: A Reference Biography,* edited by Merrill D. Peterson, 214–32. New York: Charles Scribner's Sons, 1986.

———. "Jefferson: The Making of an Architect." In *Jefferson and the Arts: An Extended View,* edited by William Howard Adams, 159–86. Washington, DC: National Gallery of Art, 1976.

———. *Thomas Jefferson's Architectural Drawings.* Charlottesville: University Press of Virginia, 1961.

Nichols, Frederick D., and Ralph E. Griswold. *Thomas Jefferson: Landscape Architect.* Charlottesville: University of Virginia Press, 1978.

O'Donovan, Bill. "A Secret American Historic Site." *Colonial Williamsburg,* winter 2014, 69–74.

O'Neal, William Bainter. *An Intelligent Interest in Architecture: A Bibliography of Publications about Thomas Jefferson as an Architect, together with an Iconography of the Nineteenth-Century Prints of the University of Virginia.* Vol. 6 of *The American Association of Architectural Bibliographers: Papers.* Charlottesville: University Press of Virginia, 1969.

———. *Jefferson's Fine Arts Library: His Selections for the University of Virginia Together with His Own Architectural Books.* Charlottesville: University Press of Virginia, 1976.

———. "The Workmen at the University of Virginia: 1817–1826." *Albemarle County Historical Society* 17 (1958–59): 5–48.

Onuf, Peter S., ed. *Jeffersonian Legacies.* Charlottesville: University Press of Virginia, 1993.

———. *The Mind of Thomas Jefferson.* Charlottesville: University of Virginia Press, 2007.

———. "The State of the World." In *The Private Jefferson,* 7–16. Boston: Massachusetts Historical Society, 2016.

Onuf, Peter S., and Nicholas P. Cole, eds. *Thomas Jefferson, the Classical World, and Early America.* Charlottesville: University of Virginia Press, 2011.

Palladio, Andrea. *Andrea Palladio: The Complete Illustrated Works.* Edited by Howard Burns. New York: Universe, 2000.

Peterson, Merrill D. *The Jefferson Image in the American Mind.* New York: Oxford University Press, 1960.

———, ed. *Thomas Jefferson: A Reference Biography.* New York: Charles Scribner's Sons, 1986.

———, ed. *Visitors to Monticello.* Charlottesville: University Press of Virginia, 1989.

Pickens, Buford. "Mr. Jefferson as Revolutionary Architect." *Journal of the Society of Architectural Historians* 34, no. 4 (December 1975): 257–79.
Pierson, William H., Jr. *American Buildings and Their Architects: The Colonial and Neo- Classical Styles.* Garden City, NY: Doubleday, 1970.
Randall, Henry S. *The Life of Thomas Jefferson.* 3 vols. 1858. Reprint, Freeport, NY: Books for Libraries Press, 1970.
Randolph, Sarah N. *The Domestic Life of Thomas Jefferson.* 1871. Reprint, New York: Harper, 1978.
Rasmussen, William M. S. "Drafting the Plans." In *The Making of Virginia Architecture,* edited by Charles Brownell et al. Charlottesville: University Press of Virginia for Virginia Museum of Fine Arts, 1993.
Rasmussen, William M. S., Charles Brownell, and Richard Guy Wilson. "Idea, Toll, Evidence." In *The Making of Virginia Architecture,* edited by Brownell et al. Charlottesville: University Press of Virginia for Virginia Museum of Fine Arts, 1993.
Rayner, B. L. *Sketches of the Life, Writings, and Opinions of Thomas Jefferson.* New York: A. Francis and W. Boardman, 1832.
Reed, B. Bernetiae. *The Slave Families of Thomas Jefferson.* Greensboro, NC: Sylvest-Sarah, 2006.
Reinberger, Mark, and Elizabeth McLean. *The Philadelphia Country House: Architecture and Landscape in Colonial America.* Baltimore, MD: Johns Hopkins University Press, 2015.
Reinhold, Meyer, ed. *The Classic Pages: Classical Readings of Eighteenth-Century Americans* University Park: Pennsylvania State University, 1975.
———. "The Classical World." In *Thomas Jefferson: A Reference Biography,* edited by Merrill D. Peterson, 135–56. New York: Charles Scribner's Sons, 1986.
Rice, Howard. *Thomas Jefferson's Paris.* Princeton, NJ: Princeton University Press, 1976.
Rowland, Ingrid D., and Thomas Noble Howe. *Vitruvius: Ten Books on Architecture.* Cambridge: Cambridge University Press, 1999.
Schneider, Herbert W. "The Enlightenment in Thomas Jefferson." *Ethics* 53, no. 4 (July 1943): 246–54.
Scully, Vincent. "American Houses: Thomas Jefferson to Frank Lloyd Wright." In *The Rise of an American Architecture,* edited by Edgar Kaufmann Jr. New York: Praeger and the Metropolitan Museum of Art, 1970.
Seale, William. *The President's House.* Washington, DC: White House Historical Association, 1986.
———. *The White House: The History of an American Idea.* Washington, DC: American Institute of Architects Press in association with The White House Historical Association, 1992.
Self, Robert L., and Susan R. Stein. "The Collaboration of Thomas Jefferson and John Hemings: Furniture Attributed to the Monticello Joinery." *Winterthur Portfolio* 33, no. 4 (1998): 231–48.
Smith, Margaret Bayard. *The First Forty Years of Washington Society.* Edited by Gaillard Hunt. New York: Scribners, 1906.
Spahn, Hannah. *Thomas Jefferson, Time, and History.* Charlottesville: University of Virginia Press, 2011.
Stanton, Lucia C. *Free Some Day: The African-American Families of Monticello.* Charlottesville, VA: Thomas Jefferson Foundation, 2000.
———. *Those Who Labor for My Happiness: Slavery at Monticello.* Charlottesville: University of Virginia Press, 2012.
Stein, Susan R. *The Worlds of Thomas Jefferson at Monticello.* New York: Harry N. Abrams, 1993.
Stillgoe, John. In *The Poetics of Space: The Classic Look at How We Experience Intimate Places,* by Gaston Bachelard, vii–x. 1996. Boston: Beacon, 1998.
Summerson, John, *The Architecture of the Eighteenth Century.* London: Thames and Hudson, 1986.
Sutcliffe, Anthony. *Paris: An Architectural History.* New Haven, CT: Yale University Press, 1993.
Sweetman, John. "Nature and Art in Enlightenment Culture." In *The Enlightenment World,* edited by Martin Fitzpatrick et al. New York: Routledge, 2004.

Tavernor, Robert. *Palladio and Palladianism.* London: Thames and Hudson, 1991.
Thompson, Ian. *In the Sun King's Garden.* New York: Bloomsbury, 2006.
Thompson, James C. *Thomas Jefferson's Enlightenment.* Alexandra, VA: James C. Thompson, 2013.
Thornton, Anna Maria. Diary. September 18–22, 1802. Papers of Mrs. William Thornton, Library of Congress. Quoted in *Visitors to Monticello,* edited by Merrill D. Peterson, 33–35. Charlottesville: University Press of Virginia, 1989.
Thornton, Tamara Plakins. *Cultivating Gentlemen: The Meaning of Country Life among the Boston Elite, 1785–1860.* New Haven, CT: Yale University Press, 1989.
Tzonis, Alexander, and Liane Lefaivre. *Classical Architecture: The Poetics of Order.* Cambridge, MA: MIT Press, 1988.
Upton, Dell. *Architecture in the United States.* Oxford: Oxford University Press, 1998.
———. "Imagining the Early Virginia Landscape." In *Earth Patterns: Essays in Landscape Archaeology,* edited by William M. Kelso and Rachel Most. Charlottesville: University Press of Virginia, 1990.
———. "New Views of the Virginia Landscape." *Virginia Magazine of History and Biography* 96, no. 4 (October 1988): 403–70.
Von Kalnein, Wend. *Architecture in France in the Eighteenth Century.* New Haven, CT: Yale University Press, 1995.
Waddell, Gene. "The First Monticello." *Journal of the Society of Architectural Historians* 46, no. 1 (March 1987): 5–29.
Ward, Peter. *A History of Domestic Space: Privacy and the Canadian Home.* Toronto: UBC, 1999.
Wells, Camille. *Material Witnesses: Domestic Architecture and Plantation Landscapes in Early Virginia.* Charlottesville: University of Virginia Press, 2018.
———. "Virginia by Design: The Making of Tuckahoe and the Remaking of Monticello." In *Material Witnesses: Domestic Architecture and Plantation Landscapes in Early Virginia,* by Wells, 147–75. Charlottesville: University of Virginia Press, 2018.
Wenger, Mark R. "Jefferson's Designs for Remodeling the Governor's Palace." *Winterthur Portfolio* 32, no. 4 (Winter 1997): 223–42.
———. "Town House and Country House." In *The Chesapeake House,* edited by Cary Carson and Carl R. Lounsbury, 120–55. Chapel Hill: Colonial Williamsburg Foundation and University of North Carolina, 2013.
———. "Two Aspects of Jefferson's Domestic Architecture." Typescript copy, 1991.
Williams, Rebecca Yancey. *The Vanishing Virginian.* New York: Dutton, 1942.
Wills, Gary, ed. *Thomas Jefferson: Genius of Liberty.* New York: Viking Studio, 2000.
Wilson, Douglas L. "Dating Jefferson's Early Architectural Drawings." *Virginia Magazine of History and Biography* 101, no. 1 (January 1993): 53–76.
———. *Jefferson's Books.* Charlottesville, VA: Thomas Jefferson Foundation, 1996.
Wilson, Douglas L., and Lucia Stanton, eds. *Jefferson Abroad.* New York: Modern Library, 1999.
Wilson, Gaye, and Sharon McElroy, eds. *Thomas Jefferson's Monticello.* Charlottesville: Thomas Jefferson Foundation, 2018.
Wilson, Richard Guy, ed. *Thomas Jefferson's Academical Village: The Creation of an Architectural Masterpiece.* Charlottesville: University Press of Virginia, 2009.
———. "Thomas Jefferson's 'Bibliomanie' and Architecture." In *American Architects and Their Books to 1848,* edited by Kenneth Hafertepe and James F. O'Gorman, 59–89. Amherst: University of Massachusetts Press, 2001.
Winterer, Caroline. *American Enlightenments.* New Haven, CT: Yale University Press, 2016.
Worsley, Giles. *Classical Architecture in Britain: The Heroic Age.* London: Yale University Press, 1995.

Wright, Louis B. "Thomas Jefferson and the Classics." *Proceedings of the American Philosophical Society* 87, no. 3 (1943).

Wundram, Manfred, and Thomas Pape. *Andrea Palladio: 1508–1580, Architect between the Renaissance and Baroque.* Cologne, Germany: Taschen, n.d.

Zaborney, John J. *Slaves for Hire: Renting Enslaved Labor in Antebellum Virginia.* Baton Rouge: Louisiana State University Press, 2012.

Zerbe, Jerome, and Cyril Connolly. *Les Pavillons: French Pavilions of the Eighteenth Century.* New York: Macmillan, 1962.

ILLUSTRATION CREDITS

Author's collection: fig. 14, fig. 15, fig. 16

Author's photographs: fig. 1, fig. 2, fig. 6, fig. 44, fig. 48, fig. 53, fig. 54, fig. 55, fig. 56, fig. 57, fig. 58, fig. 60, fig. 61, fig. 62, fig. 63, fig. 65, fig. 66, fig. 67, fig. 72, fig. 73, fig. 77, fig. 83, fig. 88, fig. 89, fig. 90, fig. 94, fig. 98, fig. 101

Nat Case (INCase, LLC): fig. 8, fig. 59, fig. 91

Coolidge Collection of Thomas Jefferson Manuscripts, Massachusetts Historical Society: fig. 9 (K-133), fig. 11 (K-67), fig. 13, fig. 17 (K-146), fig. 21 (K-32), fig. 23 (K-206), fig. 25 (K-217), fig. 26 (K-185), fig. 27 (K-186), fig. 31 (K-220), fig. 33 (K-193), fig. 37 (K-196), fig. 38 (K-197), fig. 50 (K-31), fig. 68 (K-177), fig. 76

Rachel Fletcher, *Infinite Measure* (2013): fig. 43

Historic American Buildings Survey, Prints and Photographs Division, Library of Congress, Washington, DC: fig. 7 (HABS VA,10-BED.V,1- FF]sheet 12 of 22])

The Huntington Library, San Marino, California: fig. 22, fig. 28

Jefferson's Poplar Forest: fig. 3, fig. 4, fig. 5, fig. 47, fig. 75, fig. 84, fig. 85, fig. 86, fig. 100

L. Diane Johnson, *Jefferson's Poplar Forest:* fig. 99

Nancy Marion drawings: Appendix C: Jefferson's Typology of Octagon Designs (pages <ooo>–<ooo>)

Mesick Cohen Wilson Baker Architects: fig. 39, fig. 40, fig. 41, fig. 42, fig. 46, fig. 49, fig. 52, fig. 69, fig. 70, fig. 71, fig. 79, fig. 80, fig. 92, fig. 93, fig. 97 (with Office of the Architect of the University of Virginia)

Print Collection, The New York Public Library: fig. 30

Princeton University Jefferson Papers Project: fig. 20 (1938 photostat, location and ownership unknown)

Rieley & Associates, Landscape Architects: fig. 47

Thomas Jefferson Foundation at Monticello: fig. 12, fig. 18, fig. 87

Nicholas Phillip Trist Papers, Southern Folklife Collection, Wilson Library, University of North Carolina at Chapel Hill: fig. 29

Special Collections, University of Virginia: fig. 24 (N-255), fig. 32 (N-496), fig. 34 (N-255), fig. 35 (N-350), fig. 36 (N-351), fig. 45 (N-372), fig. 64, fig. 74, fig. 81, fig. 82, fig. 95, fig. 96

INDEX

Page numbers in italics indicate photographs or illustrations.